Flavors of Greece

BLACK
Sea

YUGOSLAVIA

BULGARIA

TURKEY

ALBANIA

MACEDONIA

Thesalonika

Sea of
Marmara

THASOS

Mt. Athos

Mt. Olympus •

TURKEY

• Meteora

SPORADES

Metsovon

CORFU

LESSOS

Aegean Sea

IONIAN
ISLANDS

CHIOS

Athens

PELOPONNESE

SAMOS

Corinth

ZAKINTHOS

Náfplion

THE CYCLADES

DODECANESE

KOS

• Kalamata

Ionian Sea

SANTORINI

RHODES

Sea of Crete

Kanea

Iraklion

CRETE

Mediterranean Sea

N

Flavors of
GREECE

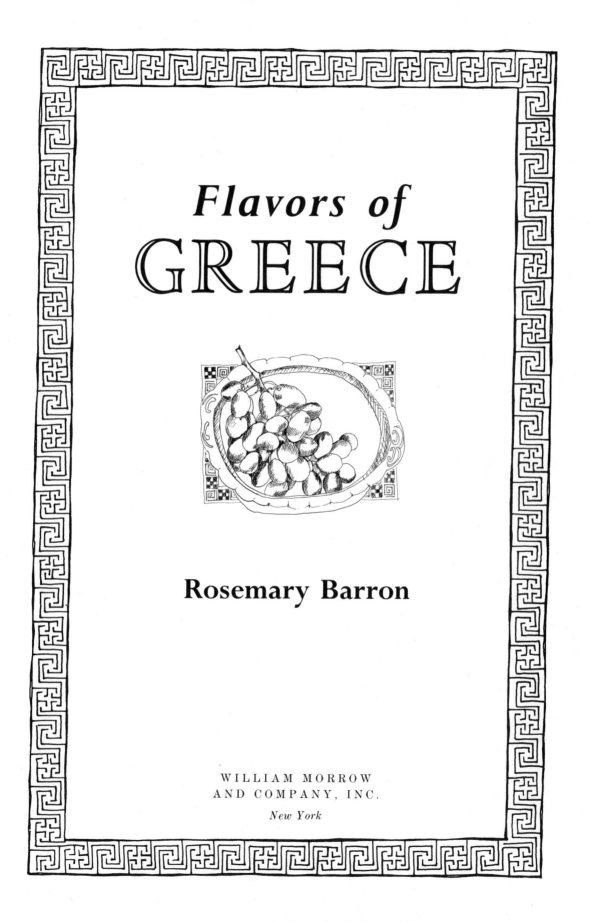

Rosemary Barron

WILLIAM MORROW
AND COMPANY, INC.
New York

Library of Congress Cataloging-in-Publication Data

Barron, Rosemary.
    Flavors of Greece / by Rosemary Barron.
        p.   cm.
    Includes bibliographical references.
    ISBN 0-688-07087-6   1. Cookery, Greek.   I. Title.
TX23.5.G8B37   1991
641.59495—dc20   90-48594
                                                                                  CIP

Printed in the United States of America

First Edition

1 2 3 4 5 6 7 8 9 10

BOOK DESIGN BY RICHARD ORIOLO

For Cordell

Acknowledgments

I could not have written this book without the encouragement and help of many people. I am indebted to Pat Herbert, whose patience, calm, and generous spirit helped me through every step of the way to its publication.

My thanks to Tanya Gaines and Joshua Golden, for testing and perfecting the bread recipes, and for sharing with me their insights into Greek life and cooking; to Christoforos Veneris, for his information and advice while I lived on Crete; to Walt Emery, for enlightening me as to the functions of a computer.

For their aid in my research in Greece over the years I thank Christine Helliwell (Los Angeles), George Panagiotopoulos (Crete), Stelios Petropoulos (Santorini), Tony Spiridakis (California), Catherine Vanderpool (American School of Classical Studies, New York), Helen Speronis (Olympic Airways, Athens), Nikos Skoulas, Evi Kouletsi, Lisa Thanopoulos, and all the other people in the Greek National Tourist Organization in Athens and the United States who gave me their time. My special thanks to Meredith Pillon (New York), always ready to help with any problem, however small, and to Carol Reed and her daughter, Christina, for making much of the research enjoyable.

I also offer special thanks to my agent, Fred Hill, who somehow always managed to say the right words at the right time; to my patient editor, Ann Bramson; to Irene Varounis and Janene Spencer, for their illustrations that so perfectly capture the essence of Greek food; to Brian Hagiwara, for his dazzling jacket photograph; to Richard Oriolo, for his attractive book design; to Laurie Orseck, ever supportive; to copy editor Judith Sutton; to Maria Charalambidis, for explaining the vagaries of modern Greek to me.

For their invaluable advice and support at appropriate moments, I thank Gertrude Harris, Terence Murphy, Penni Wisner, Peter and Marcie Layton, Paul Preuss and Nancy Rilett, and my heartfelt gratitude to Gloria Capel.

Foreword

Those who know Greece, even if only on a brief acquaintance, are aware that there is a vigorous culinary tradition in the country, with a distinct identity and character. There is a robust regional and local cuisine and an informed and lively interest in food and flavor. All these aspects are linked, in an amazing continuity of tradition, with the ancient world of over two thousand years ago.

Ancient Greece is universally accepted as the cradle of Western civilization, with its highly developed political and social system and rich intellectual and cultural life. In such a civilization could it have been possible that food and its preparation would not have been taken seriously? A remote possibility indeed. In fact, the ancient Greeks regarded cooking as both an art and a science and throughout the ancient world Greek chefs were accorded the status and reputation that French chefs now enjoy. The principles and practice of fine cooking and gastronomy as we know them in Europe and the United States today were first established in the abundantly stocked and highly creative kitchens of ancient Greece, and modern Greeks still enjoy the foods and tastes that inspired the chefs of antiquity.

What makes the style and flavor of Greek food essentially different from that of other Mediterranean countries? To discover that we need to take a brief look at the country's history, since Greek cooking is greatly influenced by the twists and turns of its turbulent past.

Until around 3500 B.C. the early inhabitants of Greece grilled the food they had gathered, hunted, and fished over wood fires, baked it in glowing embers, or, like their Etruscan neighbors, cooked it in clay ovens. But with the advent of what has been called the "Greek miracle"—the budding of the sophisticated Minoan civilization on the islands of Crete and Santorini— Greek cuisine began to develop a strongly individual style.

At the height of its influence (around 1700 to 1400 B.C.) the Minoan state dominated the Aegean, and its culture spread throughout the Mediterranean. Trade links with North Africa brought dates and onions to the islands and forests were cleared to make way for widespread planting of vines and olives. Then, as now, Crete was a true "Garden of Eden," producing some of the richest honey and sweetest fruits to be found anywhere, so it is no coincidence that the first candies were made in Minoan kitchens. The well-known Mediterranean candy *membrillo*, made from quince paste, is almost undoubtedly Minoan in origin, although it is often thought to come from Spain. Quinces were grown on Crete before the days of the ancient Greeks and archaeological research has established that the Minoans made pastes from fruits.

The creative and organizational skills of the Minoans, and their systematic approach to land cultivation and trade, laid the foundations for the successful economy of classical Greece and, as the Greek civilization developed, so also did a culinary culture. Gastronomy became a subject for serious study, and skilled technicians were required to put into practice the food theories formulated by scholars. These technicians, soon highly regarded as chefs, developed many of the cooking techniques and basic sauces we still use. Just as importantly, civilized Greek society developed the framework in which we enjoy food—the art of dining and of dinner party conversation.

As classical Greece declined and the Roman Empire grew in power and influence, Rome supplanted Athens as the center of the civilized world. Educated and affluent Romans, anxious to improve their gastronomic and cultural standards, employed Greek teachers for their children and Greek chefs in their kitchens. Under the tutelage of Greek chefs the Romans developed their own distinctive cuisine and laid the foundations of Italian cooking, which, of course, has many similarities with Greek food.

Later, the expansion of the Byzantine Empire, with its center in Constantinople (now Istanbul), spread the influence of Greek cooking northwards and eastwards throughout the Balkans and the area that is now Turkey. Even today many Turkish and Eastern Mediterranean communities rely on Greek bakers and pastry cooks for a variety of breads, pastries, and candies. In its turn Greek cuisine absorbed Balkan and Eastern influences.

Then came the "dark years" for Greece when she found herself at the mercy of a succession of invaders. Parts of the country were occupied in turn by Franks, Venetians, and Ottomans, who all influenced native food, and smaller invasions—for example, by the Vlachs and Slavs—brought new flavorings, such as paprika, to occupied towns and villages.

After the fall of Constantinople in 1453 A.D. Greece was occupied by the expansionist Ottoman Empire. This occupation naturally brought a renewed Eastern influence to bear on Greek food, although this influence was

Introduction

It is almost impossible for me to think of Greece without thinking of the colors, sights, aromas, and, above all, the flavors of Greek cooking. So many of my happy memories of the country are linked with food enjoyed in the company of good Greek friends or of new food experiences associated with out-of-the-way or exotically beautiful places—high in the mountains, by the glistening blue Aegean Sea, or in medieval ports, picturesque villages, or the heart of cosmopolitan Athens.

As a visitor I was automatically awarded the status of a *xsénos*, which means a "stranger-friend"; with this comes, for any traveler to Greece, the "protection of the gods" and a magnificent welcome to match. Such a welcome always includes the sharing of food. You are not just given food by Greeks but asked to share with them the food they enjoy (somehow there is always enough!). In few other countries are food and its traditions so much part of the fabric of life, playing an important role in the rituals associated with birth and death and everything in between.

Whether the occasion is an ordinary family supper or a splendid festive celebration the dining table is the place to enjoy each other's company. Good food entwines people in a bond that remains long after the meal is finished. The preparation of food for others, a generous and loving activity, is experienced at its most lavish and hospitable at a Greek table; no one is ever turned away.

Feasting and fasting, richness and frugality, especially among traditional and religious Greeks, is still the pattern of gastronomic life; food cannot truly be valued unless, at some other time, it has been denied. Hence, the strict observance of the Lenten and Advent fasts, and the explosion of rich ingredients and exotic flavors lavished on Easter and Christmas meals.

For me, Greek food is beautiful in its honesty, its healthy indifference to trends (although many basic tenets of traditional Greek cooking are now both medically approved and highly fashionable) and in its ability to promote a feeling of well-being in everyone at the table. Even the most sophisticated world-traveled Greek approaches a village table laden with foods such as wild greens, spit-roasted lamb, and sweet cheese pies with relish and enthusiasm. At such a feast he instinctively feels in touch with generations of Greeks who have enjoyed these traditional aromas and tastes before him; these are the flavors of home and here he knows he will find good companionship and a special communal pleasure and appreciation.

Greek food is inspired by the heady perfumed fragrances that float on the Greek air; these aromatic scents are echoed in many of the dishes I have included in this book. Then there is the color and novelty of Greek food. On shopping trips to the market, shapes, textures, and colors assault the senses, excite and entice—glossy multicolored vegetables and lush juicy fruits; plump nuts and seeds; boxes of dried fruits; strange-shaped sausages and meats from every part of an animal; sea-fresh fish you have never seen before; barrels of salted fish and *taramá*; hard and soft cheeses, crumbly white or creamy golden, some wrapped in animal skins; and more kinds of olives and beans than you ever imagined. Even the water in Greece seems special; Greeks say that some dishes, particularly those based on vegetables, cannot be made properly outside Greece because the water is not the same.

Dining in Greece is an activity that stimulates all the senses; the food is aromatic, pungent, and colorful and it is consumed with great gusto. Whether the meal is eaten at home, in a *tavérna*, or at a restaurant, it is accompanied by animated conversation, and appreciation of the food is loud and unequivocal!

In this book you will find no "haute cuisine" but much fine food. Many recipes are simple, based on good fresh ingredients; many are highly flavored and aromatic; all taste even better when shared with friends. Most of these dishes are straightforward to prepare and do not call for unreasonable culinary artistry and skill. And each recipe is in some way personal to me and evokes wonderful memories of the person who gave it to me.

Greek food is not generally fussy—its magic lies in its very simplicity, and in the way professional chefs or village, *tavérna*, or family cooks understand how to combine fresh natural flavors and ingredients to produce a finished dish far greater in texture and taste than the sum of its parts. Greeks tend to plan each day's meal around whatever foods are fresh and in season. Unfortunately, this sensible principle makes it difficult to plan ahead more than one or two days.

For us menu planning becomes easier if we bear in mind some of the Greek traditions and customs associated with dining. The meal itself is a social event, so much of the work is done ahead and, with the exceptions of *mezé* and salad preparation, relatively little last-minute attention is required.

In the villages the traditional way of dining is still observed, and very pleasant and relaxed it is. A table is set up in a courtyard and on it is spread a variety of *mezéthes* for guests and family to nibble on for an hour or two while they chat and wind down. Every meal is preceded by *mezéthes*, "to prepare the stomach for the onslaught to come," as one ancient Greek writer explained. When the *mezéthes* are finished, bread, salad, and a main course are placed in the center of the table. Vegetables are usually served later, separate from the main course.

Family and guests alike are expected to serve themselves to the food provided and to pass their wine glasses to the host to be filled. But there are strict rules of etiquette at work here, very different from our own. For example, taking large helpings of everything at the start of the meal, to show appreciation of the food, would actually be an insult to the host, implying that there might not be enough food to go around! Instead, the diners help themselves to the same dish several times, proving to the host that they are enjoying themselves and the food he offers.

When we serve Greek food at home, these customs can pose problems. Our guests, used to spending less time relaxing before dinner, can easily misjudge the pace of the meal and become quite full just on *mezéthes*! Thus, it is better to serve just a few *mezethákia* such as olives, *féta* cheese, salted almonds, and peppered figs with drinks. Then, at the table, serve two or three more substantial *mezéthes* as a first course.

In traditional Greek homes no separate first or soup courses are served (a soup is usually served as a complete meal), so the main course is served immediately after the *mezéthes*. Fresh fruit or perhaps pudding or ice cream usually completes the meal. After the meal, and away from the dining table, Greeks often enjoy honey-rich pastries, candies, or syruped fruits (*glyká*) with coffee. For us these treats make delectable desserts.

If you find balancing your Greek menu a problem you may find my menu planner (page 476) helpful. As you become more familiar with Greek food, however, you will begin to recognize instinctively which dishes complement each other best.

I hope my recipes will pay some tribute to the wonderful spirit of friendliness that has engulfed me, and warms any visitor, in Greece; that they will revive happy memories in those who have already traveled to Greece or her islands and in the Greeks who now live abroad. Perhaps too they will persuade others to visit that beautiful and hospitable country and experience the delights of Greek food for themselves.

The Greek Kitchen

Ingredients

Olives / Eliés

For modern Greeks olives and bread are the basic necessities of life, as they have been for centuries. The olive groves of modern Greece—still, mysterious, and peaceful places—date back to around 450 B.C. when olive oil was first recognized as a valuable export commodity and the land given over to olive cultivation. As the British writer Lawrence Durrell put it, olives have "a taste older than meat, older than wine. A taste as old as cold water."

Modern methods of picking and curing olives have come to Greece in recent years but their use is still far from widespread. Consequently, most Greek producers, using centuries-old methods, still supply olives of a very high standard and a great diversity of flavor. In each olive-producing area the local people delight in the flavor variation that makes their olives different from others and, they claim, better!

Olives thrive in the Mediterranean climate of long hot summers and mild winters with only short periods of frost. The differences in flavor and texture are to some extent influenced by their situation—olives grown on the arid rocky hillsides, for example, tend to be small and the richest flavored, while those grown on the coastal plains are fatter and fleshier.

The taste is also affected by the degree of ripeness when an olive is picked and by the curing method used. In the two-stage curing process the olives are first soaked in water for 3 to 30 days to remove any bitterness, then immersed in brine, the strength of the brine determining the saltiness of the cured olive. Occasionally the olives are packed into rock salt rather than steeped in brine.

Olives are usually harvested in the fall and considered sufficiently cured by early spring. They are then packed in either fresh brine, brine and vinegar, olive oil, or olive oil and vinegar for storage. They can be used straight from the pot or marinated in herbs, lemon juice or vinegar, and olive oil to serve as a *mezé*.

It is worth seeking out imported Greek olives to give an authentic flavor to the recipes in this book. Here is a list of those more commonly available in Greek stores and in good supermarkets and specialty shops:

Ámfissa From the olive groves surrounding Delphi. Picked when ripe, Amfissa olives are round and black with a mellow, pleasantly nutty flavor. Perfect with cheese and crusty country bread.

Atalánti Large, luscious, and fruity olives in shades of purple and greenish-purple. Exquisitely flavored, they can be served straight from their brine or sprinkled with a few drops of red-wine vinegar, olive oil, and a little dried *rígani* or thyme.

Cracked Green The ubiquitous countryside olives, picked just before their color changes from light to dark green. Strong and sharp, they are an ideal *mezé* to serve with *oúzo*. Or marinate them for a few hours in olive oil, a few drops of red-wine vinegar, bay leaves, a little crushed coriander seed, and slivered garlic.

Elítses Tiny, sweetly flavored olives, similar in appearance and taste to Niçoise olives—a favorite on Cretan *mezé* tables.

Ionian Green Grown on the Ionian islands, picked young, and cured in a light brine. Lovely mild, mellow olives to serve just as they are. Or sprinkle with lemon juice, olive oil, and a little finely chopped preserved lemon and parsley.

Kalamáta Probably the most famous Greek olives: glossy black, almond-shaped, and with a distinctive flavor from the red-wine vinegar used in the curing. Good Kalamátas are meaty and firm, at their best four to five months after curing, but can be kept longer. Named for the town of Kalamata (at the entrance to the Messenia Valley in the western Peloponnese), they are the perfect olive for many salads, and especially good marinated.

Náfplion Grown in the eastern Peloponnese and picked in September when young and underripe. Their mild and slightly nutty flavor is good in salads and Náfplion is the traditional olive to serve with *taramosaláta*. Occasionally I like to mix them with a little finely chopped preserved lemon, olive oil, and crushed coriander seeds.

Thásos Grown on the island of Thasos in the northern Aegean, these olives are salt-cured (a process that produces a wrinkled skin and concentrated flavor), then stored in olive oil. They are excellent with *myzíthra* cheese.

When buying olives be guided by your nose! Regardless of the curing method used, good olives smell fresh and intriguingly complex, never over-whelmingly salty. Left in the storage solution, they can be kept for months, although all are best eaten as soon as possible after buying.

Olive Oil / Elaiólatho

Three significant factors influence the quality of olive oil: the growing conditions, the timing of the harvest, and, probably the most important, the way they are harvested—the olives should be picked, sorted, and pressed with care and precision, preserving as much of the fine natural flavor as possible.

Cold-pressed olive oil is made by spreading olive pulp on mats that fit in layers into a wooden press. A weight is placed on the top mat and the pressure releases the oil into a vat below. Extra-virgin olive oil (defined by its low acidity, less than 1 percent) is made from the pulp of just-ripe olives and has the best flavor for salads. The pressed oil, standard cold-pressed or extra-virgin, is left to settle for a few days to a week, then decanted into crocks, ready for the kitchen.

There have, of course, been modern advances in olive production—picking and oil extraction is now mechanized and there are chemicals avail-able to "persuade" the olives to ripen and fall. But a machine cannot distinguish among ripe, just-ripe, and underripe olives nor strip trees on rocky hillsides where the best-tasting olives grow. Nor can mass production, relying on chemicals to accelerate filtering, "improve" flavor, and lengthen shelf life, yield an oil with anything approaching the rich quality, beautiful green-gold color, and fruity flavor of oils produced by traditional methods.

Fine olive oil is expensive, but there is no substitute for it in good cooking. When buying olive oil, use the same discernment as you would when buying wine. Look for a young oil, with a fruity, immediately recog-nizable, olive aroma and taste and a good balance of flavor, and buy only a small quantity at first. Although the best village oil does have a distinctive green-gold color, it is a mistake to use only the color criterion when buying—unscrupulous producers have been known to alter the color with additives. Buy only from markets where there is a high turnover and where the oil has been carefully stored in airtight containers, away from heat or sunlight. In your own kitchen, store olive oil in a dark cool place—it does not require refrigeration.

Greeks appreciate fine olive oil and demand high standards from commercial brands. I recommend Agouréleo Extra-Virgin (Peloponnese brand), which I consider to be one of the best extra-virgin olive oils currently sold in the United States. Among the less expensive refined oils I would suggest you look for those made from Kalamáta or Ámfissa olives.

It's worth keeping both extra-virgin and refined olive oil on hand. Use the extra-virgin oil in salads and in dishes requiring a last-minute addition of oil; use the less expensive refined oil in cooked dishes or for deep-fat frying (refined oil is more suitable for heating and has none of the "debris" left in extra-virgin oils).

Sea Salt / Aláti tis Thálassas

Salt was important in the ancient world, both to enliven frugal diets and as a preservative, but in recent years we have become more aware of the health risks associated with too much salt. However, it is possible to use salt to gain maximum taste advantage without endangering health. For example, adding lemon juice to salt strengthens its flavor, so you can use less salt but retain the taste, and relatively small quantities of strongly salted foods (such as olives) satisfy the body's natural requirements for this important mineral.

Sea salt, the type commonly used in Greece, is a wonderful enhancer of flavor, and it also contains other trace minerals beneficial to health. When a villager explains how to make a dish, salt is never far from the top of his or her list of ingredients. It is considered a digestive, an appetizer, and a wonderful balancer and mellower of flavors. It also deepens color and aroma and has the effect of drawing out liquids—which is why villagers always add salt to grilled food after cooking, not before.

Sea salt is more expensive than other types but you use less of it. It's a good idea to keep two varieties of sea salt in your kitchen—fine-grain for most cooking, and coarse-grain for some dishes and for the table.

Vinegar / Xsíthi

Only wine vinegar, mainly that made from red wine, is used in the Greek kitchen and it's a commodity that's taken seriously. As much care is taken over vinegar making as wine making and often the village winemaker has a dual role as the local supplier of good vinegar. In one old village house I once occupied a huge earthenware pot stood in a corner of the courtyard. This contained the village vinegar supply and during the day villagers would stop by for a ladleful of vinegar, sometimes bringing a little wine to top up the pot.

One of the first "food additives," vinegar is a digestive, a preservative, and a versatile flavoring agent. There is an enormous difference in flavor between good- and poor-quality wine vinegars, and it is an important distinction since the quality of the vinegar affects the quality of the dishes and sauces made with it. The quality depends primarily on the quality of the wine converted or soured by the vinegar "mother"—a self-perpetuating colony of harmless bacteria that float around in the wine while slowly acidifying it.

To make your own wine vinegar Stand a large glazed earthenware crock on a shelf or in a corner, and add leftover red wine whenever you have any available. When you have about 1 pint, add ¼ cup good-quality red-wine vinegar, loosely cover the crock to keep it dust-free but open to the air, and leave undisturbed for a week or two. A "mother" will form. Continue adding red wine, tasting occasionally to see if you are satisfied with the vinegar. Once you are, decant most of it into bottles and seal. Add more red wine to the "mother," which will continue to grow—eventually you will need to break it up and donate bits to your friends!

If you cannot find aged red-wine vinegar imported from Greece, or make your own, substitute Italian balsamic vinegar, but use less than is called for in the recipe.

Wine in Cooking / Krasí sti Magirikí

Wine does not feature in Greek recipes as often as you might expect. As an old winemaker on the island of Santorini once told me, wine is made to drink! However, red wine's ability to tenderize tough cuts of meat is used to full effect in casseroles, and traditional nectar-sweet wines are used to flavor sweet dishes. Madeira can be used in place of sweet Greek wines such as Samos or Mavrodaphne, which can sometimes be difficult to find.

Yogurt / **Yiaóurti**

Fresh milk, a controlled temperature, and the help of two friendly bacteria (*lactobacillus bulgaricus* and *streptococcus thermophilus*) are the essential requirements for making yogurt. A rich source of minerals and vitamins, especially vitamin B, yogurt can also taste wonderful. The best deliciously thick and creamy versions have a refreshing taste and luxurious texture, totally different from the thin and lusterless product that too often passes as yogurt on our supermarket shelves.

Yogurt is used throughout the Balkan region and the Middle East as a tenderizer, to enrich stews, to make sauces, and in salads, desserts, and cakes. And the food-curious visitor to Greece very soon discovers what I consider to be the best snack in the world—a plate of thick white sheep's milk yogurt covered with fragrant Hymettus honey.

The best yogurt I have ever tasted was made in the small Cretan village of Vrisses. It was sold in unglazed flat-bottomed bowls for which each customer paid a deposit; if you brought back the bowl all you had to pay for next time was the yogurt. That memorable yogurt was made from sheep's milk but village yogurt is also made from goat's milk which gives a different, less creamy, sharper flavor.

The easiest way to ensure that you have a good supply of flavorful yogurt is to make it yourself. Despite the complicated instructions often given for yogurt making, it's really very simple. All you need is good-quality fresh milk, a few tablespoons of live yogurt starter, and a fairly warm (about 65°F to 75°F) draft-free spot.

Live yogurt starter can be bought in Greek or health food stores. Once you have made your first batch, you save some of it to use as a starter for the second batch, and so on. The taste of your finished yogurt depends largely on this starter—one- to two-day-old starter will produce a mildly sweet version, five- to six-day-old starter a sharper, tarter one. Every month or two you will need a new starter (the bacteria gradually lose their potency). Taste is also affected by the length of time yogurt is incubated—the longer you leave it, the stronger the result.

Both the texture and flavor of Greek yogurt is difficult to reproduce outside the countries of the Near East. I find half-and-half gives a similar smooth, thick, and creamy consistency, but this may not appeal to dieters. Experiment with the milk you have available to find what works best for you. Yogurt added to cooked dishes or salads must be thick; thin yogurt can be strained for a few hours to remove excess water. Left longer to strain, it becomes a delicious creamy cheese.

Yogurt
Yiaoúrti
Makes 1 quart

1 quart half-and-half or milk
3 tablespoons live yogurt starter

Heat the milk to just under a boil and pour into a glass, china, or earthenware bowl. Let cool, uncovered, to about 106°F to 110°F (you should be able to comfortably leave your finger in the milk for a count of 5). A skin will have formed on the surface (this makes a special treat later, with honey). To retain the skin, push a little of it to one side and spoon the yogurt into the milk. For yogurt with a textured crust, cover the bowl loosely, if at all; for yogurt without a crust, cover the bowl with a plate. Set aside for 8 to 12 hours in a warm draft-free spot, such as an oven with a pilot light, until thick and creamy. Cover and refrigerate for up to 4 days. (Remember to make another batch of yogurt before finishing the bowl.)

Do not be put off if your first few attempts are disappointing. Your yogurt may not set—in which case make sure that the incubating spot is warm enough and the temperature is constant; if your yogurt still does not set, you need to begin again with a new starter. Or it may curdle—the most common causes of curdling are incubating yogurt in a place that is too warm or for too long a period.

Strained Yogurt Line a sieve with 2 layers of cheesecloth and set over a bowl. Pour in 1 quart yogurt, pull up the sides of the cheesecloth, and tie together to make a bag. Hang the bag over the bowl in a cool place and let drain for 3 hours. Do not drain the yogurt in the refrigerator or it will set firm rather than just thickening. Give the bag an occasional squeeze to remove as much water (whey) as possible. (You can use the whey in a soup or casserole.) Refrigerate in an airtight container for up to 5 days. (Makes about 3 cups.)

Yogurt Cheese Strain 1 quart yogurt and return the bag to the sieve. Open the cheesecloth and stir in ¼ to ½ teaspoon fine-grain sea salt if liked. Fold the cheesecloth over the yogurt, place a heavily weighted plate on top, and set aside for 2 hours. Transfer to the refrigerator and leave another 2 hours. Dry the cheesecloth bag with paper towels and, leaving the cheesecloth in place, refrigerate the yogurt cheese in an airtight container for up to 4 days.

For breakfast, serve with honey, fresh fruit, and crusty bread. For lunch, sprinkle with olive oil, a little freshly ground pepper, and/or finely chopped fresh herbs such as parsley and oregano. (Makes about 1½ cups.)

Cheeses / Tyriá

Greece produces relatively few types of cheese but each has a distinctive, direct honesty of flavor. In the villages cheese is made according to local traditions that determine its unique character. For this reason, Greek cheeses are rarely named: to a villager, cheese is cheese! Some of the finest Greek cheeses come from the island of Crete, where sheep and goats graze on herb-covered foothills and where cool mountain temperatures provide an ideal environment for storing and ripening cheese to perfection. Below is a short guide to the cheeses referred to in this book, as well as the ones a visitor to Greece is most likely to find. Most are available here from Greek or Middle Eastern grocery stores:

Anthótyro A soft, delicate, very pale yellow cheese, made from goat's milk—a specialty of the island of Crete. Soured or aged *anthótyro* is the cheese that gives Cretan pies their unique flavor. You can make a decent substitute by adding finely grated *féta* to sieved cottage cheese (use 1 part *féta* to 4 parts cottage cheese).

Féta The most famous Greek cheese, sometimes known in Greece as farmhouse cheese. Made from sheep's milk, *féta* is white and crumbly with a slightly sour, salty flavor—a pleasant, moderately priced table cheese. In isolated villages it is still made traditionally by pouring fresh unpasteurized sheep's milk into large leather pouches that are left hanging through the heat of the day. This process quickly curdles the milk, separating it into curds and whey. The curds are scooped out and packed into small baskets, the whey combined with salt to make brine, and the cheese is then stored in this brine for a week or two.

Although cheesemakers throughout Greece use the same basic method to make *féta*, there are marked regional variations. A good *féta* has a flaky texture and a mildly salty, fresh flavor. When you buy *féta* ask for some of the brine in which it is stored—the cheese can be refrigerated in this for up to two weeks longer, but without it your *féta* will last only a few days. Buy only Greek or Bulgarian *féta*; many other countries now make this cheese but do not always use the distinctively flavored sheep's milk and the result is a vastly inferior product. *Féta* is best eaten young (ripened for a month or two); if ripened longer it becomes unpleasantly salty. Enjoy *féta* just as it is or sprinkle it with a little olive oil and dried *rígani* or fresh oregano and serve it as a *mezé* or with grilled dishes. With the exception of Shrimp in a Pot with Féta Cheese (page 148) and Baked Eggplants with Tomatoes and Féta Cheese (page 267), I do not recommend using *féta* in cooked dishes, as cooking dissipates its fresh flavor.

Graviéra A mild-tasting, slightly salted cheese made from sheep's or cow's milk. Similar in both texture and flavor to gruyère cheese, *graviéra* is used mostly in sauces (page 208 and page 321). The best *graviéra* is produced in the mountains, and this is served as a traditional and delicious accompaniment to fresh or poached fruits (pages 386 and 387).

Halloúmi I have not been successful in finding Cretan or island cheese in the United States but have occasionally come across *halloúmi* from Cyprus. This salty cheese is often flavored with coriander or mint. It is very good grilled and sprinkled with lemon juice as a *mezé*.

Kephalotýri Named for its headlike shape, *kephalotýri* is a hard, pale yellow cheese made from unpasteurized sheep's or goat's milk. The curds are rubbed with salt, then returned to the mold for three days for a rind to form. Young *kephalotýri* is a good table cheese; one around eight months old or more makes excellent Fried Cheese (page 47), and aged *kephalotýri* is perfect for grating over *macarónia* dishes.

Kasséri *Kephalotýri*'s milder and creamier cousin, known to Greeks as "factory cheese" since it is reconstituted from the curds of *kephalotýri*. However, it is often a perfectly acceptable, good-tasting cheese.

Kopanistí This cheese is ripened in earthenware crocks called *kopanistí*—hence the name. It is a blue cheese, made only on the islands. Freshly made curds are cut and wrapped in cloth, then left to dry to develop a bluish-green mold. This mold, along with salt, is kneaded into the curds and left to ripen. With a light peppery flavor, *kopanistí* is a perfect *mezé* cheese, a wonderful complement to Thásos olives.

Métsovo Also excellent for the *mezé* table are two cheeses made in the Pindus mountain village of Métsovo. One type of *métsovo* is a light flaky goat's milk cheese flavored with whole black peppercorns, the other an unusual smoked sheep's milk cheese.

Megíthra *Megíthra*, made on the Cycladic islands, is one of the few Greek cheeses that has anything added to the curds. When the curds are cut for the first time, herbs, usually oregano or thyme, are mixed in, and the curds are pressed into a goatskin and left to mature for four months or more.

Myzíthra Made from the whey from *féta* or *kephalotýri*. Fresh sheep's or goat's milk is added to the whey, then the curds are separated and poured into muslin-lined baskets, with light weights placed on top. After one or two days this young fresh *myzíthra*, sometimes known as *anári*, is ready to enjoy. During the fall, winter, and early spring these flavorful unsalted cheeses, still displaying the indentations of the baskets, are sold in every Greek market. Unfortunately, young *myzíthra* is not exported, but fresh Italian ricotta is a reasonable substitute—or you can make your own (recipe follows). The *myzíthra* widely available in the United States is a pale yellow semi-hard cheese with a mildly nutty, almost buttery flavor. This is aged *myzíthra*, about three months old, and a perfect grating cheese for *macarónia* dishes.

Toulomotýri Matured for three months encased in animal hide, *toulomotýri* does not look like the most appetizing cheese in the world. But if you visit Greece and are offered a chance to sample this glorious cheese please do so. It is a pure white sheep's curd cheese, semi-soft, a little sour, even strangely musty—truly delicious with sweet wine and fruit. The whey left over from making *toulomotýri* is used to make *manoúri*, a cheese that is similar to *myzíthra* but with a tangier flavor.

Fresh Cheese
Myzíthra
Makes about 1¼ cups

2 quarts half-and-half

Juice of 1 small lemon, strained

Line a sieve with 2 layers of cheesecloth and set over a bowl. Bring the half-and-half to a boil in a stainless steel saucepan. Immediately remove from the heat, add the lemon juice, and stir with a wooden spoon until the curds separate from the whey. If they do not separate, return the saucepan to very low heat and stir until they do. Pour slowly through the cheesecloth and set aside for 15 minutes to drain. Refrigerate the whey for later use in soups or casseroles. Fold the cheesecloth over the curds, place a weighted plate on top, and let drain for 1 hour. For a firmer cheese, refrigerate overnight with the weight in place. Dry the cheesecloth bag with paper towels and refrigerate it in an airtight container. For the freshest flavor, use within 2 days but it can be kept for up to 5 days.

Serve with honey, fresh fruit, and crusty bread. Or sprinkle with olive oil, *rígani* (page 14), a little fine-grain sea salt, and cracked black pepper, and serve with olives and bread.

Butter / Voútiro

In the hot Greek climate fresh sweet butter is a rare commodity. But when you do find it, made from sheep's or goat's milk and rather like English clotted cream in texture, it tastes wonderful. According to some Greeks, goat's milk butter, which quickly develops a rather "high" aroma and flavor, is an essential flavoring for *macarónia* (page 313).

In Greek cooking butter does not generally play an important flavoring role, except in pastries. Unsalted butter can be used but clarified butter is the traditional choice and produces the finer flavor. Butter can be clarified in large quantities and, once processed, it keeps for several months in the refrigerator.

To clarify butter Melt 2 pounds butter in a heavy saucepan over low heat. When it begins to foam, gently stir in ¼ cup cracked wheat. Cook over low heat until the butter no longer steams (this indicates that all the water is expelled), removed from the heat, and set aside for 30 minutes. Carefully decant into a container, leaving the salt and other residues on the bottom of the saucepan with the cracked wheat. You can also clarify butter by straining it through 3 layers of cheesecloth, but decanting produces the clearest, most satisfactory, result.

Herbs and Spices / Vótana ke Arómata

It would be difficult to imagine Greek food without the characteristic aromatic pungency of a wide range of fresh herbs and spices. Parsley, cori-

ander, and mint, fresh from the kitchen garden, are used in large quantities; wild herbs (*rígani*, marjoram, thyme, sage, and fennel), with a fresh concentrated strength, are gathered from the dry rocky hillsides.

Listed below you will find information on the herbs and spices most commonly used in the Greek kitchen and in these recipes.

Various factors, such as climate, soil, time of year, and length of storage, all affect the pungency of any herb or spice you use. Thus, I have given guidance on seasonings for each dish but feel free to adjust the amounts specified—let your own taste be the final judge.

Ánithos (Dill) Quickly glancing at bunches of fresh herbs in a Greek market, it is easy to mistake the gentle fronds of dill for fennel; their seasons overlap. But dill is earlier and a darker green. In early spring dill is a favorite flavoring in soups or dishes made with *avgolémono* sauce.

Dáfni (Bay Laurel) An indispensable flavoring in both savory and sweet dishes, bay laurel is pungent and strong. Its Greek name is a legacy from myth—Daphne had the misfortune to be turned into a bay laurel tree by the sun god Apollo! Buy imported bay leaves—the California variety can taste acrid.

Dendrolívano/Arismári (Rosemary) Rosemary grows wild throughout Greece and the best aromatic rosemary, with beautiful tiny purple-blue flowers, is said to grow on the dry hills close to the sea. Rosemary is used in Greek cooking mainly to aromatize roasts and grilled meats and fish—a few sprigs of fresh rosemary make a perfect basting brush.

Kímino (Cumin) Cumin is a member of the same botanical family as fennel, caraway, dill, and coriander. For the sweetest, most pungent flavor, buy the dried seeds whole, and grind them when needed. In Greek cooking cumin gives a very special character to roast pork and lentil dishes.

Koriandrón (Coriander) Coriander has been cultivated in Greece since antiquity. Fresh coriander leaves are a stimulating aromatic in dried bean dishes and vegetables cooked *à la grecque* (pages 256 to 258); the pulverized dried seeds are a popular flavoring for pork (pages 224, 226, 227, and 230). Ground coriander quickly loses its perfumed pungency, so store the seeds whole and pulverize them only when needed. The ancients believed a cordial of fresh coriander, garlic, and wine to be an effective aphrodisiac. Dried coriander seeds are also used to preserve meat (*pastoúrmas*, page 469) and to flavor sausages (page 238).

The Greek Kitchen

13

Maidanós/Petrosélino/(Parsley) Few savory Greek dishes do not require parsley. Flat-leaf parsley, which is measured by the handful in Greek cooking, has a more delicate appearance and milder flavor than the more common curly-leaf variety. Greeks regard parsley as a true tonic (it contains iron, minerals, and vitamins A and C) and consider it a natural deodorizer, absorbing the smell of other strong flavors such as wine, garlic, and vinegar. Take a minute or two to strip the leaves from the parsley stems before use to prevent any trace of bitterness in your finished dish.

Mandzurána (Marjoram) Pot marjoram (*origanum onites*) is the type most commonly used in Greek cooking. It is a smaller, more delicate herb than its botanical cousin sweet or "garden" marjoram (*origanum hortensis*), which has a markedly different flavor. There can be confusion over the two so be sure to check which one you are buying if you wish to avoid disappointment in your finished dish. Marjoram is the essential flavoring in many lamb dishes and in *loukoúmia* (Turkish delight).

Márathon (Fennel) In spring, new shoots of fennel flavor an exquisite bread (page 343). Later, the silky fronds are added to salads, wild greens, pies, and beet dishes. During early fall the seeds are collected and dried, to be used in fish dishes, sweet breads, and pork dishes all through the year. The flavor is similar to licorice.

Rígani (Oregano) Greek oregano is a stronger sharper version of the familiar imported Italian herb. The word *oregano* is from the Greek, meaning "joy of the mountains," and *origanum heracleoticum*, the herb known to the ancient Greeks, covers the hills and mountain slopes of Greece and perfumes the air. You can find large bunches of dried *rígani* in Greek stores; it is worth seeking out to give an authentic flavor to these recipes. Italian oregano (*origanum vulgare*) can be substituted but will not provide the characteristic pungency associated with *rígani*.

Thiósmos/ Méntha (Mint) Several varieties of this deliciously refreshing herb are popular in Greece. Water mint is the type most commonly used in cooking dishes such as stuffed tomatoes. Peppermint, spearmint, lemon mint, and corn mint are all used to make fragrant herbal teas. Our nearest equivalent for cooking is fresh garden mint (use only the young tender leaves). Dried spearmint is delicious in *tsatsíki* (page 73).

Throúmbi (Savory) There are two types of this fragrant herb. Winter savory (*satureia hortensis*) is a favorite herb for flavoring grilled dishes, especially lamb. Delicate summer savory (*satureia thymbra*) is not used in Greek cooking but to make a soothing tea.

Thymári (Thyme) The thyme most widely available in Greece, the type that covers the dry limestone hills and is the source of the wonderful fragrance of Hymettus honey, is too strong to be used in cooking. But in the hillside villages, a gentler, sweeter version grows and this is used a great deal in cooking. It flavors game and pork as no other herb can.

Vasilikós (Basil) Pots of sweetly fragrant basil, believed to keep flies away, are a common sight in Greece, but this herb is rarely used in cooking except in cakes and breads celebrating important religious events. The reasons for this are lost in folklore and myth, although basil's Greek name, meaning "kingly," may give us a clue; but it is also known as the "devil plant" and is associated with misfortune.

The herbs detailed above are all grown in Greece, but it was trade in other aromatics that helped create the wealth on which classical Greece thrived. These were mainly spices, some introduced through trade with Egypt, others brought back from eastern military campaigns by Alexander the Great.

Kanélla (Cinnamon) Produced from the bark of the cinnamon tree this heady spice is used to maximum advantage in the Greek kitchen. A favorite flavoring in lamb dishes (it is essential for magnificent *moussakás*), it also lends a delectable fragrance to cakes, syrups, cookies, and pies. Whole cinnamon sticks can be stored almost indefinitely; ground cinnamon is easier to use but be sure to buy only small quantities at a time since it quickly loses its pungency.

Moskhokário (Nutmeg and Mace) Deep-yellow nutmegs are the hard seeds of a soft fruit; mace is the nutmeg's lacy reddish-orange natural covering. Nutmeg, rich and pungent, is best stored whole and grated as needed; mace has a milder, less acrid flavor, and ground mace is fine for cooking. Both impart a lovely fragrance to sauces and casseroles.

Moskokárfi (Cloves) Spicy cloves, the unopened flower buds of the clove tree, have a powerful fragrance. Whole cloves are used to perfume syrups, decorate cookies, and impart an unforgettable fragrance to beef casseroles; ground cloves add a delicious flavor to cookies.

The Greek Kitchen

Pipéri (Pepper) Pungent black pepper is generally preferred to the stronger, less subtle white. Invest in a good-quality pepper mill—ready-ground pepper is no substitute for freshly ground. I find it useful to have three pepper mills: one for black pepper, one for white, and one for a mixture of the two.

Vaníllia (Vanilla) Vanilla, the dried pod of a tropical orchid, is a relative newcomer to the Greek kitchen (used only since the medieval period!) but is an essential flavoring in many cakes and pastries. Buy only good-quality pure vanilla extract. You also can make vanilla sugar by keeping a vanilla bean in a jar of granulated or superfine sugar.

Xsilokérata (Carob) Carob is now better known as "health-food chocolate," a substitute for the real thing. But at other times in its long history, it had considerable economic importance (its seeds were the original carat measurement used by jewelers). In antiquity, carob was a favorite flavoring in confections. On Crete, the world's largest exporter of carob, it is now mostly used in wine production or to make syrup.

In addition to these aromatic flavorings, such spices as caraway seeds, paprika, aniseed, allspice, cayenne pepper, mustard seeds, and dry mustard appear in many Greek dishes.

With the exception of cinnamon, all spices should be bought whole if possible and ground in a spice grinder or electric coffee grinder as required. Buy in small quantities and store in airtight jars away from the light to minimize loss of the spice's oil. It is this oil that aromatizes and flavors food.

Capers / Kápari

In the spring, the small tender leaves of the spindly wall-hugging caper bush, a native of the eastern Mediterranean, are picked; in early summer the tight flower buds, varying in size from tiny currants to small olives, are gathered. Leaves and buds are thoroughly cleaned and dried, then pickled in white wine vinegar aromatized with bruised fennel seeds. The capers can be eaten after one month or stored in the pickling liquid for up to a year. Capers give incomparable zest and character to grilled foods (especially lamb), beef casseroles, and fish dishes. Sprinkled with a little olive oil they can also be served as part of a *mezé* table. Buy small imported capers; some of the larger ones on the market are actually nasturtium buds.

Nuts / Karýthia

Almonds (*amígdala*) have probably been cultivated in Greece for as long as the grape, the fig, and the olive and they feature in many ancient and traditional recipes. Eaten instead of meat and dairy products during religious fasts they are also symbols of long life and happiness. For festive sugar-coated almonds—and to flavor preserves—the Jordan, or "bitter," almond is used. For all other purposes the "sweet" almond is the type of choice.

Almonds are the central ingredient in rich Greek cakes (page 375), in Garlic Almond Sauce (page 421), and in a soft marzipan candy called *amígdalotá*. Pounded with sugar to a sweet paste, they are also used to make *soumátha*, a delicious syrupy drink. On Crete almonds are believed to prevent a hangover and are eaten in large handfuls before any serious *rakí* drinking begins. These nuts are also sold on every street corner, either salted or coated with honey.

Karýthia is the Greek word for nuts but it is also the name for the walnut, popular throughout Greece. During fall newly ripe walnuts are everywhere—served with *oúzo* or *rakí*, made into cakes, sprinkled over desserts, and pounded into a creamy sauce (page 425). Very young walnuts are preserved for the winter—either in salt and vinegar to serve as a *mezé* or in honey to nibble with coffee.

Waxy white pine nuts (*koukounária*), from the cones of the stone pine, are a delicate and essential ingredient in a favorite *piláfi* (page 302) and make a delicious sauce (page 426). Since the stone pine bears fruit only every three years and the nuts have to be extracted from their tough outer covering by hand, pine nuts are expensive even in Greece.

Hazelnuts (*foundoúki*), sold by every street vendor, are used to make wonderful cookies. On the vendor's tray there are also purple-skinned, green-fleshed pistachio nuts (*fistíkia*); their delicate sweet perfume scents elegant creamy desserts (page 407) and often replaces sesame seeds in *pastéli*, a popular candy.

Store-bought ground nuts are, of course, easy for the cook. But in terms of moistness and flavor it is worth shelling, skinning, and grinding nuts yourself. The skins are easily removed after dipping the nuts into boiling water, and a food processor or blender makes short work of grinding (use a clean coffee grinder for small quantities or treat yourself to an antique nut grinder).

Honey / Méli

According to legend, honey was literally a lifesaver for Zeus, the king of the ancient Greek gods. His father, Chronos, had a nasty habit of murdering his male offspring to prevent them threatening his omnipotence and power. Keeping the baby Zeus quiet, therefore, was vital; spoonfuls of sweet and fragrant honey did the trick! Perhaps this is why honey-candied fruits were once a favorite sacrificial offering to the gods.

For Greeks the best honey comes from Mount Hymettus; clear and thick, it is perfumed with the thyme blossom that covers the mountain slopes. Most Greek honeys have a herbal bouquet although a few hint at the more floral notes of almond or citrus blossom. Honey contains natural minerals and trace elements beneficial to health and its aroma and pungency are so satisfying that only small amounts are needed. So, for a variety of reasons, honey is a healthier sweetener than sugar.

Honey and bread is a quick, nutritious snack; add honey to yogurt and you have a meal fit for the gods. Pungent blends of honey and vinegar are traditional flavorings for Greek casseroles, vegetables, and fish, and what would a *phýllo* pastry be without its luscious drenching of honey syrup? You should be able to find Hymettus honey in Greek and Middle Eastern stores but if this proves difficult, unfiltered herb or orange blossom honey are good substitutes.

Lemons / Lemónia

The clear sharp tang of lemon was unknown to the ancient Greeks; this lovely fruit made its first appearance in Greece at the time of the thirteenth-century Crusades. But it would be difficult now to imagine Greece without its profusion of lemon trees, or a Greek meal without the color and piquant flavor lemons bring.

Lemon juice is an essential ingredient in many marinades and sauces, and it is the perfect complement to rich fruity olive oil. A small bunch of lemon leaves makes an exquisitely perfumed basting brush for grilled foods, and lemon zest and juice give a refreshing pungency to syrups and savory dishes. And what would a platter of tiny fried fish, *kephtéthes*, or *souvlákia* be without their garnish of bright lemon wedges? Oil extracted from lemon zest is also a fragrant flavoring in sweet pies and cakes, and pretty rolled strips of peel make a luscious candy.

To make the most of versatile lemons it's a good idea to invest in three inexpensive kitchen implements—a zester (to remove tiny strips of zest), a wooden reamer (to quickly juice a lemon), and a stripper (to remove small sections of zest for flavoring or garnish). Empty lemon halves, pierced with a skewer and dipped into olive oil, make perfect natural basters for grilled fish and other dishes.

From every Greek lemon harvest some fruit is set aside to be preserved. Lightly treated with salt and stored in olive oil, lemons acquire a lively and distinctive flavor, perfect as a last-minute addition to casseroles, beans, and liver and fish dishes. Save the olive oil used as a preservative—it adds a delicious flavoring to salads and grilled dishes.

Preserved Lemons

5 large lemons (unsprayed if possible)

5 tablespoons coarse-grain sea salt or kosher salt

Kalamáta olive oil, to cover the lemons

Sprigs of dried rígani (page 14), marjoram, or thyme or large bay leaves

If you have unsprayed lemons you need only to rinse them well. Otherwise, cover the lemons with boiling water and set aside to cool. Drain, then cover with cold water. Set aside for 2 days, changing the water 3 or 4 times. Dry the lemons, cut off a thin slice from each end, and cut lemon into ¼-inch slices. Remove any seeds with the point of a small knife, spread the slices on a plate, and sprinkle with the salt. Cover and refrigerate 24 hours.

Layer the slices in glass or earthenware jars and pour over any of the brine (salt water) left on the plate. Place the herb sprigs or bay leaves on top of the lemons, wedging them under the rims of the jars, and pour over enough olive oil to cover. The sprigs keep the slices immersed and flavor the olive oil. Cover tightly with plastic wrap and let sit at room temperature for at least 2 weeks. Refrigerate after opening, and use within 3 months.

Oranges / Portokália

Navel and Seville are the types of oranges generally found in Greek kitchens. Navel oranges, large, juicy, sweetly perfumed, and thick-skinned, are

on every dining table during their season. The skins are made into candies (below) or a spoon sweet (page 384), or the zest (orange rind) dried to flavor cakes and casseroles). To dry the zest, remove the orange part of the skin in long strips and dry in a very low oven or in the sun. Hang the strips in the kitchen—they will add a lovely scent to the room—and break off pieces as you need them. (Treat lemon zest the same way.)

Seville oranges have a bitter flavor so cannot be eaten straight from the tree. Tiny ones, however, are preserved whole in a thick honey or sugar syrup as a delicious spoon sweet. The juice from larger oranges is used in dishes such as Pork in Aspic (page 44).

The blood orange, not widely popular on the Greek mainland, is more appreciated on the islands. Similar to a navel orange in taste, the flesh of a blood orange is a startling deep blood red. Its juice makes an unusual mayonnaise and a vibrantly colored drink.

Orange extract is used to flavor cookies and cakes; orange blossom infused to make a headily perfumed essence or "water" to flavor syrups, and also made into an exquisite spoon sweet (page 400). There is no substitute for orange extract or orange flower water; the best brands are available in specialty shops.

Candies / Zakharotá

Candies are a legacy of antiquity. The word is derived from *Candia*, the ancient name for Crete, where it was considered that the best honey and honeyed fruits originated. The candies so beloved by the ancients were sweet and fragrant, and many of these are still made in Greece in exactly the same way. The most popular are *pastéli* (Honey Sesame Candies) (page 414), Moustalévria Candies, flavored with cinnamon (page 411), sugared almonds, *loukoúmia* (Turkish Delight), and a sweet paste made from the quince. A more modern candy, very simple and economical to produce at home, can be made from the peel of oranges, lemons, or grapefruit.

· *Candied Citrus Peel* / Portokalófloutho glykó

Cut oranges into 8 or 10 lengthwise segments, lemons into 6, and grapefruit into 12. Remove the flesh with a small paring knife. Place the peels in a large saucepan, cover with cold water, and bring to a boil. Drain and repeat the process 3 times. Drain, cover with cold water, and set aside for 2 hours.

Drain, thoroughly dry with paper towels, and pack peels into a measuring cup. Measure out an equal quantity of sugar and set aside.

Thread a trussing or other large needle with thin kitchen twine and tie a large knot at the end. Roll each piece of peel into a spiral and thread onto the string, passing the needle through the roll so it will not unravel. Thread no more than 18 rolls onto each length of string, and tie the 2 ends together.

Place the sugar and half its volume of water in a large sugar pan or heavy saucepan. Slowly bring to the boil, stirring until the sugar is dissolved. Simmer 5 minutes, then add the strings of peel. Simmer uncovered for 30 minutes or until a needle will easily pierce the rolls. Remove from the syrup and let cool.

Carefully pull out the twine. The rolls will be left intact. Boil the syrup until it just reaches the light thread stage (230°F) on a candy thermometer. Stir in the juice of 1 small lemon and pour this syrup over the rolls. Store the syrup in a covered container for up to 1 month.

To serve, remove the rolls from the syrup and coat each one with honey, preferably Hymettus, or granulated sugar.

Pots, Pans, and Kitchen Tools
Tsoukália, Tigánia, ke Ergalía Kouzínas

The most important, and most frequently used, tool in the Greek kitchen is the mortar and pestle. Greek cooks like to have three—a large walnut mortar in which to pound and blend *salátes*, a large marble mortar and pestle for pulverizing nuts and spices, and a small brass or wooden mortar and pestle for bruising herbs. A food processor or blender could do this work quickly and easily, but these machines cannot produce the fine flavor that traditional equipment seems to be able to. I find too that the delectable aromas released into the air when herbs and spices are pounded with oils are wonderfully satisfying.

Your repertoire of pots and pans should include the following:

An enameled cast-iron casserole with a tight-fitting lid, for long slow oven baking. The best is called a *doufeu*. It has an indented lid that can be filled with water to keep the food moist during slow baking. Without the water, the *doufeu* can be used as an ordinary heavy casserole.

The Greek Kitchen

21

Heavy cast-iron sauté pans, the plainer and heavier the better. (Fancy surfaces soon wear out and also prevent meat from browning properly.) You need one medium-sized and one large one.

A cast-iron omelet pan. In Greece a traditional shallow cast-iron pan is preferred as it can be taken straight to the table.

Also useful is a round aluminum baking dish (*tapsí*), about 2 to 3 inches deep and 15 inches in diameter, available in Greek and Middle Eastern stores.

For cooking and serving traditional dishes, nothing can beat earthenware pots. They should be glazed on the inside (the glazes on any pots available in the United States comply with government safety regulations). If kitchen space is limited choose one deep casserole with a lid and one oval or round baking dish. If you can store more, add a deep bean pot (similar to a *cassoulet* pot), a rectangular dish (for baked *macarónia* dishes), and an unglazed clay pot (which I find produces a wonderful flavor in potatoes and beets).

Pickles and vinegar are best stored in stoneware jars. Stoneware is not, in fact, available in Greek villages but it is a much better material for long-term storage than porous earthenware. Small stoneware or glazed earthenware jars with tight-fitting stoppers are the most effective containers for dried herbs and spices. You may also like to collect special storage jars for specific ingredients, such as salt-glazed containers for sea salt or a jar with a tap at the base for vinegar.

Three good knives should be a minimum requirement in any serious cook's kitchen: a large chopping knife, a flexible filleting knife, and a paring knife.

The utensil I would least like to be without is the food mill. Unlike a food processor or blender, a food mill produces a delicious texture in soups and vegetable dishes and it can process larger quantities at one time.

A hinged double grill saves work too, making the grilling of small fish and pieces of meat simple.

And a few more:

A balloon whisk and small sauce whisk

A colander and several sizes of sieve

A wide pastry brush, for *phýllo*

Heavy baking sheets

Coffee-making equipment

Bríki long-handled, small brass coffeepot; the 4- or 6-cup size is the most useful

Flintzáni tiny coffee cups

Mílos tou kafé a magnificent coffee grinder, usually brass, but older ones are often made of copper.

There are other kitchen tools, dishes, and storage pots in common use in Greek village kitchens of interest to serious cooks elsewhere. All have their origins in antiquity but are in daily use in the village. If you enjoy exploring markets you may like to look for a few of the following:

Bread-making equipment

Skáfi a wooden trough for mixing and kneading the dough, usually about 3 feet long and 2 feet wide

Kóskino a large shallow sieve, for sifting flour

Petrómilos a large millstone with a wooden handle, for grinding flour

Típari a carved wooden seal about 6 inches in diameter, used to imprint "offering" bread for the church

Casseroles

Kapamás *or* lópas a glazed earthenware casserole with sloping sides and a conical lid; it gives its name to the dish *kapamás* (page 158)

Píthos a beautiful tall earthenware bean pot

Tséntsero a deep earthenware casserole with an elegant lid

Tsoúka a round earthenware baking dish without a lid, for baking foods in the *foúrnos*

Tsoukáli a smaller version of the *tsoúka*, but with a lid and sometimes a handle

Grilling equipment

Soúvles 12- to 18-inch long skewers, often with elaborate cast metal animals at one end, for *souvlákia*

Foufoú a beautiful little clay brazier, based on a design used by the Minoans and still to be found in Cretan villages; for grilling small birds and fish

Mangáli a deep metal tray on legs, standing about 2 feet high, for *souvlákia*. The ends of the skewers (*soúvles*) rest on the sides of the *mangáli*, so no metal grill is needed

Cheese-making equipment

Tríkon a deep basket with slightly sloping sides, made in many sizes—the smallest holds a ½-kilo cheese; the largest, a cheese weighing several kilos; lined with muslin, the *tríkon* is then filled with curds and left on a tray to drain

Kopanáki wooden paddle for kneading and shaping the curds

And in village courtyards you may be lucky enough to find:

Kazáni (colloquial Arabic name) or *lébes* (Greek) the ubiquitous iron cooking pot, used on a tripod over an open fire

Pithária unglazed storage pots, some standing 4 feet high, and decorated with simple but beautiful designs dating from antiquity

Stámnos a gorgeous squat pot with two handles at the neck, for storing liquids such as vinegar or wine

Sourátha similar to the *stámnos*, but with a spout on one side of the neck for easier pouring; with a *sourátha* you do not need to master the difficult trick of tilting the large *stámnos* over your shoulder

Amoúrghi an earthenware cooking pot with cups attached on both sides, to hold the ingredients to be added to the pot later in the cooking

Hýdria a large earthenware jar with three handles, for carrying and storing water

Kakavé a three-legged pot, which gives its name to the dish *kakaviá* (fish soup)

Skoúpa the appropriately named brush for sweeping the courtyard

My neighbor on the island of Crete, Irina, keeps a traditional kitchen, still using many of these ancient cooking tools. The entrance to her house is through a pretty paved courtyard that serves as an extension of both kitchen and sitting room; on warm days a large dining table is set up here, shaded from the fierce midday sun by a beautiful trellised vine.

Built into the far side of the courtyard wall is a beehive-shaped oven (*foúrnos*) where all the family baking is done. Nearby are propped a long-handled wooden rake and paddle, used for removing baking trays and red-hot embers, and in one corner is a pile of kindling (the rest of the wood, mostly olive, is neatly stacked on the roof). In the corner a small blackened alcove encloses a fireplace and metal tripod supporting a large encrusted black cauldron with a gleaming interior, and a grill rests against the stones surrounding the fire. A small opening in the wall leads to a small stone building where the grape press, olive press, and huge storage jars (*pithária*) for wine, olive oil, olives, vinegar, and pickles are kept.

Inside the small kitchen, a double burner (fueled by bottled gas) occupies one shelf; this is used mainly to make coffee—a concession to progress that most villagers have made. Four small wall cupboards hold bowls and kitchen tools; casseroles and saucepans are stored outside. Three mortars of varying sizes stand against one wall. A tiny pantry extends beyond the kitchen where preserves, preserved meats, pickles, yogurt, and cheeses are stored, and bunches of herbs and smoked sausages dangle from the ceiling.

A short walk from the house brings you to the delightful kitchen garden where Irina grows the herbs and all the vegetables she needs. Caper bushes cover the surrounding low stone walls and the lush greenery of asparagus and artichoke plants contrasts vividly with the barren hills beyond. In one corner of the garden is a well, tapping a natural spring, and beyond the garden is a small field where Irina's father grows wheat. Along the hillside, beyond the wheatfield, are the vines and olive trees that have provided Irina's family with their basic necessities for centuries.

The Greek Kitchen

For me the simplicity of Irina's traditional kitchen was a revelation. I quickly discovered that I could produce superb food with very little sophisticated equipment and that there is a wonderful satisfaction in working with traditional tools in an atmosphere of calm, tranquillity, and order.

About the Recipes

There is a marked gender bias in the preparation and serving of food in Greece. This does not, of course, affect the flavor of the food but it does influence any selection of recipes. The oral tradition in the kitchen, passing recipes from mother to daughter, is still very strong, but men also take a keen interest in food and have their own oral tradition, passing on knowledge and skill in spit roasting, grilling, and oven (*foúrnos*) baking from father to son. In hotels, restaurants, and *tavérnas* most chefs are male and, while they have a broad overview of their country's food, their knowledge is often confined to the professional, rather than the domestic, kitchen.

My experience of food and cooking in Greece falls somewhere among all these categories. I learned a great deal about grilling and roasting, for example, from good male cooks in the village where I lived. Through their experience and knowledge I also began to appreciate the particular culinary skills of Greek hunters and fishermen.

And since I lived in a village, I was always welcome in family kitchens—traditionally the woman's domain and a place where men are rarely seen. Here I learned just how pleasurable and creative food preparation can be, and how skilled Greek women cooks are at a range of remarkable vegetable cookery and at bread and pastry making.

Occasionally Athens would lure me. In this cosmopolitan city I enjoyed the company of urban Greek friends, many from families returned from Asia Minor. They too have their food preferences and particular flavoring skills in the kitchen. And I have to thank the chefs, on the mainland and on the beautiful islands, who shared with me their professional secrets and taught me much about the Greek attitude to food, to cooking, and to flavor. These combined experiences, city and country, domestic and professional, provided me with the inspiration and information for this selection of recipes.

I have tried to be completely scrupulous in crediting the recipes, but it has not been an easy task! Few people, especially villagers, could be persuaded to give me a recipe I could actually write down, preferring instead to give me an idea (albeit lovingly descriptive) of the "essence" of a dish.

Or they would give me a list of ingredients calling for "a little of this, more of that," until the flavor was "just right." Details about traditional dishes such as *stifátho* (page 172) or *fassolátha* (page 79) tended to follow these lines—how on earth could anyone not know the best way to make and flavor these familiar dishes?

My recipes are the result of tasting and more tasting, until I was satisfied I had reproduced an authentic Greek flavor. Most of the recipes have been adapted to a greater or lesser degree to suit our kitchens and tastes. Where I have used a recipe exactly as it was given me, or stressed a technique or ingredient in the way it was stressed to me, I have said so and credited the cook who passed the recipe on to me. These were usually the recipes of the chefs, who understood my need for a concise explanation. However, even they tended to answer the question "Why?" with the response, "Because that is the way it has always been done."

Appetizers and First Courses

Mezéthes ke Orektiká

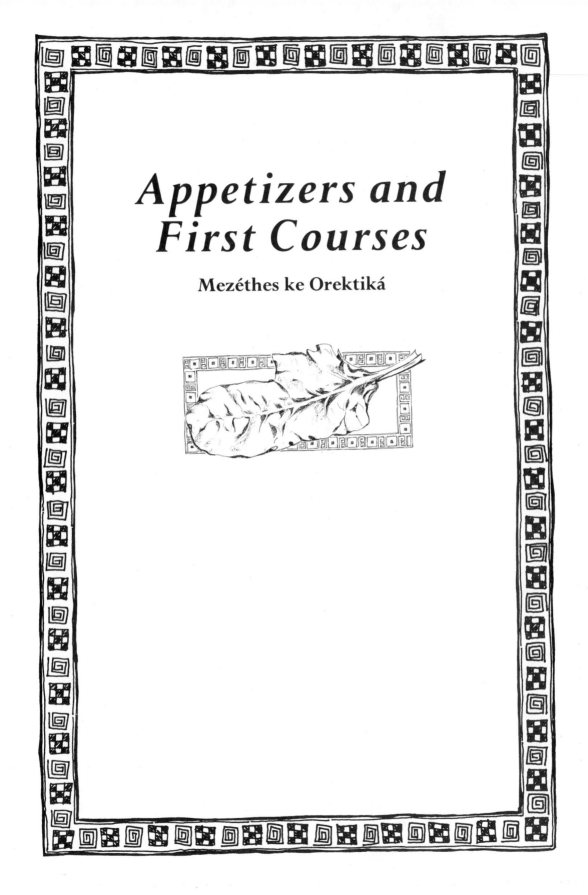

Philosophers the ancient Greeks may have been, but they were practical too. They knew, for example, that drinking wine on an empty stomach is not a sensible idea. With characteristic creative logic they made it impossible in Greek society to indulge in such a barbaric practice—by the simple expedient of making delectable mouthfuls of solid food available wherever and whenever drinks were served. From this practical precaution stems the tradition and culture of the *mezé*, now, as then, an integral part of the fabric of Greek social life.

Mezéthes is usually translated as "appetizers" and, of course, these tempting little dishes are served with drinks as hors d'oeuvre and many make imaginative first courses. But the translation hardly does justice to the sheer range, ingenuity, and delight of *mezéthes* nor to their fundamental place in Greek tradition.

Mezéthes are available in cafés at any time; for many Greeks meeting friends to enjoy a refreshing drink and a *mezé* platter makes a relaxing break in the busy working day. In Greek homes *mezéthes* are automatically offered to all visitors, whether friends or strangers.

Guests are expected to help themselves to as much as they like from the *mezé* platter and it's the host's duty to make sure empty dishes are replenished with more, or different, *mezéthes* as necessary. This is not just politeness but an important social ritual. By providing food, drink, stimulating conversation, and an easy relaxed atmosphere the host demonstrates his ability to satisfy both the physical and spiritual needs of his guests. At the *mezé* table the food is colorful, intensely aromatic, and highly flavored and the conversation is similarly exuberant, dramatic, and high-spirited.

In his writings, the philosopher Plato gives us a good idea of the range of tastes and textures offered by a well-balanced *mezé* table. Laid out before the guests, he says, were platters of radishes, olives, beans, green vegetables, figs, cheese, fresh garbanzo beans, and myrtle. Here are foods both sweet and savory, fresh and preserved, crunchy and tender, and flavors subtle and strident. The same principle of contrasts is evident in good *mezé* platters today—fresh and preserved vegetables, crunchy nuts, soft creamy *salátes*, pickles, tiny savory pies and miniature meat patties, crumbly cheese, morsels of fried fish, octopus, or smoked eel, and fresh or dried fruit—the list is practically endless.

Mezéthes are perfect for buffets and picnics, make unusual first courses, and are ideal as light lunches. A traditional *mezé* table might comprise twenty-five dishes or more but for our purposes twelve to sixteen will create a spectacular display. It does take time to organize and cook a good variety of *mezéthes*, but the pickled and preserved dishes can be prepared months ahead and many others one or two days before serving. You need provide only a small quantity of each *mezé* but do make sure each is decorated with an attractive edible garnish that enhances both its flavor and appearance.

Mezéthes are served everywhere in Greece, from the tiniest bar to the smartest hotel and are one of the most enjoyable features of Greek life. Some of the best *mezéthes* I've tasted were in one of the crowded *mezé* cafés in the back streets of Athens, around the ancient Athinas market. These high-ceilinged, marble-floored cafés ring with the buzz and bustle of humanity, all chaos and confusion. With an attractive *mezé* table, *oúzo*, *rakí*, or wine to drink, and the stimulating company of good friends you can create something of the atmosphere of those vibrant cafés.

Small Appetizers

Mezethákia

Serves 8

At the sight of a tray of *mezethákia*—small *mezéthes*— tastebuds tingle and eyes light up in anticipation! The bite-sized morsels, in a seductive array of colors, textures, and flavors, are tidbits par excellence and Greek cooks assemble *mezethákia* platters with consummate artistry and skill. On a well-balanced platter you'll find something crunchy (peppery radishes, perhaps, or fresh walnuts), something refreshing (tiny fingers of cucumber or melon or juicy tomato wedges), something salty (olives, capers, pickled eggplants), savories such as crumbly fresh cheese or tiny fried fish, and sweet treats like dried figs or tiny plump currants.

---

2 large ripe tomatoes

Large pinch of sugar

Sea salt to taste

1 English hothouse cucumber

12 olives, Ámfissa, Thásos, or cracked green

12 Marinated Olives (page 33) or Kalamáta olives

8 ounces féta cheese, cut into slices or cubes

*12 radishes, stems trimmed to 1 inch, a few
small leaves left in place*

AND 2 OR MORE OF THE FOLLOWING

24 Salted Almonds (page 34)

4 to 8 Peppered Dried Figs (page 35)

8 Pickled Tiny Eggplants (page 440)

8 toursi peppers (page 439)

24 capers, drained

*8 salted anchovy fillets, rinsed and patted dry, or small
sardines packed in olive oil (page 460)*

8 slices smoked ham or sausage (page 238)

A few minutes before serving, core the tomatoes, cut them each into 6 or 8 wedges, and sprinkle with sugar and salt. Peel the cucumber and cut it in half, lengthwise, then into ½-inch slices to make half-moons.

Keeping each ingredient separate, arrange the *mezethákia* on a large platter, either in concentric circles or as triangular wedges.

Marinated Olives

Eliés Marinátes

Makes about 3 cups

A small barrel of these glistening aromatic olives is a familiar sight in Greek homes. They are easy to prepare and the pungent herbs used in the marinade make the fleshy *Kalamáta* olives irresistible. After the olives are eaten, the olive oil can be used in salad dressings.

1 pound Kalamáta olives

¼ cup dried rígani *(page 14)*

1 tablespoon dried rosemary

½ tablespoon dried thyme

1 teaspoon dried marjoram

2-inch strip of orange zest

3 sprigs of dried rígani *or thyme, each about 3 inches long*

Kalamáta olive oil, to cover the olives

Spread the olives between layers of paper towels and blot dry to remove most of the brine. Mix together the olives, dried herbs, and orange zest in a bowl. Loosely pack into a glass jar, lay the herb sprigs on top, and add olive oil to cover. Cover tightly and store for 2 days to 1 week.

Salted Almonds

Amigtdhála Alatisména

Makes 2 cups

Traditional Greek wisdom says that eating salted almonds when you take a drink (or several!) will keep you sober. I have not put this tip to serious test myself so cannot vouch for its success, but I do know that once you've tasted the delicious sweet-sour flavor of these almonds you'll be in no hurry to buy commercially prepared ones again.

———

2 cups unblanched almonds

Juice of 2 lemons

3 tablespoons coarse-grain sea salt

Heat the oven to 325°F. Combine the almonds and lemon juice in a nonreactive bowl and set aside for 10 minutes; stir the almonds with a wooden spoon occasionally so they are evenly coated.

Arrange the almonds on a baking sheet in a single layer and sprinkle with the salt. Bake 20 minutes or until lightly browned, stirring once or twice. Let cool and serve, or store in small airtight containers for up to 1 month.

Peppered Dried Figs
Síka Piperáta

If possible, use fleshy juicy figs imported from southern Greece for this simple *mezé,* and prepare 3 days ahead for the richest flavor.

---

24 good-quality, moist dried figs

¼ cup coarsely cracked black peppercorns

12 to 18 imported bay leaves

Trim the fig stems. Gently roll each fig in the pepper to lightly coat.

Cover the bottom of a glass jar with a few of the bay leaves, or make an overlapping circle of leaves on 2 layers of plastic wrap. Then make alternate layers of figs and bay leaves, finishing with a layer of leaves. Gently press down on the leaves with the palm of your hand, then tightly cover the jar or pull the edges of the plastic wrap together into an airtight package. Store at room temperature for up to 1 month. Serve the figs on a bed of bay leaves.

Smoked Fish Salad

Tsirosaláta

Serves 6 to 8

There is a long tradition of preserving fish in Greece and markets display a variety of brightly colored smoked fish, stacked in decorative layers in wooden crates and barrels. There may also be whole anchovies packed in salt, fish roe in beeswax, sardines in olive oil, bonito in brine, or young mackerel or octopus, dried in the sun. Look for preserved fish in Greek grocery stores; this recipe is for smoked fish but you can also use bonito, sardines, or anchovies.

---

1 large smoked mackerel or herring or 2 small smoked mackerel (about 12 ounces)

2 tablespoons aged red-wine vinegar

FOR SERVING

1 tablespoon capers, drained

1 tablespoon extra-virgin olive oil, or to taste

Cracked black pepper to taste

2 tablespoons snipped fresh dill or chervil or 1 tablespoon coarsely chopped flat-leaf parsley

Elítses or Niçoise olives, drained

Hold the mackerel by its tail above an open flame until the skin blisters and breaks. (Or broil in a preheated broiler until the skin blisters.) Peel off the skin and discard the head and tail. With a thin-bladed knife make a slit along the underside of the fish, open it like a book, and, with your palm, firmly press to flatten it. Discard the backbone and skeleton. Place the fillets in a bowl, add 1½ tablespoons of the vinegar, and cover with cold water. Set aside for 10 minutes.

Remove the fillets, discarding the liquid, thoroughly dry with paper towels, and cut into thin strips or bite-sized pieces. Arrange on a platter and sprinkle with the capers, olive oil, pepper, dill, olives, and the remaining ½ tablespoon vinegar.

Tiny Fried Fish

Maríthes Tighanités

Serves 6 to 8

When ordering a drink at a beachside *tavérna* the visitor to Greece is often agreeably surprised to discover that, along with a glass of wine or *oúzo*, the waiter has brought an appealing platter of crisply fried tiny fresh fish. In Greece pickerel, sardines, and anchovies are favorites for this delightful *mezé* but for us more readily available whitebait make a good substitute. It's important to choose glossy-looking very fresh fish since the whole whitebait is eaten, including the bones and head.

---

1 pound tiny whitebait

½ cup all-purpose flour

½ tablespoon coarse-grain sea salt, or more to taste

1 tablespoon cracked black pepper, or more to taste

Extra-virgin olive oil, for frying

FOR SERVING

2 large lemons, cut into wedges

Rinse the fish, drain between layers of paper towels, and blot dry. Combine the flour, salt, and pepper in a bowl, add the fish, and toss to coat.

Pour a ½-inch layer of olive oil into a large heavy skillet set over low heat. When hot but not smoking, raise the heat to medium low and add enough fish to fill the skillet without overcrowding. Fry until golden brown, turning once, and drain on paper towels. Repeat with the remaining fish.

To serve, pile on a warm platter, surround with the lemon wedges, and sprinkle with additional salt and pepper if desired.

Kephtethákia

Makes approximately 4 dozen *kephtethákia*
or 3 dozen *kephtéthes*

Kephtethákia—small, highly flavored meat croquettes or patties, traditionally made with lamb or pork, and fried or baked in good olive oil—are popular on *mezé* tables whatever the occasion. Equally delicious served warm or cold, tiny *kephtethákia* (about the size of marbles) are the perfect tidbit to serve with *oúzo*. Make them egg-sized instead and they become *kephtéthes*, which, served with a green salad, make an enjoyable and economical main course.

———

1½ cups minced onion

1 pound lean lamb or beef or a mixture of both,
finely ground

1 large potato, peeled and grated

½ cup fresh bread crumbs

2 eggs, lightly beaten

1 tablespoon aged red-wine vinegar, or more to taste

¼ cup finely chopped flat-leaf parsley

Sea salt and freshly ground black pepper to taste

1 tablespoon ground cumin or 1½ tablespoons ground coriander or ½ tablespoon ground cinnamon or ¼ cup finely grated kasséri *or parmesan cheese*

All-purpose flour, for dredging

Olive oil, for frying or baking

FOR SERVING

Juice of 1 large lemon

Combine the onion and ½ cup water in a small saucepan, bring to a boil and simmer until the liquid has evaporated, about 6 minutes. Combine the onion, meat, potato, bread crumbs, eggs, vinegar, parsley, and a generous amount of salt and pepper in a large bowl and add one of the spices or the cheese. With a wooden spoon or your hand, mix until well blended. Add additional vinegar, salt, and/or pepper to taste; the mixture should be highly flavored. Cover and refrigerate for 1 hour.

Moisten your hands with cold water and pat them barely dry. Form the meat mixture into ¾-inch patties (or 1½-inch patties for *kephtéthes*), flattening each slightly between your palms, and lightly dredge with flour.

To fry, pour a ¼-inch layer of olive oil into a heavy skillet set over medium-low heat. When the oil is hot but not smoking, add just enough *kephtethákia* (or *kephtéthes*) to fit comfortably in a single layer. Fry until golden brown on both sides and drain between 2 layers of paper towels. Repeat with the remainder.

To bake, heat the oven to 325° F and warm 2 or more heavy baking sheets. Brush with olive oil and arrange the *kephtethákia* 1 inch apart on the sheets. Lightly brush with olive oil and bake 20 to 25 minutes (25 to 30 minutes for *kephtéthes*), turning once to brown on both sides. Drain between layers of paper towels.

To serve, arrange on a platter and sprinkle with the lemon juice.

Note For a buffet or first course, form the meat mixture into 1-inch patties and cook as directed. To serve, combine the following:

> *1 small head of romaine lettuce, rinsed and cut into chiffonade (thin ribbons) just before serving*
>
> *6 scallions, trimmed, the best green parts left intact, and thinly sliced*
>
> *¼ cup coarsely chopped flat-leaf parsley*
>
> *1 tablespoon dried* **rígani** *(page 14)*

Arrange this salad on a platter. Sprinkle with the strained juice of 1 lemon and extra-virgin olive oil, salt, and pepper to taste. Pile the *kephtethákia* on top.

Potato Kephtethákia

Patatokephtethákia

Makes approximately 30 *kephtethákia*
or 24 *kephtéthes*

In the charming Cretan village of Aghios Nikolaos picturesque white-washed houses dazzle in the clear light and a brilliant sun dances off the bluest of seas. At his bustling café George serves his customers a mouth-watering variety of traditional Cretan *mezéthes* but his great specialty is these flavorful *kephtethákia*. Potato *kephtethákia* may not be sophisticated eating, but the taste is superlative. Serve with a variety of other *mezéthes* and khórta (page 294) for a traditional meal, or include them in a buffet or picnic. Larger potato *kephtéthes* and a salad of wild leaf greens (page 295) make an unusual light lunch.

---

1 pound boiling potatoes

2 tablespoons unsalted butter, melted

1 egg yolk

*3 tablespoons fresh mint leaves or 3 tablespoons
chopped fresh dill*

4 scallions, trimmed and finely chopped (about ⅓ cup)

2 tablespoons finely chopped flat-leaf parsley

1 tablespoon fresh lemon juice

Sea salt and freshly ground black pepper to taste

¼ cup fine bulgur, optional

All-purpose flour, for dredging

About ¼ cup olive oil, for baking

Scrub the potatoes and cut larger ones in half or into quarters. Place in a saucepan with cold salted water to cover, bring to a boil, cover, and simmer 15 minutes or until just cooked. Drain, and as soon as the potatoes are cool enough to handle, peel them. Pass through a food mill fitted with the fine disk into a large bowl. Or mash with a potato masher or fork, then push through a sieve into a large bowl. Tear the mint leaves into small pieces. Combine the melted butter and the egg yolk and add to the potatoes, with the mint, scallions, parsley, lemon juice, and salt and pepper. Lightly mix with a fork, and refrigerate.

If using the bulgur, combine it with 2 tablespoons flour in a food processor and process until the mixture has a sand-like consistency. Spread the mixture, or plain flour, on a plate. Heat the oven to 375°F and place 2 baking sheets in the oven to heat. Moisten your hands with cold water and pat barely dry. Shape spoonfuls of the potato mixture into ¾-inch balls for *kephtethákia*, or a little larger for *kephtéthes*. Flatten slightly between your palms and lightly dredge with the bulgur mixture or flour. Brush the hot baking sheets with olive oil and arrange the *kephtethákia* 1 inch apart on them. Lightly brush with olive oil and bake 15 to 20 minutes, turning once to brown on both sides. Drain between layers of paper towels.

Pile on a platter and serve hot or warm.

Potato Kephtethákia with Cheese
Polpétes

On Crete, two favorite cheeses are used to flavor potato *kephtethákia:* either aged *myzíthra* cheese or the fresh, slightly sour-tasting, *anthótyro*. Anthótyro is available only in Greece, but *féta* makes a delicious substitute.

Omit the parsley and use dill rather than mint. Add ⅓ cup finely grated aged *myzíthra* cheese, or ¼ cup finely grated *féta* cheese, and ½ cup well-drained cottage cheese, passed through a sieve, to the potato mixture. Chill, shape into *kephtethákia* or *kephtéthes*, and bake and serve as above.

Potato Kephtethákia with Tomatoes
Polpétes me Domatés

Make these beautiful little *kephtethákia* when tomatoes are in season. Core, peel, and seed 2 large ripe tomatoes. Cut into dice, place in a sieve set over a bowl, and sprinkle with a large pinch of sugar and small pinch of salt. Set aside for at least 30 minutes, then press the tomatoes gently but firmly against the sides of the sieve to remove as much juice as possible. Combine tomato with the potato or potato-cheese mixture just before shaping.

(continued)

Potato and Vegetable Kephtethákia
Polpétes Lakhaniká

Add a purée of spinach, cauliflower, or fresh fava beans to either the potato mixture or the potato-cheese mixture. For each 1 cup of potato mixture, add ½ cup vegetable purée.

Note To fry *kephtethákia*, use a light olive oil. To deep-fry, form the mixture into small round patties no more than 1 inch in diameter. Heat the oil until hot but not smoking, and fry the *kephtethákia* a few at a time until golden brown. Drain between layers of paper towels.

To pan-fry, pour a ¼-inch layer of oil into a heavy skillet set over medium-low heat. Heat until hot but not smoking, and fry the slightly flattened *kephtethákia* in batches until golden brown on both sides. Drain between layers of paper towels and serve hot or warm.

Lamb's Liver with Lemon Juice and Rígani

Sikotákia Tikhanitá

Serves 10

Thin squares of tender lamb's liver, lightly fried in a well-flavored olive oil, are a classic of Greek cuisine. Justly so, since that treatment lifts humble liver into the realms of the sublime! If lamb's liver is unavailable, you can substitute calf's liver, although of course the dish will be less authentic.

---

1 pound lamb's or calf's liver

All-purpose flour, for dredging

5 tablespoons Kalamáta olive oil

1 teaspoon paprika

Coarse-grain sea salt and cracked black pepper to taste

Strained juice of 1 large lemon

FOR SERVING

*2 tablespoons dried rígani (page 14), briefly pounded
in a small mortar*

⅓ cup coarsely chopped flat-leaf parsley

1 small red onion, cut into thin rings

Trim off any membrane from the liver, cut it into thin slices, and cut the slices into 2-inch squares. Lightly dust with flour and shake off the excess.

Heat ¼ cup of the olive oil in a large heavy skillet and fry the liver over medium-low heat until light brown and slightly crusty on both sides, about 4 minutes. (It should still be moist in the center.) Sprinkle with the paprika, salt and pepper, and half the lemon juice. Reduce the heat to low and cook 1 minute longer.

Transfer to a warm platter and sprinkle with the remaining 1 tablespoon olive oil and the lemon juice, salt and pepper to taste, and the onion, *rígani*, and parsley. Serve at once.

Pork in Aspic

Piktí

**Serves 12 to 14 as a first course,
8 as a light lunch**

Acommon sight in village kitchens in fall and winter is a sturdy tripod supporting a well-used blackened pot from which steams the most tantalizing spicy aroma. In the pot, pork and pig's feet simmer gently with herbs and spices. A good *piktí* takes time to prepare, but it is an important traditional dish and will repay all your effort. Prepare it at least four hours before serving so it will have time to set. It makes a beautiful buffet centerpiece, garnished with olives, radishes, cucumber, and cherry tomatoes. It can also be served as an elegant first course, accompanied by toasted whole-wheat bread and black olives or Black Olives and Lentil Saláta (page 49). For a satisfying lunch serve it with Beet Salad with Allspice (page 246), black olives, and crusty bread.

---

2 pig's feet, cut into pieces by the butcher

2 pounds lean bone-in pork (any cut), trimmed of fat

12 black peppercorns

1 tablespoon sea salt

4 bay leaves

3 whole cloves

1/2 teaspoon dried red pepper flakes

1 tablespoon dried rosemary or sage leaves

1/4 to 1/2 pound lean mild ham, optional

3 to 5 tablespoons white-wine vinegar

2 egg whites

2/3 cup finely chopped flat-leaf parsley

Rinse the pig's feet and pork, place in a stockpot, and add water to cover. Bring to a boil and remove any surface froth with a slotted spoon. Add the peppercorns, salt, bay leaves, cloves, red pepper flakes, and rosemary. Reduce the heat, cover, and simmer 1 hour.

Add the ham, cover, and simmer 2 to 3 hours longer, or until the meat is falling off the bones. Strain, and set aside the meat and bones to cool; discard the seasonings. Strain the stock through 2 layers of cheesecloth into a bowl, let cool, and refrigerate uncovered until cold.

Remove and discard the surface layer of hardened fat. Heat the stock just until it has liquified, then measure it. You should have 4 cups; if necessary, reduce by rapid boiling. Let cool, add 3 tablespoons of the vinegar and the egg whites, and stir with a wooden spoon. Bring to a boil over medium-low heat, stirring constantly, until the egg whites set and become stringy. Simmer a few minutes longer.

Set a fine-meshed sieve lined with 2 layers of cheesecloth over a bowl and strain the stock. You should have about 2 cups of clear straw-colored aspic. Taste, add more vinegar if desired; the aspic should be quite tangy. Loosely cover and refrigerate.

Remove the meat from the bones and discard the fat, sinew, and bones. Cut the ham and the meat from the pig's feet into tiny dice and the remaining meat into ¼-inch dice. Once the aspic has begun to thicken and adhere to the sides of the bowl, stir in the meat and parsley. Transfer the mixture to an oiled 4-cup mold, cover, and refrigerate until set, or for up to 3 days.

To serve, dip the mold in a bowl of boiling water for 5 seconds. Invert a serving plate on top and, holding the plate firmly in place, turn upside down to unmold.

Note If you can find bitter Seville oranges, substitute ¼ cup orange juice and the juice of 1 lemon for the vinegar to make a slightly different version of this traditional dish.

Snails in Vinegar

Salingária me Xsíthi

Serves 3

This rather startling *mezé* is a specialty of the island of Crete. The islanders enjoy it with plenty of crusty bread and copious quantities of robust local red wine, together with two or three other *mezéthes* such as olives, marinated vegetables, and *khórta* (page 294) to complement the taste and texture of the snails.

———

2 tablespoons coarse-grain sea salt

24 cleaned snails in their shells, boiled 15 minutes and their protective skins removed (page 472)

2 tablespoons extra-virgin olive oil

Boiling water, to cover the snails

½ cup aged red-wine vinegar

FOR SERVING

¼ cup coarsely chopped flat-leaf parsley

Spread the salt on a plate, press the rim of each snail into it, and set aside.

Add the olive oil to a large heavy skillet that will hold all the snails in a single layer and heat it over low heat. Add the snails and gently roll them around with a wooden spoon so they heat through. Add enough boiling water to barely cover the snails and simmer until the water has evaporated, about 12 minutes. Take care not to let the snails burn. Add the vinegar, cover, and cook over very low heat for 5 minutes or until reduced by half, occasionally shaking the skillet.

Transfer the snails to a warm platter or individual plates, spoon over the sauce, sprinkle with the parsley, and serve.

....

....

....

Fried Cheese

Saganáki

Serves 6

*S*aganáki means "two-handled frying pan"—this savory *mezé* is named for the dish in which it was originally cooked. It should be served bubbling hot: have ready some olives, *kephtethákia* (page 38), and one or two *salátes*—then bring on your *saganáki* centerpiece with a flourish!

½ pound **kephalotýri** *or* **kasséri** *cheese*

All-purpose flour, for dredging

Extra-virgin olive oil, for frying

FOR SERVING

Strained juice of 1 large lemon

Finely chopped flat-leaf parsley

Cracked black pepper to taste

Cut the cheese into ¼-inch slices with a sharp thin-bladed knife or cheese wire, and cut each slice into rectangles approximately 1½ by 2 inches. Dredge with flour, shaking off any excess, and set aside.

Cover the bottom of a heavy skillet with a thin layer of olive oil, and heat over medium-low heat just until the oil sizzles when you drop in a crumb of cheese; don't allow the oil to reach smoking temperature. Fry the cheese slices, a few at a time, on both sides until golden brown and crusty, about 6 minutes. Drain between layers of paper towels and keep warm in a low oven until all the slices are fried.

Transfer to a warm platter, sprinkle with the lemon juice, parsley, and pepper, and serve immediately.

Salátes

Greek *salátes* bear little resemblance to what we know as salads. Most are purées made from fresh or dried vegetables, blended with herbs, spices, and olive oil. Sometimes nuts are substituted for vegetables; the popular *taramosaláta* is made from the puréed roe of the mullet fish. With a culinary history stretching back into antiquity, *salátes* are attractive additions to a buffet table and offer a variety of interesting flavors and textures. The best *salátes* are still made the traditional way, using a large walnut mortar, which imparts its own special flavor. Blenders and food processors make speedy and simple work of them but tend to mash the ingredients into a smoother, blander texture than most Greeks would like. Serve two or three *salátes* on a *mezé* table, accompanied by warm *píta* or crusty bread and fresh or preserved *mezethákia* such as cucumbers and olives.

Salátes are appealing to busy cooks, as many can be made ahead of time, giving the flavors time to mellow and deepen. They also are versatile: Some, such as Fresh Fava Bean Saláta (page 50), can be served as unusual first courses. Or, to serve with drinks, spread one or two contrasting *salátes* on toast for quick and simple canapés.

Black Olives and Lentil Saláta

Elaiosaláta

**Serves 10 to 12 as a *mezé*,
8 as a first course**

All over Greece olives appear in an infinite variety of guises. In this attractive *saláta*, the magnificent flavor of oil-cured black olives is at its powerful best. Ideal as a spread for canapés, it's especially good with savory appetizers and Tiny Cracked Potatoes (page 76).

———

*1 cup green lentils, picked over, rinsed, and soaked for 30
minutes in cold water to cover*

½ cup imported oil-cured black olives, pitted

2 tablespoons capers, rinsed and patted dry

2 small salted anchovy fillets (page 460), rinsed and patted dry

2 tablespoons dried rígani (page 14)

1 large clove garlic, finely chopped

Juice of 1 large lemon

¼ cup extra-virgin olive oil, or more to taste

FOR SERVING

Oil-cured olives

1 teaspoon dried rígani, briefly pounded in a small mortar

Coarsely chopped flat-leaf parsley

Drain the lentils and place in a large saucepan with cold water to cover by 3 inches. Bring to a boil, cover, and simmer 30 minutes, or until they are soft but not disintegrating. Drain and set aside to cool; shake the colander once or twice to make sure all the lentils dry.

Place the olives, capers, anchovies, *rígani*, garlic, and lentils in a food processor or blender container. With the machine running, add half the lemon juice, then add the olive oil in a thin steady stream. Add more lemon juice or olive oil to taste and process just until the mixture is thick and creamy.
(continued)

Spread on a platter and place the olives in the center. Sprinkle with the *rígani* and parsley, and serve.

To make the traditional way Fit a food mill with the fine disk and press all the ingredients through into a large wooden mortar. Pound 5 minutes, or until well mixed. Add half the lemon juice and then add the olive oil drop by drop, pounding constantly, until you have a thick, creamy purée. The more olive oil you use, the better the flavor. Add more lemon juice to taste.

Note To store, refrigerate for up to 24 hours in an airtight container or store for up to 6 months in small sterilized jars, with a thin layer of olive oil on top of the purée to "seal" it. Before serving, stir in the olive oil.

Fresh Fava Bean Saláta

Favá

**Serves 8 as a *mezé*,
4 as a vegetable dish**

There's no doubt that shelling and skinning fava beans is labor-intensive, but don't let that stop you from making this wonderful classic dish. The earthiness of the beans is sharpened by the lemon juice and yogurt, olive oil gives a creamy texture, and fragrant dill lends pungency. The combination produces a *mezé* of surprisingly fine flavor and texture. Or try it as a side dish for roast or grilled pork or lamb.

---

3 pounds fresh fava beans in their pods

6 scallions, trimmed, with 2 inches of green left intact

5 to 6 tablespoons extra-virgin olive oil

2 tablespoons finely chopped fresh dill

Pinch of sea salt

1/2 teaspoon freshly ground black pepper

Strained juice of 1 small lemon

1/4 cup Strained Yogurt (page 8)

FOR SERVING

Fresh dill sprigs

4 to 8 Elítses or Niçoise olives

Shell the beans, remove their skins, and set aside. Coarsely chop the scallions, then finely chop 2 tablespoons and set aside for garnish.

Heat 2 tablespoons of the olive oil in a large heavy skillet over low heat and sauté the scallions for 5 minutes, or until soft. Add the beans, cover, and cook 5 minutes longer, shaking the skillet occasionally.

Transfer the beans and scallions to a food processor or blender container and add the dill, salt, and pepper. With the machine running, add most of the lemon juice, 3 tablespoons of the yogurt, and 2 tablespoons of the remaining olive oil, and process to a purée. If the purée seems too thick, add a few tablespoons of water. Add lemon juice, yogurt, or olive oil for a sharper, lighter, or deeper flavor (in that order).

Spread on a platter and sprinkle with the reserved scallions and the remaining olive oil and lemon juice. Garnish with the dill sprigs and olives and serve at room temperature.

To make the traditional way Prepare the beans in the same way, but finely chop the scallions before sautéing with the beans and dill. Pound the sautéed bean mixture in a large wooden mortar for 10 minutes before adding the remaining ingredients. To obtain a creamier purée, double the quantity of olive oil.

Fava Bean Saláta

Favá

Serves 8 to 10 as a *mezé*,
6 as a vegetable dish

The success of this traditional country *saláta* depends on the quality of the olive oil you use—the better the oil, the richer the flavor. The base is a melting mixture of finely diced carrot, celery, onions, and garlic and bay leaf, sweetened by long slow cooking in the olive oil. It's a distinctive dish that never fails to please, and it improves in flavor if made a day or two ahead. Serve as a *mezé*, with bowls of yogurt and *khórta* (page 294), or as a side dish for roast or grilled meats. If using fava beans seems too time-consuming, you can substitute canned or dried butter beans, although the dish will lose some authenticity of flavor.

----

*1 1/2 cups dried fava or butter (large lima) beans, soaked
overnight in water to cover, or 2 15-ounce cans butter beans,
drained and rinsed*

1/3 cup extra-virgin olive oil

1/2 cup finely chopped onion

1 clove garlic, finely chopped

1/3 cup finely diced carrot

1/3 cup finely diced celery

1 bay leaf, crumbled

2 1/2 tablespoons finely chopped flat-leaf parsley

Sea salt to taste

1/2 teaspoon freshly ground black pepper, or more to taste

*1 thick slice coarse-grain white or whole-wheat bread, crust
removed and soaked for 5 minutes in 1 to 3 tablespoons
extra-virgin olive oil (to taste)*

Juice of 1 small lemon

FOR SERVING

Large pinch of paprika

Drain the dried beans and place in a large saucepan with cold water to cover. Bring slowly to a boil, drain, and rinse. Rinse out the saucepan, return the beans to the pan, and add cold water to cover by 3 inches. Bring to a boil, reduce the heat, cover, and gently simmer 25 to 30 minutes, or until soft. Drain, reserving ½ cup of the cooking liquid. Remove the fava bean skins with your fingers and spread the beans between layers of paper towels to dry.

Heat 2 tablespoons of the olive oil in a large heavy skillet. Sauté the onion, garlic, carrot, celery, and bay leaf over medium-low heat for 15 to 20 minutes, or until dark golden brown, stirring occasionally with a wooden spoon.

Stir in 2 tablespoons of the parsley, the salt, pepper, beans, and reserved cooking liquid. (If using canned beans, add ½ cup water.) Cook for 2 to 3 minutes, or until the liquid has evaporated.

Transfer to a food processor or blender container and add the bread. With the machine running, add about two thirds of the lemon juice and 2 tablespoons of the olive oil, and process until thick and smooth. Add a few tablespoons of water if the purée seems too thick, and add salt, pepper, olive oil, and/or lemon juice to taste.

Serve on a platter, sprinkled with the remaining parsley and olive oil and the paprika.

To make the traditional way Pound the cooked vegetable-bean mixture and the bread in a large wooden mortar for 5 minutes. Slowly add about two thirds of the lemon juice and then ¼ cup of the olive oil. Pound for 5 minutes longer, and add salt, pepper, olive oil, and/or lemon juice to taste.

Garbanzo Beans and Garlic Saláta

Revithosaláta

Serves 10

The best *revithosaláta* has a thick creamy consistency, a spicy coriander tang, and a pleasing pale mustard color. The flavors of garlic and olive oil, although not overpowering, should be detectable. Serve with *mezethákia*, vegetable appetizers, a bowl of yogurt, and warm *píta* bread.

1½ cups dried garbanzo beans, soaked overnight in water to cover

2 large cloves garlic, chopped

1 teaspoon ground coriander or ½ teaspoon ground cumin

½ teaspoon sea salt, or more to taste

½ teaspoon freshly ground black pepper, or more to taste

5 tablespoons Kalamáta olive oil

Strained juice of 2 lemons, or to taste

FOR SERVING

Finely chopped flat-leaf parsley

1 tablespoon dried rígani (page 14), crumbled

1 teaspoon paprika

Drain the beans and place in a large saucepan with cold water to cover. Bring slowly to a boil, drain, rinse. Rinse out the saucepan, return the beans to the pan, and add cold water to cover by 3 inches. Bring to a boil, reduce the heat, cover, and gently simmer for 50 minutes or until soft. Drain, reserving ½ cup of the cooking liquid and a few whole beans for garnish.

Place the beans, garlic, coriander, salt, and pepper in a food processor or blender container. With the machine running, gradually add ¼ cup of the olive oil and most of the lemon juice. Add more salt and pepper and the remaining lemon juice if desired and process until smooth and creamy. For a thinner consistency, gradually add some or all of the reserved cooking liquid. (If you plan to store the *saláta*, add all the reserved liquid—it will thicken on standing.)

Spread on a platter and sprinkle with the parsley, *rígani*, and reserved whole beans. Combine the paprika and remaining 1 tablespoon olive oil and sprinkle over the *saláta*.

Note To store, refrigerate in an airtight container for up to 2 days.

Fish Roe Saláta

Taramosaláta

**Serves 10 to 12 as a *mezé*,
8 as a first course**

The ancient Greeks were very fond of this smooth sharp fish pâté and it's just as popular in Greece today. Barrels of salted dried mullet roe, the basic ingredient of *taramosaláta*, are a familiar sight in busy fish markets. For the Greeks, *taramosaláta* is a winter dish, especially popular during the Lenten fast when no meat or dairy products are eaten. For us, with jars of *taramá* readily available in Greek and Middle Eastern stores, it can be a year-round treat. Versions vary from region to region, even from cook to cook—some favor the use of just bread, others use potatoes instead, yet others both. Experiment until you find your favorite combination of ingredients, texture, and flavor. Best made just before serving, *taramosaláta* is an attractive buffet dish; served on small plates, garnished with radishes, olives, and cucumber, it makes an elegant first course for a dinner party.

(continued)

1 10-ounce jar **taramá**

¼ cup minced onion

3 to 4 cups fresh bread crumbs (made from densely textured white bread, crusts removed)

Juice of 1½ lemons

½ cup extra-virgin or Kalamáta olive oil, or more to taste

FOR SERVING

12 Náfplion olives or other Greek green olives

Finely chopped flat-leaf parsley

Place the *taramá* in a bowl, cover with cold water, and break up any lumps with your fingers. Set aside for 30 minutes.

Line a sieve with 2 layers of cheesecloth and drain the *taramá* over a bowl. Gently squeeze the cheesecloth "bag" to remove as much of the salty water as possible; discard the water. Place the *taramá*, onion, and 3 cups of the bread crumbs in a food processor or blender container. With the machine running, add the juice of 1 lemon, then add the olive oil in a thin steady stream and process until the *taramosaláta* has the consistency and texture of thick cream. Add a little cold water if it is too thick, or additional bread crumbs if too thin. If you prefer a sharper flavor, add some or all of the remaining lemon juice; for a more mellow taste, add more olive oil.

Serve on a platter, surrounded with the olives and sprinkled with the parsley.

To make the traditional way With a large wooden mortar and pestle, pound the *taramá*, about 3½ cups of the bread crumbs, and the onion for 5 minutes, or until well mixed. Slowly add the lemon juice and ⅔ cup olive oil, and pound 5 minutes longer. Add a little cold water if the mixture seems too thick, or additional bread crumbs if too thin.

Note You can substitute 1½ cups mashed potatoes for the bread crumbs or use a mixture of potatoes and bread crumbs. Use a mortar and pestle— potatoes lose their firm texture if processed.

Eggplant Saláta

Melitzanosaláta

⊠

Serves 10 to 12

For this wonderful *saláta* eggplants are first broiled or grilled, then the soft cooked flesh is scooped from the shells and mixed with an aromatic blend of tomato, *rígani*, onion, garlic, lemon juice, and seasoning. Your food processor will make fast work of this unusual dish—but a smoky flavor is essential, so the eggplants must be broiled or grilled, not baked.

———

1 large ripe tomato, peeled, seeded, and diced

3 or 4 large unblemished eggplants (about 3 pounds)

1 tablespoon dried rígani (page 14)

2 tablespoons finely chopped sweet or mild onion

1 to 2 cloves garlic, crushed

Sea salt and freshly ground white pepper to taste

Juice of 1 small lemon

¼ cup Strained Yogurt (page 8)

¼ cup coarsely chopped flat-leaf parsley

¼ cup extra-virgin olive oil

FOR SERVING

6 small capers, drained and rinsed

Large pinch of paprika

Heat the broiler. Drain the diced tomato in a sieve.

Trim the stem ends from the eggplants, make 6 small slits in each eggplant, and place on the broiler tray 2 to 3 inches from the heat source. Broil until the skins scorch, carefully turning so that they brown evenly on all sides, about 15 minutes. Test by inserting the point of a knife into the center of each eggplant—they should be very soft. Let cool.

When the eggplants are cool enough to handle, carefully scrape out the flesh from the skins and, with a teaspoon, remove and discard as many of the seeds as possible (there's no need to be too fussy!). Gently squeeze the flesh between paper towels to remove excess moisture.

Place the *rígani*, onion, garlic, salt and pepper, and lemon juice in a food processor or blender container and process a few seconds, until well mixed and finely chopped but not pulverized. Add the tomato, eggplants, and about 3 tablespoons each of the yogurt and parsley, and pulse 2 or 3 times to mix. Add the olive oil in a thin steady stream, continuing to pulse—but stop before the mixture is smooth. Add salt and pepper, lemon juice, and/or olive oil to taste. Transfer to a serving bowl, cover tightly, and chill at least 1 hour.

To serve, spoon the remaining yogurt on top of the *saláta* and sprinkle with the capers, paprika, and the remaining parsley.

To make the traditional way Grill the eggplants over the embers of a wood fire. Let cool, remove the flesh and seeds, and cut the flesh into fine dice. Pound the onion, garlic, and salt and pepper in a large wooden mortar for 5 minutes. Add the eggplant, tomato, *rígani*, lemon juice, yogurt, and parsley. Pound 5 minutes longer, or until well pulverized. Add the olive oil in a thin steady stream, still pounding, until the mixture is thick and well combined. Although the quantities of the other ingredients remain the same, 2 or 3 tablespoons more olive oil are needed to obtain the right consistency—this is one reason why traditionally made *melitzanosaláta* has a deeper, more interesting flavor.

Sweet and Spicy Tomato Saláta

Domatosaláta Pikantikí

Serves 6

Anastasia, a friend on the island of Khios, taught me how to make this appetizing *saláta*. The dish has a charm all its own, especially when served in a shallow bowl with a swirl of creamy white yogurt and a sprinkling of glossy fresh parsley or coriander leaves for garnish. You can also use the *saláta* as a rich tomato sauce, perfect with baked or grilled fish, meat *piláfi* and *macarónia* dishes.

¼ cup extra-virgin olive oil

1 cup finely chopped onion

3 pounds firm ripe tomatoes, peeled and diced,
juices reserved

1 tablespoon tomato paste diluted with 2
tablespoons water

1½ teaspoons ground cinnamon, or to taste

1 large clove garlic, finely chopped

Sea salt to taste

½ teaspoon freshly ground black pepper, or more to taste

Pinch of cayenne pepper

2 tablespoons aromatic honey, such as Hymettus

1 to 2 tablespoons aged red-wine vinegar or 1 tablespoon
balsamic vinegar

FOR SERVING

2 tablespoons Strained Yogurt (page 8), optional

Finely chopped flat-leaf parsley or a few fresh
coriander leaves

Heat the olive oil in a large heavy skillet and sauté the onion over medium-low heat for 10 minutes or until soft; do not let it brown. Add the tomatoes and their juices, tomato paste, cinnamon, garlic, cayenne pepper, salt, and pepper. Raise the heat and boil uncovered 30 to 40 minutes, or until most of the liquid has evaporated, stirring occasionally with a wooden spoon. The purée should be thick enough to remain separated for a few seconds when you draw the spoon across the bottom of the skillet. Add the honey, reduce the heat, and cook, stirring occasionally, for 10 minutes longer, or until thick and slightly syrupy. Be careful not to let it burn. Remove from the heat and set aside to cool.

Stir in 1 tablespoon of the vinegar, taste, and add more cinnamon, salt, pepper, cayenne, and/or vinegar if desired.

Transfer to a shallow bowl, add a swirl of the yogurt in the center, sprinkle with the parsley, and serve.

Note To store, refrigerate for up to 1 week in an airtight container or store for up to 3 months in small sterilized jars "sealed" with a thin layer of olive oil. Use this oil in salad dressings or other dishes, or stir into the *saláta* before serving.

Eggplant and Other
Vegetable Appetizers

Eggplant Appetizers

Melitzánes Mezéthes

Eggplants are such a characteristic ingredient of Mediterranean cuisines that it's surprising to learn that they are not native to the region but instead originated in tropical Asia. In Greece, eggplants form the basis of an infinite variety of simply prepared delicacies—baked, they lend a subtle earthy flavor and richness to casseroles and other dishes; stuffed with aromatic or spicy fillings, they become satisfying main courses; and puréed into delicate creamy *salátes* they have pride of place on a good *mezé* table. For simple snacks eggplant slices can be fried plain in olive oil or dipped in fritter batter and fried.

Visit any Greek market in early summer and displayed before you is the abundance, variety, and splendor of the exotic eggplant: skillfully stacked in huge geometric piles, glossy skins gleaming in the sun, small round eggplants nestle next to thin elongated varieties and bulbous pear shapes. Their variegated colors create a feast for the eye, ranging from pure pearly white and white streaked with green to the deepest velvet purple and black.

Reject any eggplants with bruised or wrinkled skins and check that the stem end looks fresh and the prickly calyx firm and bright. Fresh eggplants feel heavy in your hand and the skins should be glossy and tight. Size and shape do not affect flavor, so choose according to the requirements of your recipe.

Eggplants contain a bitter juice that must be removed before cooking. Cut the vegetable in half or into slices or dice, sprinkle the cut surfaces with salt, and let drain in a colander for thirty minutes to an hour. The cut surfaces will then be covered by droplets of pale brown liquid, which you can remove by patting the pieces dry with paper towels. Remove as much moisture as you can. This salting and drying process not only seasons the eggplant but also prevents it from absorbing too much olive oil during cooking. Eggplant and olive oil are, however, natural partners so do not be tempted to skimp on the amounts called for in these recipes. A Greek friend says that olive oil helps the "shy" eggplant to discover its "true talkative personality"—and I agree with him!

Broiled Eggplants

Melitzánes Skháras

An informal supper that always pleases friends is simplicity itself to prepare: broiled eggplants, a tasty fish *mezé*, juicy olives, *féta* cheese, plenty of bread, and a glass or two of *oúzo*. Each guest receives a whole eggplant and, according to taste, adds a dressing of olive oil, lemon juice, and seasonings to the eggplant's delicious smoky-flavored flesh. Sighs of delight are not uncommon once guests begin to eat!

---

1 4- to 6-inch long eggplant per person

Heat the broiler.

Trim the ends from each eggplant and make 6 small slits in the skin to allow moisture to drain during broiling. Place on a broiling pan 2 to 3 inches from the heat and broil, using tongs to turn carefully, until lightly charred and blistered on all sides, about 10 minutes. Drain briefly on paper towels.

Slit open each eggplant from one end to the other, taking care not to let any charred pieces of skin fall aside, and press the ends to open them slightly. Arrange on a platter or individual plates and serve immediately.

Fragrant Eggplants with Olives
Melitzánes Aromatikés

Serves 4

Turning everyday ingredients into special treats is a traditional Greek skill, as this popular *mezé* demonstrates. Eggplant slices are simply fried, grilled, or broiled but the last-minute addition of good red-wine vinegar, succulent olives, bright green parsley, and perfumed *rígani* creates a colorful dish with a highly unusual flavor. Serve with thick yogurt in which to dip the eggplant slices.

---

*3 medium eggplants (about 1¼ pounds),
each around 2 inches in diameter*

Sea salt to taste

Extra-virgin olive oil, for frying or broiling

FOR SERVING

3 tablespoons aged red-wine vinegar, or to taste

1 dozen Elítses or Niçoise olives, drained

2 tablespoons finely chopped flat-leaf parsley

1 tablespoon dried rígani *(page 14),
briefly pounded in a small mortar*

Cracked black pepper to taste

Trim off the ends from the eggplants and cut into ¼-inch slices. Sprinkle with salt and set aside for 1 hour to sweat.

To grill or broil, arrange a grill rack about 3 inches above hot coals, or heat the broiler. Thoroughly dry the eggplant slices with paper towels and brush on both sides with olive oil. Grill or broil 1 to 2 inches from the heat source until dark golden brown on both sides; don't worry if they blacken in places. To fry, cover the bottom of 1 or 2 large heavy skillets with a thin layer of olive oil and heat over medium-low heat. Fry the eggplant slices, a few at a time, until golden brown on both sides. Drain between paper towels.

Arrange the slices in an attractive pile on a platter. Just before serving sprinkle with the vinegar, olives, parsley, *rígani*, and salt and pepper. Serve hot, warm, or at room temperature (within 1 hour of cooking).

Eggplant with Zucchini and Artichoke Hearts

Tighanitá Lakhaniká

**Serves 12 as a *mezé*,
6 as a light lunch**

In early summer, when zucchini and artichokes are at their crunchy best, these delectable vegetable fritters appear on *tavérna* tables throughout Greece, as part of a *mezé* table, or as a simple lunch. Garlic adds the finishing touch—these fritters are traditionally served with a powerful garlicky sauce.

---

3 medium eggplants, about 1 pound

Sea salt

1 pound medium zucchini

12 small or 6 medium artichokes

1 lemon, cut in half

All-purpose flour, for dredging

2 cups fresh fine bread crumbs

3 eggs

Freshly ground black pepper to taste

Extra-virgin or Kalamáta olive oil, for frying

FOR SERVING

⅓ cup coarsely chopped flat-leaf parsley

1 tablespoon dried rígani (page 14)

Finely grated zest of ½ lemon

Juice of 1 large lemon

1 dozen Elítses or Niçoise olives, drained

*Garlic Almond Sauce (page 421)
or Garlic Potato Sauce (page 422)*

Trim off the stem ends of the eggplants and cut into ¼-inch lengthwise slices. Cut these crosswise in half or into quarters, sprinkle with 1 tablespoon salt, and set aside for 30 minutes to sweat. Wipe the -inch slices. Sprinkle with 1 tablespoon salt and set aside.

Prepare a large bowl of ice water. Trim the stems of the artichokes and remove the tough outer leaves. With a sharp knife, slice off the top third of each artichoke to expose the choke. Scoop out the fuzzy part with a small spoon and trim off any remaining leaves from the heart. Cut larger hearts in half or into quarters. Rub all the cut surfaces with half a lemon, place in the bowl of ice water, and add the lemon halves to the bowl.

Spread the flour on one plate and the bread crumbs on another. Break the eggs into a small bowl, add salt and pepper to taste, and lightly beat together with a fork. Place 2 large heavy skillets over low heat and add olive oil to make a thin layer. With paper towels, dry enough eggplant slices to make a single layer in the skillets. Lightly dust with flour and shake off any excess. Dip the slices first in the egg mixture, then in the bread crumbs, to coat on both sides. When the oil is hot but not smoking, fry the eggplant slices until light golden brown on both sides, about 6 minutes. Drain between layers of paper towels, and repeat with the remaining eggplant and the zucchini slices.

Add enough olive oil to one of the skillets to make a ¼-inch layer. When the oil is hot, fry the artichoke hearts until light golden brown on all sides. Drain between layers of paper towels. Chop the parsley, *rígani*, and lemon zest together until well mixed.

To serve, arrange the vegetables on a platter and sprinkle with the lemon juice, olives, and the parsley mixture. Serve hot, warm, or at room temperature, with the garlic sauce.

Note For greater speed, you can deep-fry the vegetables in olive oil, but be sure to keep the temperature of the oil just below smoking.

Island Eggplants

Nisiótikes Melitzánes

**Serves 8 to 10 as a first course,
6 as a vegetable dish**

This hearty eggplant dish from the Greek islands, with its combination of robust contrasting flavors, reflects the Turkish occupations of medieval times. Serve cold as an elegant appetizer or buffet dish or warm as an unusual accompaniment to grilled meats and egg dishes. If possible, make a day ahead to give the flavors time to mellow.

1½ pounds medium round eggplants

Sea salt

6 ribs celery, rinsed and tough strings removed

2 red bell peppers, roasted and peeled (page 460)

½ cup extra-virgin or Kalamáta olive oil, or to taste

2 large onions, quartered and thinly sliced

1 large clove garlic, minced, optional

6 large ripe tomatoes, peeled and diced, juices reserved

1 teaspoon honey

*1 tablespoon tomato paste diluted with 2
tablespoons water*

3 tablespoons dried rígani (page 14)

½ teaspoon freshly ground black pepper, or more to taste

*1 pound tiny potatoes, baked in a clay pot (page 273) or boiled
until barely tender, optional*

½ cup finely chopped flat-leaf parsley

2 dozen Elítses or Niçoise olives, rinsed and pitted

¼ cup capers, rinsed and coarsely chopped

4 salted anchovies, rinsed and finely chopped

FOR SERVING

Juice of 1 large lemon

Trim the ends from the eggplants and cut into ¾-inch cubes. Sprinkle the cut surfaces with 1 tablespoon salt and set aside in a colander 30 minutes to sweat. Cut the celery into large julienne (matchsticks) and blanch in boiling water for 1 minute. Drain under cold running water, and set aside. Remove the cores and seeds from the bell peppers and wipe with paper towels to remove any remaining seeds. Slice lengthwise into thin strips.

Heat 3 tablespoons of the olive oil in a large skillet and sauté the onions over low heat for 10 minutes, or until soft. Add the garlic, tomatoes and their juices, honey, tomato paste, *rígani*, and salt and pepper. Raise the heat and lightly boil 15 to 30 minutes, or until reduced by half. The sauce should remain separated for a second or two when a wooden spoon is drawn across the bottom of the skillet.

Meanwhile, in another large skillet, heat 3 tablespoons of the remaining olive oil over medium heat. Thoroughly dry the eggplants with paper towels and fry 10 to 15 minutes or until golden brown on all sides. Drain between layers of paper towels and set aside.

Add the celery, peppers, potatoes, parsley, olives, capers, anchovies, and eggplant to the tomato sauce. Stir just to combine and cook over very low heat for 5 minutes. Add salt, pepper, and/or the remaining 2 tablespoons olive oil to taste.

To serve, arrange on a platter or individual plates and sprinkle with the lemon juice.

Note If you intend to reheat the dish, don't add extra salt until just before serving; the salty olives, anchovies, and capers will flavor the other ingredients.

Other Vegetable Appetizers

Tiny Stuffed Vegetables

Mikrá Yemistá Lakhaniká

**Serves 12 to 15 as a *mezé*,
8 as a first course**

These tiny stuffed vegetables are miniature works of art, masterpieces of the Greek kitchen. The vegetables used may be tomatoes, eggplants, bell peppers, onions, artichokes, zucchini, or squash. The main criteria for selection are that they add splashes of brilliant color to the *mezé* table and are the best available.

For a large gathering, buffet, or picnic these vegetables are a gift. They look spectacular and they're very long-suffering—staying fresh and delicious even in hot sunshine and after the first wave of guests has descended on the table! Although the preparation is fairly time consuming most of it can be done ahead of time. Any of the meatless fillings for stuffed vegetables given on pages 107 and 110 can be used but my own favorite is the following recipe. Its tantalizing herbal aroma reminds me of villages in the rugged Greek mountains where these highly flavored tiny treats are a specialty.

2 firm round eggplants, no more than 3 inches long

Sea salt

2 zucchini, 2 to 3 inches long

3 small patty pan squash or other squash suitable for stuffing, about 2 inches in diameter

3 small bell peppers, green, red, or yellow or a combination of all three

6 boiling onions, about 1½ inches in diameter

4 large cherry tomatoes

½ teaspoon sugar

½ to ¾ cup extra-virgin olive oil (to taste)

1 small onion, finely grated

1 large clove garlic, minced

1½ teaspoons ground cinnamon or 1 tablespoon ground coriander

Freshly ground black pepper to taste

2 cups cooked long-grain rice

¼ cup finely chopped flat-leaf parsley

2 tablespoons rígani (page 14), briefly pounded in a small mortar

½ cup currants or small dark seedless raisins, optional

Juice of 1 lemon

FOR SERVING

Lemon wedges

Slice off the stem ends of the eggplants, cut lengthwise in half, and sprinkle the cut sides with 2 teaspoons salt. Set aside for 30 minutes to sweat.

Fill a large saucepan with water and bring to a boil. Meanwhile, rinse the zucchini and other squash and rub with a kitchen towel to remove any fuzz. Slice off the stem ends of the patty pan squash and remove a thin slice from the base of each so they stand upright. Add the zucchini and other squash to the boiling water and lightly boil for 5 minutes, or until barely soft. Drain on paper towels. (Retain the boiling water for the next stage.)

(continued)

Slice off the tops of the bell peppers, remove the cores and seeds, and rinse the tops and peppers. Peel the onions, slicing off the root and stem ends. Add the peppers, pepper tops, and onions to the boiling water. Lightly boil the peppers for 5 minutes or until slightly softened, the onions 3 or 4 minutes longer, or until just soft, and drain.

Slice off the tops of the tomatoes and set aside. With a small spoon, scoop out the seeds, sprinkle the insides with the sugar and a pinch of salt, and invert on paper towels to drain. With the point of a small paring knife, push out the centers of the boiled onions, leaving shells of 2 layers. Finely chop the centers.

Heat the oven to 325°F. Place a heavy skillet over medium-low heat and add 3 tablespoons of the olive oil. Dry the eggplants with paper towels and fry until the cut sides are golden brown and the skin is dark and wrinkled, about 12 minutes. Drain on paper towels.

Cut the zucchini lengthwise in half and carefully scoop out the flesh, leaving ¼-inch shells. Scoop out the flesh of the eggplants and patty pan squash. Discard the eggplant seeds and finely dice all the flesh.

Heat 2 tablespoons of the remaining olive oil in a heavy skillet. Add the chopped onion, grated onion, and garlic, and sauté over low heat until soft. Add the tomato dice, eggplant pulp, cinnamon, and pepper, stir with a wooden spoon, and cook 1 to 2 minutes. Add the rice, parsley, *rígani*, currants, and half the lemon juice, and gently stir to mix. Add salt and pepper, cinnamon, and/or lemon juice to taste; the mixture should be highly flavored.

Arrange all the vegetable shells in a single layer in a large shallow baking dish. Loosely fill with the rice mixture, taking care not to split the shells. Replace the tops of the tomatoes and peppers and sprinkle all the vegetables with the remaining lemon juice and olive oil to taste. Add 1 cup water to the dish and bake uncovered for 1 hour, or until the vegetables are soft; reduce the oven temperature to 300°F if the vegetables start to brown. If necessary, add a little more water to the dish.

Let the vegetables cool in the baking dish, then transfer to a serving platter. Surround with lemon wedges and sprinkle with pan juices and olive oil to taste. Serve at room temperature.

Note If you prefer to use less olive oil, the eggplants can be cut in half and added to the boiling water with the zucchini. Boil 5 minutes and drain on paper towels. Because this dish has an overall mellowness, the rich flavor of eggplant prepared in olive oil is not essential to its success.

Aromatic Giant Beans

Fassólia Gigántes

**Serves 10 to 12 as a *mezé*,
4 as a light lunch**

This is one of my favorite Greek dishes and one I always associate with impromptu village gatherings in cool courtyards. Whatever the occasion, these beans are always present! Long slow cooking in olive oil sweetens and mellows the vegetables and the dish has a very special nutty flavor.

---

5 tablespoons Kalamáta olive oil

1 cup thinly sliced onion

½ cup finely diced celery

¾ cup finely diced carrot

1 pound ripe tomatoes, peeled and diced, juices reserved

1 teaspoon honey

1 tablespoon ground coriander

2 tablespoons dried rígani (page 14)

1 large clove garlic, finely chopped

*½ pound (about 2½ cups) dried butter (large lima) beans or
fava beans, soaked and cooked (page 53), or 2 15-ounce cans
butter beans, rinsed*

Sea salt and freshly ground black pepper to taste

FOR SERVING

Juice of ½ small lemon, or to taste

Heat 3 tablespoons of the olive oil in a large heavy skillet. Sauté the onion, celery, and carrot over medium-low heat for 20 minutes, or until light golden brown, stirring occasionally with a wooden spoon. Add the tomatoes and tomato juices, honey, coriander, *rígani,* and garlic, and stir well. Simmer until the sauce becomes thick and syrupy and stays separated a few seconds when the spoon is drawn across the bottom of the skillet. Gently stir in the beans, salt (canned beans may not need added salt), and a generous sprinkling of pepper, cover, and simmer 5 minutes longer.

Transfer to a shallow bowl, sprinkle with the lemon juice and the remaining 2 tablespoons olive oil, and serve hot, warm, or cold.

Three Marinated Salads

Lakhaniká Diáfora Marianáta

**Serves 10 as a *mezé*,
5 to 6 as a light lunch**

This enticing trio of vegetable salads captures all the unmistakable fragrance and flavors of the eastern Mediterranean. Serve with plenty of crusty bread to mop up the delicious sauces.

———

2 pounds fava beans in their pods

*1 pound thin asparagus, steamed or lightly boiled
(page 243)*

*4 medium artichoke hearts, lightly boiled just until tender and
cut into quarters (page 65)*

*⅓ cup coarsely chopped flat-leaf parsley, stems removed and
tied in a bundle*

Strained juice of 3 lemons, or to taste

Coarse-grain sea salt and cracked black pepper to taste

Large pinch of ground mustard

1 cup extra-virgin olive oil, or to taste

2 tablespoons snipped fresh chervil, optional

*2 tablespoons coarsely chopped fresh oregano leaves or 1
tablespoon dried* **rígani** *(page 14)*

FOR SERVING

*1 red bell pepper, roasted and peeled (page 460), seeded and
cut into thin strips*

Fill a large saucepan with lightly salted water and bring to a boil. Shell the beans, reserving 2 pods. Add the pods and parsley stems to the boiling water and boil 5 minutes. Add the beans and boil 2 minutes longer. Drain, discarding the pods and parsley stems. While the beans are still warm, remove the skins. Drain between layers of paper towels and pat dry.

Divide the lemon juice among 3 nonreactive bowls; add salt and a generous amount of pepper to each. Add the mustard to one of the bowls, divide the olive oil among the bowls, and add the chervil (or 1 tablespoon of the parsley) and artichokes to the bowl with the mustard. Add the (remaining) parsley and asparagus to the second bowl, and the oregano and fava beans to the third. Gently stir each mixture, tightly cover, and set aside for 1 hour.

To serve, taste each sauce and add lemon juice, salt, and/or pepper if necessary; the sauces should be highly-seasoned. Arrange the vegetables attractively on a flat platter or on individual plates, keeping them separate. Garnish the fava beans with strips of bell pepper.

Yogurt and Cucumber Salad

Tsatsíki

Serves 8 as a *mezé*, 4 as a salad

Variations of this crisp refreshing salad are popular throughout an area stretching from northern India to the Balkans and Greece. In the Greek version large amounts of garlic and flat-leaf parsley are used or, better still, fresh mint which gives a light fragrant flavor. Serve *tsatsíki* as soon as possible after preparing or it will become watery. Delicious as part of a *mezé* table, *tsatsíki* also nicely complements *kephtéthes, souvláki,* grilled meats, and fried liver (page 43).

(continued)

*1 large English hothouse cucumber or 2 small cucumbers,
peeled, cut lengthwise in half, and seeded*

1 tablespoon sea salt, or more to taste

1¼ cups Strained Yogurt (page 8)

2 tablespoons Kalamáta olive oil

1 tablespoon fresh lemon juice

Freshly ground white pepper to taste

2 to 5 large gloves garlic, minced (to taste)

*¼ cup fresh mint leaves or ¼ cup coarsely chopped flat-leaf
parsley or 2 tablespoons dried mint, crushed*

Using a knife, food processor, or mandoline, slice the cucumber into julienne (matchsticks). Sprinkle with salt and set aside in a colander for 1 hour to drain.

Combine the yogurt, olive oil, lemon juice, pepper, and garlic in a large bowl. Cover and refrigerate.

Just before serving, beat the yogurt sauce with a wooden spoon until smooth. Tear the mint into small pieces. Dry the cucumber by gently squeezing it between paper towels; don't worry if the cucumber bruises—it is more important to avoid a watery salad. Combine with the yogurt mixture and mint, add salt and pepper to taste, and serve.

Leeks the Classic Way

Klassiká Prása

Serves 12 as a *mezé*,
6 as a first course

This simple dish features traditional ingredients of the ancient Greek cuisine—spicy coriander, perfumed bay leaves, sweet honey, pungent vinegar, and rich olive oil. A popular *mezé* since the days of Homer, it looks beautifully elegant and has an unusual sour-sweet flavor.

12 thin leeks (¹/₂ inch diameter) or 6 thick leeks (1 inch diameter)

¹/₃ to ¹/₂ cup extra-virgin olive oil (to taste)

1¹/₂ tablespoons whole coriander seeds, crushed

3 bay leaves

1 teaspoon cracked black pepper

2 tablespoons aromatic honey, such as Hymettus

¹/₄ cup aged red-wine vinegar

¹/₂ cup currants or small dark seedless raisins

Coarse-grain sea salt to taste

FOR SERVING

2 tablespoons finely chopped flat-leaf parsley

Slice off the roots and green tops of the leeks. Cut a lengthwise slit halfway through each leek, keeping the original shape intact. Hold upright under running water and gently pull the layers apart one at a time to wash out any grit or dirt. Shake off excess water, drain between layers of paper towels, and blot dry.

Place a skillet large enough to hold the leeks in a single layer over low heat, and add ¹/₃ cup of the olive oil, the coriander seeds, bay leaves, and pepper. Cook for 1 minute, or until the coriander is aromatic. Add the leeks, turning to coat with the oil and spices.

Combine the honey and vinegar and add to the leeks along with the currants. Cover and bring just to a boil; reduce the heat to very low and simmer 10 to 15 minutes, or until the leeks are tender but still slightly firm in the center.

Transfer to a serving dish and set aside to cool. Add salt to taste and the remaining olive oil if desired. Sprinkle with the parsley and serve warm or at room temperature.

Note Twelve tender celery ribs can be substituted for the leeks. Remove the tough strings with a paring knife and cut wide ribs in half lengthwise. Cut into 5-inch pieces. Boil 1 minute in lightly salted water, drain, and add to the aromatic olive oil.

Tiny Cracked Potatoes
Patátes Antinaktés

**Serves 8 to 10 as a *mezé*,
3 to 4 as a vegetable dish**

This simple but superbly aromatic dish is a perfect *mezé* with yogurt, *khórta* (page 294), *kephtethákia* (page 38), and Fried Cheese (page 47), or serve it with grilled meats and chicken.

———

1½ pounds tiny new potatoes

¼ cup Kalamáta olive oil

⅓ cup aged red-wine vinegar

¼ cup coriander seeds, lightly crushed

Sea salt and cracked black pepper to taste

¼ cup coarsely chopped flat-leaf parsley

1 tablespoon small capers, rinsed and patted dry

1 tablespoon finely grated lemon zest

Scrub the potatoes and pat dry. With a mallet or heavy meat pounder, firmly tap each potato to crack it slightly, taking care not to break it apart.

Heat the olive oil in a large skillet with a tight-fitting lid. Add the potatoes in a single layer, cover, and cook 15 minutes over low heat, or until light golden brown, shaking the skillet frequently.

Drain off most of the oil from the skillet. Add the vinegar, coriander, salt, and a generous amount of pepper to the potatoes, cover, and cook over very low heat for 15 minutes, or until the potatoes are tender. Take care not to let the potatoes burn. Chop the parsley, capers, and lemon zest together to mix.

Transfer the potatoes to a warm platter and sprinkle with the parsley mixture. Serve hot, warm, or at room temperature.

Soups

Soúpes

For Greeks an ideal one-dish meal is a large bowl of aromatic and hearty soup, accompanied by crusty bread, plenty of local wine, juicy olives, peppery radishes, and soft crumbly cheese. From classical times Greeks have believed in the fortifying powers of good soups and they have a particular reverence for bean soups, which they believe develop physical and mental stamina. These substantial winter soups are especially popular during the Lenten fast.

At the other extreme, the Greek cook is also adept at creating a variety of delicate broths that make light and elegant first courses. These are usually laced with *avgolémono*, giving them a beautiful pale lemon color.

The most exquisitely flavored soup of this type is *mayirítsa*, the Easter soup made from the innards of the Paschal lamb and flavored with fresh dill and *avgolémono*. Served at the midnight breakfast of Easter morning and at Easter Sunday lunch, *mayirítsa* is a treat not to be missed. It's difficult to reproduce with complete success outside Greece, but if you are in Greece at Easter, don't miss the opportunity to sample it.

An introduction to Greek soups is not complete without some reference to fish soups, staple food on Greek tables, especially on the islands. The most popular of these is *kakaviá*, almost certainly the original of the famous Marseilles *bouillabaise* and introduced into France by occupying Greeks of classical times. You will not, however, find a recipe for this soup in my selection. This is not an oversight but a recognition of the fact that it is almost impossible to reproduce *kakaviá* with any kind of authenticity outside Greece since the requisite variety of fish is not available. But if you visit Greece be sure to seek out *kakaviá* and discover its delights for yourself!

Bean and Vegetable Soup

Fassolátha

Serves 6 to 8

For the Greeks of antiquity *fassolátha* was the staple winter food—not only delicious and aromatic, but nourishing, filling, and easy to make with ingredients to hand. It's still the most popular winter soup in Greece today and it is served in large shallow bowls, accompanied by *féta*, olives, a green salad, crusty bread, and a robust red wine. For best results use top-quality olive oil—it's essential for an authentic flavor.

---

2 cups dried black-eyed beans or cannellini or great northern beans, soaked for 4 hours in water to cover

½ cup extra-virgin olive oil, or to taste

2 cups finely chopped onion

1½ cups finely diced carrot

1 cup finely chopped celery rib

½ cup lightly chopped celery leaves, optional

2 large cloves garlic, finely chopped

2 tablespoons dried thyme or rígani (page 14) or a mixture of both

1 cup finely chopped flat-leaf parsley

Sea salt and cracked black pepper to taste

8 cups water or Meat Broth (page 467) or a mixture of both

3 large ripe tomatoes, peeled and diced, juices reserved

2 tablespoons tomato paste diluted with 3 tablespoons water

FOR SERVING

Aged red-wine vinegar or lemon juice, optional

(continued)

Drain the beans and place in a large saucepan. Add cold water to cover by 3 inches, bring slowly to a boil, drain, and rinse. Set aside.

Rinse out the pan, set over medium-low heat, and add ⅓ cup of the olive oil. Heat the oil and add the onion, carrot, and celery rib. Sauté 30 minutes, or until pale gold, stirring occasionally with a wooden spoon. Add the celery leaves, if using, the garlic, thyme, half the parsley, the pepper, beans, and water. Bring to a boil, cover, and simmer 1 hour, or until the beans are soft but not disintegrating. Meanwhile, sprinkle the tomatoes with salt and set aside for 15 minutes.

Stir the tomato paste and tomatoes into the soup, season with salt and pepper, and simmer 5 minutes longer. Stir in the remaining parsley, olive oil, and the vinegar if desired. Serve hot.

Bean and Vegetable Soup with Spinach
Fassolátha me Spanáki

Thoroughly wash 1 8-ounce bunch of young spinach leaves, discard the tough stems, and slice the leaves into chiffonade (thin ribbons). Add to the soup with the tomatoes. Sprinkle 1 tablespoon aged red-wine vinegar over each bowl of soup when serving, and provide each guest with a small bowl of croutons (page 462).

Green Lentil Soup
with Sorrel

Fakés Soúpa

Serves 6

Lentil and onion soup does not sound exotic—but add the richness of honey-sweetened ripe tomatoes, the strong sharp tang of sorrel, and a swirl of yogurt and you have a soup in an entirely different class. This trick of adding wild greens to bean soups is a common village practice and works well in softening the texture of their lentils and improving their flavor.

¼ cup extra-virgin olive oil

1 cup finely chopped sweet Bermuda onion

1½ cups green lentils, picked over, rinsed, and soaked for 10 minutes in water to cover.

5 cups fat-free broth (Chicken, Meat, or Vegetable, pages 461, 467, and 473) or water

2 large ripe tomatoes, peeled, seeded, and cut into small dice

½ teaspoon honey

Sea salt and cracked black pepper to taste

½ pound fresh sorrel

FOR SERVING

½ cup Strained Yogurt (page 8)

Heat the olive oil in a heavy saucepan and sauté the onion over low heat for 10 minutes. Drain the lentils and add to the saucepan with the broth. Bring slowly to a boil, cover, and simmer 40 minutes, or until the lentils are soft. (Keeping the heat low prevents an unattractive froth from forming.)

Meanwhile, place the tomatoes in a colander set over a bowl, sprinkle with the honey and salt, and set aside to drain. Wash the sorrel in several changes of cold water, strip the leaves from the stems, and discard any bruised or discolored parts of the leaves.

Drain the lentils over a bowl and set aside the cooking liquid. Transfer the lentils to a food processor or blender container, in batches if necessary, and pulse, adding enough reserved cooking liquid (and water if needed) to make a light soup. Return the soup to the rinsed-out saucepan.

Slice the sorrel into chiffonade (thin ribbons) and reserve a few choice strips for garnish. Add the sorrel and the tomatoes to the soup and season with pepper. Simmer 3 minutes, or just until the sorrel is soft. Add salt and pepper to taste.

Serve in individual bowls with a spoonful of yogurt in the center of each, and sprinkle with the reserved sorrel.

Aromatic Yellow Split-Pea Soup

Aromatikí Soúpa

Serves 4

This savory cumin-flavored soup looks elegant, comforts on cold days, and yet is surprisingly refreshing in warm weather.

———

1 cup yellow split peas, picked over and rinsed

¼ cup Kalamáta olive oil

½ cup finely chopped onion

½ cup finely diced carrot

½ cup finely diced celery

1 tablespoon ground cumin, or more to taste

4 to 4½ cups fat-free Chicken Broth (page 461) or water

Sea salt and freshly ground white pepper to taste

FOR SERVING

¼ cup Strained Yogurt (page 8)

Juice of 1 lemon

Coarsely chopped flat-leaf parsley

Cover the split peas with cold water and set aside. Heat the olive oil in a large heavy saucepan and sauté the onion, carrot, and celery over medium heat until golden brown, about 20 minutes, stirring occasionally with a wooden spoon. Stir in the cumin and cook 1 minute longer. Drain the split peas and add with 4 cups of the broth. Bring to a boil, cover, and gently simmer 40 minutes or until the peas are soft.

Purée the soup in a food processor or blender or push through the medium disk of a food mill. Add water or additional broth if necessary to make a light soup. Return to the rinsed-out saucepan, add salt and pepper, and heat slowly. Add more cumin if desired (you should be able to taste the cumin but its flavor should not be overpowering).

Divide the soup among warm individual bowls and place a spoonful of yogurt in the center of each. Sprinkle with lemon juice and parsley and serve hot or warm.

Variations

- Add 2 peeled and diced ripe tomatoes to the puréed soup and simmer 5 minutes. Omit the lemon juice.
- Serve with golden-brown croutons (page 462) rather than yogurt, and sprinkle each serving with the parsley and lemon juice and 1 teaspoon finely chopped Preserved Lemon (page 19).

Country Tomato Soup

Khoriátiki Soúpa

Serves 4

The gentle slow cooking of chopped onion, celery, and carrot, perfumed with thyme, creates a fragrant base for this colorful country soup. Make it when tomatoes are at their sweetest and serve with olives, *féta*, crusty bread, and a green salad.

———

2 tablespoons extra-virgin olive oil

1 cup finely chopped onion

¼ cup finely diced celery

¼ cup finely diced carrot

1 tablespoon dried thyme

1½ pounds ripe tomatoes, peeled and diced,
juices reserved

1 teaspoon honey

Sea salt and cracked black pepper to taste

4 cups Chicken Broth (page 461) or water

⅓ cup small kritharáki *or ¼ cup medium-grain bulgur*
(available from Greek or Middle Eastern stores, see Note)

1 cup watercress leaves, rinsed and coarsely chopped

2 tablespoons finely chopped flat-leaf parsley

FOR SERVING

Finely grated kasséri, kephalotýri, *or parmesan cheese*

Warm the olive oil in a large heavy saucepan over low heat and sauté the onion, celery, carrot, and thyme until pale golden brown, about 25 minutes, stirring occasionally with a wooden spoon. Stir in the tomatoes and their juices, honey, and salt and pepper, and simmer 4 minutes, or until the tomatoes are soft. Add the broth and bring to a boil. Add the pasta and simmer 4 minutes, or until the pasta is almost cooked. Add the watercress

and simmer 1 minute longer. Stir in the parsley and serve immediately, with small bowls of the grated cheese.

Note If using the bulgur, bring a small pan of water to a boil over medium heat. Add the bulgur, boil 1 minute, drain, and rinse under cold running water. Set aside.

Chicken Avgolémono Soup

Avgolémono Soúpa

Serves 6 to 8

Atraditional favorite in Greek homes and *tavérnas, avgolémono* soup has its origins back in antiquity. It's a most delicious and refreshing soup—light, nourishing, and elegant enough to serve at a dinner party. My version is based on a rich chicken broth enhanced with saffron, which gives a delicate but distinctive flavor. The addition of rice makes a more substantial soup.

8 cups fat-free rich Chicken Broth (page 461)

⅓ cup short-grain rice, optional

4 eggs, separated

Juice of 2 large lemons

Sea salt and freshly ground white pepper to taste

FOR SERVING

2 tablespoons finely chopped flat-leaf parsley

Bring the broth to a boil in a large pot, add the rice, cover, and simmer 15 minutes, or until the rice is cooked.

Five minutes before ready to serve, whisk the egg whites in a large bowl with a wire whisk or an electric mixer until stiff. Whisk in the yolks, add the lemon juice, and whisk 1 minute longer. Hold a ladleful of the hot broth about 12 inches above the bowl and slowly add it to the eggs and lemon

juice, whisking constantly. (This trick helps prevent curdling the egg mixture, because by the time the broth reaches the bowl it is hot but not boiling). Off the heat, whisk the egg and lemon juice sauce into the soup. Do not return the soup to the heat. Add salt and pepper to taste, sprinkle with the parsley, and serve at once.

Note Once the egg and lemon juice flavoring is added the soup must not be reheated.

Avgolémono Soup with Kephtéthes
Avgolémono Soúpa me Kephtéthes

Serves 8

This delicate and delicious soup is satisfying without being heavy—ideal for a light lunch. For convenience both the broth and the tiny crisp *kephtéthes* can be made in advance, but do not combine them until 10 minutes before serving.

½ pound lean lamb, finely ground

1 egg yolk, lightly beaten

¼ cup finely chopped onion

2 tablespoons finely chopped flat-leaf parsley

¼ cup fresh fine bread crumbs, soaked for 5 minutes in 1 tablespoon milk

½ tablespoon aged red-wine vinegar

Sea salt and freshly ground black pepper to taste

1 tablespoon olive oil, or more to taste

8 cups Meat Broth (page 467)

2 egg yolks

Juice of 2 lemons

FOR SERVING

Finely chopped flat-leaf parsley

Heat the oven to 375°F.

Combine the lamb, egg yolk, onion, parsley, bread crumbs, vinegar, and salt and pepper, and mix until thoroughly blended. Moisten your hands with cold water and pat barely dry. Shape the meat mixture into small balls the size of your thumbnail; you should have about 3 dozen.

Lightly brush a baking sheet with olive oil and place in the oven for 2 minutes to heat. Arrange the *kephtéthes* on the baking sheet and bake 15 to 20 minutes, or until golden brown. Drain between layers of paper towels.

Bring the broth to a boil in a large saucepan. Add the *kephtéthes,* reduce the heat, cover, and gently simmer 10 minutes; do not let the broth boil. Using a whisk, whisk the egg yolks in a large bowl until pale and frothy, add the lemon juice, and whisk 1 minute longer. Hold a ladleful of the hot broth about 12 inches above the bowl and slowly add it to the eggs, whisking constantly.

With a slotted spoon, transfer the *kephtéthes* to a warm soup tureen or divide among warm individual bowls. Off the heat, lightly whisk the egg and lemon juice mixture into the soup. Add salt and pepper to taste, stir in the parsley, ladle the soup over the *kephtéthes*, and serve.

The Monks' Onion Soup

Monarchó Soúpa

Serves 4

Staple fare in Byzantine monasteries, this soup is based on the humblest ingredients. It was served to the monks to remind them of the virtues of the simple religious life, removed from worldly extravagance. Although it is simple, and easy to prepare, this onion soup has a delicious flavor and makes a warming winter meal.

(continued)

2 tablespoons unsalted butter

¼ cup extra-virgin olive oil

3 large onions, quartered and thinly sliced (about 6 cups)

Sea salt and freshly ground black pepper to taste

*2 slices whole-wheat bread, crusts removed, and cut into
½-inch dice*

3 egg yolks

*3 tablespoons aged red-wine vinegar or 2 tablespoons balsamic
vinegar*

FOR SERVING

Finely chopped flat-leaf parsley

Pinch of ground cinnamon

Heat the butter and 1 tablespoon of the olive oil in a large, preferably nonaluminum, saucepan and sauté the onions over low heat for 20 minutes, occasionally stirring with a wooden spoon; don't let the onions color. Cover, reduce the heat, and cook 50 minutes longer, stirring once or twice. If the onions begin to stick, sprinkle with 1 or 2 tablespoons water. They will reduce almost to a purée, but should remain very pale. Add 4 cups water, salt, and pepper, and bring to a boil over medium heat. Cover, reduce the heat, and simmer for 15 minutes.

Heat the remaining olive oil in a heavy skillet and fry the diced bread over medium-low heat until golden brown on all sides. Drain these croutons between layers of paper towels.

Just before serving, whisk the egg yolks with the vinegar in a large bowl. Hold a ladleful of the hot soup about 12 inches above the bowl and slowly add it to the eggs, whisking constantly; whisk 10 seconds longer. Off the heat, stir the egg mixture into the soup. Add salt and pepper to taste.

Divide the soup among warm individual bowls and sprinkle with the croutons, parsley, and cinnamon. Serve at once.

Note For a more substantial soup, substitute Chicken or Meat Broth (pages 461 and 467) for some or all of the water.

Light Meals

Yévmata Elláfra

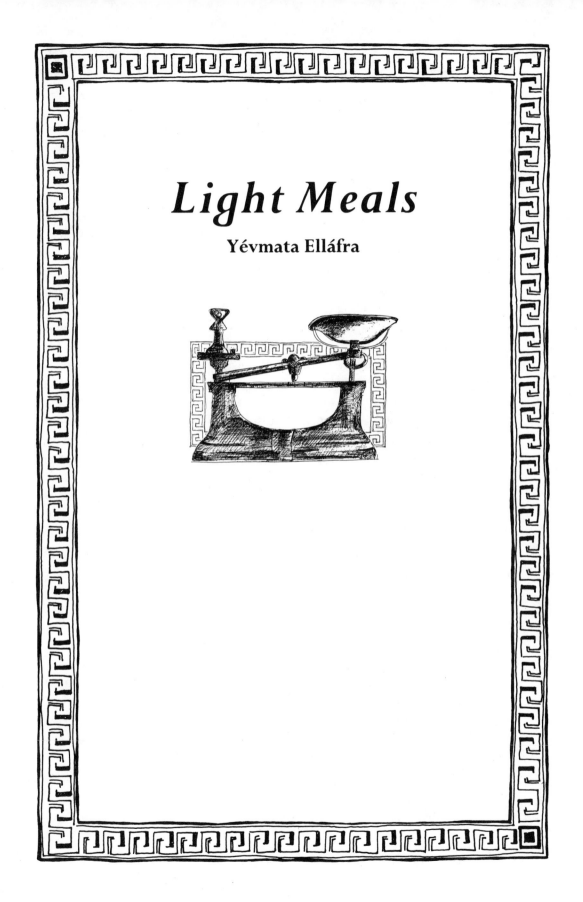

Greek cooks have a special talent for creating quick and appetizing snacks and light meals. Often the clue to their enchantment is the sheer simplicity of ingredients and the perfect freshness of the ingredients used.

The satisfying Greek egg dishes are a good example of this skill. I have been delighted by a homey platter of creamy aromatic eggs on a laden *tavérna* table, a *frittata* of zucchini in the cool shade of a perfumed summer garden, and, at a country café buzzing with local gossip, a fragrant herbed omelet enveloping tiny browned diced potatoes.

In summer a colorful variety of stuffed vegetables are served as light meals, and *tavérnas* display tempting trays of vegetable shells bulging with spicy rice or meat fillings. In the villages stuffed vegetables with an olive oil and lemon juice or tomato sauce are slowly baked to a moist mellowness in the baker's oven, producing a wonderful richness of flavor. The amount of olive oil used in the following stuffed vegetable recipes may seem high. But the pungency of good-quality olive oil is essential to flavor both vegetable and filling—without it you will not achieve the richness and depth of taste that's characteristic of these aromatic country meals.

Savory pies, made with crumbly pastry or *phýllo*, are favorite snacks and light meals too. Every bus or train station and every town square has its pie shop, selling tiny pastries concealing mouthfuls of spicy meat, cheese, chicken, or wild greens. Honeyed nuts or sweet custard fillings are popular too.

Many of the following recipes can be prepared in advance and reheated or served cold, and several, notably the pies, freeze very well. Remember too that many *mezéthes* and vegetable dishes can also be served as light meals or tasty snacks.

The Villager's Eggs
Avgá Khoriátiki

Serves 2

An omelet made with just-laid eggs and a handful of pungent fresh wild herbs is a favorite country snack. Villagers are especially fond of wild asparagus, mallow, wild chervil, purslane, wild leeks, zucchini flowers, and wild artichokes in their omelets and we can enjoy some of these country flavors too. I have found wild chervil in Chinese markets, purslane in a Tennessee potato field, and mallow alongside a footpath in Marin County.

½ pound wild asparagus or thin young asparagus

2 tablespoons extra-virgin olive oil

1 tablespoon fresh lemon juice

Coarse-grain sea salt and cracked black pepper to taste

4 eggs, lightly beaten

FOR SERVING

Coarsely chopped flat-leaf parsley

Lemon wedges

Break off the tough ends of the asparagus stalks at the point where they snap easily and discard. Blanch the asparagus in boiling water for 5 seconds, rinse under cold running water, drain between layers of paper towels, and blot dry. Cut into 2-inch pieces.

Warm the olive oil in a seasoned 9-inch omelet pan or heavy skillet and sauté the asparagus over medium-low heat until barely tender. Sprinkle with the lemon juice and salt and pepper. Pour the eggs over the asparagus and tilt the pan to distribute evenly. Reduce the heat to low.

When the omelet is lightly set, lift one edge with a spatula to allow any still-liquid egg to flow underneath. Slide out onto a plate, invert the pan over the plate, and, firmly holding both, invert once more so the omelet is upside down in the pan. Cook 20 seconds longer, or until set, and invert onto a warm serving platter.

Sprinkle with the parsley and serve at once with the lemon wedges.

(continued)

Light Meals

91

Note To season an omelet pan, sprinkle 2 tablespoons salt over the bottom of the pan and set it over low heat for 5 minutes. The salt will turn light brown as it absorbs all the extraneous substances that inevitably stick to the surface of kitchen utensils. Discard the salt and thoroughly wipe out the pan with paper towels.

Cheese Omelet

Omeléta Tyrí

Serves 2

In this tasty dish garlic is used to flavor the cooking oil, giving a robust taste to the omelet; the crunchy oven-dried bread crumbs add an unusual nutty texture. Serve with a tomato or bean salad or Beet Salad with All-spice (page 246).

---

2 tablespoons extra-virgin olive oil

1 clove garlic, cut into 3 pieces

3 tablespoons dried fine bread crumbs

2 ounces féta *cheese, crumbled, or aged* myzíthra, *grated*

4 eggs

Freshly ground black pepper to taste

FOR SERVING

1 tablespoon finely chopped flat-leaf parsley

1 tablespoon thinly sliced scallion

2 teaspoons fresh oregano, chopped, or 1 teaspoon dried rígani
(page 14), crumbled

6 Elítses or Niçoise olives, drained

Lemon wedges

Heat the olive oil in a seasoned 9-inch omelet pan or heavy skillet. Sauté the garlic a minute or two over medium-low heat and discard. Add the bread crumbs to the pan and fry until pale golden brown, stirring occasionally. Lightly whisk together the cheese, eggs, and pepper and pour over the bread crumbs, tilting the pan to distribute evenly.

When the omelet is lightly set, lift one edge with a spatula to allow any still-liquid egg to flow underneath. Slide the omelet out onto a warm plate, invert the pan over the plate, and, firmly holding both, invert once more so the omelet is upside down in the pan. Cook 20 seconds longer, or until set, and invert onto a warm serving platter.

Chop the parsley, scallion, and oregano together just to mix and sprinkle over the omelet, along with the olives. Serve at once with the lemon wedges.

Sausage and Potato Omelet

Omeléta me Loukhánika ke Patátes

Serves 2

Make this substantial and spicy omelet with *pastoúrmas* sausages (page 235) or Country Sausages (page 238) and whatever fresh herbs are available. Serve with a salad of wild greens (page 295) and Shepherd's Bread (page 335) or Olive Bread (page 339).

———

3 tablespoons extra-virgin olive oil

Two 4- to 5-inch sausages, casings discarded, cut into ½-inch slices

2 medium boiling potatoes, peeled if desired, cooked and cut into ½-inch dice (about 1½ cups)

5 eggs, lightly beaten

Cracked black pepper to taste

FOR SERVING

2 tablespoons coarsely chopped flat-leaf parsley or fresh coriander or fresh dill

Large pinch of ground paprika

Lemon wedges

(continued)

Heat 1½ tablespoons of the olive oil in a seasoned 9-inch omelet pan or heavy skillet (page 92) and sauté the sausages until lightly browned on both sides. Drain between layers of paper towels and wipe the pan clean.

Heat the remaining 1½ tablespoons olive oil in the pan and sauté the potato dice over medium-low heat until golden brown on all sides, about 6 minutes. Add the sausages and lightly stir to mix. Pour in the eggs, reduce the heat to low, and tilt the pan to distribute the eggs evenly. Season with pepper (the sausages are salty). When lightly set, lift one edge with a spatula to allow any still-liquid egg to flow underneath. Slide the omelet onto a warm plate, invert the pan over the plate, and firmly holding both, invert once more so the omelet is upside down in the pan. Cook 20 seconds longer, or until set, and invert onto a warm serving platter.

Sprinkle with the parsley and paprika and serve at once with the lemon wedges.

Variations Add 1 roasted, seeded, and peeled red bell pepper (page 460), cut into strips, or 1 cup fried diced eggplant or zucchini, or 1 leek, thinly sliced and sautéed, to the pan with the potato.

Saffron Eggs with Lamb's Kidneys

Avgá me Néfra apo Arnáki

Serves 2

Ifirst came across this surprising dish one Easter in a village on the island of Paxos. This was the specialty of the village café and I must say I had my reservations about sampling it, but it tasted superb. It is a highly unusual dish with a bold conjunction of distinctive flavors—try it! With crusty bread and a wild greens salad (page 295), purslane salad (page 292), or green salad it's an ideal lunch or supper when you'd like a meal that's quick and easy but out-of-the-ordinary.

———

2 or 3 small lamb's kidneys

Sea salt

2 tablespoons aged red-wine vinegar

3½ tablespoons extra-virgin olive oil

6 large flat mushrooms, preferably wild, trimmed and cut into ¼-inch slices

¼ teaspoon saffron threads

1 tablespoon hot water

½ teaspoon fresh thyme or oregano, finely chopped

1 teaspoon whole coriander seeds, pulverized

½ teaspoon freshly ground black pepper

1 teaspoon honey

4 eggs

FOR SERVING

1 tablespoon finely chopped flat-leaf parsley

1 tablespoon finely chopped chives

Slice each kidney horizontally in half to expose centers. Cut out the valves and discard. Cut the kidneys lengthwise into ¼-inch slices and place in a bowl with ½ teaspoon salt, 1 tablespoon of the vinegar, and water to cover. Set aside for 30 minutes.

Heat 1 tablespoon of the olive oil in a skillet and sauté the mushrooms over medium-low heat for a minute or two. Once they have released some of their water, raise the heat to medium and cook, stirring occasionally, until most of the liquid has evaporated. Set aside.

Heat the saffron in a small dry skillet until aromatic, crumble into the hot water, and set aside. Drain the kidneys and rinse in several changes of cold water until the water remains clear; thoroughly dry with paper towels.

Heat 1 tablespoon of the remaining olive oil in a skillet and sauté the kidneys over medium heat until lightly browned, about 3 minutes. Sprinkle with the thyme, coriander, salt, and pepper. Combine the honey and remaining vinegar and add with the mushrooms. Cover, shake gently to mix, and cook 1 minute over low heat. Uncover, raise the heat, and cook, stirring, for 1 minute, or until most of the liquid has disappeared. Set aside and keep warm.

Strain the saffron water, discarding the saffron and reserving the liquid. Lightly beat the eggs and add the strained saffron water, salt, and pepper. Add the remaining 1½ tablespoons oil to a seasoned 9-inch omelet pan or heavy skillet (page 92) set over medium-low heat. Pour in the eggs and cook, stirring with a fork, until lightly set. Reduce the heat and spoon the warm kidney and mushroom mixture over the eggs.

Sprinkle with the parsley and chives and serve immediately.

Country Vegetable Omelet
Sfongáta

Serves 2

A fragrant dish of vegetables and eggs flavored with Mediterranean cheese, a *sfongáta* is essentially a *frittata*. You can use eggplants, potatoes, grilled bell peppers, onions, beans, leeks, or zucchini—whatever you have available. If you include tomatoes your *sfongáta* will have a soft and creamy texture. A *sfongáta* made without tomatoes, which is easier to maneuver, is usually turned over to brown on both sides. Garnish with tiny olives and parsley, and serve with country bread, slices of *féta* or *myzíthra* cheese, and a salad of wild greens (page 295).

---

5 small firm zucchini (about 1 pound)

Coarse-grain sea salt

5 tablespoons extra-virgin olive oil

1 shallot, finely chopped

1 small clove garlic, minced

2 large ripe tomatoes, peeled, seeded, and diced

Pinch of sugar, optional

5 eggs

2 tablespoons finely grated kephalotýri or parmesan cheese

Freshly ground black pepper to taste

1 teaspoon fresh oregano or marjoram, finely chopped

FOR SERVING

2 tablespoons coarsely chopped flat-leaf parsley

6 Elítses or Niçoise olives, drained

Trim the zucchini and cut into large julienne (¼-inch-thick matchsticks). Sprinkle with 1 teaspoon salt and set aside for 30 minutes to drain.

Heat 3 tablespoons of the olive oil in a seasoned 9-inch omelet pan or heavy skillet (page 92). Dry the zucchini with paper towels and sauté over medium-low heat until light golden brown, about 8 minutes. Drain on paper towels. Wipe out the skillet and set aside.

Heat 1 tablespoon of the remaining oil in a heavy skillet, and cook the shallot and garlic over low heat until soft. Add the tomatoes, sugar, and a pinch of salt and gently boil 1 minute. Set aside.

Whisk together the eggs, cheese, and pepper. Heat the remaining olive oil in the omelet pan over low heat and spread the zucchini over the bottom of the pan. Sprinkle with the oregano, pour the egg mixture over the zucchini, and cook until the eggs are lightly set. Using a slotted spoon, spoon the tomato mixture over the eggs, and season to taste.

Sprinkle with the parsley and olives and serve.

Baked Eggplants to Make the Sultan Swoon

Imam Bayildí

**Serves 12 as a first course,
6 as a vegetable dish**

*I*mam Bayildí is of Turkish origin, and there are many stories about how the dish acquired its name. Some say the sultan fainted in blissful pleasure at his first taste of this rich and spicy eggplant dish, others that he was overcome by the beauty of the young woman who served it to him. Whatever its origin, it is delectable. *Imam Bayildí* is ideal for a large party since it is best made a day ahead to give the flavors time to mellow and deepen. Serve warm for a first course, hot as a side dish for grilled meats, or cold as part of a buffet.

12 thin eggplants, about 4 inches long, or 6 medium
eggplants (about 2½ pounds)

Coarse-grain sea salt to taste

¾ to 1 cup extra-virgin olive oil (to taste)

1½ pounds onions, quartered and thinly sliced

2 large cloves garlic, finely chopped

1½ pounds ripe tomatoes, peeled and diced, juices reserved

½ cup currants or small dark seedless raisins

1 tablespoon ground allspice

¾ cup finely chopped flat-leaf parsley

Freshly ground black pepper to taste

1 tablespoon honey

Juice of 2 lemons

2 tablespoons dried rígani (page 14)

Slice off the ends of the eggplants and cut lengthwise in half. Sprinkle the cut sides with salt and set aside for 30 minutes to sweat.

Heat ¼ cup of the olive oil in a heavy skillet and sauté the onions over low heat until soft and pale golden brown, about 15 minutes, stirring occasionally. Add the garlic and tomatoes with their juices and boil until most of the liquid has evaporated, about 10 minutes. Stir in the currants, allspice, most of the parsley, and salt and pepper to taste, and set aside.

Heat the oven to 325°F. Thoroughly dry the eggplants with paper towels. Place a large heavy skillet over medium-low heat, add 3 tablespoons of the remaining olive oil, and fry half the eggplants until the cut sides are a deep golden brown and the skins are dark and wrinkled, about 10 minutes. Drain between layers of paper towels. Add 2 tablespoons of the remaining oil to the skillet, fry the remaining eggplants, and drain on paper towels. With a small spoon, scoop out the eggplant centers, leaving ¼-inch-thick shells. Discard most of the seeds, finely dice the flesh, and stir into the onion and tomato mixture.

Arrange the eggplant shells in a heavy baking dish just large enough to accommodate them. Divide the filling among them, heaping it a little in the center for an attractive appearance. Combine the honey, lemon juice, and olive oil to taste and drizzle over the eggplants. Sprinkle with the *rígani*, salt, and pepper. Pour ½ cup water into the dish and bake uncovered 45 minutes. Add a little more water to the dish if it appears to be drying out.

Arrange the eggplants on a platter or on individual plates, spoon over any cooking liquid, and sprinkle with olive oil to taste and the remaining parsley.

Note To serve as a main course use large round eggplants, 5 or 6 inches long and increase the filling by half. Or add 1½ cups Perfect Pilaf (page 301) or lightly browned, finely ground lamb, or a mixture of both, to the filling, adding more currants and allspice to taste; place 1 thin tomato slice on top of each eggplant, to prevent the rice from drying out during baking. Bake uncovered at 325°F for 1 hour.

Imam Bayildí in Grape Leaves
Imam Bayildí me Ambelófila

Using 12 small thin eggplants, fry the eggplants and prepare the filling as directed above. Line a heavy baking dish, just large enough to hold the eggplants in a single layer, with fresh or canned grape leaves that have been blanched in boiling water (3 seconds for canned leaves, 5 seconds for fresh), glossy sides facing down. (You will need about 12 large leaves or 18 medium leaves.) Divide the filling among the eggplants and arrange them in the baking dish. Cover with a second layer of blanched grape leaves, glossy sides facing up. Pour the lemon juice, honey, and olive oil mixture over the eggplants; omit the *rígani*. Add ½ cup water to the dish and bake uncovered at 325°F for 1 hour. Add a little more water to the dish if necessary.

To serve, discard the top layer of grape leaves and carefully transfer the eggplants to a platter or individual plates. Serve with lemon wedges.

Stuffed Eggplants with Tomato Cinnamon Sauce

Yemistés Melitzánes

⊠

Serves 4

These subtly spiced stuffed eggplants are easy to make. If possible, prepare and bake them a day ahead and gently reheat before serving. This gives the rich flavors a chance to deepen and brings out all the pungent fragrance of herbs and spices. Bell peppers can be substituted for eggplants—in that variation cumin becomes the dominant spice.

———

2 large or 4 medium eggplants (about 1½ pounds)

Sea salt

¾ cup Kalamáta olive oil, or to taste

½ cup finely chopped onion

½ pound lean lamb, finely ground

1 to 1½ teaspoons ground cinnamon (to taste)

¾ cup long-grain rice

1½ cups fat-free Chicken or Meat Broth (page 461 or 467) or water

⅓ cup small dark seedless raisins

⅔ cup finely chopped flat-leaf parsley

1 large ripe tomato, peeled and cut into 8 slices

1 teaspoon sugar

Cracked black pepper to taste

1 cup Tomato Sauce (page 431), made with cinnamon and parsley, and ½ cup water or ¼ cup tomato paste diluted with 1¼ cups water

FOR SERVING

Juice of 1 lemon

(continued)

Slice off the ends of the eggplants and cut lengthwise in half. Dust the cut sides with salt and set aside for 30 minutes to sweat.

Heat 3 tablespoons of the olive oil in a deep skillet and sauté the onion over low heat until pale golden, about 12 minutes, stirring occasionally. Add the lamb, raise the heat, and cook until lightly browned, breaking up any lumps with a wooden spoon. Stir in the cinnamon, 1 teaspoon salt, and the rice. Add the broth, bring to a boil, cover, reduce the heat, and simmer until the liquid has disappeared from the surface, about 20 minutes. Set aside.

Heat the oven to 325°F. Thoroughly dry the eggplants with paper towels. Warm ¼ cup of the remaining olive oil in a heavy skillet and fry the eggplants over medium-low heat until the cut sides are golden brown and the skins are dark and wrinkled, about 10 minutes. Drain between layers of paper towels. With a small spoon, scoop out the flesh, leaving ¼-inch-thick shells. Discard most of the seeds and finely dice the flesh. Stir the eggplant dice, raisins, and half the parsley into the rice mixture.

Arrange the eggplant shells in a heavy baking dish, just large enough to accommodate them. Divide the filling among the shells. Place a tomato slice on top of each, sprinkle with the sugar, salt, a generous amount of pepper, and the remaining olive oil. Pour the tomato sauce and water into the dish and bake uncovered 1 hour, basting occasionally with the sauce. Add more water if the dish is in danger of drying out.

To serve, remove the eggplants from the dish with a slotted spoon and set aside. Pour the sauce onto a warm platter, arrange the eggplants on top, and sprinkle with the lemon juice and the remaining parsley. Serve hot or warm.

Stuffed Bell Peppers with Tomato Cumin Sauce
Yemistés Strongilés Piperiés

Substitute 8 medium green and/or yellow bell peppers for the eggplants, cumin for the cinnamon, and ½ cup coarsely chopped celery leaves for the raisins. Slice off the tops of the peppers, discard the cores and seeds, and rinse out to remove any remaining seeds. Blanch the tops and shells in boiling water for 5 minutes, and drain well. Fill the peppers and replace the tops. Arrange them in a heavy baking dish just large enough to hold them. Sprinkle with the sugar, salt and pepper, and olive oil, and add the sauce and water. Cover and bake 1 hour, basting the peppers occasionally with the sauce.

Serve sprinkled with the lemon juice and parsley.

Note The peppers can also be simmered in a heavy saucepan on top of the stove. Bring the sauce to a boil, cover, reduce the heat, and simmer 45 minutes to 1 hour, until tender.

Stuffed Eggplants with Green Grape Sauce

Yemistés Melitzánes me Agourítha

Serves 6

This Cretan version of stuffed eggplants is one of my favorite dishes—substantial enough to feed the hungriest family yet impressive enough for an elegant dinner. The rice filling is spiced with cloves, sharpened by the sauce made from underripe green grapes, and exotically colored and aromatized with saffron. The grape leaves protect the eggplants from drying out in the oven and, of course, impart a subtle flavor to the dish. Serve with bowls of Strained Yogurt (page 8), radishes, and tiny black Elítses olives, and a salad of wild greens (page 295).

(continued)

3 large or 6 medium eggplants (about 2 pounds)

Sea salt

*1 cup yellow split peas, picked over, rinsed, and soaked for 2
hours in water to cover*

1 cup extra-virgin olive oil, or to taste

1 medium onion, grated

½ pound lean lamb, finely ground

1 teaspoon saffron threads

½ teaspoon ground cloves

1 teaspoon cracked black pepper, or to taste

½ cup long-grain rice

*1¼ cups fat-free Chicken or Meat Broth
(page 461 or 467) or water*

*⅓ cup finely chopped chives or the best green parts
of scallions*

*⅓ cup Green Grape Sauce (page 430) or the juice of
1 large lime*

1 cup finely chopped flat-leaf parsley

¼ cup packed brown sugar

Juice of 1 large lemon

*16 fresh or canned grape leaves, blanched in boiling water
(3 seconds for canned leaves, 5 seconds for fresh) and drained*

Slice off the ends of the eggplants and cut lengthwise in half. Sprinkle the
cut sides with salt and set aside for 30 minutes to sweat.

Drain the split peas, place in a medium saucepan with water to cover by
2 inches, and bring to a simmer over medium heat. Reduce heat and simmer
20 minutes, or until just tender. Drain and set aside.

Meanwhile, heat 3 tablespoons of the olive oil in a heavy skillet and sauté
the onion over medium-low heat until golden brown, about 12 minutes. Add
the meat, raise the heat, and cook until lightly browned, breaking up any
lumps with a wooden spoon. Gently heat the saffron in a small dry skillet
until aromatic, and crumble it into the lamb mixture. Stir in the cloves,
pepper, 1 teaspoon salt, and the rice. Add the broth and bring to a boil,
without stirring. Cover, reduce the heat to low, and cook 15 to 20 minutes,
or until all the liquid has been absorbed by the rice.

Heat the oven to 325°F. Thoroughly dry the eggplants with paper towels. Place a large skillet over medium-low heat, add 3 tablespoons of the remaining olive oil, and fry the eggplants until the cut sides are dark golden brown and the skins are dark and wrinkled, about 10 minutes. (Fry in 2 batches if necessary, adding 2 tablespoons additional olive oil before frying the second batch.) Drain between layers of paper towels. Scoop out the flesh with a small spoon, leaving ¼-inch-thick shells. Discard most of the seeds and cut the flesh into small dice. Combine the eggplant dice, split peas, chives, Green Grape Sauce, ¾ cup of the parsley, and the lamb and rice mixture. Season to taste with salt and pepper.

Arrange the eggplant shells in a heavy baking dish just large enough to hold them. Divide the filling among the eggplant shells, heaping the filling in the centers. Combine the sugar, lemon juice, and 1 cup water, and pour into the baking dish. Add more water if necessary to come halfway up the sides of the eggplant shells. Sprinkle the remaining olive oil over the eggplants and cover with the grape leaves, glossy sides facing down.

Bake uncovered 50 minutes to 1 hour, or until the grape leaves are dry and wrinkled, basting frequently with the liquid in the pan. Add a little more water if the dish is in danger of drying out.

To serve, discard the grape leaves, arrange the eggplants on a warm platter, pour over the pan juices, and sprinkle with the remaining parsley. Serve hot or warm.

Stuffed Onions with Green Grape Sauce
Yemistá Kremíthia me Agourítha

Served in ancient Greece, this spicy dish is still popular today. Substitute 4 large onions for the eggplants. Peel them, slice off the root and stem ends, and cook in boiling water for 10 minutes; drain. Push out the centers to leave shells of 3 layers, and separate these to make 12 shells. Finely chop 1 of the centers and add it to the rice mixture. (Reserve the remaining centers for another use.)

Arrange the onion shells in a heavy baking dish and divide the filling among them. Pour the sugar–lemon juice mixture over the onions and sprinkle with the olive oil; omit the grape leaves. Bake uncovered until the filling is golden brown, about 1 hour, basting frequently with the liquid in the pan. Serve hot or warm, with the syrupy pan juices poured over.

Serve 2 or 3 per person as a main course or, for an unusual vegetable to accompany grilled meats, omit the lamb, and serve 2 to each person.

(continued)

Stuffed Bell Peppers with Green Grape Sauce
Yemistés Strongilés Piperiés me Agourítha

Substitute 12 small to medium red, yellow, and/or green bell peppers for the eggplants. Slice off the tops, discard the cores and seeds, and rinse out to remove any remaining seeds. Blanch the tops and shells in boiling water for 5 minutes and drain. Divide the filling among the peppers and replace the tops. Add the sugar–lemon juice mixture and sprinkle with the olive oil; cover with leaves if desired. Bake uncovered 1 hour, basting frequently with the liquid in the pan. Serve hot or warm, with the pan juices.

Stuffed Bell Peppers Avgolémono

Yemistés Strongilés Piperiés Avgolémono

**Serves 8 as a first course,
5 as a main course**

In this recipe a perfumed rice filling is enhanced with *avgolémono* to produce a dish that's both sweetly aromatic and exquisitely beautiful. Choose small bell peppers for a first course, medium-sized ones for a main course—or substitute zucchini or onions if you prefer.

———

½ cup extra-virgin olive oil

2 tablespoons unsalted butter

*3 shallots, finely chopped, or 6 scallions, white part only,
finely chopped (about ⅓ cup)*

1½ cups long-grain rice

1 teaspoon saffron threads

5 cups fat-free Chicken Broth (page 461) or water

1 teaspoon sea salt, or to taste

*16 small or 10 medium yellow, green, and/or
red bell peppers*

⅔ cup small dark seedless raisins

⅔ cup lightly toasted pine nuts

1 tablespoon dried rígani (page 14)

⅔ cup finely chopped flat-leaf parsley

*3 tablespoons finely chopped Preserved Lemon (page 19)
or the strained juice of 1 lemon, or to taste*

Freshly ground black pepper to taste

3 eggs

Strained juice of 2 large lemons

Heat 2 tablespoons of the olive oil and the butter in a heavy saucepan and sauté the shallots over low heat until soft, about 5 minutes. Add the rice and cook 1 minute, stirring with a wooden spoon, until opaque. Heat the saffron in a small dry skillet until aromatic and crumble it into 1 cup of the broth. Add the saffron broth, 2 cups of the remaining broth, and the salt to the rice. Raise the heat and boil uncovered for 8 minutes, or until the liquid has disappeared and holes appear in the surface of the rice. Remove from the heat, cover with 2 layers of paper towels and a tight-fitting lid, and set aside for 30 minutes in a warm place such as the back of the stove.

Fill a large saucepan with water and bring to a boil. Slice the tops off the peppers, discard the cores, and rinse off the seeds from both tops and shells. Add to the boiling water, cover, and boil 5 minutes. Drain and set aside.

With a fork, lightly mix the raisins, pine nuts, *rígani*, ½ cup of the parsley, the Preserved Lemon, and pepper into the rice. Add salt and lemon juice to taste. Loosely fill the pepper shells with this mixture and replace the tops. Arrange in a heavy saucepan just large enough to hold them, pour the remaining olive oil and broth over, and bring to a boil. Cover, reduce the heat, and simmer 40 minutes to 1 hour, until the peppers are soft, adding water if the liquid in the saucepan reduces to less than 1 cup.

Ten minutes before serving the peppers, whisk the eggs in a large bowl for 2 minutes, or until pale and frothy. Slowly add the lemon juice and whisk 1 minute longer. Remove the peppers from the pan, reserving the cooking liquid, and keep warm. Add 1 cup of the reserved liquid to the egg mixture in a slow steady stream, whisking constantly. Transfer the sauce to a small heavy saucepan or the top of a double boiler set over hot water. Stir over low heat until the sauce thickens enough to coat the back of the spoon, about 5 minutes; do not allow to boil.

Arrange the peppers on a warm platter or individual plates and pour over the sauce. Sprinkle with the remaining parsley and serve immediately.

Stuffed Zucchini Avgolémono
Yemistá Kolokíthia Avgolémono

Substitute 5 medium zucchini, 4 to 5 inches long (to serve as a main course), or 8 small zucchini, 3 inches long (to serve as a first course), for the peppers, and make half the amount of filling. Trim the ends of the zucchini and rub them with a kitchen towel to remove any fuzz. Blanch in boiling water (5 minutes for large zucchini, 3 minutes for small) and drain. Cut lengthwise in half and scoop out the centers with a small spoon and arrange in a baking dish. Finely chop the flesh and add it to the rice mixture. Add salt, pepper, and lemon juice to taste. Fill the zucchini, pour over the remaining olive oil and broth, and bake uncovered in a preheated 350°F oven until tender, about 40 minutes; add water if liquid in the dish reduces to less than 1 cup. Make the sauce and serve immediately.

Stuffed Onions Avgolémono
Yemistá Kremíthia Avgolémono

Substitute 5 large onions (to serve as a main course) or 16 small boiling onions (to serve as a first course) for the peppers. Peel, and slice off both ends. Blanch in boiling water (10 minutes for large onions, 5 minutes for small), drain, and let cool slightly. Push out the onion centers, leaving shells of 2 layers. If using large onions separate the layers to make 10 shells. Arrange the shells in a heavy baking dish. Fill the shells with the rice mixture, piling it high. Pour over the remaining olive oil and broth, and bake uncovered in a preheated 325°F oven until tender, about 40 minutes for small onions, 1 hour for large, occasionally basting with the broth. Make sure there is always at least 1 cup of cooking liquid in the dish; add water if necessary. Make the sauce and serve hot.

Note For a meat filling sauté 12 ounces finely ground lean lamb in 2 tablespoons olive oil until lightly browned. Drain on paper towels and sprinkle with a little salt and lemon juice. Stir into the cooked rice mixture with a fork.

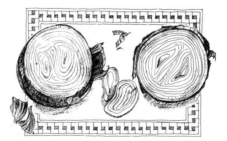

Baked Stuffed Tomatoes and Peppers

Yemistés Domátes ke Piperiés

**Serves 8 as a first course,
4 as a main course**

Huge shallow trays of beautiful stuffed vegetables—tomatoes and multicolored bell peppers, zucchini, eggplants, and onions—await the hungry visitor to any *tavérna*. In this recipe either garbanzo beans or pine nuts can be used to provide an unusual texture. Currants or raisins add a gentle sweetness and fresh mint or *rígani*, a hillside fragrance. Although the vegetables take some time to prepare, they can be baked ahead of time. Serve cold with yogurt, olives, and lemon wedges for a perfect summer lunch.

---

8 small or 4 large ripe tomatoes

1/2 tablespoon sugar

Sea salt

*8 small or 4 medium green bell peppers, roasted, seeded,
and peeled (page 460)*

1/2 cup extra-virgin olive oil, or more to taste

1 medium onion, grated

1 teaspoon ground allspice

1 teaspoon freshly ground black pepper

2 cups cooked long-grain rice

*1/2 cup crumbled cooked garbanzo beans or lightly
toasted pine nuts*

*1/4 cup fresh mint, torn into small pieces at the last minute, or
1 tablespoon dried rígani (page 14), crumbled*

1/2 cup currants or small dark seedless raisins

1/2 cup finely chopped flat-leaf parsley

Juice of 1 lemon

1/2 cup fresh whole-wheat bread crumbs

Heat the oven to 325°F. Slice off the tops of the tomatoes and set aside. Scoop out the pulp with a small spoon, discard the seeds, and dice the pulp. Set aside with the juices. Sprinkle the sugar and salt into the tomato shells, invert onto paper towels, and set aside to drain.

Slice off the tops of the peppers, discard the cores, and wipe the seeds off the tops and shells. Drain on paper towels.

Warm ¼ cup of the olive oil in a heavy skillet and sauté the onion over low heat until golden brown, about 12 minutes, stirring occasionally. Add the tomato dice and juices, allspice, pepper, and 1 teaspoon salt, and cook 5 minutes, or until most of the liquid has evaporated. With a fork, stir in the rice, garbanzo beans, mint, currants, and ¼ cup of the parsley. Season to taste. Loosely fill the tomatoes and peppers, replace their tops, and arrange them in a heavy baking dish. Sprinkle with the lemon juice and the remaining olive oil; sprinkle the bread crumbs over the tomatoes. Add 1 cup water to the dish and bake uncovered 40 minutes to 1 hour, until the vegetables are soft and slightly darkened, basting occasionally with the liquid in the pan. Add a little more water to the dish if it appears to be drying out. Let the vegetables cool in the dish.

To serve, arrange the vegetables on a platter and sprinkle with the cooking liquid, olive oil if desired, and the remaining parsley.

Baked Stuffed Eggplants, Tomatoes, and Peppers
Diáfora Parayemistá

Choose slightly smaller tomatoes and peppers, and add 4 round eggplants, about 4 inches long. Trim off the stems of the eggplants, cut lengthwise in half, and fry in 2 to 3 tablespoons olive oil until the cut sides are golden brown and the skin is dark and wrinkled. Scoop out the flesh with a small spoon, discard the seeds, and dice the pulp. Add the eggplant dice, an additional ½ cup cooked rice, ¼ cup lightly toasted pine nuts, and salt and pepper to taste to the filling. Arrange the vegetables in a heavy baking dish, divide the filling among them, and replace the tomato and pepper tops. Sprinkle with the lemon juice and olive oil if desired. Sprinkle the bread crumbs over the tomatoes. Add 1 cup water to the dish and bake uncovered for 1 hour, basting frequently with the liquid in the pan. Let the vegetables cool in the dish.

Arrange on a large platter or individual plates, pour over the pan juices, and serve with lemon wedges.

Stuffed Cabbage Leaves
in Tomato Sauce

Lakhanodolmáthes me Sáltsa Domátas

Serves 4

In the winter months cabbages, cheap and at their best, are used for a variety of salads and family meals, and this is one of the most popular dishes. The Greek affection for cabbage has a long history: Hippocrates is said to have prescribed it as a cure for colic and Pythagoras to have composed a eulogy on this humble vegetable! Serve with Perfect Pilaf (page 301) or Pilaf with Green Lentils (page 306).

One 1½- to 2-pound white or green cabbage

¼ cup extra-virgin olive oil

1 small onion, finely chopped

½ pound lean pork or beef, finely ground

1 teaspoon ground allspice, or to taste

¼ cup lightly toasted pine nuts

¼ cup currants

1½ cups cooked long-grain rice

Sea salt and freshly ground black pepper to taste

2 tablespoons fresh mint leaves, or to taste

¼ cup finely chopped flat-leaf parsley

Juice of 1 lemon or 2 tablespoons white-wine vinegar

*1½ cups Tomato Sauce (page 431) made with
parsley and bay leaves*

Discard any torn or discolored outer cabbage leaves and, with a sharp paring knife, cut out as much of the core as possible. Cook, covered, in boiling water for 5 minutes to drain, and set aside.

Heat 2 tablespoons of olive oil in a heavy skillet and sauté the onion over low heat until soft, about 6 minutes. Raise the heat, add the meat, and sauté until lightly browned, breaking up any lumps with a wooden spoon. Add the allspice, pine nuts, currants, rice, and salt and pepper. Chop the mint and 2 tablespoons of the parsley together and add to the meat along with the lemon juice. Stir with a fork until well mixed. Add allspice, salt and pepper, and/or mint if desired; the mixture should be highly flavored.

Turn the cabbage upside down. Separate 16 to 20 leaves from the core with a paring knife by pulling each one down and off. Trim out and discard any thick spine, and lay the leaves flat between layers of paper towels to dry.

Lay a cabbage leaf on your palm (or on a flat surface), spine side up, and place 1 heaped tablespoon filling on the bottom third of the leaf. Fold over both sides and, keeping the filling in place with your thumb, firmly roll up from the leaf base to tip; repeat with remaining leaves and filling. As you finish each stuffed leaf, place it seam side down in a heavy sauté pan large enough to hold all the *dolmáthes* in a single layer, pressing the rolls tightly against each other.

Pour over the tomato sauce and add enough water to barely come to the top of the *dolmáthes*. Place a heatproof plate slightly smaller than the pan on top and set a weight (such as a large can of fruit) on top of the plate. Slowly bring to a boil, reduce the heat, and gently simmer 1 hour. Add a little more water if the liquid begins to disappear from the surface. Remove from the heat and set aside for 5 minutes with the weight still in place.

Transfer the *dolmáthes* to a warm platter and pour over the sauce and the remaining 2 tablespoons olive oil. Sprinkle with the remaining parsley and serve hot or warm.

Fried Cheese Pies
Tyrópittes Tighanités

Makes 1½ to 2 dozen pies;
Serves 8 as a *mezé*, 4 to 6 as a lunch dish

These tiny fried pies are a real taste of Greece. Made with an orange-flavored pastry, they conceal a sweet cheese filling, perfumed with fresh mint. Whenever I serve them to guests, either as a *mezé* or light lunch, they seem to disappear very quickly! Fry them in olive oil for the most authentic flavor, or, if you prefer, bake them.

PASTRY

2 cups unbleached all-purpose flour

1 teaspoon sea salt

½ teaspoon superfine sugar

2 tablespoons light olive oil

1 egg white, lightly beaten

About ⅓ cup strained fresh orange juice

FILLING

¼ cup fresh mint leaves

*2 cups fresh myzíthra cheese (page 11), crumbled, or
small-curd cottage cheese, drained and pressed through a fine sieve*

½ cup finely grated féta cheese

1 whole egg plus 1 egg yolk, lightly beaten

2 tablespoons honey

2 tablespoons unsalted butter, melted

½ to 1 teaspoon ground cinnamon (to taste)

Olive oil, for frying

FOR SERVING

Sifted confectioner's sugar

Ground cinnamon

Flavors of Greece

114

To make the pastry, combine the flour, salt, sugar, olive oil, egg white, and 3 tablespoons of the orange juice in a large bowl. Knead for 5 minutes, adding more orange juice if needed to make a smooth and elastic dough. Tightly wrap in plastic wrap and refrigerate for 1 hour.

To make the filling, finely chop the mint leaves and mash together all the filling ingredients with a wooden spoon until well mixed but not smooth.

Divide the dough in half, rewrap 1 portion, and return to the refrigerator. Roll out the pastry on a lightly floured surface and cut out circles with a 4-inch round cutter; or cut into 2- by 4-inch rectangles. Place 1 heaped tablespoon of filling in the centers of half the 2-inch circles, or of all the large circles or rectangles. Brush the edges of the pastry with the remaining orange juice. Cover the 2-inch circles with the remaining small circles, or fold the 4-inch ones in half to make half-moons; fold rectangles in half to make 2-inch squares. Crimp the edges with a fork to seal. Repeat with the remaining pastry and filling.

Pour a ½-inch layer of olive oil into a large heavy skillet, or heat olive oil in a deep-fat fryer. When the olive oil is hot but not smoking, fry the pastries over medium heat until deep golden brown on both sides; or deep-fry until golden. Drain on paper towels, arrange on a warm platter, sprinkle liberally with the confectioner's sugar and cinnamon, and serve hot or warm.

Note To bake, preheat the oven to 350°F. Arrange the pastries 2 inches apart on lightly oiled baking sheets and bake 15 minutes. Lightly beat 2 egg yolks with 2 tablespoons olive oil and brush the pastries with this glaze; bake 10 minutes longer, or until deep golden brown. Or you can also make squares or circles with a little of the filling exposed in the center (page 369) and bake these.

Baked Cheese and Spinach Pies

Spanakópittes me Tyrí

Makes 1½ to 2 dozen pies

These little pastries, filled with a creamy nutmeg-spiced spinach mixture, are perfect picnic food. You can make them with either pastry dough or with *phýllo* and they freeze beautifully.

---

1 recipe Pastry (page 114) or 1-pound package phýllo *dough,*
(page 357), thawed if frozen

FILLING

1½ pounds fresh spinach

½ cup extra-virgin olive oil

4 scallions, trimmed, the best green parts left intact,
and thinly sliced

¼ teaspoon grated nutmeg

Sea salt to taste

1 teaspoon cracked black pepper, or to taste

¾ cup small-curd cottage cheese, drained and pressed
through a fine sieve

¾ cup crumbled féta *cheese*

½ cup coarsely chopped flat-leaf parsley

2 egg yolks, lightly beaten (for pastry pies), or ¼ cup unsalted
butter, melted (for phýllo *pies)*

If using *phýllo,* remove the package of dough from the refrigerator and set aside unopened.

Rinse the spinach in several changes of cold water, discard the stems and any bruised or tough leaves, and place in a heavy saucepan. Cover and cook, with just the water that clings to the leaves, for 1 minute, or until wilted and barely soft. Drain, pressing the greens against the sides of the colander to remove as much liquid as possible. Finely chop the spinach and set aside.

Warm ¼ cup of the olive oil in a heavy skillet and sauté the scallions over low heat until soft, about 5 minutes. Stir in the spinach, nutmeg, salt, and pepper and cook 2 minutes. Remove from the heat and drain off any liquid. Add the cottage cheese, *féta* cheese, and parsley, and gently mash together with a fork. Season to taste with salt and pepper.

Heat the oven to 350°F. Make the pies with the pastry as directed on page 114 or the *phýllo* as directed on page 366. Arrange 2 inches apart on lightly greased baking sheets. Brush pastry pies with the remaining olive oil, *phýllo* pies with a mixture of the olive oil and the melted butter. Bake pastry pies 15 minutes, brush with the beaten egg yolks, and bake 10 minutes longer, or until deep golden brown. Bake *phýllo* pies 15 to 20 minutes, or until deep golden brown. Serve hot or warm.

Note If tender young beet greens are available, you can make the country version of these pies. Substitute 2 pounds greens for the spinach. Place in a saucepan, add ¼ cup water, and cook 3 minutes or until just soft.

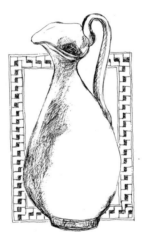

Sesame Spinach Pies
Spanakópittes

Makes 1½ to 2 dozen pies
Serves 8 as a *mezé*, 4 to 6 as a lunch dish

These delicious sesame-topped miniature pies and some good fresh cheese are the perfect nibbles to accompany a glass of wine. Or serve them the Cretan way, as a side dish with roast or grilled pork. Wild greens provide the most authentic country flavor, but you can substitute beet greens or spinach.

---

1 recipe Pastry (page 114)

FILLING

3 pounds young water spinach (vlita, page 294) or beet greens or 2 pounds young fresh spinach

½ cup extra-virgin olive oil

2 medium onions, quartered and thinly sliced

1 teaspoon ground cumin

½ cup fresh dill or sprigs of fennel, coarsely chopped

1 teaspoon medium-grain sea salt, or to taste

1 teaspoon cracked black pepper, or to taste

Juice of 1 small lemon

2 egg yolks, lightly beaten

1 cup sesame seeds

Rinse the greens in several changes of cold water and discard the stems and any tough or discolored leaves. Boil the water spinach, covered, in ½ inch of water for 5 minutes, or until barely tender. (Boil beet greens in ½ cup water for 2 minutes, spinach in a few tablespoons water for 1 minute.) Drain and press the greens firmly against the side of the colander to remove excess water.

Heat ⅓ cup of the olive oil in a heavy skillet and sauté the onion over low heat until soft, about 10 minutes. Stir in the cumin. Finely chop the greens, and add to the onions with the dill. Cook 2 minutes longer, and add the salt, pepper, and lemon juice; the mixture should be highly seasoned.

Heat the oven to 350°F. Make the pies as directed on page 115 and arrange 2 inches apart on lightly oiled baking sheets. Brush with the remaining olive oil and bake 15 minutes. Brush with the beaten egg yolks, liberally sprinkle with the sesame seeds, and bake 8 minutes longer, or until deep golden brown. Serve hot or warm.

Variations

- Add 1 cup cooked rice and ¼ cup currants to the filling.
- Add ½ cup drained small-curd cottage cheese, pressed through a sieve, and ¼ cup toasted pine nuts to the filling.
- Increase the amount of dill or fennel to 1 cup and use 2½ pounds water spinach or beet greens

Note To freeze, spread uncooked pies in a single layer on a baking sheet and freeze. Remove from the baking sheet and store in freezer bags. Defrost before baking.

Marjoram Meat Pies

Kreatópittes

Makes 1½ to 2 dozen pies
Serves 8 as a *mezé*, 4 to 6 as a lunch dish

These spicy pastry parcels are a treat, especially good in late spring when lamb has a delicate succulent flavor and marjoram leaves are at their most fragrant. If you have the patience, you'll achieve the best texture and flavor if you chop the meat by hand.

———

(continued)

PASTRY

2 cups unbleached all-purpose flour

1 teaspoon sea salt

2 tablespoons olive oil

1 egg, lightly beaten

3 tablespoons red-wine vinegar or yogurt, preferably homemade (page 8)

3 to 4 tablespoons cold water

FILLING

½ cup extra-virgin olive oil

2 large onions, chopped

1½ pounds lean lamb or beef or a mixture of both, finely chopped or ground

¼ cup dry red wine or 2 tablespoons red-wine vinegar

½ teaspoon coarse-grain sea salt, or to taste

1 teaspoon cracked black pepper, or to taste

1 teaspoon ground cinnamon

¼ teaspoon ground cloves

½ cup finely chopped flat-leaf parsley

2 tablespoons fresh marjoram, chopped, or 1 tablespoon dried rígani (page 14), crumbled

½ cup lightly toasted pine nuts

2 egg yolks beaten with 1 tablespoon water

½ cup sesame seeds, optional

To make the pastry, sift the flour into a large bowl and add the salt, olive oil, egg, and vinegar. Knead for 5 minutes, adding enough of the cold water if needed to make a smooth and elastic dough. Tightly wrap in plastic wrap and refrigerate for 1 hour.

To make the filling, heat 3 tablespoons of the olive oil in a large heavy skillet and sauté the onion over medium-low heat until golden brown, about 15 minutes, stirring occasionally. Add the meat and cook until lightly browned, breaking up any lumps with a wooden spoon. Add the wine and boil until almost evaporated. Stir in the salt, pepper, cinnamon, and cloves, cover, and simmer 15 minutes over very low heat. Add 1 or 2 tablespoons water if the mixture starts to dry out; or, if there is still liquid remaining in the pan, uncover for the last few minutes to let it evaporate. Add the parsley, marjoram, and pine nuts. Season to taste and set aside to cool.

Heat the oven to 350°F. Roll out the pastry on a lightly floured surface, and cut out circles with a 4-inch round cutter or cut into 2- by 4-inch rectangles. Place 2 scant tablespoons of filling in the center of each shape and brush the edges of the pastry with water. Fold the circles in half to make half moons or fold the rectangles in half to make 2-inch squares. Crimp the edges with a fork to seal.

Arrange the pies 2 inches apart on a lightly oiled baking sheet and brush with the remaining olive oil. Bake 10 minutes, then brush with the egg yolks and lightly sprinkle with the sesame seeds. Bake 15 minutes longer, or until deep golden brown. Serve hot or warm, or cool to room temperature on racks.

Note These can be made with *phýllo*, but the filling must be moister. Add 2 peeled and diced tomatoes to the meat along with the spices, or add 1 cup drained cottage cheese, pressed through a sieve, with the pine nuts. Shape into triangles, rolls, or rectangles as directed on page 366 or into 1 large pie as directed on page 126, and bake as directed in each recipe.

Aromatic Lamb Phýllo Rolls

Arnáki Tiligméno me Phýllo

Serves 6

There are several versions of this delicious and versatile dish. It can be made as small rolls for a buffet or lunch, or as one large round or rectangular pie. It's composed of an aromatic meat layer topped with a spicy cheese mixture, and wrapped in *phýllo* to make a neat package for baking. Although it sounds complicated it's not really too difficult to make, and you can prepare the filling a day ahead and refrigerate overnight if you prefer. Greeks are fond of even more exotic versions, with an extra layer of *piláfi*, spinach, or rice or, perhaps, sautéed diced eggplants. Serve with a salad of wild leaf greens (page 295) or a green salad.

(continued)

5 tablespoons extra-virgin olive oil

6 tablespoons unsalted butter

1 large onion, finely chopped

1½ pounds lean lamb, finely ground

2 large ripe tomatoes, peeled and diced

1 teaspoon honey

1 tablespoon ground cinnamon, or to taste

½ teaspoon sea salt, or to taste

1 teaspoon cracked black pepper, or to taste

¼ cup reduced Meat Stock (page 467) or robust red wine

1½ tablespoons fresh marjoram or 2½ tablespoons dried
rígani (page 14), crumbled

⅓ cup finely chopped flat-leaf parsley

1 cup fresh myzíthra (page 11) or small-curd cottage cheese,
drained

⅓ cup finely grated féta cheese

½ teaspoon grated nutmeg

2 egg yolks

12 sheets phýllo (from a 1-pound package, page 357)

FOR SERVING

Confectioner's sugar

Ground cinnamon

Warm 1 tablespoon of the olive oil and 2 tablespoons of the butter in a heavy skillet and sauté the onion over low heat until soft, about 8 minutes. Raise the heat, add the meat, and sauté until lightly browned, breaking up any lumps with a wooden spoon. Add the tomatoes, honey, cinnamon, salt, and ½ teaspoon of the pepper, and bring to a boil. Add the stock, bring to a boil, reduce the heat, and simmer 15 minutes, or until almost all the liquid has evaporated. Add the marjoram and parsley, and additional cinnamon, marjoram, and pepper to taste (do not add salt at this point, as the cheese mixture is salty). Set aside, or refrigerate for up to 24 hours.

Heat the oven to 375°F. Press the *myzíthra* through a sieve or food mill into a bowl. Combine with the *féta*, nutmeg, remaining ½ teaspoon pepper, and the egg yolks, cover, and set aside.

Combine the remaining 4 tablespoons butter and olive oil in a small saucepan, and melt over very low heat. Brush a heavy baking sheet with some of this mixture. Lay the *phýllo* sheets one on top of another and cut in half crosswise to make 24 sheets. Tightly rewrap half the sheets and refrigerate. Lay 1 of the remaining sheets on a clean work surface, with a long end facing you, and brush lightly with the butter mixture. Lay a second sheet on top, brush it with the mixture, and repeat with a third sheet. Lay another sheet on top. Divide the meat mixture into 6 portions. Place 1 portion on the bottom third of the top *phýllo* sheet and shape it into a sausage about 8 inches long. Divide the cheese filling into 6 portions and spread 1 portion over the meat. Fold the bottom edges of the *phýllo* layers over the filling, then fold over the 2 sides, and roll up to make a firm neat parcel. Place on the baking sheet and repeat with the remaining *phýllo* and filling.

Brush the rolls with the remaining butter mixture and bake 25 to 30 minutes, or until deep golden brown. Drain on paper towels, sprinkle liberally with the confectioner's sugar and cinnamon, and transfer to a warm platter.

Note To make one large round or rectangular pie, use a 1-pound package of *phýllo* and additional melted butter and olive oil as needed for brushing the sheets. Assemble the pie as directed on page 126. Bake 35 to 45 minutes, or until deep golden brown. Sprinkle liberally with the confectioner's sugar and cinnamon and serve warm.

Cretan Chicken Pie

Tzoulamás

Serves 10 to 12

At a wedding feast high in a remote mountain village on Crete, this pie was the magnificent centerpiece to the wedding buffet table laid out in the village square. Around us were snow-capped mountain peaks, in the distance a brilliant blue sea glistening in the sunlight. No wonder the *tzoulamás* tasted wonderful! But it tastes almost as good in less romantic settings, can be prepared ahead, and even freezes well, so don't miss out on it.

A traditional *tzoulamás* is made with layers of crisp pastry (fried in olive oil before the pie is assembled), mildly spiced chicken and rice, fresh mountain cheese, and hot goat's butter. My version replaces the fried pastry with *phýllo*, the *anthótyro* cheese with *féta* and cottage cheese, and the goat's butter with unsalted butter and lemon juice. Begin the meal with *mezéthes* such as Eggplant Saláta (page 57) or *taramosaláta* (page 55).

———

One 5- to 6-pound chicken, cut into serving pieces, skin and excess fat removed and giblets reserved

1 large onion, chopped

2 carrots, unpeeled, cut into thick slices

1 large bunch flat-leaf parsley, stems removed and tied in a bundle, leaves finely chopped

Sea salt

Freshly ground white pepper to taste

5 tablespoons extra-virgin olive oil

4 shallots, minced

1 tablespoon ground cumin

1 cup long-grain rice

6 bay leaves

Juice of 2 lemons

¼ cup finely chopped Preserved Lemon (page 19) or the finely grated zest of 1 lemon

1 large clove garlic, finely chopped

¼ cup capers, rinsed

One 1-pound package phýllo, *thawed if frozen*

8 ounces unsalted butter

½ cup grated féta cheese

2 cups small-curd cottage cheese, drained

1½ cups small dark seedless raisins

1 cup lightly toasted pine nuts

Place the chicken pieces, giblets, onion, carrot, parsley stems, broth, and salt and pepper to taste in a large saucepan. Bring slowly to a boil, cover, reduce the heat, and simmer 40 minutes, or until the chicken is cooked. Strain over a bowl, and strain the cooking liquid once more through cheesecloth. Set aside 2 cups of the liquid (and refrigerate the rest for another use). Discard the vegetables and all the giblets except the liver.

Warm ¼ cup of the olive oil in a heavy saucepan and sauté the shallots over low heat for 10 minutes, or until soft. Add the cumin and cook 1 minute, or until aromatic. Stir in the rice, reserved stock, the bay leaves, and ½ teaspoon salt and bring to a boil without stirring. Cook uncovered for 8 minutes, or until holes appear in the surface of the rice and the liquid has evaporated. Remove from the heat, cover with 2 layers of paper towels and a tight-fitting lid, and set aside for 30 minutes in a warm place.

Remove the chicken from the bones and cut the meat into almond-sized pieces. Cut the liver into tiny dice. Place the chicken and liver in a bowl and sprinkle with half the lemon juice and pepper to taste. Set aside 2 tablespoons of the parsley and add all but 1 tablespoon of the Preserved Lemon, the garlic, 3 tablespoons of the capers, and a pinch of salt to the remaining parsley. Chop to mix. Combine with the chicken, using your fingers to make sure each piece is coated. Cover and set aside. (The chicken can be prepared ahead and refrigerated overnight.)

Heat the oven to 375°F. Remove the package of *phýllo* from the refrigerator and set aside unopened. (If you have refrigerated the filling, remove it too.) Melt 12 tablespoons of the butter over very low heat and add the remaining 1 tablespoon olive oil. With a fork, mash the *féta* and cottage cheeses together in a small bowl.

(continued)

Divide the *phýllo* sheets into 2 portions, tightly rewrap one, and refrigerate. Lightly brush a 10-inch square or round baking pan with the butter mixture. Line with 1 *phýllo* sheet, gently pressing it into the sides of the pan, and brush the sheet with the butter mixture. Repeat with the remaining unrefrigerated sheets of pastry, but do not brush the last sheet. If you are using a round pan, turn it 60° each time you add a sheet. Spread the rice mixture over the *phýllo* and spread the chicken and parsley mixture over it. Scatter the cheese mixture over it as evenly as possible, then sprinkle the raisins and pine nuts over the cheese. Sprinkle with a few tablespoons of chicken stock if the filling seems dry. Taste the filling and season if necessary. Fold the edges of the *phýllo* over the filling and brush with the butter mixture.

Remove the second portion of *phýllo* from the refrigerator. Lay 1 sheet over the filling, letting the edges hang over the sides of the pan. Lightly brush with the butter mixture, and continue layering until all the sheets are used; do not butter the last sheet.

Carefully ease your fingers down between the edge of the pie and the sides of the pan, pull the bottom edges of the pie towards the center, and tuck the top sheets in around the bottom of the pie. Liberally butter the top sheet and, with a sharp knife, score the top 2 sheets of *phýllo* into rectangles or diamond shapes for serving. Do not score a round pie—this would make it impossible to remove from the pan. Bake 35 to 45 minutes, or until deep golden brown.

While the pie is baking, heat the remaining 4 tablespoons butter in a small saucepan over very low heat for 10 minutes, or until foamy and nutty brown; don't let it burn. Strain through cheesecloth into a small bowl, add the remaining lemon juice, and set aside in a warm place. Chop the reserved parsley and remaining 1 tablespoon capers and Preserved Lemon together.

When the pie is done, immediately cut through the score marks to the bottom of the pan. Serve from the pan or arrange the pieces on a platter. Transfer a round pie to a serving platter. Invert a large plate over the baking pan, turn upside down, remove the pan, and invert a serving platter over the bottom of the pie. Hold firmly and turn right side up. Carefully make a small hole in the center of the pie, pour over the brown butter, and sprinkle with the parsley mixture. Serve at once.

Fish and Seafood

Psária ke Psariká Thalássina

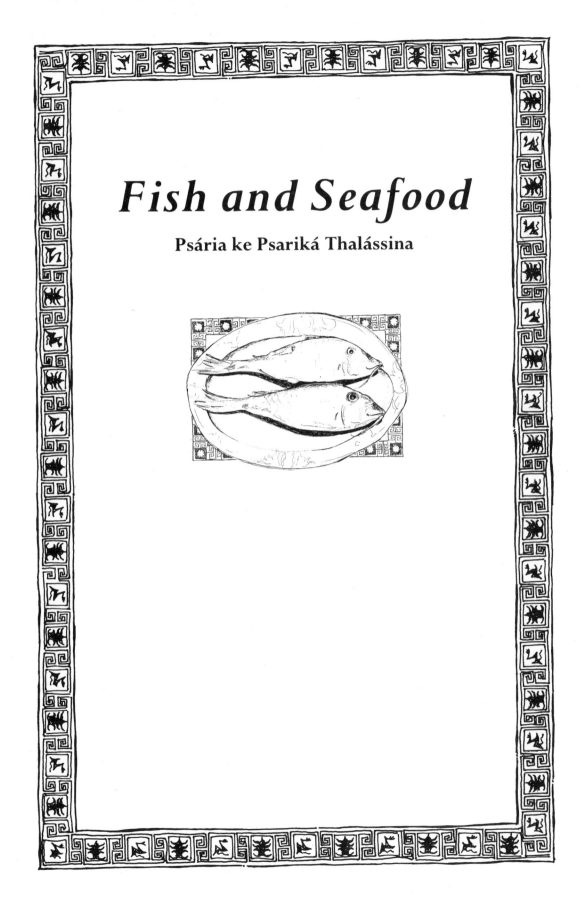

For me any mention of Greek fish dishes immediately conjures up images of harborfront *tavérnas* by a sparkling azure sea on a day shimmering with heat and brilliant sunlight. Seated at a rickety table under the welcome shade of a pine tree, you choose the fish that takes your fancy, then relax with an *oúzo* and *mezéthes* while it's prepared. Your anticipation of the treat ahead mounts as a bewildering array of fish dishes, their mouthwatering aromas filling the air, are served to tables around you.

The sheer variety of fish readily available in Greece is amazing. The Greek cook has the choice of over thirty different kinds of fish, plus shellfish and the cephalopods such as octopus and squid, and makes good use of them all. Situated in the warmest part of the Mediterranean, Greece and her islands have enjoyed a wonderfully rich sea harvest since ancient times.

Methods of preparation and presentation have changed remarkably little over the centuries. Fish is always served complete with its head—to Greeks this is the tastiest and most nutritious part. They also prefer many fish dishes to be served warm rather than hot, a practice that many visitors to Greece are not used to.

Most of the dishes included here are very simple to prepare. And, although we may not have the Greek cook's wide choice of fish, in many of these dishes almost any kind of fish steak or whole fish can be substituted.

Crusty Baked Fish

Psária Plakí sto Foúrno

Serves 4

This gloriously aromatic dish is a concoction of olive oil, parsley, tomatoes, and garlic with a crunchy crusty top. Village cooks say *psária plakí* should be made only with John Dory (page 465) but almost any firm-fleshed fish can be baked this way, using either the whole fish, steaks, or fillets. You can make a lighter version by substituting white wine or fish or chicken stock for some of the olive oil. Serve with lemon wedges.

---

2 firm-fleshed white fish such as John Dory, porgy, or bass, about 1¼ pounds each, cleaned and scaled (page 461) or 4 fillets, 6 to 8 ounces each

Coarse-grain sea salt and cracked black pepper to taste

Juice of 1 lemon

1 cup extra-virgin olive oil or ⅓ cup extra-virgin olive oil and ⅔ cup Fish or Chicken Broth (pages 463 and 461) or dry white wine

3 tablespoons finely chopped fresh oregano or thyme or 2 tablespoons dried rígani (page 14), crumbled

2 medium onions, cut in half and thinly sliced

1 large clove garlic, finely chopped

1¼ pounds boiling potatoes, peeled and cut into thin slices (boiled 10 minutes if fillets are used)

6 large ripe tomatoes, peeled and cut into slices

3 bay leaves, broken in half

12 Elítses or Niçoise olives, rinsed and pitted

FOR SERVING

¼ cup coarsely chopped flat-leaf parsley

Lemon wedges

(continued)

Dry the fish with paper towels. Make 2 deep parallel incisions on either side of the whole fish. Rub whole fish inside and out, fillets on both sides, with salt and pepper, half the lemon juice, and 1 tablespoon of the olive oil. Sprinkle the cavities of the whole fish, or both sides of the fillets, with 2 tablespoons of the oregano, cover, and set aside for 30 minutes to marinate.

Heat 2½ tablespoons of the remaining olive oil in a heavy skillet and sauté the onions over low heat until pale golden, about 12 minutes. Stir in the garlic, cook 1 minute longer, and set aside.

Heat the oven to 350°F. Brush a heavy deep baking dish with 1 tablespoon of the remaining olive oil. Dry the potato slices with paper towels and arrange about two thirds of them in the bottom of the baking dish. Cover with the onion slices and lay the fish on top. Cover with the tomato slices, and sprinkle with any remaining marinade, the bay leaves, and salt and pepper. Arrange the remaining sliced potatoes on top, leaving the tomato slices partially exposed.

Pour the remaining lemon juice and 3½ tablespoons olive oil over the potatoes, cover, and bake 30 minutes. Reduce the oven temperature to 325°F, uncover, and bake 20 to 30 minutes longer, or until golden brown and crusty. Gently press the olives into the potato-onion crust and bake 5 minutes longer.

Sprinkle with the parsley and the remaining 1 tablespoon oregano and serve at once.

Corfiot Baked Fish

Bourthéto

Serves 4

This Corfu island specialty is one of the few hot and spicy dishes in Greek cuisine. The Corfiots use small, bony fish, the cheapest in the market. For our taste fillets of any firm-fleshed white fish such as bass, porgy, or halibut are probably a better choice—and easier to eat. Or try a popular island alternative—*bourthéto* made with octopus. This colorful country food, traditionally cooked in a shallow earthenware dish, is easy to make and perfect for a leisurely summer lunch.

4 firm-fleshed white fish, about 14 ounces each, cleaned and
scaled (page 461), or 4 fillets, 6 to 7 ounces each

Juice of 1 small lemon

Sea salt and freshly ground black pepper to taste

1 large bunch flat-leaf parsley, stems reserved,
leaves finely chopped

½ to ¾ cup extra-virgin olive oil (to taste)

3 large mild onions, quartered and thinly sliced

1 large clove garlic, finely chopped

¼ cup aged red-wine vinegar

1 tablespoon honey

⅓ cup dry red wine

1 teaspoon cayenne pepper, or to taste

4 large ripe tomatoes, peeled, seeded, and diced

3 bay leaves

1 teaspoon fresh thyme, finely chopped

FOR SERVING

24 Elítses or 12 Niçoise olives, rinsed and pitted

Dry the fish with paper towels. Rub whole fish inside and out, fillets on both sides, with the lemon juice and salt and pepper. Place in a shallow dish along with the parsley stems, pour ¼ cup of the olive oil over, cover, and set aside for 1 hour to marinate.

Heat 3 tablespoons of the remaining olive oil in a large heavy skillet and cook the onions, covered, over low heat until very soft, about 30 minutes; reduce the heat if the onions begin to brown.

Heat the oven to 350°F. Stir the garlic into the onions. Combine the vinegar and honey, add to the skillet, and boil until syrupy. Add the wine and boil 1 minute longer. Stir in the cayenne pepper, tomatoes, bay leaves, thyme, and half the parsley, and pour into the baking dish. Remove the fish from the marinade, discarding the parsley stems, and lay the fish on top of the onions. Sprinkle with the remaining olive oil, cover, and bake 20 (fillets) to 30 minutes (whole fish), or until the fish is an even white all the way through.

Sprinkle with the olives and remaining parsley and serve hot.

Fish and Seafood

Baked Fish with Garlic and Vinegar

Psári sto Foúrno me Xsíthi

Serves 4

This is a popular way of cooking a plump whole fish, especially for a small dinner party. The ingredients produce an interestingly sweet but mildly piquant flavor, and the finished dish is elegant and polished. Whole cloves of garlic and sprigs of herbs support the fish in the baking dish and impart fragrance and flavor. The only other requirements are a salad, wine, and plenty of bread to mop up the delicious sauce and roasted garlic.

One 3- to 3½ pound sea bass or other firm-fleshed white fish,
cleaned and scaled, scored (pages 461 and 471)

1½ tablespoons coarse-grain sea salt, or to taste

1 tablespoon cracked black pepper

2 bay leaves

24 cloves garlic (unpeeled), feathery skin rubbed off and
stem ends trimmed

6 sprigs of dried rosemary, thyme, or rígani

1¼ cups extra-virgin olive oil

⅓ cup aged red-wine vinegar

FOR SERVING

Coarsely chopped flat-leaf parsley

Thásos or Kalamáta olives

Dry the fish with paper towels and rub inside and out with half the salt and pepper. Place the bay leaves inside the cavity, cover, and set aside for 1 hour.

Heat the oven to 325°F. Liberally brush a heavy baking dish just large enough to hold the fish with some of the olive oil. Lay the garlic cloves in the baking dish in a single layer, brush with olive oil, and bake, uncovered,

20 minutes. Lay the rosemary sprigs over the garlic and lay the fish on top. Whisk together the vinegar and remaining olive oil. Pour half this mixture over the fish and sprinkle with the remaining salt and pepper. Add ¼ cup water to the baking dish, cover loosely with aluminum foil, and bake 15 minutes. Remove the foil and bake 25 to 40 minutes longer, until the fish is an even white all the way through; baste the fish and garlic frequently with the remaining vinegar and olive oil mixture, and add a little more water to the dish if the garlic is in danger of burning.

Transfer the fish to a warm platter and surround with the garlic. Spoon over the pan juices and any remaining oil and vinegar sauce, sprinkle with the parsley, and serve the olives in bowls.

Baked Sole in Grape Leaves

Glósses Foúrnou se Ambelófila

Serves 4

Dover sole is a favorite choice for this dish but other flat fish such as flounder or slender fillets of bass make fine substitutes. John Dory fillets (page 465) or whole sardines are also delicious cooked this way. The layers of grape leaves keep the delicate fish moist and infuse the dish with their subtle and unique fragrance.

---

8 fillets of sole, 4 or 5 ounces each, or 4 larger fish fillets

Juice of 1 lemon

Sea salt and freshly ground black pepper to taste

⅓ to ½ cup extra-virgin olive oil (to taste)

Fresh or canned grape leaves, to make 2 layers in the baking dish, blanched in boiling water (3 seconds for canned leaves, 5 seconds for fresh) and drained

FOR SERVING

Finely chopped flat-leaf parsley

12 Elítses or 8 Niçoise olives, rinsed and pitted, optional

Lemon wedges

(continued)

Fish and Seafood

Dry the fillets with paper towels. Sprinkle both sides with half the lemon juice and salt and pepper, and set aside for 30 minutes.

Heat the oven to 325°F. Brush a shallow earthenware or enamel-lined cast-iron baking dish just large enough to hold the fillets in a single layer with some of the olive oil, and cover the bottom of the pan with half the grape leaves, glossy sides up. Brush the leaves with olive oil, lay the fillets on top, and sprinkle with the remaining lemon juice and olive oil. Cover with the remaining grape leaves, glossy sides down, and sprinkle with 2 tablespoons water. Bake uncovered for 20 minutes, or until the fillets are an even white all the way through.

Discard the top layer of grape leaves. Spoon the pan juices over the fish, sprinkle with the parsley, olives, and pepper, and serve with the lemon wedges.

Fish Spetsai-Style
Psári Spetsiótiko

Serves 4

From the charming island of Spetsai, famous for its fragrant pinewoods, comes this good country dish. The fish is smothered in an aromatic tomato sauce flavored with cinnamon, cloves, and garlic, topped with a layer of bread crumbs, and baked until golden and crisp. It can be served hot or cold. Fried or grilled eggplants are a good accompaniment, and resin-flavored *retsína* is the perfect wine to complement the fish.

―――――

Two 1½ pound porgies, cleaned and scaled, scored (pages 461 and 471), or 4 fillets of white-fleshed fish such as bass, about 7 ounces each

Juice of ½ lemon

Coarse-grain salt and cracked black pepper to taste

½ cup extra-virgin olive oil

1 small onion, finely chopped

2 to 4 cloves garlic, finely chopped

8 large tomatoes, peeled and diced, juices reserved

1 teaspoon honey

One 3-inch cinnamon stick, broken in half, or 1 teaspoon ground cinnamon

3 whole cloves or ¼ teaspoon ground cloves

¼ cup coarsely chopped flat-leaf parsley

½ cup dry white wine

½ cup dried coarse bread crumbs

1 teaspoon dried **rígani** *(page 14), crumbled*

Dry the fish with paper towels. Rub whole fish inside and out, fillets on both sides, with the lemon juice, salt and pepper, and 2 tablespoons of the olive oil. Cover and set aside.

In a heavy skillet heat 2 tablespoons of the remaining olive oil over low heat and sauté the onion until soft, about 6 minutes. Add the garlic, tomatoes with their juices, honey, cinnamon, cloves, and half the parsley. Raise the heat to medium-low and simmer until the cooking liquid is reduced by half. Add the wine and boil 1 minute. Strain the sauce through a coarse sieve into a large bowl, pressing on the solids to extract as much liquid as possible. Measure, and add water if necessary to make 3 cups. Season to taste with salt and pepper. Place the fish in the sauce, turn once or twice to coat, and set aside for 30 minutes.

Heat the oven to 325°F.

Brush a baking pan just large enough to hold the fish with some of the remaining olive oil, place the fish in it, and pour over the sauce. Sprinkle with olive oil and bake, uncovered, 20 minutes. Baste the fish with the sauce and sprinkle with the bread crumbs and remaining olive oil. Bake 15 minutes longer, or until the fish is an even white all the way through and the sauce is thick and syrupy.

Sprinkle with the *rígani* and remaining parsley and serve hot or warm.

Sea Bass with Vinegar and Rosemary

Lavrákia Marináta

Serves 4

Sea bass is a favorite *tavérna* dish—best eaten, say the Greeks, at an open-air restaurant close by the sea. The fish, glistening and plump, looks beautiful, while sweet rosemary lends a subtle fragrance. Here the dusting of flour keeps the fish from splitting and flaking during frying and cuts down fish odors in the kitchen. Garbanzo flour, available in Greek and health food stores, gives just the right traditional nutty flavor.

Four 1 to 1¼-pound sea bass, cleaned and scaled (page 461),
or 4 fillets, about 7 ounces each

Juice of ½ lemon

1 teaspoon coarse-grain sea salt, or to taste

½ tablespoon cracked black pepper, or to taste

¼ cup garbanzo flour and 2 tablespoons all-purpose flour or 6
tablespoons all-purpose flour

¾ to 1 cup extra-virgin olive oil (to taste)

1 large clove garlic, cut into slivers, optional

⅓ cup aged red-wine vinegar

2 tablespoons hot water

2 tablespoons fresh rosemary

4 bay leaves

FOR SERVING

Small sprigs of fresh rosemary

Elítses or Niçoise olives

Wipe the fish with a damp cloth and rub whole fish inside and out, fillets on both sides, with the lemon juice and half the salt and pepper. Dust with 2 tablespoons of the flour, cover, and set aside for 30 minutes.

Place a large heavy skillet over medium-low heat and add half the olive oil. Dust the fish again with 2 tablespoons of the remaining flour and shake off any excess. When the olive oil is hot but not smoking, fry the fish on both sides just until pale golden, about 15 minutes for whole fish, 10 to 12 minutes for fillets. Check for doneness by inserting a thin knife blade into the thickest point of the fish; it should be an even white all the way through. Drain between layers of paper towels. Strain the frying oil through 2 layers of cheesecloth to remove any residue and set aside.

Wipe out the skillet with paper towels and return to low heat. Sprinkle the remaining 2 tablespoons flour over the bottom of the skillet and stir a minute or two with a wooden spoon until deep golden brown. Whisk in the reserved frying oil and the remaining olive oil. Add the garlic and cook, stirring 1 minute longer, or until the flour is a deep nutty brown. The flour and oil will not blend together, but the flour will flavor and color the oil. Add the vinegar, water, rosemary, bay leaves, and remaining salt and pepper, whisk to mix, and simmer 3 minutes.

Return the fish to the skillet, cover, and heat through. Transfer to a warm platter, pour over the sauce, and surround with the rosemary sprigs. Serve hot or warm, with black olives.

Note To serve cold, add ½ cup dry white wine or 1 cup strained Tomato Sauce (page 431, made with parsley and bay leaves) along with the vinegar. Let the sauce cool, then transfer the fish and sauce to a shallow glass or china dish, add olive oil to cover, tightly cover, and refrigerate overnight or up to 3 days before serving. Turn the fish in the marinade once or twice. Serve as a *mezé* or lunch dish.

Red Mullet in Savory Sauce

Barboúnia me Sáltsa Savóri

Serves 4

Red mullet has always been highly prized in Greece. One ancient manuscript lists a two-pound mullet at the same price as two dozen slaves. Nowadays large red mullet are popular and therefore more expensive, but it's the smaller fish that have the sweeter flavor. In Greece the liver and cheeks are considered a delicacy—I prefer to do without the liver unless the fish is very fresh. This dish tastes equally delicious hot or cold; the piquant sauce also marries well with fillets or steaks of bass, halibut, or porgy.

———

8 red mullet, 8 to 10 ounces each, cleaned and scaled (page 461), or 4 fillets of bass or porgy, about 7 ounces each

1 teaspoon coarse-grain sea salt, or to taste

½ tablespoon cracked black pepper, or to taste

½ cup extra-virgin olive oil

1 large clove garlic, cut into slivers

⅓ cup aged red-wine vinegar

1 teaspoon honey

6 large ripe tomatoes, peeled, seeded, diced, and drained in a colander for 30 minutes

¼ teaspoon ground cinnamon

¼ cup currants or small dark seedless raisins, soaked for 30 minutes in 1 tablespoon hot water

4 bay leaves

1 tablespoon fresh thyme, finely chopped, or ½ tablespoon dried thyme, crumbled

FOR SERVING

¼ cup coarsely chopped flat-leaf parsley

2 salted anchovy fillets (page 460), rinsed, patted dry, and finely chopped

Wipe the fish with a damp cloth and rub whole fish inside and out, fillets on both sides, with half the salt and pepper. Cover and set aside for 30 minutes.

Place a large heavy skillet over medium-low heat, add ¼ cup of olive oil, and heat until hot but not smoking. Fry the fish on both sides until pale golden, about 15 minutes for whole fish, 10 to 12 minutes for fillets. Check for doneness by inserting a thin knife blade into the thickest part of the fish—it should flake easily and be an even white all the way through. Drain between layers of paper towels.

Drain off the olive oil and wipe out the skillet with paper towels. Add 2 tablespoons of the remaining olive oil and sauté the garlic over low heat just until fragrant; don't let it color. Combine the vinegar and honey and add it to the skillet, raise the heat, and boil until reduced to about 3 tablespoons. Add the tomatoes, cinnamon, currants, bay leaves, thyme, and remaining salt and pepper, lower the heat, and simmer 3 minutes. Return the fish to the skillet, cover, and heat through.

Transfer to a warm platter, pour over the sauce and remaining 2 tablespoons olive oil, and sprinkle with the parsley and chopped anchovies. Serve hot, warm, or cold.

Note To serve cold, add ½ cup dry white wine to the skillet once the vinegar is reduced, boil 1 minute, and then add the tomatoes and remaining ingredients. Let the sauce cool, transfer the fish and sauce to a glass or china dish, add olive oil to cover, tightly cover, and refrigerate overnight or up to 3 days. Turn the fish in the marinade once or twice. Serve as a *mezé* or light lunch dish.

Grilled Fish

Psária Skháras Khoriátika

Serves 4

Few treats can equal the splendor of a freshly-caught fish grilled over an aromatic charcoal fire and served with a scattering of fresh herbs. Walk along any Greek harborside and you'll find *tavérnas* whose specialty is the daily creation of this culinary masterpiece.

For grilling, Greeks choose a variety of fish and seafood, including red mullet, the colorful members of the bream family, bonito, tuna, and sword-fish, delicious little sardines, and lobster, shrimp, octopus, cuttlefish, and squid. Before grilling, fish is often steeped in a well-flavored marinade.

The charcoal should be produced from hardwood (olive wood and vine clippings make the best); it should be moderately hot and have reached what the Greeks call the "digested stage," i.e., lightly covered with grey ash.

Herbs, both fresh and dried, are a fundamental way of flavoring grilled fish, but how you use them is more important than which herbs you choose. Don't be tempted to just throw a handful of bay leaves onto the fire—the acrid smoke they produce will not enhance the flavor of the fish! Sprigs of fresh herbs such as thyme, rosemary or oregano are used as basting brushes, in marinades, and in sauces; dried *rígani* is used in marinades and at serving time.

The most common problems with grilled fish are drying up and breaking. Guard against this by choosing plump and succulent fish of at least 1½ pounds in weight (smaller fish are better fried), brush both fish and grill liberally with olive oil before grilling, and take special care over cooking times (this depends on the thickness of the fish, not its length).

———

*Two 1¾- to 2¼-pound or one 3½-pound firm-fleshed fish,
cleaned and scaled (page 461), or 4 fish steaks, at least
½ inch thick (about 8 ounces each)*

Juice of 1 lemon (reserve 1 juiced lemon half)

Sea salt and cracked black pepper to taste

¼ to ⅓ cup extra-virgin olive oil (to taste)

6 sprigs of fresh oregano

3 bay leaves

Purslane Salad (page 292) or watercress sprigs

Dry the fish with paper towels and score fish larger than 2 pounds so they cook evenly. With a sharp knife, make two or three deep 2-inch parallel diagonal incisions on each side of the fish. (The heads are always left intact on fish prepared for the grill—the cheeks taste particularly good.) Rub whole fish inside and out, steaks on both sides, with half the lemon juice, salt, and pepper, and 1½ tablespoons of the olive oil. Scatter the oregano and bay leaves over and set aside while you prepare the fire.

Set a grill rack 4 to 5 inches above hot coals and brush with olive oil, or brush a hinged double grill with olive oil. Brush the fish with some of the remaining olive oil. Combine the remaining lemon juice and olive oil to make a basting sauce. Pierce the lemon half with a skewer and use it as a "baster," dipping it in the sauce. Grill the fish on both sides until cooked through, about 10 minutes for steaks, up to 15 minutes for smaller whole fish and 25 minutes for larger fish, basting liberally with the sauce.

Spread the Purslane Salad over a warm platter and arrange the fish on top. Sprinkle with the remaining basting sauce, salt, and pepper and serve immediately.

Grilled Marinated Fish

Psári Skháras

Serves 4

Traditionally used by village cooks to preserve freshly caught fish, aromatic marinades inspired by a variety of ingredients continue to add a delightful flavor to grilled fish. Swordfish steaks are particularly good with the marinades given here. Either with give any grilled fish an authentic Greek taste, whether you serve it simply garnished with fresh herbs or accompanied by one of the suggested sauces, along with a salad of wild greens (page 295) and Olive Bread (page 339).

(continued)

Fish and Seafood

*Two 1¾- to 2¼-pound or one 3½-pound firm-fleshed fish,
cleaned and scaled, scored (pages 461 and 471), or 4 fish
steaks, at least ½ inch thick (about 8 ounces each)*

Juice of 1 small lemon (see Note)

Sea salt and freshly ground black pepper to taste

½ cup extra-virgin olive oil

MARINADE 1

1 large mild onion, thinly sliced

2 tablespoons aged red-wine vinegar

Pinch of cayenne pepper

FOR SERVING

Coarsely chopped fresh coriander leaves or flat-leaf parsley

*Black Olives and Lentil Saláta (page 49)
or Anchovy Sauce (page 436)*

MARINADE 2

3 shallots, finely chopped

4 sprigs of parsley

2 sprigs of fresh thyme

Juice of ½ lemon

2 bay leaves

FOR SERVING

Finely chopped flat-leaf parsley

Peloponnese Honey Sauce (page 435) or latholémono *sauce
(4 parts extra-virgin olive oil to 1 part fresh lemon juice,
whisked together, with finely chopped fresh thyme or parsley to taste)*

Dry the fish with paper towels. Rub whole fish inside and out, steaks on both sides, with the lemon juice and salt and pepper. Place in a shallow china or glass dish and add all the ingredients for either of the marinades and ¼ cup of the olive oil. Cover and set aside for 1 hour.

Prepare the fire and set a grill rack 4 to 5 inches above the coals. Brush the grill or a hinged double grill with olive oil. Remove the fish from the marinade, strain the marinade, and combine with the remaining ¼ cup of olive oil. Remove any onion or herbs sticking to the fish and grill on both sides until cooked through, about 10 minutes for steaks, up to 15 minutes for smaller whole fish and 25 minutes for larger whole fish. Baste occasionally with the marinade.

Transfer to a warm platter, sprinkle with the coriander or parsley, and drizzle with the remaining marinade mixture. Serve immediately and pass the *saláta* or sauce separately.

Note Reserve 1 of the juiced lemon halves for a "baster" (pierce it with a skewer and dip it in the marinade) or use sprigs of dried *rígani* or fresh thyme as a basting brush.

Pan-Seared Bonito with Beet Greens

Palamítha Psití me Khórta

Serves 4

For centuries Greeks have enjoyed this ancient dish, which brings land and sea together in perfect harmony: from the sea, the rich strongly flavored oily fish and from the land, the earthy country tones of beet greens. The combination creates a colorful succulent dish that looks enticingly exotic, but is very easy to prepare. Surprising as it may sound, a good dry red wine complements the flavors in this dish best.

---

4 bonito, tuna, or swordfish steaks, about 8 ounces each

Coarse-grain salt to taste

1 tablespoon cracked black pepper, or to taste

¼ to ⅓ cup red-wine vinegar (to taste)

4 bay leaves

2 sprigs of fresh or dried thyme

½ teaspoon ground paprika

⅓ to ½ cup extra-virgin olive oil (to taste)

1 pound beet greens

1 large clove garlic, cut into thin slivers

FOR SERVING

1 tablespoon small capers, rinsed   *(continued)*

Wipe the fish steaks and rub with salt, ½ tablespoon of the pepper, and 1 tablespoon of the vinegar. Place in a shallow china or glass dish with the bay leaves and thyme, and sprinkle with ¼ teaspoon of the paprika and 1 tablespoon of the olive oil. Cover and set aside for 1 hour to marinate.

If the beet greens are young and tender, with bright green leaves, just strip the leaves from the stems. If the greens are older, with dark green leaves, remove the tough stems. Blanch the leaves in boiling water for 3 minutes and drain in a colander, pressing out excess moisture.

Heat a heavy cast-iron skillet over medium-low heat, and add 2 tablespoons of the remaining olive oil. Remove the fish from the marinade, discarding the bay leaves and thyme, and sear on both sides until the fish is an even white all the way through, about 8 to 10 minutes. Transfer to a warm platter, cover, and keep warm.

Wipe out the skillet with paper towels, return to low heat, and add 1 tablespoon of the remaining olive oil. Sauté the garlic until golden. Add 3 tablespoons of the remaining vinegar to deglaze the pan; it will almost immediately reduce by half. Slice the fresh greens into thin ribbons or coarsely chop the cooked greens and add to the skillet with salt and the remaining ½ tablespoon pepper. Stir with a wooden spoon until tender greens are just cooked or cooked greens are hot.

Transfer to a platter and arrange the fish on top. Sprinkle with the capers, remaining ¼ teaspoon paprika and vinegar, and olive oil to taste. Serve at once.

Shellfish and Crustaceans

Ostraka ke Ostrakíthi

Greeks revel in subtle and innovative blends of taste and texture, but they also know when to leave well enough alone—and the shellfish and crustaceans available to them, deliciously fresh from the sea, need very little help from the cook.

Cockles and scallops are eaten raw as *mezéthes* or made into *piláfi* or soup. Mussels are removed from their shells, coated with egg and bread crumbs, and deep-fried, to be served as a *mezé,* with *macarónia,* or in *piláfi.*

Shrimp is popular throughout Greece and her islands. The fishermen baste them with lemon juice, olive oil, and coarse-grain sea salt and grill them—nothing could be more delicious.

Lobster is the prize catch of the Mediterranean and many Greeks prefer their lobster simply boiled and served with a good mayonnaise or a light *latholémono* sauce—but charcoal-grilled lobster is popular too.

Spiny Lobster with Latholémono Sauce

Astakós me Latholémono

Serves 4

Greeks prefer the flavor of spiny lobster to that of the larger North American lobster. This smaller variety, also known as rock lobster, is the most common in Greek waters, and it's readily available on our West Coast. In Greek homes and *tavérnas* lobster is always presented very simply, with olive oil, lemon juice, and a scattering of fresh parsley or oregano—an especially lovely treat on a warm summer's day.

¼ cup vinegar

1 tablespoon sea salt

2 live spiny (rock) or small North American lobsters,
1 to 1¼ pounds each

Juice of 1 lemon

Large pinch of ground mustard

Sea salt and freshly ground black pepper to taste

½ cup extra-virgin olive oil

FOR SERVING

Finely chopped fresh oregano or flat-leaf parsley

Fill a large saucepan with water and bring it to a boil over high heat; add the vinegar and salt. Add the lobsters, bring back to a boil, reduce the heat slightly, and cook 6 minutes longer. Drain and blot dry.

Devein the lobsters and discard the small sac beneath the heads. Cut in half along the length of the body. Take out the olive-green livers and, if there is any, the bright orange coral. Mash the coral (and liver, if liked) to a paste with half the lemon juice, the mustard, and salt and pepper. Whisk in the olive oil to make a creamy sauce, and add the remaining lemon juice to taste.

Remove the meat from the tails and chop it into small pieces. Toss with 2 tablespoons of the sauce and replace in the shells. If using North American lobsters, crack the claws (only the tail meat of the spiny lobsters is eaten). Arrange the lobsters attractively on a platter and sprinkle with the oregano. Serve the sauce separately.

Grilled Lobster

Astakós tis Skhára

Serves 4

Small lobsters are the best choice for grilling; their meat stays moist and sweet. If you can prepare your fire using woody rosemary bush branches or olive hardwood you will enjoy grilled lobster with a very special flavor. Better still, have some branches of rosemary ready to throw on the fire just before grilling the lobsters and use several sprigs of rosemary tied together as a basting brush.

———

Coarse-grain sea salt

6 tablespoons wine vinegar

4 live small North American or spiny (rock) lobsters

¾ to 1 cup extra-virgin olive oil (to taste)

1 teaspoon honey

½ teaspoon ground coriander

Cracked black pepper to taste

Juice of 1 lemon

Fill a large saucepan with water and bring to a boil over high heat; add 1 tablespoon salt and ¼ cup of the vinegar. Add the lobsters, bring back to a boil, reduce the heat slightly, and boil 3 minutes longer. Drain and blot dry.

Set a grill rack 3 inches above charcoal and brush it with olive oil.

Combine the remaining vinegar, ⅓ cup of the olive oil, honey, coriander, and salt and pepper and brush the lobsters liberally with this sauce. Grill 20 to 30 minutes, basting and turning frequently, until the shell can be easily separated from the flesh. Leave the shells in place, but devein each lobster, and discard the small sacs beneath the heads. Remove the orange coral, if there is any, and mash to a paste with the lemon juice and remaining olive oil.

Arrange the lobsters on a serving platter. Serve the remaining sauce separately, and have plenty of napkins on the table.

Shrimp in a Pot with Féta Cheese

Garíthes Youvétsi

Serves 4

This is a pretty—and convenient—dish for a dinner party. It can be prepared a few hours ahead of time and baked at the last minute. Serve in individual earthenware dishes for a beautiful presentation and have plenty of country bread on the table for your guests to mop up the delicious sauce.

———

1½ pounds shrimp in the shell

½ cup extra-virgin olive oil

2 onions, quartered and thinly sliced

1 large clove garlic, finely chopped

*4 medium ripe tomatoes, 4 of them peeled, seeded, and diced,
the remaining 3 peeled, cored, and cut into thin slices*

½ teaspoon honey

¼ teaspoon cayenne pepper, optional

½ teaspoon ground cumin

1 tablespoon dried rígani (page 14), crumbled

½ cup coarsely chopped flat-leaf parsley

1 cup dry white wine

Coarse-grain sea salt to taste

½ tablespoon cracked black pepper, or to taste

¾ pound féta cheese, cut into 8 slices

FOR SERVING

Lemon wedges

Flavors of Greece

Remove the legs from the shrimp and devein (but do not remove from the shell). Rinse and dry between layers of paper towels. Heat 2 tablespoons of the olive oil in a heavy skillet, add the shrimp, cover, and cook 4 minutes over medium-low heat, occasionally giving the skillet a vigorous shake. Transfer the shrimp and oil to a bowl, tightly cover, and refrigerate. Wipe out the skillet.

Heat the oven to 350°F. Heat ¼ cup of the remaining olive oil in the skillet and sauté the onion over low heat until soft, about 8 minutes. Add the garlic, diced tomatoes, honey, cayenne pepper, and cumin, raise the heat to medium, and simmer until most of the liquid has evaporated, about 10 minutes. Add the *rígani,* about ⅓ cup of the parsley, the wine, salt, and pepper. Cook, stirring occasionally, 8 minutes; the sauce should remain separated for a few seconds when a wooden spoon is drawn across the bottom of the skillet.

Divide the sauce among 4 individual ovenproof dishes. Peel the shrimp, catching any juices in the bowl. Arrange the shrimp on top of the sauce and sprinkle with the juices. Cover with the tomato and *féta* cheese slices, sprinkle with the remaining 2 tablespoons olive oil, and bake until heated through, about 15 to 20 minutes.

Sprinkle with the reserved parsley and serve hot with the lemon wedges.

Sea Urchins

Achiní

Serves 4

Until recently any cookbook mention of sea urchins would have been of purely academic interest. Now that these fascinating sea creatures are in greater demand, they are farmed in California and Oregon and are far more widely available.

Greeks have enjoyed eating sea urchins since before the time of Homer. They gather only the females since it is the females that yield the distinctive coral (roe) and gather sea urchins only at around the time of the full moon, when, for some mysterious reason, they contain the greatest number of eggs.

Serve sea urchins in the shell so guests can scoop out the coral for themselves, or gently detach the coral from the sides of each shell and serve it on small dishes, and offer *oúzo, rakí,* or a jug of chilled dry white wine to drink.

---

4 dozen very fresh sea urchins (page 471)

FOR SERVING

Lemon wedges or aged red-wine vinegar

To prepare a sea urchin, wrap one of your hands in a heavy cloth and grip the shell, soft side facing upwards. Insert a blunt-ended knife into the mouth in the center of this soft side and, with a circular motion, gently scoop out the mouth and the top third of the shell; the shell cracks easily, so care is needed. As you finish preparing each sea urchin, rinse it in a bowl of water; the loose inner gray mass should float out, leaving the roe adhering to the inside of the shell. Check that no spikes have found their way into the shell, and set aside; or scoop the roe out onto a small platter.

Serve immediately, or tightly cover and refrigerate no more than an hour or two. Serve with the lemon wedges.

Octopus, Squid, and Cuttlefish

Khtapóthi, Kalamária, ke Soupiés

Octopus, squid, and cuttlefish (the cephalopods) are everyday food in Greece. Inexpensive and nutritious, they appear on *tavérna* menus everywhere, especially on the islands.

Small squid and cuttlefish are the tastiest and the most tender. As a *mezé*, these tiny creatures are fried whole to crisp perfection and served just with a little lemon juice and salt. For a main course squid may be slowly simmered in an aromatic wine or ink sauce.

Larger squid are usually stuffed—popular in Greece are stuffings made with rice, shallots, spinach, and tomatoes; bread crumbs, olives, pine nuts, and currants; or rice, parsley, currants, and pine nuts—and simmered until they are tender and the flavors have blended beautifully. Cuttlefish can also be stuffed, but it is easier to cut cuttlefish into pieces before cooking. It's from cuttlefish ink that the pigment sepia is extracted (the Greek name for cuttlefish is *soupiés*).

Perhaps the best way to try octopus for the first time is grilled (page 152). In Greece not only the octopus itself but also the ink sacs are considered *mezé* delicacies. Large ink sacs are fried; small ones roasted in an eggplant or onion shell in the embers of a fire. Check the Glossary for more information on mastering the art of cleaning and preparing these traditional delicacies.

Grilled Octopus
Khtapóthi sti Skhára

Serves 6

The taste of octopus grilled over the embers of a wood fire always reminds me of beach parties in Greece on balmy star-lit nights. Guests are greeted with a glass of *oúzo* or *rakí* and while they chat the charcoal burns down to just the right dull glow and the octopus marinates in olive oil, lemon juice, and *rígani*. Grilling takes just a few minutes and the octopus, cut into small pieces, is served as a *mezé*, accompanied by bowls of olives and cheese. Or serve it as a main course with a pilaf and Beets Island-Style (page 244), or *khórta* (page 294).

One 5- to 7-pound octopus, tenderized (page 468)

2 cups dry white wine or water

1¼ cups extra-virgin olive oil

Juice of 2 lemons

12 sprigs fresh oregano or rosemary, leaves stripped from the stems, and stems reserved, or ¼ cup dried rígani (page 14)

1 tablespoon coarse-grain sea salt, or to taste

1 tablespoon cracked black pepper

FOR SERVING

Lemon wedges

1 cup coarsely chopped flat-leaf parsley

One day ahead, remove the eyes, mouth, and inside of the head of the octopus if it has not already been done. Rinse well in several changes of water and place in a large saucepan with the wine, adding water, if necessary, to cover. Bring slowly to a boil, cover, reduce the heat, and simmer 1¼ hours (for a 5-pound octopus) to 1¾ hours (for a 7-pound octopus). Drain, thoroughly rinse, cover tightly, and refrigerate overnight.

Prepare the fire. Cut up the octopus: sever the legs from the body and leave whole; cut the body (head) lengthwise in quarters; and peel off the skin to expose the pale pink flesh—the suckers come off easily with the skin.

Whisk together 1 cup of the olive oil, the lemon juice, and *rígani* leaves

in a shallow bowl. Add the octopus pieces and turn to coat with the marinade. Set aside.

Set a grill rack 4 inches above the hot coals, and brush with olive oil. Throw the herb stems on the fire. Remove the octopus pieces from the marinade, sprinkle with the salt and pepper, and grill a few minutes on either side, or until browned, brushing once or twice with the marinade. Arrange on a warm platter and surround with the lemon wedges. Sprinkle with the parsley and the remaining olive oil.

Cuttlefish in Ink Sauce

Soupiés me Sáltsa Melánis

Serves 4

At any time of year Crete's largest city, Heraklion, boasts a spectacular market, vibrant with color, bustling with noise, and overflowing with produce from all over the island. In spring and fall Greek cooks head first for the fishermen's stalls, which are piled high with towers of gleaming cuttlefish. Bargaining with stallholders, they reject the large cuttlefish and choose instead the small ones. Cuttlefish are the most tender and easily prepared of all cephalopods and a favorite food on the islands, especially when cooked with this creamy inky sauce.

———

3 pounds cuttlefish, preferably small, of a similar size

⅓ cup extra-virgin olive oil

2 large mild onions, quartered and thinly sliced

½ cup dry white wine

⅓ cup finely chopped flat-leaf parsley

½ tablespoon fresh oregano, finely chopped, or dried **rígani**
(page 14), crumbled

Coarse-grain sea salt and cracked black pepper to taste

FOR SERVING

1 tablespoon finely chopped Preserved Lemon
(page 19), optional

Lemon wedges   (continued)

Fish and Seafood

Rinse the cuttlefish. Small ones (4 to 5 inches) can be left whole. Prepare larger ones as follows: Gently pull off the head with the tentacles still attached, then carefully slash the center front of the body with a sharp knife. Remove the 2 small black ink sacs, and check to make sure they contain no sand—try to avoid rinsing them, or they will lose too much ink. Set aside 8 sacs, and discard the rest. Rinse off any ink from the cuttlefish. Remove the single bone, discard everything else from inside the body, and rub off the brownish outer skin. Rinse again, cut into long 1-inch-wide strips, and place in a colander to drain.

Slice off and discard the part of the head that contains the eyes, and rinse the head. Slice it open so it unfolds into a strip, with the tentacles on one side. Discard the beak, and thoroughly rinse and rub the tentacles to remove any sand. Cut into 1-inch pieces and add to the colander.

Heat ¼ cup of the olive oil in a large heavy skillet and sauté the onion over low heat until soft, about 6 minutes. Add the cuttlefish and cook, stirring occasionally, until any liquid has evaporated and the cuttlefish and onion begin to color, about 15 minutes. Place the ink sacs and ½ cup water in a small bowl and gently rub the sacs to expel all the ink. Strain through a fine strainer into the skillet, add the wine, and raise the heat to medium low. Cook, stirring frequently, until all the liquid has evaporated and the cuttlefish are coated with a creamy sauce, about 15 minutes. Stir in about ¼ cup of the parsley, season with salt and a generous amount of pepper, and cook 1 minute longer.

Chop the Preserved Lemon, remaining parsley, and a large pinch of salt and pepper together to mix. Transfer the cuttlefish to a platter, or serve directly from the skillet, sprinkled with the lemon mixture and the remaining olive oil. Serve at once with the lemon wedges.

Chicken and Game

Kotópoula ke Kinígi

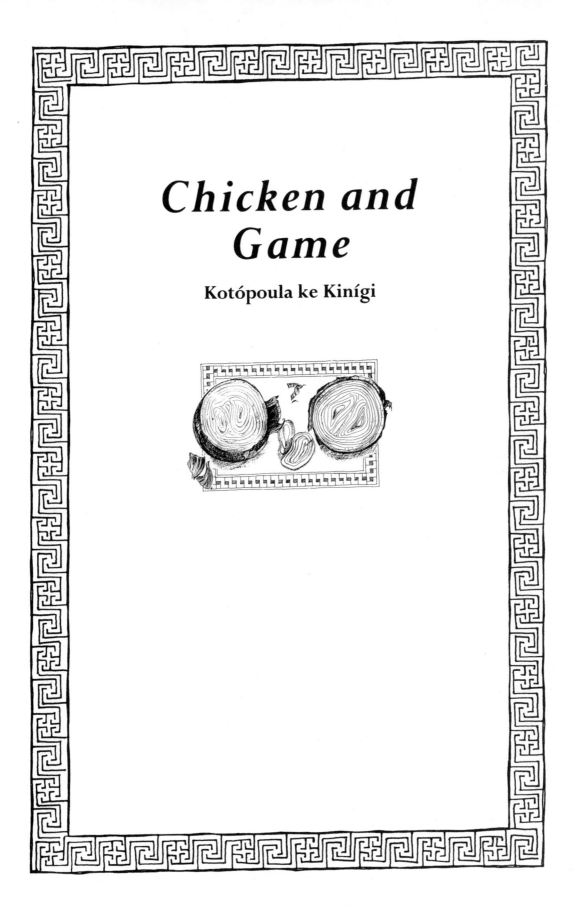

Sizzling on spits, scented with lemon and fruity olive oil, glistening and golden-roasted—that's how Greeks like chicken best. That's also how the traveler to Greece most often remembers chicken—the pungent aroma of mountain herbs as chicken spit roasts assails the senses and sets the taste buds racing. Greek chickens may not be as plump as our own but they are invariably free range and have a superb flavor and texture.

But Greeks also enjoy a variety of chicken casseroles and baked dishes. These are traditional dishes, meant to be baked in the village oven, but they are easily adapted to our ovens and slow cookers. Greek ways to flavor chickens may come as a surprise: Many feature the strong use of Eastern spices—Chicken in a Pot (page 158), for example, includes cloves and cinnamon, and just the aroma of this heartening dish envelops you in a comforting warmth of gastronomic expectation. Also spiced, with cumin, allspice, and cloves, is Chicken and Okra (page 160), a colorful dish to make in early summer when this vegetable is at its best. Other chicken dishes are tied to seasonal change—in spring, the clear lemony fragrance of a poached Chicken with Avgolémono Sauce (page 164) and, in fall, the creamy coriander-and-walnut-flavored sauce enrobing a braised chicken (page 162) are delights.

For us chicken is commonplace: for Greeks in rural communities rabbit, hare, and game birds in season are everyday fare. Simple spit-roast rabbit or game birds are popular at village feasts and the spicy *stifátho,* made with rabbit, hare, or even snails, and sweetened with large quantities of onions, is a favorite winter meal. Greece lies on the migratory path between northern Europe and Africa and from September through November Greek skies are darkened with flocks of birds on their way to the sun. At this time of year the "hunter's pot" (page 178) may contain quail, woodcock, partridge, or pigeon, gently braised under a covering of grape leaves and fragrant with herbs. Duck, particularly wild duckling from the Macedonian lakes, is a popular spring food—cooked Thessalia-style (page 182), scented with juniper berries, cloves, and orange zest, it's a dish fit for the gods!

Roast Chicken with Rígani and Garlic

Kotópoulo Riganáto

Serves 4 to 6

Pungent *rígani* grows in wild abundance on the mountain slopes of Greece. The Greek cook's favorite herb, it's in strong evidence in this aromatic roast chicken. This is a dish for garlic lovers too—the amount used is generous! Cook the chicken whole for elegance, cut into serving pieces for speed and convenience.

---

2 pounds roasting potatoes, cut lengthwise into quarters

One 4- to 5-pound chicken, whole or cut into serving pieces,
skin and excess fat removed

Juice of 1½ lemons

⅓ to ½ cup extra-virgin or Kalamáta olive oil (to taste)

½ tablespoon coarse-grain sea salt, or to taste

6 cloves garlic (unpeeled), lightly crushed

¼ cup dried rígani (page 14), crumbled

Cracked black pepper to taste

6 bay leaves

1 tablespoon unsalted butter

1¾ cups fat-free Chicken Broth (page 641)

½ teaspoon Dijon mustard

1 teaspoon honey

FOR SERVING

½ cup coarsely chopped flat-leaf parsley

Heat the oven to 375°F. Rub the chicken with the juice of 1 lemon, 3 tablespoons of the olive oil, and the salt. Place the chicken in a deep heavy baking dish and surround with the potatoes and garlic in a single layer.

(continued)

Sprinkle the chicken with the *rígani*, pepper, bay leaves, and the remaining olive oil and dot with the butter. Add 1 cup of the broth, and roast, uncovered, 15 minutes. Reduce the oven temperature to 350°F and roast until tender: about 1 hour longer for a whole chicken, 40 minutes longer for chicken pieces; baste the chicken and potatoes frequently, adding more broth to the dish if necessary.

Transfer the chicken, potatoes, and garlic to a serving platter and keep warm. Strain the pan juices into a small saucepan, remove the fat with a spoon, and add any remaining broth. If there is more than about 1½ cups liquid, reduce it by rapid boiling. Combine the mustard, honey, and half the remaining lemon juice and stir into the sauce. Add salt, pepper, and lemon juice to taste, and heat to warm.

Pour sauce over the chicken and potatoes just to moisten, and sprinkle with the parsley. Serve the remaining sauce separately.

Chicken in a Pot

Kapamá Kotópoulo

Serves 4 to 5

On a morning stroll through a traditional Greek village visitors are often welcomed by the warm, comforting aromas of *kapamás* wafting from private kitchens or the baker's oven. These are no ordinary stews: they are rich and colorful creations cooked slowly so that flavors blend and the meat becomes so tender that you could eat it with a spoon. *Kapamá kotópoulo,* a classic country dish, is flavored with cloves and cinnamon, marjoram and bay leaves, tomatoes, onions, and honey; you can use this recipe to make glorious casseroles of lamb or hare, too. The real secret of these wonderful stews is that the ingredients are packed in closely together and a tight-fitting lid locks in the spicy flavor during baking. Serve with fried eggplant slices, *piláfi* and grated *kasséri* cheese.

One 4- to 5-pound chicken, cut into serving pieces, skin and
excess fat removed and giblets reserved

2 tablespoons extra-virgin olive oil

1 tablespoon unsalted butter

1 large onion, chopped

8 large ripe tomatoes, peeled and diced

1 teaspoon honey

3 bay leaves, broken into pieces

1 tablespoon dried marjoram or rosemary, crumbled

4 whole cloves

One 3-inch cinnamon stick or 1 teaspoon ground cinnamon

½ to 1 cup Chicken Broth (page 461) or water

1 teaspoon cracked black pepper, or to taste

¼ cup all-purpose flour

1 clove garlic, finely chopped

1 teaspoon coarse-grain sea salt, or to taste

⅓ cup pine nuts

⅓ cup finely chopped flat-leaf parsley

12 Ámfissa or Niçoise olives, rinsed and pitted

Heat the oven to 325°F. Discard the chicken liver. Rinse the remaining
giblets and trim off the membranes. Heat the olive oil and butter in a heavy
skillet and sauté the chicken and giblets over medium-low heat until lightly
browned. Drain between layers of paper towels and transfer to a heavy
casserole.

Drain off most of the fat from the skillet, add the onion to the pan, and
sauté until soft, about 5 minutes. Add the tomatoes, honey, bay leaves,
marjoram, cloves, cinnamon, ½ cup of the broth, and pepper, and simmer 5
minutes. Pour over the chicken.

Mix the flour with a little water to make a thick paste and spread the top
rim of the casserole and inner rim of the lid with it. Place the lid in position,
smooth the paste to make a good seal, and bake 15 minutes. Reduce the oven
temperature to 300°F and bake 2½ hours longer.

(continued)

Chicken and Game

Meanwhile, pound the garlic and salt together in a mortar or bowl until blended. Add the pine nuts and half the parsley, pound until well mixed, and set aside. (You can use a food processor, but process only until the nuts are chopped, not ground.)

Lift off the casserole lid, using a blunt-ended knife to break the seal, and wipe the rim. Transfer the chicken pieces to a serving bowl and keep warm. Strain the sauce into a saucepan, pressing against the solids with a wooden spoon to extract as much liquid as possible; discard the solids. Add broth or water to the sauce if needed to make 2 cups. Bring to a simmer, add the parsley mixture and the olives, and season to taste; the sauce should be highly flavored.

Pour the sauce over the chicken, sprinkle with the remaining parsley, and serve.

Chicken and Okra

Kotópoulo me Bámies

Serves 4 to 6

In early summer when okra is at its best, this intriguing dish appears on *tavérna* menus all over Greece. The colorful combination of golden chicken and onions, pale green okra, and vivid red tomatoes, spiced with cumin, cloves, and allspice, makes this a perfect party dish. Adding the okra at the end of the cooking time keeps it whole and deliciously juicy. If okra is unavailable you can substitute green beans, leeks, or artichokes. Potatoes in a Clay Pot (page 273) makes a good side dish.

———

1½ pounds okra, trimmed and rinsed

Juice of 2 large lemons

1 tablespoon coarse-grain sea salt, or to taste

One 4- to 5-pound chicken, cut into serving pieces and skin and excess fat removed, or 3 whole chicken breasts, skinned and split in half

½ to ¾ cup Kalamáta olive oil (to taste)

2 cups thinly sliced onions

1 teaspoon ground allspice

½ tablespoon ground cumin

6 whole cloves

6 large ripe tomatoes, peeled, seeded, and diced

1 teaspoon honey

1½ tablespoons dried thyme, crumbled

1 cup fat-free Chicken Broth (page 461) or dry white
wine or water

1 tablespoon cracked black pepper, or to taste

½ cup coarsely chopped flat-leaf parsley

Spread the okra on a baking sheet in a single layer, sprinkle with half the lemon juice and 2 teaspoons of the salt, and set aside for 1 hour.

Heat the oven to 375°F. Heat 3 tablespoons of the olive oil in a large heavy skillet and sauté the chicken over medium-low heat until lightly browned on all sides. Drain between layers of paper towels and transfer to a baking dish.

Drain off most of the oil from the skillet, reduce the heat to low, and sauté the onion 10 minutes, or until soft. Stir in the allspice, cumin, cloves, and tomatoes. Raise the heat to medium, bring to a boil, and boil until the liquid is reduced by one third. Add the honey, thyme, broth, a pinch of salt, and ½ tablespoon of the pepper. Simmer a few minutes longer and pour over the chicken. Cover and bake chicken pieces 35 minutes, chicken breasts 20 minutes.

Meanwhile, rinse the okra and dry with paper towels. Heat 3 tablespoons of the remaining olive oil in a large heavy skillet and sauté the okra over low heat until it begins to change color, rolling it gently around the skillet with a wooden spoon. Drain between layers of paper towels.

Add the okra to the baking dish; firmly but carefully shake the dish to combine the ingredients. Bake, uncovered, 15 minutes longer.

Add some or all of the remaining lemon juice to the baking dish; its flavor should be quite distinct. Add the remaining salt, pepper, olive oil to taste, and the parsley. Shake gently to mix all the ingredients together and serve at once.

Chicken with Walnut and Coriander Sauce

Kotópoulo me Sáltsa Karythión

Serves 4 to 6

I first tasted this unusual dish in a tiny *tavérna* in the mountains of Northern Greece, as all around me the villagers gathered the fall harvest from the ancient walnut trees in the village square.

Freshly gathered walnuts give the best flavor but plump older walnuts (blanched to remove any bitterness) can be substituted. Greeks like the creamy sauce with a slightly coarse nutty texture, but use a food processor to produce a smooth version if you prefer. Serve with *piláfi* and a zucchini dish.

½ cup extra-virgin olive oil

One 4- to 5-pound chicken, cut into serving pieces and
skin and excess fat removed

1 cup dry white wine

3 bay leaves

1½ cups hot fat-free Chicken Broth (page 461) or water

Sea salt and freshly ground black pepper to taste

1 cup walnut halves or pieces (if not freshly gathered, blanch
in boiling water for 1 minute)

2 tablespoons whole coriander seeds, crushed, or
½ tablespoon ground coriander

1 large clove garlic, minced

Pinch of cayenne pepper

Juice of 2 lemons, or to taste

3 large eggs

FOR SERVING

¼ cup coarsely chopped flat-leaf parsley

Heat the oven to 350°F. Heat ¼ cup of the olive oil in a heavy skillet and lightly brown the chicken pieces on all sides. Drain between layers of paper towels and transfer to a heavy casserole.

Drain off the oil from the skillet, add the wine, and boil 1 minute, stirring in the browned bits from the bottom of the pan. Pour over the chicken, and add the bay leaves, broth, and salt and pepper. Cover and bake 45 minutes or until tender.

Meanwhile, in a large wooden mortar or bowl, pound the walnuts, coriander, garlic, and cayenne pepper to a fairly smooth paste. Add the remaining ¼ cup olive oil and half the lemon juice drop by drop, pounding constantly, until well mixed. (Or you can do this in a food processor, using the pulse switch; do not overprocess.) Season to taste and set aside.

Transfer the chicken to a serving platter and keep warm. Strain the liquid from the casserole, measure 1½ cups, and combine it with the walnut sauce. Set aside.

Whisk the eggs in a large bowl with a whisk or an electric mixer until pale and frothy. Gradually add the remaining lemon juice, beating constantly. Stir in the walnut sauce. Transfer to a heavy saucepan and heat slowly, stirring with a wooden spoon, until creamy and a little thickened, about 5 minutes; don't let it boil.

Pour the sauce over the chicken and sprinkle with the parsley. Serve at once.

Chicken with Avgolémono Sauce

Kotópoulo Avgolémono

Serves 4

The taste of this classic spring-time dish is fresh and clean, the flavors light and fragrant: zesty lemon, delicate dill, and mild, vitamin-rich lettuce. Serve with Potatoes in a Clay Pot (page 273) or boiled new potatoes, and a dry white wine to enhance the subtle flavor. As a variation try *arnáki fricassé,* a popular version made with boned lamb instead of chicken.

One 3½-pound chicken, cut into serving pieces and skin and excess fat removed

2 cups fat-free Chicken Broth (page 461) or water

2 carrots, cut into large pieces

1 rib celery, cut into large pieces

3 bay leaves

6 black peppercorns

6 scallions, trimmed, with 2 inches of green left intact

2 tablespoons extra-virgin olive oil

2 heads of romaine or endive lettuce, trimmed of outer leaves and tough ribs and cut into ¼-inch-wide ribbons (about 8 cups)

½ cup coarsely chopped fresh dill

Sea salt and freshly ground white pepper to taste

Juice of 2 large lemons

3 eggs, separated

Combine the chicken, broth, carrots, celery, bay leaves, and peppercorns in a large heavy saucepan. Slowly bring to a boil, cover, reduce the heat, and simmer 40 minutes or until the chicken is tender.

Meanwhile, slice the scallions lengthwise in half and cut into 1-inch-long pieces. Warm the olive oil in a large heavy skillet and sauté the scallions over low heat until soft, about 2 minutes. Add the lettuce, cover, and cook, stirring once or twice, until wilted, about 2 minutes. Stir in the dill, salt and pepper, and half the lemon juice. Add the cooked chicken to the skillet and set aside.

Strain the cooking broth into a bowl. Whisk the egg whites in a large bowl with a whisk or an electric mixer until they hold soft peaks. Add the yolks and whisk 1 minute longer. Slowly add the remaining lemon juice and the broth, whisking constantly. Transfer to a medium saucepan and gently heat over low heat, stirring constantly with a wooden spoon, until creamy and slightly thickened, about 5 minutes; don't let the sauce boil.

Pour the sauce over the chicken, place the skillet over low heat, and heat to warm through—do not boil. Season to taste, transfer to a warm serving dish, and serve at once.

Chicken and Game

Marinated Chicken with
Tiny Onions and Vinegar

Kotópoulo Marináto me Xsíthi

Serves 4

This ancient recipe brings together traditional ingredients favored by Greek cooks for centuries. Honey and vinegar blend to produce a sweet-and-sour sauce and the piquant theme is repeated in the garnish of capers, parsley, and lemon zest. This delicious dish makes for easy entertaining too—much of the work can be done ahead of time. Serve with Pilaf with Green Lentils (page 306).

One 3- to 4-pound chicken, cut into serving pieces and skin and excess fat removed

2 tablespoons extra-virgin olive oil

1 tablespoon fresh lemon juice

1 teaspoon coarse-grain sea salt, or to taste

1 teaspoon freshly ground black pepper, or to taste

2 bay leaves

1 sprig of fresh thyme or rosemary

2 tablespoons unsalted butter

1 pound tiny boiling onions, peeled (page 472)

¼ cup aged red-wine vinegar

1 teaspoon honey diluted with 1 tablespoon hot water

4 large ripe tomatoes, peeled, seeded, and diced

¼ cup small dark seedless raisins, soaked in 2 tablespoons hot water for 30 minutes

FOR SERVING

¼ cup finely chopped flat-leaf parsley

1 tablespoon capers, rinsed

1 teaspoon grated lemon zest

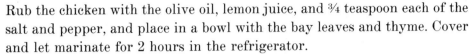

Rub the chicken with the olive oil, lemon juice, and ¾ teaspoon each of the salt and pepper, and place in a bowl with the bay leaves and thyme. Cover and let marinate for 2 hours in the refrigerator.

Melt the butter in a heavy saucepan and add the chicken, marinade, including the herbs, and onions. Turn the chicken and onions to coat with the butter, cover tightly, and cook 40 minutes over low heat, or until the chicken is tender; add 2 tablespoons water if the butter begins to brown. Transfer the chicken to a warm platter, cover, and keep warm.

Pour off the pan juices, remove the fat with a spoon, and reserve; discard the bay leaves and thyme. Add the vinegar to the saucepan, raise the heat to medium high, and reduce to a syrup by rapid boiling. Add the honey and tomatoes and boil gently 1 minute. Add the raisins, reserved pan juices, and remaining ¼ teaspoon pepper, and reduce the heat.

Chop the parsley, capers, lemon zest, and remaining ¼ teaspoon salt together. Spoon the onions and tomatoes around the chicken, sprinkle with the parsley mixture, and serve.

Bay-Scented Chicken with Figs

Kotópoulo me Dáfni ke Síka

Serves 4

Bay trees and bushes flourish in Greece and the leaves are widely used in Greek cooking—a dozen leaves impart a pungent perfume to this dish. The chicken and figs are cooked separately so that their individual flavors remain distinct. Serve with Pilaf with Currants and Pine Nuts (page 302).

(continued)

One 3- to 4-pound chicken, cut into serving pieces and skin
and excess fat removed

2 tablespoons extra-virgin olive oil

1 teaspoon coarse-grain salt, or to taste

1 teaspoon freshly ground black pepper, or to taste

1 tablespoon unsalted butter

12 bay leaves

4 ripe figs, rinsed, or 4 dried figs, soaked in ½ cup dry red
wine or water for 30 minutes

2 tablespoons aged red-wine vinegar

1 teaspoon honey

¼ cup dry red wine

½ cup Chicken Broth (page 461) or water

24 Elítses or 12 Niçoise olives, rinsed and pitted

FOR SERVING

Sprigs of watercress

Rub the chicken with the olive oil and ¾ teaspoon each of the salt and pepper and place in a bowl. Sprinkle with the bay leaves, cover, and refrigerate for 2 to 4 hours.

Heat the oven to 325°F.

Melt the butter in a flameproof baking dish over low heat. Add the chicken, bay leaves, and 2 tablespoons water. Cover and simmer 2 to 3 minutes. Transfer to the oven and bake 30 to 40 minutes, basting occasionally, until the chicken is cooked; if the butter begins to brown, add 2 tablespoons water.

Meanwhile, trim the stems from the figs, cut lengthwise in half, and arrange in a baking dish, cut sides up. Add 3 tablespoons water (or the liquid remaining from soaking dried figs) and bake fresh figs 20 minutes, dried figs 10 minutes.

Transfer the chicken to a platter and keep warm. Discard the bay leaves. Add the vinegar to the dish and reduce the cooking liquid by rapid boiling to 2 tablespoons. Add the honey, wine, and broth, and reduce to ½ cup. Add the olives and heat to warm.

Spoon the sauce over the chicken, surround it with the figs, and garnish with the watercress sprigs.

Spit-Roasted Chicken

Kotópoulo tis Sóuvla

Serves 4

Homer relates that Ulysses enjoyed a spit roast or two on his homeward journey after the Trojan War. Modern Greeks have certainly inherited his love of them! Turn a corner in any Greek city and you'll meet with the enticing smell and sight of a turning spit threaded with sizzling golden-brown chickens. For a successful spit roast you need a plump young chicken, a patient cook to baste it constantly, and a good hardwood fire to sear the skin but keep the meat juicy.

———

Two 2½- to 3-pound chicken, excess fat removed

Juice of 1 large lemon

¼ cup extra-virgin olive oil

1 teaspoon sea salt

1 teaspoon freshly ground black pepper

1 tablespoon finely chopped fresh oregano or flat-leaf parsley

FOR SERVING

About 4 cups watercress sprigs

Lemon wedges

24 Elítses or 12 Ámfissa or Niçoise olives

Kephalotýri *or mild* **féta** *cheese, cut into slices*

Rub the chickens with the lemon juice and 2 tablespoons of the olive oil. Set aside for 1 hour.

Prepare the fire. Fasten the wing tips over the chicken breasts with short metal or wooden skewers. Insert the spit into each chicken to dissect the wishbone and tie the drumsticks and tail together; the chickens will now revolve with the spit.

Brush the chickens with the remaining 2 tablespoons olive oil, and place the spit about 12 to 15 inches above the hot coals. Roast 10 minutes, frequently turning the spit, catching the juices in a pan held under the chicken.

(continued)

Chicken and Game

Raise the spit 2 to 3 inches and roast 30 to 45 minutes longer, turning the spit and basting with the juices, until deep golden brown. The juices will gradually darken and become very aromatic; to prevent them from burning, add a few tablespoons of water to the pan. To test for doneness, pierce the thickest point of one chicken thigh with a skewer or knife; the juices should run clear. Sprinkle the chickens with salt and pepper.

Strain the pan juices into a small saucepan. Heat to warm and stir in the oregano. Carve the chicken into serving pieces.

Line a platter with the watercress, place the chicken on top, and surround with the lemon wedges. Serve the sauce, olives, and cheese separately.

Spit-Roasted Mountain Rabbit

Kounélli tou Vounoú

Serves 4 to 5

Mountain villagers in Greece are practiced in the art of creating memorable feasts from simple foods. Spit-roasted rabbit, a variety of salads, olives, cheese, country bread, and wild pears, all washed down with fiery *raki,* make for splendid—and lively—village celebrations. Eggplant dishes are particularly good with spit-roasted rabbit. If *raki* is not to your taste, choose a full-bodied red wine.

One fresh 5-pound rabbit, prepared by the butcher
(see Note)

1 tablespoon wine vinegar

Juice of 1 lemon

3 sprigs of fresh thyme

2 bay leaves, broken into pieces

2 shallots, thinly sliced

4 juniper berries, lightly crushed

⅓ cup extra-virgin olive oil

½ cup Chicken Broth (page 461) or white wine

1 tablespoon Dijon mustard

1 teaspoon cracked black pepper, or to taste

Sea salt to taste

2 tablespoons finely chopped flat-leaf parsley

Rub the rabbit all over with the vinegar, then rinse it and dry with paper towels. Place in a glass or china dish with the lemon juice, thyme, bay leaves, shallots, juniper berries, and olive oil. Tightly cover and marinate for 12 to 48 hours in the refrigerator, occasionally turning the rabbit in the marinade.

Prepare the fire.

Secure the rabbit to the spit and set it about 12 to 15 inches above medium fire. Set a pan on a rack underneath to catch the juices. Add the broth to the marinade and baste the rabbit with this mixture. Roast, turning and basting, until the rabbit is cooked, about 50 minutes. To test for doneness, pierce the thickest part of one thigh with a skewer or knife; the juices should run clear.

Strain the pan juices and any remaining marinade into a small saucepan. Add the mustard, pepper, salt, and parsley, and heat to warm. Cut the rabbit into serving pieces, arrange on a warm platter, and pour over just enough sauce to moisten. Serve the remaining sauce separately.

Note This recipe can also be made with rabbit pieces rather than a whole rabbit. Use a hinged grill to hold the pieces and grill over a medium-low fire for 15 to 20 minutes, basting frequently and turning occasionally.

Rabbit with Small Onions

Kounélli Stifátho

Serves 6

*S*tifátho is a favorite family casserole in winter: rich and sustaining, spiced with cumin, cloves, and cinnamon, it's a dish full of character. Although it's traditionally made with wild rabbit, I have made delicious chicken, beef, and pork versions and a neighbor on Crete makes a remarkable snail *stifátho*! The most important ingredient, however, is onions—large quantities are essential to produce the characteristic rich sweet sauce. Like most stews, *stifátho* can be made ahead of time and it tastes even better when reheated.

———

3 pounds small boiling onions, about ¾ to 1 inch in diameter

*1 5-pound rabbit, cut into 8 serving pieces and
excess fat removed*

All-purpose flour, for dredging

⅔ cup extra-virgin olive oil, or to taste

½ cup aged red-wine vinegar

2 cloves garlic, finely chopped

6 large tomatoes, peeled, seeded, and diced

1 teaspoon honey

One 2-inch cinnamon stick

1½ tablespoons ground cumin

8 whole cloves

1 teaspoon ground allspice

4 bay leaves

*Zest of 1 orange, removed in large strips and tied
together with kitchen string*

2 tablespoons tomato paste diluted with ½ cup water

1 cup red wine

Sea salt to taste

½ tablespoon cracked black pepper, or to taste

FOR SERVING

¼ cup finely chopped flat-leaf parsley

Slice the root end off each onion and remove the feathery outside layer of skin. Blanch the onions in boiling water for 5 minutes, drain, and peel. Set aside.

Heat the oven to 350°F. Rinse the rabbit pieces and pat dry with paper towels. Lightly dredge with flour. Heat ¼ cup of the olive oil in a large heavy skillet and lightly brown the meat on all sides. Drain between layers of paper towels and transfer to an earthenware or enamel-lined cast-iron casserole.

Add the onions to the skillet and sauté 10 minutes, or until lightly browned. Transfer to the casserole.

Drain off the oil from the skillet and add the vinegar. Boil 1 minute, scraping up the browned bits from the bottom and sides with a wooden spoon. Add the garlic, tomatoes, honey, cinnamon, cumin, cloves, allspice, bay leaves, and orange zest, and boil 1 minute. Stir in the tomato paste, red wine, and remaining olive oil and season with salt and pepper. Pour over the meat, cover tightly, and bake 20 minutes. Reduce the oven temperature to 300°F and bake 1½ hours longer; if the liquid in the casserole reduces to less than 2 cups, add hot water as necessary.

Discard the orange zest and season to taste. Sprinkle with the parsley and serve hot.

Marinated Hare with Juniper Berries
Lagós Stifátho

Serves 6 to 8

This is a wonderful cold-weather dish, strongly spiced and rich in flavor. The marinade can also be used with great success for other meats, such as beef. Serve with a *piláfi* or *macarónia* dish and *khórta* (page 294) or a green salad.

———

One 7- to 8-pound hare, skinned, cut into 12 to 14 serving
pieces (page 171), trimmed and excess fat removed

1½ cups aged red-wine vinegar

6 cloves garlic

6 juniper berries, lightly crushed

6 whole allspice berries

3 whole cloves

12 black peppercorns

One 3-inch cinnamon stick, broken into pieces

8 bay leaves

½ cup extra-virgin olive oil, or to taste

2 pounds ripe tomatoes, peeled, seeded, and diced

1 tablespoon honey

½ tablespoon cracked black pepper, or more to taste

1 tablespoon ground paprika

2 tablespoons ground coriander

4 pounds small boiling onions, peeled (page 472)

1 cup red wine

1 tablespoon dried thyme or winter savory

Sea salt to taste

FOR SERVING

Coarsely chopped fresh coriander or flat-leaf parsley

Rinse the meat and pat dry with paper towels. Place in a china or glass bowl and add the vinegar, garlic, juniper berries, allspice, cloves, peppercorns, cinnamon, and 4 of the bay leaves. Tightly cover and refrigerate for 1 to 2 days, occasionally turning the meat in the marinade.

Heat the oven to 350°F. Transfer the meat to an earthenware or enamel-lined cast-iron casserole.

Pour the marinade (and spices) into a small pan and reduce to about ¾ cup by rapid boiling over high heat. Add ¼ cup of the olive oil, the tomatoes, honey, pepper, paprika, coriander, onions, red wine, remaining 4 bay leaves, and the reduced marinade to the meat. Cover and bake 20 minutes at 350°F. Reduce the oven temperature to 300°F and bake 2½ hours longer; add hot water as necessary if there appears to be less than 2½ cups of liquid in the casserole.

Add the thyme, salt, and remaining ¼ cup olive oil and bake 15 minutes longer. Season to taste, sprinkle with the fresh coriander, and serve hot.

Pheasant Over a Fire

Fasianós sti Skhára

Serves 4 to 6

In Khania on the island of Crete, there is a tiny *tavérna* set into the rock, and the focal point of its one cavelike room is a huge open fire over which plump pheasants often are slowly roasting. The birds are stuffed with a country mixture of bacon, mushrooms, and pine nuts and wrapped in blackberry leaves and pork fat, and the whole room fills with their heavenly aroma.

———

4 young pheasants (page 464), giblets reserved

Sea salt and freshly ground black pepper to taste

½ cup extra-virgin olive oil

2 tablespoons unsalted butter

¼ pound lean bacon, cut into tiny dice

1 pound mushrooms, trimmed and cut into small dice

½ cup pine nuts, chopped

¼ cup port wine or sweet red wine

8 thin slices pork fatback (page 462)

8 slices whole-wheat bread, crusts removed

1 clove garlic, cut into 3 or 4 pieces

2 tablespoons hot water

Prepare the fire. Rub each pheasant inside and out with salt and pepper, 2 tablespoons of the olive oil, and 1½ tablespoons of the butter. Set aside. Trim and finely chop the giblets.

Heat the remaining ½ tablespoon butter and olive oil in a heavy saucepan and sauté the giblets and bacon 2 minutes over low heat, stirring constantly. Add the mushrooms, pine nuts, and pepper and cook 2 minutes longer. Stir in the port and remove from the heat.

Stuff the pheasants with the mushroom mixture and sew up the openings or fasten with small skewers. Cover the breasts and legs with the fatback, securing it with toothpicks.

Secure the pheasants to the spit and set the spit 2 feet above medium-hot coals. Baste with olive oil, catching the juices in a pan held under the pheasants. Roast, turning the spit and basting with the pan juices, until cooked, about 50 minutes. Remove the pork fat 10 minutes before the pheasants are done to let them brown. To test for doneness, pierce the thickest part of one pheasant thigh with a skewer or knife; the juices should run clear.

Meanwhile, heat the remaining ¼ cup olive oil in a large skillet and sauté the garlic until it is pale golden and the oil is aromatic. Discard the garlic. Fry the bread until golden on both sides and drain on paper towels. Cut into triangles and keep warm.

Remove the stuffing from the pheasants with a spoon and keep warm. Pour off any juices from the cavities of the pheasants into the pan of roasting juices and add the hot water. Heat over medium-low heat, stir in the browned bits from the bottom and sides of the pan with a wooden spoon, and strain the sauce into a pitcher or gravy boat.

Carve the pheasants and arrange on a warm serving platter. Spread the stuffing on the slices of fried bread and arrange around the pheasant. Serve the sauce separately.

Hunter's Pot

Tsoukáli Kinigoú

Serves 4

This rich and herb-scented dish is traditionally made with partridge, pigeon, or guinea fowl—the spoils of a day's hunting in ancient times. I have made highly successful versions with Cornish hens and chicken. It is a sweet and fragrant casserole that will fill your kitchen with a warm "homecoming" aroma that creates a wonderful welcome for family and friends! Serve with Potatoes in a Clay Pot (page 273), fried eggplants, and a robust red wine to drink.

———

2 large partridges or 4 pigeons (squab), giblets reserved

Juice of ¹/₂ lemon

7 tablespoons extra-virgin olive oil

Sea salt and freshly ground black pepper to taste

¹/₄ pound lean bacon, finely diced

1 tablespoon unsalted butter

2 medium carrots, finely diced

1 small onion, finely chopped

3 bay leaves

1 tablespoon fresh rosemary, crumbled

1 tablespoon dried thyme, crumbled

4 cloves garlic

¹/₄ cup finely chopped flat-leaf parsley

*1¹/₂ cups dry white wine or Chicken Broth (page 461)
or a mixture of both*

*8 fresh or canned grape leaves, rinsed, blanched in boiling
water for 5 seconds if fresh, 3 seconds if canned, and drained*

¹/₂ cup fresh coarse whole-wheat bread crumbs

*20 Elítses or 8 Niçoise olives, rinsed, pitted,
and coarsely chopped*

Flavors of Greece

Rub the partridges inside and out with the lemon juice, 3 tablespoons of the olive oil, and salt and pepper. Set aside for 1 hour.

Trim the giblets. Heat 1 tablespoon of the remaining olive oil in a heavy skillet and lightly brown the bacon and giblets. With a slotted spoon, transfer to a heavy casserole. Add the butter to the skillet, lightly brown the partridges on all sides over medium-low heat, and transfer to the casserole.

Heat the oven to 375°F. Add the carrots, onion, bay leaves, rosemary, thyme, garlic, and half the parsley to the skillet and reduce the heat to low. Sauté 15 to 20 minutes, or until golden brown, stirring occasionally with a wooden spoon. Transfer to the casserole.

Add the wine to the skillet and bring to a boil, scraping up the browned bits from the bottom and sides of the skillet with a wooden spoon. Pour into the casserole, cover the partridges with the grape leaves, and tightly cover the casserole. Reduce the oven temperature to 325°F and bake 40 to 50 minutes.

Meanwhile, heat the remaining 3 tablespoons olive oil in a medium skillet. Add the bread crumbs and fry, stirring occasionally, until golden brown. Drain on paper towels.

Transfer the partridges to a warm platter, discarding the grape leaves and giblets, and keep warm. Pour the liquid from the casserole into a shallow saucepan and reduce by rapid boiling over high heat to ¾ cup; add any juices that have accumulated around the pheasants. Add the bread crumbs, olives, and remaining parsley to the vegetables in the casserole, stir just to mix, and return to the oven to heat through. Strain the sauce. Spoon the vegetables around the partridges, pour over the sauce, and serve at once.

Note You can substitute 4 whole Cornish hens or one 3½-pound chicken, cut into serving pieces and skin removed, for the partridges.

Grilled Quail

Ortíkia tis Skhára

Serves 4

Quail is a popular fall dish in Greece and, in some country *tavérnas*, it is still cooked in a traditional way. Rubbed with olive oil and herbs, the quail is wrapped in red clay and baked until the clay hardens—at the table the pot is cracked open with a dramatic flourish to reveal a perfectly cooked bird. The nearest modern equivalent is baking in parchment or in a pot tightly sealed with a flour-and-water paste. Or try this recipe, which gives the tiny birds an exquisite delicate flavor; Cornish hens can be substituted if quail is not available.

------

4 quail, livers reserved

Juice of 1 large lemon

1 teaspoon freshly ground black pepper, or more to taste

1 onion, sliced

6 sprigs of parsley

6 bay leaves

*3 sprigs of dried rígani (page 14) or
fresh oregano or marjoram*

⅔ cup extra-virgin olive oil

*4 slices whole-wheat bread, crusts removed and
cut into triangles*

½ teaspoon aromatic honey, such as Hymettus

1 teaspoon Dijon mustard

Fine-grain sea salt to taste

FOR SERVING

Sprigs of watercress

Lemon wedges

Using poultry shears or a sharp knife, split the quail along their breast-bones, turn over, and flatten by gently pressing on the backbones with the

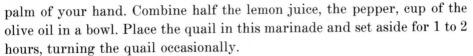

palm of your hand. Combine half the lemon juice, the pepper, cup of the olive oil in a bowl. Place the quail in this marinade and set aside for 1 to 2 hours, turning the quail occasionally.

Prepare the fire.

Arrange a grill rack over medium-hot coals and brush the grill with olive oil. Remove the quail from the marinade, leaving all the herbs in the bowl. Grill until lightly browned on both sides, about 15 minutes.

Meanwhile, heat the remaining olive oil and fry the bread over medium-low heat until golden on both sides. Dip the livers in the marinade, fry. Mash gently, spread on the fried bread, and keep warm.

Strain the marinade. Combine the honey, mustard, and remaining lemon juice in a saucepan, add the marinade, and heat to warm.

Arrange the quail on a warm platter, season with salt and pepper, pour over the sauce, and surround with the fried bread, watercress, and lemon wedges.

Duckling Thessalia-Style

Papáki Thessalías

Serves 4

Highly perfumed lemons are the secret of this sweet roasted duckling. Lemon juice is rubbed inside the duckling, and it is also used in the roasting dish so that the meat absorbs its fragrance throughout the slow cooking. Serve with Beets Island-Style (page 244) or Turnips and Grapes in Aromatic Sauce (page 252).

———

One 3-pound duckling, excess fat removed and giblets reserved

1 carrot, unpeeled, cut into large pieces

1 onion, sliced

3 bay leaves

2 sprigs of fresh thyme

Sea salt and freshly ground black pepper to taste

Juice of 1 large lemon

¼ cup extra-virgin olive oil

4 juniper berries

3 whole cloves

Zest of ½ orange, removed in thin strips

1 cup fresh coarse whole-wheat bread crumbs

¼ cup finely chopped flat-leaf parsley

⅓ cup lightly toasted pine nuts

24 Elítses or 12 Niçoise olives, soaked in hot water for 5 seconds, drained, pitted, and coarsely chopped

FOR SERVING

Sprigs of watercress

Lemon wedges

Place all the giblets except the liver in a small saucepan, and add the carrot, onion, 1 bay leaf, 1 sprig of thyme, salt and pepper, and 1½ cups water.

Bring to a boil, cover, reduce the heat, and simmer 40 minutes. Strain the broth into a bowl and set aside; discard the solids.

Rub the duckling inside and out with half the lemon juice, the olive oil, and salt and pepper. Set aside.

Heat the oven to 375°F.

Place the remaining 2 bay leaves, 1 sprig of thyme, the juniper berries, cloves, and orange zest in the duckling's cavity and sew up the opening or fasten with small skewers. Lay the duckling on its side in a heavy baking dish and add ¼ cup water to the dish. Roast, uncovered, for 20 minutes. Remove the fat with a spoon and set aside. Add the remaining lemon juice to the dish and stir in the browned bits from the bottom and sides of the dish with a wooden spoon. Roast 5 minutes longer to caramelize the juices. Pour the pan juices into a measuring cup and add enough reserved fat to make ¼ cup. Set aside.

Turn the duckling onto its other side, pour over ¾ cup of the reserved broth, and roast another 20 minutes longer, basting occasionally. Turn the duckling breast upwards and roast until deep golden brown, about 10 minutes.

Meanwhile, heat the reserved pan juices in a heavy skillet. Add the bread crumbs and cook over low heat until lightly browned and most of the liquid has been absorbed. Stir in the parsley, pine nuts, and olives and heat through. Keep warm.

Pour off the pan juices from the baking dish and remove the fat with a spoon. Add the spices and any juices from the cavity of the duckling and strain the sauce into a warm serving bowl.

Carve the duckling. Spread the bread crumb mixture on a warm serving plate, arrange the duckling pieces on top, surround with the watercress and lemon wedges, and coat with a little sauce. Serve the remaining sauce separately.

Meats

Kréata

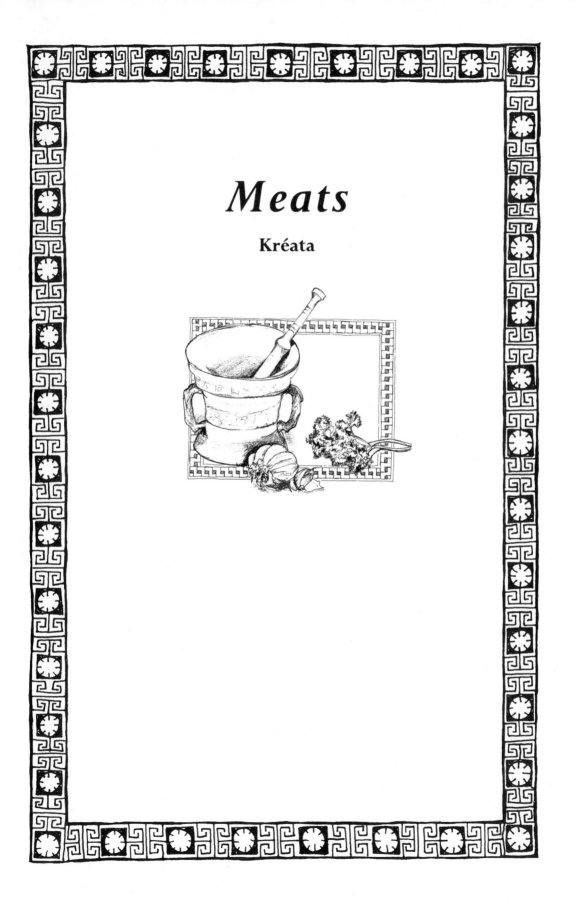

According to Greek mythology, the god Prometheus made mankind out of clay and, in opposition to Zeus, the king of the gods, stole fire for his new creation from the forge of the fire god Hephaestus. Fitting, then, that many of the best Greek meat dishes are readily associated with this gift of the ancient gods, with the crackling brilliance of living flame and the soft, lambent glow of red embers.

Spit roasting and grilling over an open fire has been an integral part of Greek life for centuries, and equipment for long-ago barbecues has been found on Minoan archaeological sites. Its popularity is undiminished today and for anyone who has visited Greece or the islands, the sizzling aroma of herb-perfumed meat roasting outdoors and the scented haze of wispy wood smoke inevitably conjures up myriad images of the country.

Tradition, custom, and experience dictate the preferred aromatics and flavorings for different meats and the types of wood used for the fire. Pine is said to give an authentic traditional taste, grapevine clippings bring out the fine flavor of game, and hardwoods such as olive, apple, pear, or cherry make perfect embers over which to grill meat to tender succulence. Charcoal of course is more convenient; the type made from softwoods like cedar or pine makes a perfect fire for the meats in this chapter, or you can just use charcoal briquets.

Easter, the most important date in the Greek Orthodox calendar, is marked not by a dish of amazing intricacy and complexity, but by a splendidly simple aromatic spit-roasted tender young lamb. Lamb, kid, and suckling pig are all favorites for spit roasting, and for these aromatic marinades are important; many of those used today are traditional recipes based on vinegar, wine, yogurt, pomegranate juice, and onion juice. An infinite variety of other meat delicacies also acquire a unique flavor when marinated and grilled, most notably *souvlákia*—small pieces of deliciously tender meat, speared on skewers, and grilled over charcoal—and *sheftaliá*—highly seasoned sausages. All over Greece *souvlákia* (from the Greek word for spit or skewer), *sheftaliá*, and a variety of other sausage snacks are sold

from *souvláki* stands—covered stalls or tiny cafés boasting a fierce grill, a makeshift counter, and, perhaps, a rickety table or two. These stands are everywhere and are never short of customers, day or night!

The Greek repertoire also includes versatile oven-baked meat dishes. In the country these dishes are still cooked in the traditional wood-burning *foúrnos*, and *foúrnos* cooking does produce a truly delectable and unique flavor, especially if clay pots are used. The meat simmers gently in its own juices, enhanced with herbs, spices, and vegetables; the result is meltingly tender meat covered with a thick aromatic sauce. While the open-air spit roasts and grilled dishes of Greece are inspired by the delicate fragrance of hillside and mountain herbs, the flavors of these oven-baked dishes are stronger and more pungent. They are characterized by heady Eastern spices and a generous use of strong flavorings. The oven-baked dishes in this chapter are traditional recipes adapted for use with modern ovens and enamel-lined cast-iron pots, but if you do possess a partly glazed clay pot, so much the better.

The Paschal Lamb

Arnáki Paskalinó

Serves 10 to 12

After the dark austerity of the Lenten fast comes the plentitude and joy of the season of rebirth. All over Greece the centerpiece of the celebratory meal, traditionally cooked by men, is spit-roasted milk-fed lamb. As early as sunrise on Easter Day coils of fragrant smoke begin to rise from pine-wood fires in preparation for the midday feast. All morning the whole lamb turns on a long spit and the cooks, using brushes made from rosemary sprigs, lemon leaves, or branches of thyme, baste the meat with olive oil. My memories of this splendid celebration always explode with brilliant color—the burning red of spring poppies, the ecclesiastical purple of wild irises, the paint-box blue skies—and above all, an atmosphere of happiness and rejoicing. Only the finest accompaniments are fit for the Paschal Lamb—spring vegetables, especially young asparagus and fava beans, a salad of Kos lettuce, and, of course, the special Easter Bread (page 348). For this roast you'll need a spit around 6 feet long to pass through the whole length of the lamb; for smaller parties this recipe works equally well with a leg of lamb.

---

1 milk-fed lamb, about 22 pounds

Juice of 2 lemons

2 cups extra-virgin olive oil

Coarse-grain sea salt and finely cracked black pepper to taste

*10 to 12 sprigs of fresh rosemary tied together to make a
basting brush or 1 branch of thyme
or dried rígani (page 14)*

FOR SERVING

Lemon wedges

Prepare the fire.

Rub the lamb inside and out with the juice of 1 lemon and sew up the stomach using a larding needle. Pierce the skin in a dozen or so places with the point of a sharp knife, and baste liberally with the olive oil.

Secure the lamb to the spit and place it about 2 feet above the glowing embers. Roast 2 to 2½ hours, slowly moving the spit closer to the embers until the lamb is only 6 inches from the heat, and catching the juices in a pan. Baste liberally at frequent intervals with the pan juices and remaining olive oil; near the end of the roasting time, add the juice of the second lemon to the pan.

To make the sauce, add a few tablespoons water to the pan juices and stir to mix. Strain into a small saucepan and gently heat to warm. Carve the lamb, arrange on a large warm platter, and sprinkle with salt and pepper. Pour some of the sauce over and surround with the lemon wedges. Serve the remaining sauce separately.

Spit-Roasted Leg of Lamb

Arnáki tis Soúvla

Serves 6

For really tender meat and a rich country flavor let the lamb marinate overnight, and be sure to baste it frequently as it roasts. The marinade given here is also very good with kid (page 192); for a different flavor, try the marinade on page 193.

———

One 5- to 6-pound leg of lamb

Red-wine vinegar, to rub over the lamb

3 tablespoons whole coriander seeds, crushed

2 tablespoons fresh rosemary, chopped

½ tablespoon freshly ground black pepper

Sea salt to taste

Juice of 2 small lemons (reserve 1 juiced lemon half)

½ cup extra-virgin olive oil

¼ to ½ cup dry red wine or water (to taste)

FOR SERVING

Sprigs of fresh rosemary

(continued)

Meats

Trim off any excess fat or tough skin from the lamb and pierce the meat in a dozen places with the point of a sharp knife. Moisten a cloth with the vinegar and wipe the lamb all over to remove any gamy flavor. Combine the coriander, rosemary, pepper, salt, and lemon juice in a bowl, and whisk in the olive oil. Rub this marinade over the lamb, cover loosely, and set aside for 4 to 6 hours at room temperature, or refrigerate overnight.

Prepare the fire.

Run the spit lengthwise through the leg and arrange it so the lamb is about 12 inches above medium-hot coals. Roast 45 minutes to 1 hour, slowly moving the spit closer to the coals, until the lamb is only 6 inches from the heat; pierce the lemon half with a skewer and use it to baste the lamb liberally at frequent intervals with the marinade, catching the juices in a pan.

Strain the pan juices and any remaining marinade into a small saucepan. Add the wine to the pan that held the pan juices, stir in any browned bits from the bottom of the pan, and strain into the saucepan. Heat to warm.

Slice the lamb, arrange on a warm platter, pour over some of the sauce, and garnish with the rosemary sprigs. Serve the remaining sauce separately.

Spit-Roasted Lamb
Variety Meats

Kokorétsi

Serves 8 to 10

Kokorétsi, made from the innards of the Paschal Lamb, are an integral part of the Easter Day feast, eaten as either a mid-morning snack or a *mezé*. The diced organ meats are marinated in herbs and spices, garlic, and lemon juice, wrapped in the lamb's intestine, and roasted over glowing charcoal. The sausages are then cut into thick slices and sprinkled with sliced onion, salt, and parsley. *Kokorétsia* are served with lemon wedges, olives, and radishes as a *mezé*.

½ pound lamb's liver

4 lamb's kidneys

2 small lamb's hearts

2 lamb's sweetbreads

Other lamb's variety meats, optional

Sea salt

1 tablespoon wine vinegar

Juice of 1 large lemon

½ teaspoon ground cumin

1 teaspoon dried thyme, crumbled

1 tablespoon dried rígani (page 14), crumbled

½ tablespoon cracked black pepper

⅓ to ½ cup extra-virgin olive oil (to taste)

4 bay leaves

1 large clove garlic, lightly crushed, optional

½ cup finely chopped flat-leaf parsley

About 8 ounces prepared lamb's intestine or
sausage casings (page 471)

About 6 ounces pork caul fat (page 470)

FOR SERVING

1 small red onion, thinly sliced

Trim off and discard all the fat, sinew, valves, and membranes from the variety meats. Dissolve 1 tablespoon salt and the vinegar in a bowl of water, and soak the meats for 30 minutes.

Drain and pat dry with paper towels. Chop the liver, kidneys, and heart into ¼-inch dice, and the other organs into smaller dice.

Combine the lemon juice, cumin, thyme, rígani, pepper, 1 teaspoon salt, and ¼ cup of the olive oil in a large bowl. Add the meats, bay leaves, and garlic, and mix together with your hands. Cover and set aside for 1 hour.

Prepare the fire.

Discard the bay leaves and garlic, and add half the parsley to the meats; mix well. Stuff the intestine or sausage casing to make 1 large or 2 small

sausages, and tie at both ends. Carefully spread out 1 or 2 sheets of caul fat and wrap the sausage(s) in it. Insert a skewer the length of the sausage(s).

Add the remaining olive oil to any marinade remaining in the bowl and baste the sausage liberally with this.

Arrange the skewer(s) 12 inches above medium-hot coals. Slowly roast thin sausages 45 minutes, plump sausages 1 to 1¼ hours, turning and basting frequently, until browned on all sides.

Cut into ½-inch slices, sprinkle with the onion, salt, and the remaining parsley, and serve immediately.

Spit-Roasted Kid

Katsíki tis Soúvla

Serves 8 to 10

Spit roasting is the best way to cook young kid, and a long marinating time produces the most tender, flavorful meat. The strong marinade in this mountain recipe includes garlic, herbs, bay leaves, orange zest, peppercorns, and juniper berries, and the meat rests in this heady mixture for 36 hours. The finishing touch is the clear sharp flavor of a sauce made from bilberries, a fruit similar to a blueberry. Bilberries are occasionally available in specialty markets; blueberries make a fine substitute. Greeks begin a festive meal like this with *mezéthes* of olives, cheese, eggplants, and beans; with the kid they enjoy Potatoes in a Clay Pot (page 273), country bread, and a green salad. A full-bodied red wine such as Naoussa is the perfect accompaniment.

One 6- to 7-pound leg of kid, prepared by the butcher

¼ cup wine vinegar

MARINADE

2 onions, sliced

3 carrots, scrubbed, cut into large pieces

2 cloves garlic (unpeeled), lightly crushed

2 sprigs each of fresh thyme and rosemary

3 sprigs of fresh summer savory, optional

6 bay leaves

1 tablespoon chopped dried orange zest (page 469)

24 black peppercorns

8 juniper berries, lightly crushed

Dry red wine, to cover the meat

1 cup extra-virgin olive oil

¼ pound bacon, cut into small dice

1 tablespoon all-purpose flour

2 cups Meat Broth or Meat Stock (page 467)

*⅓ cup fresh bilberry or blueberry syrup or ¼ cup
canned strained bilberries (see Note)*

½ tablespoon cracked black pepper, or to taste

Sea salt to taste

FOR SERVING

Watercress sprigs

Soak a cloth with the vinegar and rub the meat all over to remove any odor. Rinse and pat dry. Place all the marinade ingredients in a large nonreactive bowl, add the meat, cover, and set aside for 36 hours at room temperature.

Remove the meat, onion, and carrots from the marinade and pat dry with paper towels. Trim the meat of all fat and skin, and cut these trimmings into 1-inch pieces. Dice the onion and carrot. Set aside.

(continued)

Bring the marinade, including all the herbs and spices, to a boil in a large heavy saucepan and reduce to 2½ cups by rapid boiling. Strain and set aside.

Prepare the fire.

Run the spit lengthwise through the leg and arrange it so the kid is about 12 inches above medium-hot coals. Roast 2 to 2½ hours (20 minutes per pound), basting frequently with the reduced marinade and olive oil and catching the juices in a pan.

Meanwhile, add 2 tablespoons of the olive oil to a heavy saucepan and sauté the bacon and meat trimmings over low heat until browned. Add the diced onion and carrot and lightly brown, stirring frequently. Sprinkle with the flour, stir to mix, and cook 1 minute. Add 1¼ cups of the reduced marinade and the broth, reduce the heat, and simmer until reduced to 2 cups. Strain into another saucepan, add the syrup, pepper, and salt, and set aside.

Skim the excess fat from the pan juices and stir the juices into the sauce. Season to taste.

Slice the meat, arrange on a warm platter, surround with the watercress, and spoon over enough sauce to moisten. Serve the remaining sauce separately.

Note To make bilberry or blueberry syrup, combine 2 cups fresh berries and 2 tablespoons water in a nonreactive pan and simmer for 10 minutes. Press through a sieve, preferably plastic, measure the juice, and return to the pan. Add an equal amount of sugar and simmer 10 minutes. Strain and store in airtight jars or bottles for up to 1 month. Canned bilberries need only to be drained and pressed through a sieve.

The Villagers' Grilled Lamb

Arní Skháras Khoriátiko

Serves 4

Fresh and fragrant country herbs, perfumed lemons, and tender lean meat are the essence of this simple classic dish. Since the cooking is fast, the lamb benefits from the tenderizing and flavoring of a sharp marinade of lemon juice, pepper, and pungent bay leaves. The flavorful pan juices, to which a liberal amount of *rigani* are added, make a delicious sauce and eggplant or bean dishes are the perfect accompaniments.

———

8 small loin or rib lamb chops

Juice of 1 large lemon (reserve 1 juiced lemon half)

Cracked black pepper to taste

4 bay leaves

¼ to ⅓ cup extra-virgin olive oil (to taste)

Coarse-grain sea salt

2 tablespoons dried rígani (page 14), briefly pounded in a mortar, or 1 tablespoon dried thyme or rosemary, crumbled

FOR SERVING

Lemon wedges

Trim off most of the fat from the chops and carefully wipe them to remove any bone splinters. Place in a nonreactive bowl, sprinkle with the lemon juice, pepper, and the bay leaves, cover, and set aside for 3 to 4 hours, turning the chops occasionally.

Prepare the fire.

Set a grill rack 4 inches above the hot coals. Lightly brush the grill and the chops with the olive oil, and add the remaining oil to any marinade left in the bowl. Discard the bay leaves. Pierce the lemon half with a skewer and use this as a "baster."

Grill the lamb until browned on both sides, basting frequently with the marinade and catching the juices in a pan. Raise the grill 2 inches and grill about 5 minutes longer for rare meat, 15 minutes longer for well done. A few minutes before the chops are done, add salt, pepper, and 1 tablespoon of the *rígani* to the marinade, and baste the chops several times.

Add 2 or 3 tablespoons water to the pan juices, stir to mix, and heat; strain this sauce. Arrange the chops on a warm platter and pour over enough sauce to moisten. Sprinkle with salt, pepper, and the remaining 1 tablespoon *rígani* and surround with the lemon wedges. Serve the remaining sauce separately.

Marinated Lamb Souvlákia with Pilaf

Arní Souvlákia me Piláfi

Serves 6

This is wonderful party food—preparation can be done well ahead of time and then it takes only minutes to produce succulent *souvlákia,* grilled to a dark crust outside, tender and juicy within. To keep the meat tender, serve *souvlákia* immediately—they're ready—with bowls of radishes, olives, *féta* cheese, *khórta* (page 294), and a fresh bean or green salad.

2½ *pound lean leg of lamb*

Juice of 2 lemons

½ *cup extra-virgin olive oil*

Coarse-grain sea salt and cracked black pepper to taste

24 *(dry) bay leaves*

2 *tablespoons dried* rígani *(page 14)*

1 *teaspoon dried thyme*

PILAF

2 *ounces unsalted butter*

½ *cup crushed (broken into small pieces) vermicelli*

1½ *cups long-grain rice*

1 *teaspoon ground allspice*

1 teaspoon salt

3½ cups Lamb Broth (page 466) or water

FOR SERVING

½ cup coarsely chopped flat-leaf parsley

Finely grated zest of 1 small lemon or 1 tablespoon finely
chopped Preserved Lemon (page 19)

2 small red onions, cut into thin rings

3 lemons, cut into wedges

Cut the meat into 1-inch cubes and trim off any fat or sinew. (Reserve the bones to make broth.)

Combine the juice of 1½ lemons, ⅓ cup of the olive oil, and salt and pepper in a nonreactive bowl. Add the lamb, mix together with your hands, cover tightly, and refrigerate for 4 hours or overnight.

One hour before grilling, remove the bowl from the refrigerator.

Melt the butter in a heavy saucepan and cook the vermicelli 10 minutes over medium-low heat, or until the butter is dark nutty brown. Add the rice and allspice and cook 1 minute, stirring constantly. Add the salt and broth, raise the heat, and boil 8 minutes, or until holes appear in the surface of the rice. Turn off the heat, place 2 layers of paper towels over the top of the saucepan, and cover with the lid. Set aside for 30 minutes in a warm place such as the back of the stove.

Meanwhile, prepare the fire.

Remove the meat from the marinade and thread onto 6 lightly oiled skewers, occasionally alternating the pieces with the bay leaves. Brush liberally with the marinade.

Set the grill rack 3 inches above the hot coals and lightly brush with olive oil. Grill the *souvlákia* until browned on all sides, basting frequently with the marinade. Raise the grill 2 inches and grill 8 to 10 minutes longer, basting, until the meat is dark and crusty outside, juicy and tender inside.

Pound the *rígani* and thyme together in a small mortar until aromatic and add to the remaining marinade, along with olive oil to taste. Continue basting the *souvlákia* with this mixture.

Chop the parsley and lemon zest together until mixed, and combine with the onion, remaining lemon juice, and salt and pepper.

Spread the *piláfi* on a warm platter. Using a fork, push the *souvlákia* off the skewers onto the rice. Sprinkle with the onions, remaining marinade, and salt and pepper, and surround with the lemon wedges.

Yogurt Lamb Souvlákia
with Saffron Rice

Arní Souvlákia Yiaoúrti

Serves 6

The saffron crocus produces a deep purple flower with feathery red stamens that yield a rich yellow coloring and strong, aromatic flavor. For centuries saffron has been a highly prized commodity; the early Minoan civilization on Crete prospered through the cultivation and export of this sought-after spice. Proof of its importance to the Minoans can still be seen at the reconstructed Cretan Palace of Knossos where a fresco depicts saffron gatherers at work. Greeks now use Macedonian saffron, which has a pungent aroma; here Spanish saffron, which has an excellent flavor and strong color, is the most widely available. Accompanied by Beet Salad with Allspice (page 246) or Beets Island-Style (page 244), this delicious dish is ideal for informal dinner parties.

———

2½ pounds lean leg of lamb

Juice of 1 large onion (page 469), about ⅓ cup

1½ cups Strained Yogurt (page 8)

1 to 3 cloves garlic (to taste), minced

12 bay leaves

Coarse-grain sea salt to taste

Extra-virgin olive oil, for basting

Cracked black pepper to taste

SAFFRON RICE

1 teaspoon saffron threads

3 cups Lamb Broth (page 466) or water

¼ cup extra-virgin olive oil

1½ cups long-grain rice

1 teaspoon sea salt

FOR SERVING

About 3 cups watercress sprigs or arugula

24 Elítses or Niçoise olives, drained

¼ cup finely chopped flat-leaf parsley

3 lemons, cut into wedges

Cut the lamb into 1-inch cubes and trim off any fat or tendons. (Reserve the bones to make broth.)

Combine the onion juice, yogurt, garlic, bay leaves, and salt in a nonreactive bowl. Add the lamb and mix with your hands. Cover tightly and refrigerate for at least 12 hours, turning the lamb in the marinade 2 or 3 times.

One hour before grilling, remove the bowl from the refrigerator.

Heat the saffron in a small dry skillet over low heat until aromatic. Crumble the threads into the broth. Heat the olive oil in a heavy saucepan over medium-low heat, add the rice, and cook, stirring, 1 minute. Add the salt and the saffron broth, raise the heat, and boil 8 minutes, or until holes appear in the surface of the rice. Turn off the heat, place 2 layers of paper towels over the top of the saucepan, and cover with the lid. Set aside for 30 minutes in a warm place such as the back of the stove.

Meanwhile, prepare the fire.

Remove the meat from the marinade and thread onto 6 lightly oiled skewers. Baste with the marinade, brush liberally with olive oil, and dust with the pepper.

Set the grill rack 3 inches above the hot coals and lightly brush with olive oil. Grill the *souvlákia* on all sides until crusty, basting frequently with the marinade and olive oil. Raise the grill 2 inches and grill 8 to 10 minutes longer, basting, until the meat is dark and crusty outside, juicy and tender inside.

Spread the saffron rice in the center of a warm platter and surround with the watercress. Using a fork, push the *souvlákia* off the skewers onto the rice. Sprinkle olive oil over the salad greens and the olives and parsley over the *souvlákia*, season with salt and pepper, and surround with the lemon wedges. Serve immediately.

The Baker's Lamb
Arní me Fassólia

Serves 6

In the morning quiet of a Greek village traditionally clad women may be seen hurrying to the village baker with huge covered trays; at midday they return to pay the baker a few drachmas and to collect the now succulent stews that have been simmering in the baker's oven. This aromatic dish of new lamb and young fava beans, cooked with tomatoes and onions and spiced with cumin and *rígani,* is the spring version of a popular Greek dish that is made year-round in an infinite variety of meat, vegetable, and spice combinations. In summer and autumn chicken may be substituted for the lamb; in winter a pork and dried beans version warms and sustains. For best results, make sure the cooking is slow and steady, so that the pungent flavors of the herbs and spices can penetrate the meat and vegetables and develop a rich and highly seasoned sauce.

---

6 lean lamb chops

⅓ to ½ cup Kalamáta olive oil (to taste)

2 large onions, quartered and thinly sliced

2 pounds ripe tomatoes, peeled and diced, juices reserved

1 teaspoon honey

Sea salt

1 teaspoon cracked black pepper, or to taste

1 tablespoon tomato paste diluted with 2 tablespoons water

½ cup Meat Stock (page 467) or water

2 tablespoons ground cumin

3 tablespoons dried rígani (page 14)

*2 pounds green beans such as young favas (page 462) or
Romanos, trimmed, strings removed, and cut
into 2- to 3-inch lengths (see Note)*

1 cup coarsely chopped flat-leaf parsley

Juice of 1 large lemon, or to taste

FOR SERVING

*2 tablespoons finely chopped Preserved Lemon (page 19) or
finely grated lemon zest, blanched in boiling water
for 5 seconds*

1 large clove garlic, finely chopped

Heat the oven to 325°F. Trim off all fat and sinew from the lamb and carefully wipe the meat to remove any bone splinters.

Heat 3 tablespoons of the olive oil in a large heavy skillet and lightly brown the lamb over medium heat. Drain on paper towels and transfer to a deep glazed clay or enamel-lined cast-iron casserole at least 4 inches deep. Reduce the heat to low and sauté the onion 10 minutes or until soft. Add the tomatoes, honey, salt, and pepper, raise the heat, and boil 3 minutes or until reduced by one third. Add the tomato paste, stock, cumin, and *rígani*, stir to mix, and pour over the meat. Cover, and bake 50 minutes.

Blanch the beans in lightly salted boiling water for 1 minute. Drain and add to the casserole with the remaining olive oil. Shake gently to mix, cover, and bake 30 minutes longer. There should be about 1½ cups of sauce—if there is more, uncover the dish; if less, add a few tablespoons of water—and bake 15 minutes longer. Reserve 2 tablespoons of the parsley, and stir in the remaining parsley. Set aside in a warm place for 5 minutes.

Chop the Preserved Lemon, garlic, reserved parsley, and a large pinch of salt to mix.

Add salt, pepper, and the lemon juice to taste to the casserole; the sauce should be highly seasoned. Serve straight from the casserole, or transfer to a warm serving dish. Sprinkle with the parsley mixture and serve.

Note Unless you can find very tender young favas, shell them before using.

Variations

- Substitute 6 lean bone-in beef steaks for the lamb and use allspice instead of the cumin, dried thyme instead of the *rígani*.
- Substitute lamb shanks for the lamb chops. Popular in eastern Mediterranean countries, lamb shanks produce a rich gelatinous sauce. Have the butcher cut 4 medium shanks into 2 or 3 thick slices each. Substitute 3 tablespoons ground cinnamon for the cumin if desired.

(continued)

- Substitute chicken for the lamb. Cut 1 large chicken into 8 serving pieces and remove the skin and excess fat. Lightly brown the pieces in olive oil and bake only 15 minutes before adding the beans.
- Substitute large cubes of eggplant, cauliflower florets, small potatoes, baby zucchini, artichoke hearts, thin leeks, or cooked dried beans for the green beans. Fry the eggplant dice in olive oil until golden brown on all sides before adding to the meat; blanch the fresh vegetables in boiling water for 1 minute before adding. Cooked dried beans need no additional advance preparation.

Cinnamon Lamb Casserole
Arní Kanéllas

Serves 6

Sweet raisins and honey, spicy perfumed cinnamon, and pungent vinegar and capers—the combination of flavors in this recipe evokes the tastes of medieval cooking. Ideal for a lunch or dinner party, this casserole tastes even better if made a day ahead to allow the strong flavors a chance to mellow.

---

3 large eggplants (about 1½ pounds)

Sea salt

½ cup small dark seedless raisins

⅓ cup aged red-wine vinegar or 3 tablespoons balsamic vinegar diluted with 2 tablespoons water

3½-pounds boneless leg of lamb

½ cup Kalamáta olive oil

2 large onions, quartered and thinly sliced

2 large cloves garlic, finely chopped

2½ pounds ripe tomatoes, peeled and diced, juices reserved

1 tablespoon honey

Cracked black pepper to taste

1 tablespoon ground cinnamon, or to taste

1 cup coarsely chopped flat-leaf parsley

1 tablespoon small capers, rinsed, optional

Trim off the ends of the eggplants and cut into 1½-inch cubes. Sprinkle with 2 tablespoons salt and set aside for 30 minutes to sweat.

Combine the raisins and vinegar in a nonreactive bowl and set aside. Trim off all fat and sinew from the lamb and cut it into 1½-inch cubes.

Heat the oven to 350°F.

Heat ¼ cup of the olive oil in a large heavy skillet and lightly brown half the lamb over medium heat. With a slotted spoon, transfer to a heavy casserole. Repeat with the remaining lamb.

Reduce the heat under the skillet to low and sauté the onion until soft, about 10 minutes. Add the garlic, stir well, and transfer to the casserole.

Dry the eggplant thoroughly with paper towels. Wipe out the skillet, set it over medium-low heat, and add 2 tablespoons of the remaining olive oil. Add half the eggplant and fry until deep golden brown on all sides, about 12 minutes. Drain on paper towels and add to the casserole. Repeat with the remaining 2 tablespoons olive oil and remaining eggplant.

Add the tomatoes and their juices, honey, salt, pepper, 1 tablespoon of the cinnamon, and the raisins and vinegar to the casserole. Add ¼ cup water, cover, and bake 1 hour.

Season the sauce with salt, pepper, and additional cinnamon to taste. There should be about 1½ cups of sauce—if there is more, leave the casserole uncovered; if less, add a few tablespoons water and cover—bake 30 minutes longer.

Chop the parsley and capers together just to mix. Serve the lamb hot or warm, piled high in a shallow serving bowl, with the parsley mixture sprinkled on top.

Variations

- Substitute 1 tablespoon ground allspice for the cinnamon.
- Substitute ground cumin for cinnamon, and ⅓ cup Meat Stock (page 467) for the vinegar and raisins. To serve, sprinkle with a mixture of 3 tablespoons coarsely chopped fresh mint, ½ cup coarsely chopped flat-leaf parsley, and 2 tablespoons finely chopped Preserved Lemon (page 19).

Spring Lamb with Mountain Herbs

Arní me Vótana

Serves 6

On spring Sundays the fragrance of this immensely satisfying dish floats on the morning air of many Greek villages. My particular memory of it takes me back to the mountain village of Milia where, on trestle tables set up in a cool whitewashed courtyard, crusty bread, bowls of crisp green salad, and jugs of local rosé wine awaited a gathering of family, friends, and neighbors. At midday our hostess brought out large shallow bowls of this aromatic soup-cum-stew—a complete Sunday lunch in one pot. No haute cuisine meal, I decided, could taste more wonderful.

———

3 pounds small lamb shoulder chops

¼ cup extra-virgin olive oil

1½ pounds small boiling onions, peeled (page 472)

2 tablespoons all-purpose flour

½ cup dry red wine, optional

1 to 1½ cups Meat Stock (page 467)

6 large tomatoes, peeled and diced, juices reserved

1 tablespoon tomato paste diluted with 2 tablespoons water

1 teaspoon honey

2 tablespoons fresh rosemary, chopped, or 3 tablespoons dried rosemary, crumbled

2 tablespoons dried rígani (page 14), crumbled

1 tablespoon dried thyme, crumbled

6 bay leaves

2 large cloves garlic, finely chopped

Coarse-grain sea salt and cracked black pepper to taste

1 pound young carrots, cut into 2-inch lengths

1 pound small new potatoes, peeled if desired, and cut in half

6 small young turnips, peeled and cut in half

*¾ pound green beans such as Romanos, trimmed and
cut into 1½-inch lengths*

FOR SERVING

½ cup coarsely chopped flat-leaf parsley

Trim off all the fat from the meat and wipe it to remove any bone splinters.
Heat 4 tablespoons of the olive oil in a large heavy skillet and brown half
the lamb over medium heat. Transfer to a large heavy saucepan, and repeat
with the remaining lamb.

Reduce the heat under the skillet, add the remaining 4 tablespoons olive
oil, and sauté the onions until lightly browned on all sides, about 10 minutes. Drain between layers of paper towels and transfer to the saucepan.

Drain off most of the olive oil from the skillet and sprinkle the pan with
the flour. Stir any browned bits into the flour with a wooden spoon and
gradually add the wine, stirring vigorously. Bring to a boil, simmer 1
minute, and stir in 1 cup of the stock. Stir in the tomatoes and their juices,
tomato paste, honey, rosemary, *rígani*, thyme, bay leaves, garlic, and salt
and pepper. Transfer to the saucepan and bring to a boil over medium heat.
Cover, reduce the heat, and slowly simmer 1 hour.

Fill a large saucepan with lightly salted water and bring to a boil. Add
the carrots and potatoes and lightly boil 4 minutes. Add the turnips and
boil 1 minute longer. Drain and add to the lamb. Add more stock or water
if necessary to make about 2 cups sauce. Cover, bring to a boil, and simmer
15 minutes longer.

Bring a small saucepan of water to a boil, add the beans, cook 1 minute,
and drain. Add the beans to the casserole and shake gently to combine;
don't stir or the vegetables may break up. Simmer 15 minutes longer, or
until the vegetables are just done. Season to taste with salt and pepper.

Sprinkle with the parsley and serve.

Lamb Kléphtiko
Arní Kléphtiko

Serves 6

In this classic dish thick slices of lamb, larded with slivers of garlic and seasoned with oregano, lemon juice, and olive oil, cook gently in a tight paper parcel from which no juices or tantalizing aromas can escape. The dish probably has as many origins as there are storytellers. Village women have told me that the cooking method was devised to protect food from hungry marauding bandits who had a nasty habit of turning up at mealtimes. Village men say that meat would be left cooking gently in paper while courageous villagers went off to rout out the bandits. On their return their supper would be tender, aromatic, and cooked to perfection! Traditionally only lamb, goat, and fish are cooked this way but this wonderfully flavorful method can also be used very successfully with vegetables.

One 5- to 6-pound leg of lamb cut (by the butcher) into
1½-inch slices across the bone, or 1 boned leg of lamb cut into
1½-inch slices, or six 1-inch-thick lean lamb chops

½ cup extra-virgin olive oil, or to taste

2 large cloves garlic, cut into large slivers

Sea salt and cracked black pepper to taste

3 tablespoons coarsely chopped fresh oregano or rosemary or 2
tablespoons dried **rígani** *(page 14), crumbled*

Juice of 1 large lemon

Trim off any fat from the meat; wipe lamb on the bone to remove any tiny bone splinters. Tie a piece of kitchen string around each slice of boned lamb to keep it in shape.

Heat 3 tablespoons of the olive oil in a large heavy skillet and brown half the meat over medium-low heat. Drain on paper towels. Repeat with the remaining meat.

Heat the over to 400°F. Cut out six 12-inch squares of parchment paper. Fold each piece in half and trim the two outer corners to make 6 folded ovals. Open up the papers and divide the meat among them, placing it in the center of the bottom half of the paper. (Remove the string from the boneless lamb.) Push the garlic into creases in the meat, season generously with salt and pepper, and sprinkle with the oregano, lemon juice, and remaining 5 tablespoons olive oil. Fold the top halves of the papers over the meat and roll the edges up tightly to make neat packets that will not leak. Arrange on a large baking sheet and bake 10 minutes.

Reduce the oven temperature to 350°F and bake boneless lamb 20 minutes longer, lamb on the bone 35 to 40 minutes longer.

Place the packets on warm dinner plates. Carefully open each one by cutting the four corners with scissors and pulling back the edges of the paper.

Moussakás

Serves 8 to 10

One of the best-known Greek dishes, *moussakás* remains a popular favorite all over Greece and her islands. In *tavérnas* it's usually made in large shallow baking dishes; in a private home you may be presented with *papoutsákia,* "little shoes" of eggplant shells filled with meat sauce and cheese custard, or your own individual *moussaká* cooked in a clay pot. An authentic *moussakás* does take time, but it can be made a day ahead, and it also freezes well.

———

4 large eggplants (about 2½ pounds)

Sea salt

¾ cup extra-virgin olive oil

2 cups finely chopped onion

2 pounds lean lamb or 1 pound each of lamb and beef, finely ground

1 cup red wine, optional

6 large ripe tomatoes, peeled and diced, juices reserved

1 teaspoon honey

1 cup finely chopped flat-leaf parsley

1 cup Meat Stock (page 467)

¼ cup dried rígani *(page 14), crumbled*

2 tablespoons ground cinnamon, or to taste

1 teaspoon ground allspice, or to taste

Freshly ground black pepper to taste

2 cups milk

2 ounces unsalted butter

¼ cup all-purpose flour

1 cup small-curd cottage cheese, drained

¼ cup grated féta *cheese*

1 cup grated graviéra, *Swiss, or Gruyère cheese*

1 teaspoon grated nutmeg

5 large eggs

½ cup grated **kephalotýri** *or parmesan cheese*

½ cup fresh fine bread crumbs

Trim off the ends of the eggplants and cut into ¼-inch slices. Sprinkle with 2 tablespoons salt and set aside in a colander for 1 hour to sweat.

Heat 3 tablespoons of the olive oil in a large deep skillet and sauté the onion over medium-low heat until soft, about 6 minutes. Raise the heat, add the meat, and sauté until lightly browned, breaking up any lumps with a wooden spoon and stirring occasionally to prevent sticking. Add the wine and boil until reduced by half. Add the tomatoes with their juices and the honey, lower the heat, and simmer 10 minutes. Set aside 1 tablespoon of the parsley, and stir in the remaining parsley, the stock, *rígani,* cinnamon, allspice, and 1 teaspoon each of salt and pepper. Simmer 30 minutes, or until almost all the liquid has evaporated. Season to taste with salt, pepper, and cinnamon. Cover and set aside (or refrigerate overnight).

Heat 3 tablespoons of the remaining olive oil in a large heavy skillet (or use 2 skillets for extra speed). Thoroughly dry the eggplant slices with paper towels. Add just enough slices to make a single layer in the skillet and fry over medium heat until dark golden brown on both sides. Drain between layers of paper towels. Add 1 tablespoon olive oil to the skillet and fry another batch of eggplant; repeat with the remaining eggplant. Set aside.

Melt the butter in a heavy saucepan, add the flour, and stir with a wooden spoon until smooth. Cook, stirring, over low heat, 1 to 2 minutes, until the roux turns pale golden brown. Gradually add the milk, ½ cup at a time, stirring until smooth after each addition. Bring to a boil, stirring, and remove from the heat.

Combine the cottage cheese, *féta, graviéra,* and nutmeg, and stir into the white sauce. With a wire whisk or electric mixer, beat the eggs until pale and frothy. Thoroughly stir one third of the beaten eggs into the cheese mixture, then add the remainder all at once. Season to taste and set aside.

Heat the oven to 350°F. Arrange about one quarter of the eggplant slices in the bottom of a large 3- to 4-inch-deep baking dish, cover with one third of the meat sauce, then lightly smooth about ¼ cup of the cheese mixture over it. Make 2 more layers of eggplant, meat, and cheese, and top with the remaining eggplant. Cover with the remaining cheese mixture, sprinkle with the *kephalotýri* and bread crumbs, and bake uncovered 1 hour. If the top appears to be browning too quickly, loosely cover with a sheet of aluminum foil. (Do not press down, or you will remove the lovely crust when you take off the foil.)

Sprinkle with the reserved parsley and serve hot or warm.

To make individual casseroles Divide the eggplant, meat sauce, and cheese mixture among 8 or 10 individual baking dishes or small soufflé dishes, each about 3½ inches deep, layering the ingredients as above. Bake about 40 minutes.

To make *papoutsákia* Cut 5 large eggplants lengthwise in half, sprinkle the cut sides with salt, and sweat for 30 minutes. Dry with paper towels. Fry in olive oil until the cut sides are golden brown and the skin is dark and wrinkled, drain between layers of paper towels, and carefully scoop out the flesh from each, leaving a ½-inch shell. Fill the shells with the meat sauce and cover each with a layer of the cheese mixture. Sprinkle with the *kephalotýri* and bread crumbs and bake 40 to 45 minutes.

Moussakás with Potatoes

Use only 2 large eggplants and substitute 1 pound small new potatoes, boiled in salted water for 10 minutes and cut into ¼-inch slices, for the bottom layer of eggplant. Or omit the eggplants altogether, and substitute 3 pounds potatoes.

Moussakás with Zucchini

Substitute zucchini for eggplants: Trim 3 pounds zucchini, cut lengthwise into ¼-inch slices, and fry in olive oil until golden brown on both sides. Drain between layers of paper towels, and assemble as above.

Multicolored Moussakás

Use 1 pound new potatoes, boiled 10 minutes and sliced, as the bottom layer, and 1 pound zucchini and 1 large eggplant, sliced and fried, for the remaining layers. Proceed as directed above.

Grilled Kephtéthes

Kephtéthes sta Kárvouna

Serves 6

Spicy beef and lamb patties are a traditional centerpiece for many outdoor parties and village gatherings. These grilled *kephtéthes* are highly flavored but simple food, usually served mounded on a platter with an array of colorful garnishes for an eye-catching presentation. They are good with eggplant dishes, *tsatsíki* (page 73), *khórta* (page 294), and fried potatoes.

¾ pound lean beef, finely ground

¾ pound lean lamb, finely ground

¾ cup finely chopped onion

¼ cup finely chopped flat-leaf parsley

*2 tablespoons dried rígani (page 14), briefly pounded
in a small mortar*

1 teaspoon dried thyme, crumbled

1 tablespoon mustard seeds or ½ teaspoon ground mustard

¼ cup dry red wine or 2 tablespoons aged red-wine vinegar

1 cup fresh fine whole-wheat bread crumbs

Coarse-grain sea salt and cracked black pepper to taste

Kalamáta olive oil

FOR SERVING

2 small red onions, quartered and thinly sliced

½ cup coarsely chopped flat-leaf parsley

3 ripe tomatoes, peeled and cut into small dice

½ English hothouse cucumber, peeled and cut into small dice

Juice of ½ lemon

*1 tablespoon sumac (see Note) or 1 teaspoon paprika and
a large pinch of cayenne pepper*

Watercress sprigs

Lemon wedges   (continued)

Combine the beef, lamb, onion, parsley, *rígani,* thyme, and bread crumbs in a large bowl. Heat the mustard seeds in a dry skillet over low heat until a few pop. Pulverize them in a mortar and pestle or spice grinder. Mix this powder with the wine and add to the meat, along with salt and pepper. Knead the mixture for a few minutes, tightly cover, and refrigerate for 1 to 4 hours.

Prepare the fire.

Moisten your hands with cold water and shape the meat mixture into 12 balls, flattening each one into a ¾-inch-thick patty.

Oil a grill rack and place it 4 to 5 inches above the hot coals. Grill the *kephtéthes,* basting frequently with olive oil, until browned and crusty on both sides but still moist and pink in the center, about 8 minutes.

Combine the onion, parsley, tomatoes, cucumber, lemon juice, sumac, and salt and pepper to taste and spread this mixture over a platter. Arrange the *kephtéthes* on top, sprinkle with olive oil to taste, and surround with the watercress and lemon wedges.

Note Sumac, available from Greek, Middle Eastern, and some specialty stores, is the pulverized berry of a piquant herb. It has a coarse texture, pleasantly tangy acid flavor, and a deep auburn color.

Smyrna Sausages

Soudzoukákia

Serves 6

These spicy sausages are the legacy of the Greeks who once lived in Smyrna (now Izmir, Turkey) and brought back to their home country a taste for Eastern flavorings. Here are two versions: In the first, the *soudzoukákia* are browned and they are simmered for just a few minutes in a tomato sauce: in the second, they are marinated in the tomato sauce overnight before cooking. Either way they are a simple, tasty, and economical dish.

1 medium onion, grated

2 tablespoons cumin seeds

2 tablespoons aged red-wine vinegar

½ cup fresh fine bread crumbs

1½ pounds lean lamb, finely ground twice

¼ cup finely chopped flat-leaf parsley

1 clove garlic, minced

1 egg, lightly beaten

Sea salt

1 tablespoon cracked black pepper, or to taste

3 tablespoons olive oil

4 cups Tomato Sauce made with cumin and parsley
(page 431)

FOR SERVING

¼ cup finely chopped flat-leaf parsley

Combine the onion and ¼ cup water in a small saucepan, bring to a boil, and simmer until the water has evaporated, about 6 minutes. Take care not to let the onion burn. Meanwhile, in a dry skillet, gently heat the cumin seeds until aromatic, about 2 minutes. Pulverize them in a small mortar and pestle or a spice grinder. Sprinkle the vinegar over the bread crumbs and combine with the lamb, parsley, garlic, egg, onion, cumin, and salt and pepper. Knead the mixture for a few minutes, cover tightly, and refrigerate for 1 hour.

Moisten your hands with cold water, divide the meat mixture into 18 portions, and shape them into 2- to 2½-inch-long sausages. Flatten them slightly between your palms.

Heat the olive oil in a large heavy skillet and sauté the sausages until browned on both sides, about 12 minutes. (You can use 2 skillets for greater speed.) Drain between layers of paper towels.

Bring the Tomato Sauce to a simmer in a shallow pan large enough to hold the sausages in a single layer. Add the sausages and simmer 3 minutes or until hot. Season to taste with salt and pepper.

Transfer to a warm serving platter and sprinkle with the parsley.

(continued)

Marinated Smyrna Sausages

1 onion, grated

¼ cup red wine

½ cup fresh fine bread crumbs

1½ pounds lean lamb, finely ground twice

1½ teaspoons ground cinnamon, or to taste

¼ teaspoon ground cloves

¼ cup finely chopped flat-leaf parsley

1 egg, lightly beaten

Sea salt and cracked black pepper to taste

Olive oil, for frying

*4 cups Tomato Sauce made with cinnamon and parsley
(page 431)*

¼ cup red wine

3 bay leaves

FOR SERVING

¼ cup finely chopped flat-leaf parsley

Make the sausages and fry them as directed above, substituting the wine for the vinegar, the ground cinnamon and cloves for the pulverized cumin.

Bring the Tomato Sauce to a simmer and add the wine and bay leaves.

Place the sausages in a nonreactive bowl and cover with the sauce. Cool, tightly cover, and refrigerate overnight.

To serve, heat the sausages in the sauce and serve warm or hot, sprinkled with the parsley.

Peppery Grilled Liver
Sikóti Piperáto tis Skhára

Serves 3 to 4

For this quick and easy popular delicacy tender lamb's liver is marinated in lemon juice, mustard, and olive oil, then dusted with cracked pepper and grilled. The secret is to grill just long enough to brown the outside but keep the inside moist and pink.

———

1 pound lamb's liver, cut into ¼-inch slices

Juice of 2 lemons

½ teaspoon ground mustard

⅓ cup extra-virgin olive oil

1½ tablespoons cracked black pepper

FOR SERVING

Watercress sprigs

1 tablespoon finely chopped Preserved Lemon (page 19) or finely grated zest of 1 small lemon

¼ cup finely chopped flat-leaf parsley

½ teaspoon coarse-grain sea salt, or to taste

1 small red onion, cut into thin rings

½ teaspoon paprika

1 lemon, cut into wedges

2 ripe tomatoes, cut into wedges, or 8 cherry tomatoes

Trim off any membrane from the liver.

Whisk together the lemon juice, mustard powder, and the olive oil in a nonreactive bowl. Add the liver, cover tightly, and set aside.

Prepare the fire.

Set a grill rack 3 inches above the hot coals and lightly brush with olive oil. Remove the liver from the marinade, reserving the liquid, and sprinkle with the pepper. Grill until browned on both sides but still pink inside, about 2 minutes. *(continued)*

Meanwhile, chop the Preserved Lemon, parsley, and salt together to mix. Combine with the onion and paprika.

Arrange the liver in the center of a warm platter and surround with the watercress and lemon and tomato wedges. Spoon over a few tablespoons of the marinade and scatter over the onion mixture. Serve immediately.

Note Grilled liver is also delicious prepared with the marinade for lamb (page 197) or pork (page 225).

Piquant Garlic Beef
Sofríto

Serves 6

In this classic recipe strong red-wine vinegar, liberal amounts of perfumed mountain herbs, and a generous quantity of garlic turn modest beef stew into an outstanding dish. Richly flavored *sofríto* is an island specialty from Corfu and *tavérnas* there cook it in tightly sealed individual earthenware pots; at the table the lids are removed to release the wonderful fragrance of the beef and reveal meltingly tender cubes in a thick, garlicky herb sauce. This special dish takes very little time to prepare. Serve with Eggplant Pilaf with Glazed Tomatoes (page 304), bowls of purple and green olives and *féta* cheese, and Island Greens Salad (page 290).

───────

2½ pounds lean beef (top round or rump)
All-purpose flour, for dredging

½ tablespoon cracked black pepper, or to taste

⅓ cup extra-virgin olive oil, or to taste

1 cup aged red-wine vinegar

8 bay leaves

3 tablespoons dried thyme, marjoram, or rosemary,
or a mixture

1 cup Meat Stock (page 467) or water

Sea salt to taste

2 to 3 heads garlic (to taste), cloves separated and peeled

¼ cup all-purpose flour

FOR SERVING

Finely chopped flat-leaf parsley

24 Elítses or Niçoise olives, drained

Heat the oven to 275°F. Trim the meat of all fat and sinew and cut into 1½-inch cubes. Dredge with flour, shaking off any excess, and sprinkle with the pepper.

Heat half the olive oil in a large heavy skillet and lightly brown half the meat over medium-low heat. Drain between layers of paper towels and transfer to a large heavy casserole. Repeat with the remaining meat.

Drain off any oil from the skillet and add the vinegar. Bring to a boil, stirring any browned bits from the bottom and sides of the pan with a wooden spoon. Simmer a few minutes to reduce slightly, and pour over the meat. Add the bay leaves, thyme, stock, salt, and the remaining olive oil and shake the casserole gently to mix. Add the garlic, pushing it down among the pieces of meat so its flavor will penetrate the dish.

Combine the flour and a few tablespoons water to make a thick paste. Spread it around the top rim of the casserole and the inner edge of the casserole lid. Place the lid in position, smooth the paste to make a good seal, and bake 3 hours.

Insert a blunt-ended knife between the lid and casserole to break the seal. Remove the lid and wipe the rim of the casserole clean. Season to taste with salt and pepper; the dish should be highly seasoned. Sprinkle with the parsley and olives, and serve immediately.

To serve in individual casseroles Divide the *sofrito* equally among 6 individual casseroles, seal them, and bake 2½ hours at 250°F.

Aromatic Beef in Red Wine
Kapamás

Serves 6

This dish is said to be the invention of the nomadic tribes of antiquity who wandered all over Greece and the Balkans. That could explain the rich variety of seasonings used—the flavors of East and West are blended in a supremely aromatic and exotic concoction. After marinating for as long as 18 hours in red wine, the beef is slowly cooked in a tightly sealed pot. Prepared and cooked a day ahead, *kapamás* becomes even more intensely flavored. Serve with Garlic Potatoes with Juniper Berries (page 275), Potatoes in a Clay Pot (page 273), or a vegetable pilaf.

———

3 pounds lean beef (such as bottom round), in one piece

1½ cups sliced onion

1½ tablespoons ground allspice

2 large cloves garlic, each cut into 5 or 6 pieces

8 bay leaves

2 tablespoons dried rígani (page 14)

About 3 cups dry red wine

¼ cup lean bacon, finely diced

½ cup Kalamáta olive oil

1½ pounds small boiling onions, peeled (page 472)

¼ cup all-purpose flour, plus flour for dredging

2 pounds ripe tomatoes, peeled and diced, juices reserved

1 teaspoon honey

One 3-inch cinnamon stick, broken in half

*½ cup Meat Stock or Meat Broth
(page 467) or water*

Sea salt and cracked black pepper to taste

½ cup Thásos or Kalamáta olives, rinsed, halved, and pitted

FOR SERVING

¼ cup finely chopped flat-leaf parsley

2 tablespoons capers, rinsed

1 clove garlic, finely chopped

2 tablespoons finely grated lemon zest

Trim off any fat or sinew from the meat and cut into pieces about 2½ inches square and 1 inch thick. Combine the meat, sliced onion, allspice, garlic, 4 of the bay leaves, 1 tablespoon of the *rígani,* and the red wine in a large nonreactive bowl. Cover and set aside in a cool place for 2 to 4 hours, or refrigerate for 12 to 18 hours.

Heat the oven to 275°F. Place a large heavy skillet over low heat and sauté the bacon in its own fat for 2 to 3 minutes. Transfer to a large heavy casserole. Add ¼ cup of the olive oil to the skillet and sauté the boiling onions until lightly browned on all sides, about 10 minutes. Drain between layers of paper towels and set aside.

Remove the meat from the marinade, reserving the marinade, and pat dry with paper towels. Lightly dredge with flour, shaking off any excess. Add 3 tablespoons of the remaining olive oil to the skillet and sauté half the meat over medium heat until lightly browned on both sides, about 10 minutes. Transfer to the casserole with a slotted spoon and repeat with the remaining meat.

Meanwhile, transfer the marinade to a saucepan. Bring to a boil, lower the heat, and simmer until reduced by one third. Once the meat is browned, strain the marinade through a sieve into the skillet, and discard the solids. Bring to a boil, stirring in all the brown bits from the bottom and sides of the pan with a wooden spoon.

Add the reduced marinade, tomatoes and their juices, honey, cinnamon, stock, salt and pepper, and the remaining 4 bay leaves and 1 tablespoon *rígani* to the casserole. Gently shake the casserole to mix everything together.

Make a thick paste with the ¼ cup flour and a few tablespoons water and spread it around the top rim of the casserole and inner edge of its lid. Place the lid in position, smooth the paste to make a good seal, and bake 2½ hours.

Insert a blunt-ended knife between the lid and casserole to break the seal, remove the lid, and wipe the rim of the casserole clean. Add the onions. If there is more than about 1½ cups sauce, leave the casserole uncovered; if less, add a little water or stock and replace the lid. Bake 30 minutes longer.

Bring a small saucepan of water to a boil, add the olives, and remove the pan from the heat. Let stand for 5 minutes, then drain and rinse, add to the casserole, gently shaking to mix, and bake about 5 minutes longer. Season with salt and pepper to taste. Meanwhile, chop the parsley, capers, garlic, and lemon zest together until well mixed.

Arrange the meat and onions on a warm platter and spoon over the sauce. Sprinkle with the parsley mixture and the remaining 1 tablespoon olive oil, and serve hot.

Note If you plan to refrigerate the cooked dish overnight before serving, do not add the olives until reheating.

Country Beef
Brizóles

Serves 6

Popular country food, these spicy steaks are ideal for large parties. Greek cooks say that bone-in steaks are essential for flavor and juiciness. Delicious, attractive, and colorful, this is such an easy dish you'll find yourself making it often; try the variations with lamb or pork.

———

6 small rib-eye or other beef steaks, about 8 ounces each

Juice of 1 lemon

2 tablespoons ground coriander

¼ teaspoon grated nutmeg or ground mace

1 tablespoon dried rígani (page 14)

½ tablespoon dried marjoram

1 teaspoon coarse-grain sea salt

1 tablespoon cracked black pepper

6 large ripe tomatoes, cut in half

1 teaspoon sugar

*8 medium all-purpose potatoes, peeled if desired, and cut
lengthwise in half or into quarters*

6 large cloves garlic, each cut into 2 or 3 pieces

½ cup extra-virgin olive oil, or to taste

FOR SERVING

⅓ cup finely chopped flat-leaf parsley

Trim off all fat from the meat and wipe it to remove any bone splinters.
Place in a nonreactive bowl and pour over the lemon juice. Set aside.

Gently heat the coriander and nutmeg in a dry skillet until aromatic, and
transfer to a small mortar. Add the *rígani*, marjoram, salt and pepper, and
pound until well mixed and slightly crushed. Rub the steaks all over with
this mixture.

Heat the oven to 350°F.

Lay the steaks in a single layer in a large baking dish, spaced well apart.
Sprinkle the tomatoes with the sugar and place them between the steaks, cut
sides up. Add the potatoes, arranging them so each piece is touching a steak.
Press the garlic down among the meat and potatoes. Pour over any remaining marinating liquid, sprinkle with the olive oil, and add ½ cup water to
the dish. Bake uncovered, basting the beef and potatoes occasionally with
the pan juices, for 1 hour or until the meat is very tender and the tomatoes
are almost falling apart.

Season to taste with salt and pepper and sprinkle with the parsley.
Serve hot.

Variations

- Substitute 12 small lamb chops or 6 small shanks, trimmed of fat, for the
  beef, 3 tablespoons chopped fresh rosemary for the coriander, nutmeg,
  and marjoram, and vinegar for the lemon juice. Omit the tomatoes and
  leave the garlic cloves whole and unpeeled—diners can spread the softened garlic on the cooked meat.
- Substitute pork chops, trimmed of fat, for the beef and 1 teaspoon ground
  cumin for the nutmeg. Cut 3 small eggplants in half, sauté them in ¼ cup
  olive oil, and add to the baking dish with the potatoes and tomatoes.
  Allow an additional 15 minutes baking time.

Meats

Spit-Roasted Suckling Pig

Gourounópoulo tis Soúvla

Serves 8 to 12

The ancient Greeks worked hard to keep their gods happy and, when the occasion demanded it, a sacrifice was the best way to enlist divine help or give thanks for favors rendered—and the best sacrifice of all was a succulent suckling pig! It's still a favorite celebration dish in Greece today, especially in late summer and early fall. A true suckling pig weighs around 10 to 14 pounds and has a soft, pliant skin and mild gamey flavor. Greeks spit roast the meat without stuffing (a few bay leaves in the cavity are enough to lend a delicate fragrance to it) and baste it during cooking with a flavorful marinade so that the skin becomes crisp, brown, and sweetly scented. Serve in thick slices accompanied by Potatoes in a Clay Pot (page 273) and Beet Salad with Allspice (page 246) or an eggplant dish.

One 10- to 14-pound suckling pig, prepared by the butcher

Wine vinegar, to rub over the pig

Coarse-grain sea salt

6 bay leaves

Juice of 3 lemons

½ tablespoon cracked black pepper

1 tablespoon honey

¾ to 1 cup extra-virgin olive oil (to taste)

1 tablespoon dried thyme, crumbled

1 teaspoon dried summer savory, crumbled

FOR SERVING

Watercress sprigs

Elítses or Niçoise olives

Slices of aged **myzíthra** *cheese*

Prepare the fire.

Scrub the pig's skin with a stiff brush and lightly wipe the pig inside and out with vinegar and then with salt. Place the bay leaves in the stomach cavity and sew up the cavity using a trussing needle.

Combine the lemon juice, pepper, ½ teaspoon salt, honey, and olive oil, and set this marinade aside. Tie the forelegs and hind legs of the pig together and secure it to the spit. Pierce the skin in a dozen places, baste liberally with the marinade, and place the spit 2 feet above the hot coals. Roast, rotating the spit and basting the pig frequently, for 1½ to 2¼ hours (depending on the size of the pig); catch the juices in a pan. Gradually bring the spit closer to the coals; after about an hour of roasting, add the thyme and savory to the marinade and continue basting. Test for doneness by inserting a sharp knife into the thickest part of the pig; the juices should run clear.

Carve into serving pieces and arrange on a warm platter. Pour off as much fat as possible from the pan juices, strain the remaining liquid, and pour over the pork. Surround with the watercress, olives, and cheese.

Meats

The Winemaker's Pork

Khirinó Einopioú

Serves 4

In country districts the family pig is traditionally slaughtered on the day after the first fall rain, and the Greek pork-eating season generally runs from September through February. Legend has it that, because it is a source of formidable strength, pork is the food for warriors, and a neighbor of mine on Crete always serves this dish to the men who trample her grapes for wine making—a job that calls for great perseverance and stamina. The flavors are indeed assertive—strong garlic, scented bay leaves, the bouquet of parsley and thyme, spicy coriander and mustard. Serve this pork and mushroom dish with potatoes and a green salad.

---

4 thick boneless pork chops, 6 to 7 ounces each, trimmed of fat

2 cloves garlic, crushed

4 bay leaves, broken in half

6 sprigs of parsley

2 tablespoons coriander seeds or 1 tablespoon fennel seeds

1 tablespoon dried thyme, crumbled

About 3 cups dry red wine

1 tablespoon mustard seeds or ½ teaspoon ground mustard

Coarse-grain sea salt

½ tablespoon cracked black pepper, or to taste

1 tablespoon aged red-wine vinegar

⅓ cup extra-virgin olive oil

12 large white mushrooms, cut into quarters

FOR SERVING

24 Elítses or 12 Niçoise olives, drained

Coarsely chopped flat-leaf parsley or fresh coriander

Place the chops between 2 sheets of waxed paper. With a meat pounder or the side of a heavy knife, pound until an even ½ inch thick. Combine the pork, garlic, bay leaves, parsley sprigs, 1 tablespoon of the coriander, the thyme, and enough red wine to cover the pork in a nonreactive bowl. Cover and set aside.

Prepare the fire.

Heat the mustard seeds in a dry skillet until a few pop. Pound the mustard seeds and remaining 1 tablespoon coriander with salt and the pepper in a small mortar until pulverized. Whisk the vinegar and olive oil together in a small bowl and whisk in the pulverized spices. Remove the pork from the marinade, dry with paper towels, and brush liberally with the spiced olive oil. Reduce the marinade to ¾ cup by rapid boiling in a saucepan over high heat, and strain.

Set a grill rack 4 inches above the hot coals and brush with olive oil. Grill the pork until lightly browned on both sides, basting frequently with the oil and catching the juices in a pan. Raise the grill 2 inches and grill 10 to 12 minutes longer. (For an attractive appearance, give the chops a 45° turn on each side halfway through the cooking time to "mark" it with grill marks.) Meanwhile, brush the mushrooms liberally with the spiced oil and grill 2 to 3 minutes, turning once.

Arrange the pork and mushrooms on a warm platter. Drain off the fat from the pan juices and add the juices to the marinade. Stir in the olives and the remaining spiced olive oil, and heat through. Pour over the pork and mushrooms, sprinkle with the parsley, and serve.

Mani Pork Souvlákia

Khirinó Souvlákia Mánis

Serves 6

During the period when Greece was part of the Ottoman Empire the Muslim occupation naturally discouraged the eating of pork. This did not, however, deter the rebellious inhabitants of the isolated and mountainous Mani region at the southern tip of the Peloponnese, who continued to raise pigs throughout the centuries of occupation and developed a long tradition of pork cookery. This is a simple and easy-to-prepare dish but, what it lacks in sophistication, it more than makes up for in flavor. The meat is marinated in a blend of coriander, juniper berries, and mustard, grilled with perfumed bay leaves, and garnished with fresh coriander. Serve with *piláfi* and Beets Island-Style (page 244) or *tsatsíki* (page 73).

2½ pounds boneless lean pork from the tenderloin or leg

1 tablespoon coriander seeds

6 juniper berries

¼ cup aged red-wine vinegar

½ teaspoon ground mustard

½ cup extra-virgin olive oil

18 bay leaves, broken in half

1 tablespoon honey

Cracked black pepper to taste

Coarse-grain sea salt to taste

FOR SERVING

*Coarsely chopped fresh coriander or watercress
or purslane sprigs*

Lemon wedges

Cut the meat into 1-inch cubes and trim off any fat and sinew. Pound the coriander seeds and juniper berries in a small mortar until crushed and well mixed. Combine with the vinegar and mustard powder in a small bowl, and whisk in the extra-virgin olive oil. Combine the meat and marinade in a nonreactive bowl, mix together with your hands, and cover. Set aside for 2 to 3 hours.

Prepare the fire.

Remove the meat from the marinade. Thread the meat and the bay leaves alternately onto 6 skewers. Whisk the honey into the marinade and baste the meat liberally with this sauce, then sprinkle it with pepper.

Set a grill rack 4 inches above the hot coals and lightly brush with olive oil. Grill the *souvlákia* until lightly browned on all sides, then raise the grill 2 inches. Grill 10 to 15 minutes longer, basting frequently, or until the *souvlákia* are cooked.

Arrange on a warm platter, sprinkle with salt, pepper, and fresh coriander, and surround with the lemon wedges.

Traditional Pork and Bean Casserole

Khirinó Khoriátiko

Serves 10 to 12

Robust flavors dominate this warming winter country dish; although similar to the comforting *cassoulet* of the Languedoc region of France, this casserole almost certainly predates it. The preparation is time-consuming, so it's best to assemble it one day for final cooking the next. It's ideal to serve at a supper party, so the quantities given here are large. Pork and smoked ham are cooked with onions, garlic, red wine, and hillside herbs and tangy Eastern spices, then layered in a casserole with country sausages and dried butter beans that absorb all the rich flavors, and baked. Serve with olives, *féta* cheese, radishes, and country bread, accompanied by a red wine such as Nemea or Naousa.

———

(continued)

1 1/2 pounds dried butter (large lima) beans, soaked overnight
in water to cover, cooked and drained (page 460)
(canned beans are unsuitable for this recipe)

3 pounds boneless lean pork shoulder

1/2 cup extra-virgin olive oil, or to taste

1/4 cup finely diced lean pastourmás ham (page 469),
or pancetta, or bacon

3 cups chopped onion

3 large cloves garlic, finely chopped

1 cup red wine, optional

2 pounds tomatoes, peeled and diced, juices reserved

1 teaspoon honey

1/4 cup dried rígani (page 14)

1 tablespoon dried marjoram

1 tablespoon dried winter savory (page 14) or thyme

2 tablespoons ground coriander

5 whole cloves

4 juniper berries, lightly crushed

1/2 cup finely chopped flat-leaf parsley

Sea salt to taste

1 tablespoon cracked black pepper, or to taste

1 to 1 1/2 cups Meat Stock (page 467)

1/2 pound homemade (page 238) or commercial country
sausages, grilled or sautéed (page 239)

1 cup fresh whole-wheat bread crumbs

1/4 cup grated kasséri or parmesan cheese

Juice of 1/2 lemon

Trim off any fat from the meat and cut into 1-inch cubes. Heat 3 table-spoons of the olive oil in a heavy skillet and lightly brown half the meat over medium heat. Drain between layers of paper towels, and repeat with the remaining meat.

Drain off any fat from the skillet, add the ham, and sauté 2 to 3 minutes. Add the onion and sauté, stirring occasionally, until light golden brown, about 15 minutes. Add the garlic, cook 1 minute longer, and add the red wine. Bring to a boil and boil a minute or two, then stir in the tomatoes with their juices, honey, *rígani,* marjoram, savory, coriander, cloves, juniper berries, parsley, salt, and pepper. Simmer until the liquid is reduced by half. Add 1 cup of the stock and simmer 5 minutes longer.

Add the meat, cover, reduce the heat, and simmer 30 minutes longer; add stock or water if there appears to be less than 2 cups of sauce. Season to taste with salt, pepper, and/or additional herbs; the sauce should be highly flavored.

Heat the oven to 325°F. Slice the sausage into ½ inch-thick slices and combine with the beans.

Sprinkle 2 tablespoons olive oil over the bottom of a heavy casserole and cover with one third of the sausages and beans. Cover with a layer of half the meat mixture, then half the remaining beans, then the remaining meat. Top with a layer of the remaining beans and sprinkle with the bread crumbs and cheese. With the back of a wooden spoon, gently press down on the beans so some of the sauce rises to the surface.

Sprinkle with the lemon juice and the remaining olive oil, cover, and bake 45 minutes. Reduce the oven temperature to 300°F and bake 1 to 1½ hours longer, until a golden crust has formed. Remove the casserole lid and bake 10 minutes or until the crust is deep golden brown. Serve hot.

Pork Cretan-Style
Khirinó Kritikó

Serves 6

Affall and winter specialty on the island of Crete, this hearty dish makes the most of winter savory, a lovely mountain herb that has a particularly happy affinity with pork. In rural communities, this popular Sunday dinner dish is still cooked in the traditional way—baked very slowly overnight in the village *foúrnos*. A crisp Purslane Salad (page 292) or Wild Leaf Greens Salad (page 295) provides a refreshing complement to the richness of the pork.

———

6 thick pork loin chops, bone-in (about 8 ounces each) or
boneless (6 to 7 ounces each)

Juice of 3 lemons

3 medium eggplants

2 tablespoons coarse-grain sea salt, or to taste

2 tablespoons coriander seeds, lightly crushed

1 tablespoon cumin seeds

1½ tablespoons cracked black pepper, or to taste

2 tablespoons dried winter savory or thyme

1 tablespoon dried rígani (page 14)

8 juniper berries

½ to 1 cup extra-virgin olive oil (to taste)

4 large all-purpose potatoes, peeled and cut lengthwise in
half or into quarters

6 large tomatoes, peeled and cut in half

1 teaspoon sugar

6 large cloves garlic, feathery outer skin rubbed off

12 bay leaves

FOR SERVING

½ cup finely chopped flat-leaf parsley

Trim off any fat from the pork and wipe bone-in chops to remove any bone splinters. Combine the pork and lemon juice in a nonreactive bowl, cover, and set aside for 3 hours to marinate.

Slice off the stem ends of the eggplants. Cut lengthwise in half and sprinkle the cut sides with 1 tablespoon of the salt. Set aside for 1 hour to sweat.

Heat the oven to 325°F. Heat the coriander and cumin seeds in a dry skillet over low heat until aromatic, about 1 minute. Combine the cumin, coriander, pepper, savory, *rígani,* juniper berries, and remaining 1 tablespoon salt in a mortar and pound until slightly pulverized. Remove the pork from the marinade, reserving any juices, and rub all over with this mixture. Arrange the pork chops in a large baking dish, spaced well apart. Set aside.

Heat 3 tablespoons of the olive oil in a large heavy skillet. Thoroughly dry the eggplants with paper towels, fry until the cut sides are golden brown, about 6 minutes, and drain between layers of paper towels.

Add the potatoes to the baking dish, arranging them so each piece is touching a piece of meat. Sprinkle the tomatoes with the sugar and add to the dish, cut sides up. Add the eggplants, skin sides down, and place the garlic cloves between the pieces of meat.

Pour over the remaining olive oil and the reserved marinade and sprinkle with the bay leaves and any remaining herb mixture. Add 1 cup water to the dish and bake boneless pork 30 minutes, bone-in pork 45 minutes, basting the meat several times with the pan juices; if the liquid evaporates, add a little more water. Reduce the oven temperature to 300°F and bake 15 minutes longer, or until the pork is cooked.

Spoon the pan juices over the pork and sprinkle with the parsley.

Variation

• Substitute a 2½- to 3-pound boneless pork loin roast for the pork chops. Marinate for 3 hours in the lemon juice, turning the pork occasionally. Rub all over with the herb and spice mixture, place in the center of the baking dish, and pour over ½ cup of the olive oil. Surround with the vegetables and garlic and sprinkle with bay leaves and remaining marinating liquid including any spice mixture. Bake 1 hour at 325°F, basting frequently with the remaining oil. Bake 30 minutes longer at 300°F, or until done; do not baste again.

   Slice the pork, arrange in the center of a warm platter, and surround with the vegetables. Spoon over the pan juices.

Pork Cutlets
with Mustard Sauce

Khirinó me Sáltsa Moustárthas

Serves 4

Pork cutlets served with a tangy mustard sauce sharpened and spiced with lemon juice, garlic, and cumin are a fall and winter lunch dish. Serve with Wild Leaf Greens Salad (page 295) and vegetable *piláfi*.

---

4 boneless pork loin chops, about 6 ounces each, trimmed of all fat

Sea salt and freshly ground black pepper to taste

7 tablespoons extra-virgin olive oil

¼ cup aged red-wine vinegar and 2 tablespoons water or ⅓ cup Mavrodaphne wine or other heavy sweet wine

Juice of 1 small lemon

2 hard-boiled egg yolks, pressed through a sieve

1½ tablespoons Dijon mustard

½ tablespoon honey

½ teaspoon ground cumin

1 large clove garlic, minced

¼ cup finely chopped flat-leaf parsley

1 tablespoon dried rígani (page 14), briefly pounded in a mortar

Sprinkle the pork chops with salt and pepper and place between 2 sheets of waxed paper. With a meat pounder or the back of a wooden spoon, pound until an even ½ inch thick. Measure 3 tablespoons olive oil into a small bowl and set aside in a warm spot.

Heat the remaining ¼ cup olive oil in a heavy skillet and sauté the cutlets over medium-low heat until lightly browned on both sides. Drain off any oil and add the vinegar and water. Cover, reduce the heat, and cook for 15 minutes, or until the cutlets are evenly pale all the way through.

Meanwhile, whisk together the lemon juice, egg yolks, mustard, honey, cumin, garlic, and salt and pepper and press through a fine sieve into a bowl. Add the warm olive oil, pan juices, parsley, and *rígani* and briefly whisk to mix. Arrange the pork on a warm platter and pour over the sauce.

Souvláki Sausages

Sheftaliá

**Serves 4 as a main course,
12 as a *mezé***

These delectable, highly seasoned sausages are popular street food all over Greece, and they are the perfect spicy snack at any time of the day. Meaty parcels of ground beef and pork mixed with onions, mint, parsley, and cumin are wrapped in caul fat and threaded onto skewers—in Greece double skewers, joined at one end, are sold for just this purpose. During grilling the fat melts to reveal the moist and tasty sausages inside. Perfect with *toursí* pickles, yogurt, or *tsatsíki*, and *píta*, *sheftaliá* can be served as a main course or a *mezé*.

———

(continued)

1½ pounds lean pork or ¾ pound each of lean beef and
lean pork, finely ground twice

1 large onion, grated

2 tablespoons fresh mint leaves, finely chopped, or
1 tablespoon dried mint, crumbled

⅓ cup finely chopped flat-leaf parsley

1 teaspoon ground cumin or ½ teaspoon ground allspice

2 tablespoons aged red-wine vinegar

Coarse-grain sea salt to taste

½ tablespoon cracked black pepper, or to taste

Extra-virgin olive oil, for grilling

½ pound pork caul fat (page 470)

FOR SERVING

½ cup coarsely chopped flat-leaf parsley

2 small red onions, quartered and thinly sliced

2 lemons, cut into wedges

3 ripe tomatoes, cut into thin wedges

Combine the meat, onion, mint, parsley, cumin, 1 tablespoon of the vinegar, salt, and pepper in a large bowl. Knead for a few minutes, cover, and refrigerate for 1 to 2 hours.

Prepare the fire.

Add the remaining 1 tablespoon vinegar to a bowl of tepid water and soak the caul fat in it for 3 minutes. Separate the pieces, lay flat, and pat dry. With scissors or a sharp knife, cut into pieces approximately 4 by 3 inches.

Divide the meat mixture into 12 portions. Moisten your hands with cold water and shape 1 portion into a 2½-inch-long sausage. Lay it across a narrow end of a piece of caul fat, fold over the edge and sides, and roll up to make a firm packet. Press down on the sausage firmly but gently to flatten it slightly; take care not to let the caul casing burst. Repeat with the remaining meat and caul fat.

Lightly brush 8 skewers with olive oil. Thread 3 sausages onto 1 skewer, running the skewer through a little off-center; do not pack them closely together. Carefully insert a second skewer through the sausages, parallel to the first one, to keep the *sheftaliá* balanced during grilling. Thread the remaining sausages the same way.

Set a grill rack 4 to 5 inches above low coals and lightly brush with olive oil. Grill the sausages 10 to 15 minutes, turning them carefully so they brown evenly.

Using a fork, push the sausages off the skewers onto a warm platter. Sprinkle with some of the parsley and onion and surround with the lemon wedges. Serve the remaining parsley and onion and the tomatoes separately.

Spicy Sausages with Mustard Sauce

Loukhánika me Yéfsi Pastoúrma

Makes 10 to 12 sausages

Highly spiced with cumin, cayenne pepper, and juniper berries and scented with rosemary and thyme these sausages, which can be boiled or smoked, are exceptionally good. Although similar in flavor to the Greek delicacy *pastoúrmas,* spicy preserved veal or pork tenderloin, they are traditionally made with beef. The simple mustard sauce accompanying them is superb, and it sets off the spicy sausages to perfection. Serve as a light lunch or supper dish with potatoes or *piláfi.* Or thinly slice the sausages and serve with olives and cheese as a *mezé.*

———

(continued)

½ cup fresh whole-wheat bread crumbs
(for boiled sausages only)

½ cup (for boiled sausages) to 1 cup (for smoked sausages)
red wine or Meat Stock (page 467)

1½ tablespoons cumin seeds or 1 tablespoon ground coriander

6 juniper berries

½ teaspoon fresh rosemary

½ teaspoon dried savory or thyme

½ teaspoon cayenne pepper, or to taste

2 pounds lean beef or 1 pound each of lean beef and pork,
finely ground twice, or 2 pounds lean pork, very finely chopped

½ pound (for boiled sausages) to 1 pound (for smoked
sausages) pork fatback, (page 462), finely diced or ground

1 clove garlic, crushed

1 tablespoon each of coarse-grain sea salt and cracked
black pepper, or to taste

½ pound sausage casings or 1 prepared sheep's intestine
(for a smoked sausage, page 471)

Olive oil, for cooking the sausages

MUSTARD SAUCE

2 tablespoons mustard seeds

1 tablespoon aged red-wine vinegar

1 hard-boiled egg yolk, pressed through a sieve

1 teaspoon honey

2 tablespoons finely chopped flat-leaf parsley

1 tablespoon yogurt, preferably homemade (page 8),
or extra-virgin olive oil

Sea salt and cracked black pepper to taste

Soak the bread crumbs in the ½ cup of wine for 30 minutes.

Heat the cumin seeds in a dry skillet until aromatic. Pound the cumin, juniper berries, rosemary, savory, and cayenne pepper together in a small mortar until pulverized; or grind in a spice grinder. Combine the meat, fatback, bread crumbs (or 1 cup wine), garlic, and salt and pepper in a large bowl. Sprinkle the herb and spice mixture over, knead for a few minutes, cover, and set aside for 1 hour.

With the sausage attachment on an electric mixer or by hand, fill the casings and tie to make 4- to 5-inch sausages. If they are to be boiled, pierce each sausage in several places.

To make one long sausage for smoking, tie a knot in one end of the intestine and carefully fill with the sausage mixture. Secure with a second knot and tie the two knotted ends together. Pierce in a dozen places. Cover with a clean kitchen towel, then with a board, and place weights (such as canned fruit) on top. Let drain at least 4 hours.

To boil the sausages Bring a large pot of water to a boil, add the sausages, reduce the heat, and simmer 1 to 1¼ hours, or until cooked through. Test for doneness by piercing 1 sausage with a skewer.

To smoke the sausage(s) Follow the manufacturer's instructions for your particular type of smoker, using Mediterranean pine or lemon leaves or a mixture of both if possible. After smoking, hang the sausage(s) until needed.

To serve, lightly brush the boiled sausages with olive oil and bake 30 minutes in a 350°F oven, turning them once. Or split the sausages lengthwise, brush with olive oil, and grill or broil until lightly browned on both sides.

Smoked sausages need no cooking, but frying them in olive oil gives an even better flavor.

To make the mustard sauce Gently heat the mustard seeds in a dry heavy skillet until they begin to pop, about 4 minutes. Pulverize them in a mortar or spice grinder and transfer the powder to a bowl. Add the vinegar, egg yolk, honey, parsley, yogurt, and salt and pepper, and mix until smooth with a wooden mallet or spoon.

The sauce can be served immediately or made ahead and refrigerated for up to 2 hours.

Note For a *mezé* or to add to an omelet, slice boiled sausages into ½-inch pieces and fry in a little olive oil.

Country Sausages
Loukhánika Khoriátika

Makes 12 to 14 sausages

Sausages are as much part of the Greek diet today as they were two thousand years ago. They have long added variety to family meals, provided an effective way of preserving meat, and given the cook a chance to create novel mixtures of herbs, spices, and meats. Traditionalists say that meat for sausages should be hand chopped (to preserve the moisture in the meat). Each different region has its own favored ingredients and cooking methods, and specialty restaurants, called *kapnistéria,* cater for the popular taste in sausages and smoked meats. In this recipe the pork and beef mixture is strongly flavored with herbs, spices, and orange zest and pine nuts add a crunchy country texture. These are good thinly sliced as a *mezé,* cooked in omelets (pages 92, 93, 97) or in vegetable dishes (page 242), or just grilled and served with crusty bread and salad.

———

1 teaspoon dried thyme

2 tablespoons fennel seeds or ½ teaspoon ground allspice

1 teaspoon ground coriander

1 bay leaf, ground

2 pounds lean pork, finely diced, or 1 pound lean pork, finely diced, and 1 pound lean beef, finely ground twice

½ pound pork fatback (page 462)

1 tablespoon cracked black pepper

1 tablespoon coarse-grain sea salt, or to taste

One 2-inch strip of orange zest, blanched or dried (page 469), finely chopped

¼ cup lightly toasted pine nuts, coarsely ground

½ cup fresh whole-wheat bread crumbs, optional

1 clove garlic, crushed

3 tablespoons finely chopped flat-leaf parsley

About ¼ to ½ cup red wine or Meat Stock
(page 467), to moisten

½ pound sausage casings (page 471)

Olive oil, for cooking the sausages

FOR SERVING

Lemon wedges

Coarsely chopped flat-leaf parsley

Pound the thyme, fennel seeds, coriander, and bay leaf in a small mortar until well mixed and the fennel seeds are lightly pulverized.

Combine the meat, fatback, pepper, salt, orange zest, pine nuts, bread crumbs, garlic, parsley, and spice mixture in a large bowl. Knead for a few minutes and add enough wine to moisten. Cover and set aside for 30 minutes.

With the sausage attachment on an electric mixer or by hand, fill the casings and tie to make 4- to 5-inch sausages. Pierce each sausage in several places.

To cook the sausages, heat ¼ cup olive oil in a heavy skillet and fry the sausages over medium-low heat, turning them occasionally, until deep golden brown on all sides. Or brush the sausages with olive oil and grill or broil until browned on all sides.

To serve, surround with the lemon wedges and sprinkle with parsley.

Vegetables and Salads

Lakhaniká ke Salátes

On *tavérna* menus and at Greek family meals vegetables are often the main focus of attention. This relish for the variety and versatility of fresh vegetables, coupled with the national flair for creating exciting dishes with them, makes Greece a paradise for vegetable lovers.

At the height of the growing season Greek vegetable markets are ablaze with color—mountains of shiny multihued eggplants, piles of zucchini, baskets of scarlet and green bell peppers, leafy bunches of purple beets, fronds of salad greens in infinite variety, mounds of tiny carrots, pyramids of huge red tomatoes, creamy sheaves of fresh celery and fennel, and banks of beans in red, pink, white, and purple. From this cornucopia the cook selects the best vegetables for a range of flavorful dishes: asparagus and new potatoes, or peas, carrots, and artichokes, to serve bathed in a delicate *avgolémono* sauce, or cucumbers, beets, or zucchini to turn into sweet and spicy salads. Perhaps carrots, onions, mushrooms, celery, or cauliflower are the best choice for succulent vegetable dishes *à la grecque*—juicy tomatoes, zucchini, and eggplants to stuff or to bake in aromatic casseroles.

Beans of all sorts appear on Greek family tables at least once a week. In summer bean dishes are made from the fresh varieties available in the market, in winter many of the same dishes are made from dried beans. These range from delicate purées and simple salads for *mezéthes* to baked dishes that make substantial main courses.

The cooking method used has a great influence on the flavors of Greek vegetable cookery. Grills and griddles give the special smoky flavor essential to many eggplant dishes; *foúrnos* cooking produces a glorious texture in vegetables of all kinds, especially beans; and cooking in clay pots lends a unique earthy-sweet taste to potatoes and beets. The curious lemon astringency of grape leaves deserves special mention. Tender young leaves are stuffed with a rice mixture, while tougher leaves impart a subtle, enigmatic flavor to a wide range of grilled and baked dishes. Simply boiled or steamed vegetables are rare in Greece; most often they are served with traditional sauces such as the lemony *latholémono* and *avgolémono*, flavored vinegar sauces, or intriguing concoctions based on pine nuts, walnuts, or almonds. Many of the recipes in this chapter make perfect first courses or light lunches and suppers, as well as delicious side dishes.

Marinated Asparagus

Sparángia Latholémono

Serves 3 to 4

This superbly flavored seasonal dish requires little work but it does demand top-quality ingredients: tender young asparagus with a fresh bright color, a good fruity olive oil, and the juice of a plump fresh lemon. Choose asparagus stalks of a similar thickness for even cooking. It can be prepared several hours ahead—the longer the asparagus rests in the marinade, the more mellow the flavor. Serve plenty of bread for your guests to mop up the sauce.

---

2 pounds asparagus

Coarse-grain sea salt

Juice of 1 large lemon

4 shallots, finely chopped

1 teaspoon dried rígani (page 14)

1/3 cup coarsely chopped flat-leaf parsley

1 teaspoon cracked black pepper

2/3 cup extra-virgin olive oil, or to taste

Break off the tough ends of the asparagus stalks at the point where they snap easily and discard. Add 2 inches of water and 1 teaspoon salt to a shallow saucepan large enough to hold the asparagus in a double layer, bring to a boil, and add the asparagus. Simmer 3 to 5 minutes, or until barely tender, drain, and spread on paper towels to dry. (Or steam the asparagus as directed on page 250.)

(*continued*)

Whisk together the lemon juice, shallots, *rígani,* parsley, pepper, salt to taste, and olive oil in a large shallow bowl. Add the asparagus and gently toss to coat. Cover and set aside at room temperature for up to 1 hour, or refrigerate for up to 4 hours, but remove from the refrigerator 15 minutes before serving.

To serve, carefully toss the asparagus with the marinade once more and transfer to a platter. Season to taste with salt and pepper and serve.

Note Artichoke hearts, cauliflower florets, thin leeks, green beans, beets, and zucchini can all be prepared the same way.

Beets Island-Style
Panzária Nisiótika

**Serves 6 as a *mezé*,
3 as a vegetable dish or for a light lunch**

For this ancient dish island cooks choose small young beets, each purple-red globe nestling in glossy green leaves. Crisp leaves are a good indication of freshness but, even more important, they're packed with vitamins and minerals—so the Greeks make them an integral part of the dish. Clay-pot cooking gives the beets the best flavor but they can also be oven-baked or boiled. An appetizing light lunch or a good side dish for grilled or roasted pork or chicken, Beets Island-Style is also an attractive addition to a *mezé* table with Fried Cheese (page 47) and Lamb's Liver with Lemon Juice and Rígani (page 43).

———

*6 small beets (about 2 inches in diameter)
with their leaves*

1 small red onion, cut into thin rings

Strained juice of 1 large lemon

Coarse-grain sea salt and cracked black pepper to taste

1 teaspoon dried rígani (page 14)

⅓ to ½ cup extra-virgin olive oil (to taste)

Trim the stems and root ends from the beets. Reserve the green leaves and scrub the beets with a stiff brush under cold running water. Bake in a clay pot or baking dish (page 273), or boil 15 minutes in boiling salted water, or until just tender when pierced with the point of a knife. Drain, and when cool enough to handle, remove the skins with a small paring knife.

Place the onion in a nonreactive bowl and sprinkle with half the lemon juice, salt and pepper, and *rígani*. Toss to mix, cover, and set aside.

Remove the tough stems from the beet greens and discard any leaves that are not fresh and glossy; leave thin tender stems intact but trim to 2 inches. Thoroughly rinse, tear into pieces, and place in a saucepan. Add ¼ cup boiling water, cover, and cook 2 to 3 minutes over low heat, or until just tender; do not overcook. Drain in a colander set over a bowl, pressing the greens against the colander with the back of a wooden spoon. (Reserve the mineral-rich cooking liquid for soup stock.)

While the beets are still warm, cut lengthwise into quarters (the traditional shape) or into 1½-inch julienne (matchsticks). Combine with half the olive oil and half the remaining lemon juice and salt and pepper in a nonreactive bowl and toss to coat. Arrange the beets on one side of a platter and the greens on the other side. Sprinkle with the remaining olive oil and lemon juice and a generous amount of salt and pepper and scatter the onion over the beets. Serve warm or at room temperature.

Variations

- Coarsely chop the cooked greens. Combine with the quartered beets and add the lemon juice, olive oil, and salt and pepper; omit the onion and *rígani*.
- To serve *tavérna*-style, use only the beets; save the greens for Beet Greens Salad (page 296). Cut the cooked beets into julienne (matchsticks). Add the lemon juice, olive oil, salt and pepper, and 1 tablespoon crushed coriander seeds; omit the *rígani*. Immediately before serving, add ¼ cup fresh mint leaves torn into small pieces or ¼ cup coarsely chopped flat-leaf parsley to the beets, gently toss together, and garnish with the onion.

Beet Salad with Allspice
Panzária Kritiká

Serves 4

Allspice features strongly in Cretan cookery, and this easy-to-make salad comes from a most unlikely source—a monastery on the island, where I enjoyed a delightful culinary experience. With typically Cretan hospitality the smiling monks set before us large platters of this excellent salad, bowls of creamy fresh goat's cheese, and trays of grilled fish. You can prepare the dish up to 24 hours ahead; try it with egg dishes or grilled meats, or with cheese and fish.

6 small beets (about 2 inches in diameter)

½ tablespoon ground allspice

Coarse-grain sea salt and cracked black pepper to taste

⅓ cup Kalamáta olive oil, or to taste

Strained juice of 1 lemon

FOR SERVING

2 tablespoons fresh mint leaves or coarsely chopped fresh dill, optional

1 small red onion, cut in half and thinly sliced

¼ cup coarsely chopped flat-leaf parsley

12 Elítses or 8 Niçoise olives, drained

Heat the oven to 325°F. Trim the stems and root ends from the beets and scrub them under cold running water with a stiff brush. Line a heavy baking dish with aluminum foil (to prevent the beets from discoloring the dish), add the beets and ¼ cup water, and bake uncovered until just tender, about 40 minutes; add more water to the dish if necessary (or wrap each beet in aluminum foil and bake; allow an extra 30 minutes baking time.)

Peel the beets with a small paring knife and cut into 1½-inch julienne (matchsticks). Place in a nonreactive bowl with the allspice, salt and pepper, olive oil, and half the lemon juice, gently toss together, cover, and set aside.

Just before serving, tear the mint leaves into small pieces. Combine the onion with the parsley, mint, remaining lemon juice, and salt.

Transfer the beets to a platter and sprinkle with the onion mixture, any marinade remaining from the beets and onion, and salt and pepper to taste. Scatter the olives over the beets and serve.

Artichokes City-Style

Agináres a la Políta

Serves 6

This fresh-tasting spring vegetable dish dates from the days of the Byzantine Empire, and the "city" in question is thought to be Constantinople (now Istanbul), the glittering empire's capital. Artichokes, new potatoes, carrots, small onions, and fresh fava beans cook slowly in a tightly closed casserole from which none of the delectable flavor can escape. The dish takes some time to prepare, but it can be made a day ahead for convenience.

---

2 lemons

*12 small or 6 medium artichokes, preferably with
2 inches of stem intact*

1 tablespoon all-purpose floor

Sea salt

6 small new potatoes, peeled if desired

6 small young carrots

*12 boiling onions (about 1 inch in diameter), peeled
(page 472)*

2½ pounds young fava beans, shelled

Freshly ground white pepper to taste

¼ cup lightly packed sprigs of fresh dill

½ cup extra-virgin olive oil, or to taste

FOR SERVING

Lemon wedges

(continued)

Fill a large nonreactive saucepan with water and bring to a boil. Meanwhile, squeeze the juice from the lemons, set the juice aside, and add 2 of the lemon halves to a large bowl of ice water; whisk in the flour and 1 teaspoon salt. (Flour and salt help prevent the artichokes from discoloring.) Remove the outer leaves of the artichokes, leaving only the tender light green ones. With a sharp knife, slice off the top third of each artichoke, and scoop out the fuzzy choke with a small spoon. Peel the tough outer skin from the stems. Cut medium artichokes in half lengthwise. Rinse, rub with a lemon half, and add to the bowl of ice water.

Cut potatoes larger than 1 inch in diameter in half, and cut the carrots into ½-by 2-inch sticks.

Drain the artichokes and add to the boiling water with the potatoes and onions. Boil 2 minutes, add the carrots, and boil 2 minutes longer, then add the fava beans and cook 1 minute longer. Drain, reserving 3 cups of the cooking liquid.

Transfer the vegetables to a heavy saucepan large enough to accommodate them in a single layer, arranging the artichokes bottoms up. Add salt, pepper, most of the dill, and enough of the reserved cooking liquid to come halfway up the sides of the artichokes.

Whisk together the olive oil and two thirds of the reserved lemon juice and pour this *latholémono* sauce over the vegetables. Cut a piece of waxed paper to fit the saucepan, making a hole in the center for the steam to escape. Gently press the paper down on top of the vegetables (to prevent the artichokes from discoloring) and cover the saucepan.

Set over medium heat and bring just to a simmer. Immediately reduce the heat to very low and simmer 25 minutes, or until the vegetables are just tender; there should always be about 1 cup of liquid in the pan—add more of the reserved cooking liquid if necessary. Season the sauce to taste with the remaining lemon juice and olive oil, salt, and/or pepper. If there is more than 1 cup of sauce, pour into a small saucepan and reduce to 1 cup by rapid boiling.

Place the artichokes bottoms up in the center of a warm platter and surround with the other vegetables. Spoon over the sauce and garnish with the remaining dill. Serve hot, warm, or at room temperature, with bowls of the lemon wedges.

Note To make ahead, transfer the vegetables and sauce to a nonreactive bowl, let cool, cover, and refrigerate. Heat gently to warm or bring to room temperature before serving. Season the sauce to taste with salt, pepper, and/or lemon juice and serve.

Variations

- Add 3 peeled, seeded, and diced ripe tomatoes and ½ teaspoon sugar to the saucepan with the drained vegetables. Add only ½ cup reserved cooking liquid to the vegetables. Do not add lemon juice to the cooking liquid, but sprinkle the vegetables with 2 tablespoons lemon juice to serve.
- Serve with *avgolémono* sauce instead of *latholémono*. Add only ¼ cup olive oil and 2 tablespoons lemon juice to the vegetables. Just before the vegetables are cooked, whisk 2 egg yolks for 1 minute, whisk in the remaining lemon juice, and whisk 1 minute longer. When the vegetables are cooked, remove 1 cup cooking liquid and cover the vegetables to keep warm. Gradually whisk the cooking liquid into the egg and lemon juice mixture, whisking 1 minute longer, and transfer to the top of a double boiler set over hot water. Cook over low heat, stirring constantly with a wooden spoon, until the sauce thickens enough to lightly coat the back of the spoon, about 1 minute. Arrange the vegetables on a warm platter, pour over the sauce, garnish with the dill, and serve at once.

Asparagus and New Potatoes Avgolémono

Sparángia me Patátes ke Avgolémono

Serves 4

This is a spring dish of subtle delicacy and exquisite flavor. The gentle cooking method allows the potatoes to absorb a muted asparagus flavor; the vegetables are lightly coated with the classic *avgolémono* sauce. Serve as an elegant first course or lunch or as an accompaniment to grilled or roasted meats.

———

(continued)

Vegetables and Salads

*16 small new potatoes (about 1½ pounds), peeled if desired
and cut in half or into quarters*

1½ pounds asparagus

2 large eggs

Strained juice of 2 lemons

Sea salt and freshly ground white pepper to taste

FOR SERVING

Small sprigs of fresh chervil or flat-leaf parsley

Fill an asparagus steamer or large 2-handled pot two thirds full with lightly salted water and bring to a boil. Add the potatoes, cover, and boil for 15 minutes, or until barely tender.

Meanwhile, break off the tough ends of the stalks at the point where they snap easily. Rinse the asparagus and tie in 2 bundles with kitchen string, leaving enough string on each to loop over the handles of the saucepan.

When the potatoes are almost cooked, balance the asparagus in the saucepan, the stems immersed in boiling water. Loop the string firmly around the handles so the asparagus tips remain above the surface to steam. Cover and cook 4 minutes.

While the asparagus cooks, beat the eggs with a hand whisk or electric mixer until pale and frothy, about 2 minutes. Gradually add the lemon juice and whisk 1 minute longer. Drain the vegetables in a colander set over a bowl and keep warm. Gradually whisk ¾ cup of the cooking liquid into the egg mixture. Transfer to the top of a double boiler set over hot water and cook over low heat, stirring with a wooden spoon, until the sauce thickens enough to lightly coat the back of the spoon, about 1 minute.

Arrange the vegetables on a warm platter and sprinkle with salt and pepper. Pour over the sauce, garnish with the chervil, and serve at once.

Peas, Carrots, and Artichokes Avgolémono

Pizélia, Karótta, ke Anginares me Avgolémono

Serves 4

Excellent as a side dish with spring lamb, this is also a popular lunch dish in Greece—light but satisfying, and full of taste. With the green and orange color combination and a dressing of billowy lemon sauce, it looks marvelous.

———

8 small artichokes or 4 medium artichokes, quartered

1 pound small young carrots

1½ cups fat-free Chicken Broth (page 461) or water

½ teaspoon sugar

½ teaspoon sea salt

2 cups shelled young peas (about 1½ pounds in the pod)

2 large eggs

Strained juice of 1 large lemon

FOR SERVING

Freshly ground black pepper

Finely chopped flat-leaf parsley

Trim the artichokes as directed on page 248, cutting large artichokes into quarters, and cook in boiling salted water until tender, about 8 minutes.

Cut larger carrots into 1½- by ½-inch sticks; trim small carrots and leave whole. Bring the broth, sugar, and salt to a boil in a large heavy saucepan. Add the carrots, cover, reduce the heat, and simmer 10 minutes. Add the peas and simmer 6 minutes longer, or until the vegetables are barely tender. Add the artichokes and simmer 2 to 3 minutes.

While the artichokes simmer, beat the eggs with a hand whisk or electric mixer until light and frothy, about 2 minutes. Gradually add the lemon juice and whisk 1 minute longer. Drain the vegetables in a colander set over a bowl and keep warm. Gradually whisk ¾ cup of the cooking liquid into the egg mixture, and transfer the sauce to the top of a double boiler set over hot water. Cook over low heat, stirring with a wooden spoon using a figure-8 motion, until it thickens enough to lightly coat the back of the spoon, 1 to 2 minutes.

Arrange the vegetables on a warm platter, pour over the sauce, and sprinkle with the pepper and parsley. Serve at once.

Turnips and Grapes in Aromatic Sauce

Goggília ke Stafíli Aromatiká

Serves 4

Delicious with game, roast or grilled chicken, or lamb, this unusual dish teams the vigorous earthy flavor of young turnips with sweet pepper, grapes and currants, and a honeyed ginger sauce.

––––––––

6 to 8 small turnips (about 1½ pounds)

¼ to ⅓ cup extra-virgin olive oil (to taste)

1 small red bell pepper, cored, seeded, and cut into very thin strips

Coarse-grain sea salt and freshly ground black pepper to taste

1 cup small seedless grapes, such as Thompson

¼ cup currants or small dark seedless raisins

2 tablespoons aromatic honey

½ teaspoon ground ginger

1 tablespoon dried rosemary

3 tablespoons aged red-wine vinegar diluted with 3 tablespoons boiling water

Fill a medium saucepan with lightly salted water and bring to a boil. Trim the stems and root ends from the turnips, peel, and cut lengthwise into quarters. Boil 4 minutes, or until barely soft when pierced with the point of a knife. Drain and set aside.

Heat the olive oil in a heavy skillet large enough to hold the turnips in a single layer and sauté the pepper over medium-low heat until slightly softened, about 1 minute. Add the turnips and salt and pepper and sauté until very pale golden brown on all sides, about 5 minutes: take care not to break up the turnips when stirring. Add the grapes and currants and heat to warm through.

Combine the honey, ginger, rosemary, and vinegar, add to the skillet, and simmer until the sauce is slightly syrupy, about 2 minutes. Serve immediately.

Vegetables and Salads

Sweet-and-Sour Zucchini

Kolokitháki Glykóxsino

Serves 6

The dominant flavor in this easy dish is cinnamon, but the sprinkling of lemon juice lends just the right hint of tartness to balance the sweetness of the sauce. Serve it with grilled chicken, pork, or swordfish.

---

2 pounds zucchini, each preferably about 2 inches long

Coarse-grain sea salt to taste

½ cup small dark seedless raisins

½ cup aged red-wine vinegar

⅓ cup Kalamáta olive oil

1 tablespoon ground cinnamon

2 tablespoons aromatic honey diluted with
¼ cup hot water

½ tablespoon cracked black pepper, or to taste

FOR SERVING

½ cup coarsely chopped flat-leaf parsley

1 tablespoon dried rígani (page 14), briefly
pounded in a mortar

Strained juice of ½ lemon

Trim the zucchini and rub with a damp cloth to remove any fuzz. If large, cut into pieces 2 inches long and 1 inch thick; if smaller than 2 inches leave whole. Pat dry with paper towels and sprinkle lightly with salt. Combine the raisins and vinegar in a small nonreactive bowl.

Warm the olive oil in a heavy skillet large enough to hold the zucchini in a single layer and sauté the zucchini over low heat until just tender, about 8 minutes; stir occasionally with a wooden spoon so they cook evenly. Sprinkle the zucchini with cinnamon and add the raisins and vinegar, honey and water, and pepper. Gently shake the skillet to mix and cook until the sauce becomes slightly syrupy, about 3 minutes.

Transfer the zucchini to a platter, pour over the sauce, and sprinkle with the parsley, *rígani*, lemon juice, and salt and pepper to taste. Serve hot, warm, or cold.

Cucumber Salad with Honey and Vinegar Sauce

Angoúri Saláta

Serves 4

Along with more dramatic treasures, archaeologists working on Minoan sites have also found cucumber seeds—remnants of sumptuous royal feasts or frugal family suppers long ago. This simple salad is based on a classic recipe and features ingredients that have been accessible to Greek cooks for centuries—good olive oil, aged red-wine vinegar, and aromatic honey. Serve it with grilled meats or fish.

———

1 large English hothouse cucumber, peeled

Coarse-grain sea salt

¼ cup aged red-wine vinegar

2 tablespoons aromatic honey, such as Hymettus

1 teaspoon cracked black pepper, or to taste

2 tablespoons extra-virgin olive oil

¼ cup fresh chervil, dill, or flat-leaf parsley,
coarsely chopped

FOR SERVING

12 Elítses or 6 Niçoise olives, drained

Slice the cucumber paper-thin with a mandoline or knife, or cut into matchsticks with the french-fry disc on a food processor. Place in a bowl, sprinkle with 1 tablespoon salt, and toss to mix. Cover and set aside for 1 hour.

Combine the vinegar, honey, pepper, and a pinch of salt in a nonreactive bowl. Whisk in the olive oil. Gently squeeze the cucumber, a handful at a time, between paper towels, to remove as much moisture as possible. Add the cucumber and chervil to the vinegar sauce and mix well.

Transfer to a shallow bowl or platter, scatter the olives over, and serve.

Carrots and Onions à la Grecque
Karótta ke Kremíthi Khoriátiko

**Serves 8 as a first course,
4 as a vegetable dish or as part of a buffet**

The tiny delicately sweet Flemish carrots grown in Florida are ideal for this spicy dish, but if they are not available buy the best fresh young carrots you can find. When you make this be sure to give the flavors time to mellow and mature. Serve as part of a buffet, as a first course, or as a side dish. Celery and cauliflower are also good prepared *à la Grecque* (see the variations below).

———

¾ pound thin young carrots, cut into 2-inch lengths

¼ cup extra-virgin olive oil

2 tablespoons dried coriander seeds, lightly crushed

1 pound small boiling onions, peeled (page 472)

2 cups dry white wine

½ teaspoon ground mace

3 bay leaves

½ tablespoon aromatic honey, such as Hymettus

1 tablespoon cracked black peppercorns

Coarse-grain sea salt to taste

FOR SERVING

*3 tablespoons fresh coriander or finely chopped flat-leaf parsley
or 1½ tablespoons fresh oregano or thyme*

1 tablespoon finely grated lemon zest

Lemon wedges

Blanch the carrots in boiling salted water for 1 minute, drain, rinse, and set aside.

Heat the olive oil in a large heavy saucepan over low heat. Add the coriander seeds and the vegetables in a single layer and stir with a wooden spoon to coat with the oil. Add the wine, mace, bay leaves, honey, pepper, and salt. Bring just to a boil, cover, reduce the heat, and simmer gently 20 minutes or until tender.

Transfer the vegetables to a nonreactive bowl and measure the liquid. If there is more than 1½ cups, return it to the saucepan and reduce by rapid boiling over high heat. Pour over the vegetables and set aside until cool. Cover the bowl and shake it gently to redistribute the vegetables in the marinade, and set aside in a cool spot for 1 to 2 hours before serving.

To serve, taste the marinade; if more salt is needed, combine it with the fresh coriander. Chop the coriander, lemon zest, and salt together just until mixed.

Transfer the vegetables to a shallow serving bowl and pour over most of the marinade (strain it first if you prefer). Sprinkle with the coriander mixture and serve with the lemon wedges.

Celery à la Grecque
Sélino Khoriátiko

Substitute 1 bunch of celery for the carrots and onions and 1 tablespoon caraway seeds for the mace. Slice off the root end of the celery and rinse the stalks well. Remove the tough strings with a small sharp knife and cut the stalks on the diagonal into 2-inch lengths. Blanch 2 minutes in boiling salted water, drain, and dry on paper towels.

Simmer the celery for only 4 to 6 minutes, until it is soft but still slightly resists the point of a knife.

Garnish with finely chopped celery leaves or parsley. Celery *à la Grecque* is perfect with cold roast pork or beef.

Cauliflower à la Grecque
Kounoupíthi Khoriátiko

Substitute 5 cups cauliflower florets for the celery and use parsley as the garnish. Trim as much stem as possible from the florets and cut an "X" in the base of each with a small sharp knife. Blanch 1 minute in boiling salted water and drain. Simmer in the marinade for only 6 minutes, or until barely soft.

Mushrooms à la Grecque
Manitária Khoriátika

**Serves 6 as first course,
3 as a vegetable dish**

There are many versions of this popular dish, but most are pale imitations of the original Greek creation, with little of the rich mix of spicy and earthy flavors that are its hallmark. The intensity of flavor can be adjusted according to taste—for a lightly spiced dish prepare only two hours ahead; for more mellow taste and texture leave overnight in the marinade; the dominant cinnamon tones can be similarly exploited or subdued.

---

1 pound small white mushrooms

2 to 3 tablespoons extra-virgin olive oil (to taste)

One 3-inch cinnamon stick, broken in half

2 bay leaves

1 tablespoon coriander seeds, lightly crushed

1½ cups dry white wine

Coarse-grain sea salt to taste

1 teaspoon cracked black pepper, or to taste

FOR SERVING

Chopped fresh thyme, oregano, or coriander

Lemon wedges

Trim the mushroom stems and brush or wipe the mushrooms.

Combine the olive oil, cinnamon stick, bay leaves, and coriander seeds in a heavy skillet large enough to hold the mushrooms in a single layer, and heat over low heat. Add the mushrooms, cover, and sweat 5 minutes, or until they have released most of their liquid and are slightly darkened and aromatic; don't let them become soft.

Bring the wine to a boil in a small pan over high heat and reduce to 1 cup by rapid boiling. Add to the mushrooms along with the salt and pepper. Bring to a boil, then transfer to a nonreactive bowl and set aside to cool. Cover and set aside for 2 hours in a cool place or refrigerate overnight.

To serve, transfer the mushrooms to a shallow bowl and pour (or strain) over the marinade. Season to taste with salt and pepper. Sprinkle with the thyme and serve with the lemon wedges.

Note Thin leeks, green beans, or artichoke hearts, all blanched 2 minutes, or quartered cooked beets, can be prepared the same way for multicolored variations.

Baked Green Beans in Grape Leaves
Fassólia sto Foúrno

Serves 4

Young grape leaves appear in Crete's lively markets at the same time as fava beans, and this is the dish Cretan cooks make with the pick of the new spring crop. Since grape leaves and favas generally do not appear simultaneously in our produce markets, canned grape leaves and later beans such as Romanos or young limas in their pods make good substitutes. The leaves are not wrapped around the beans but, used to line the bottom of the baking dish and as a protective covering, they act as a flavoring agent. This dish is delicious with grilled or roasted meat or chicken.

———

2 pounds young fava, Romano, or lima beans

About 30 fresh or canned grape leaves, rinsed

¹/₃ to ¹/₂ cup extra-virgin olive oil (to taste)

Juice of 2 small lemons

Coarse-grain sea salt and freshly ground black pepper to taste

FOR SERVING

¹/₄ cup finely chopped flat-leaf parsley

(continued)

Heat the oven to 325°F. With a small paring knife, trim the ends of the beans. Remove a thin slice from each side of the fava beans, or remove the strings from Romanos or limas. Blanch in boiling salted water for 1 minute, remove with a slotted spoon, and set aside in a colander to drain. Add 6 or so grape leaves to the boiling water and blanch 5 seconds if fresh, 3 seconds if canned; with a slotted spoon, transfer to paper towels to drain. Repeat with the remaining leaves.

Cover the bottom of a deep heavy baking dish, large enough to hold the beans in a double layer, with half the grape leaves, glossy sides down. Spread the beans over the leaves and add ¼ cup of the olive oil, half the lemon juice, and 1 cup water. Sprinkle with salt and pepper and lay the remaining leaves on top, glossy sides up. Bake 50 minutes or until soft; test for doneness with a sharp knife, making sure to insert the point through a bean as well as the pod. Bake 15 to 30 minutes longer if necessary, and sprinkle with an additional ¼ to ½ cup water if the dish seems in danger of drying out.

Discard the top layer of leaves and transfer the beans to a warm platter. Sprinkle with the remaining lemon juice and olive oil and cooking liquid to taste. Season with salt and pepper and sprinkle with parsley. Serve hot, warm, or at room temperature.

Variations

• Substitute 1½ pounds white mushrooms or 2 pounds all-purpose potatoes for the beans, or a mixture of both. Trim the mushroom stems to ½ inch. Peel the potatoes if desired, cut into bite-sized pieces, and cook 5 minutes in boiling salted water. Bake mushrooms 25 minutes, potatoes or potatoes and mushrooms 40 minutes, or until tender.

Stuffed Grape Leaves with Latholémono Sauce

Dolmáthes me Latholémono

**Serves 8 as a first course,
4 as a main course**

*D*olmáthes—little rolls of savory rice in grape leaves—are popular all over Greece and there are endless variations on the theme. Tiny versions, called *dolmathákia,* are served as a *mezé,* while the larger *dolmáthes* can be first or main courses. Sometimes the filling is simply rice flavored with allspice or cinnamon; sometimes it includes meat, pine nuts, currants, and fragrant herbs. *Dolmáthes* are not difficult to make but they do take time, so it's worth knowing that they freeze well.

---

¹/₃ to ¹/₂ cup extra-virgin olive oil (to taste)

1 cup finely chopped scallions

1 cup long-grain rice

1 teaspoon ground cinnamon

Sea salt

1 bay leaf

2 cups light fat-free Chicken Broth (page 461) or water

¹/₂ cup pine nuts

¹/₂ cup currants or small dark seedless raisins

*32 medium grape leaves or 40 smaller leaves, fresh or canned,
plus extra leaves to make 1 layer in the baking dish*

*¹/₂ cup coarsely chopped fresh dill or ¹/₂ cup mint leaves,
torn in small pieces*

¹/₄ cup finely chopped flat-leaf parsley

Cracked black pepper to taste

Juice of 2 large lemons

FOR SERVING

Lemon wedges   *(continued)*

Heat 2 tablespoons of the olive oil in a heavy saucepan and sauté the scallions over low heat until soft, about 5 minutes. Add the cinnamon and rice and stir well with a wooden spoon. Add 1 teaspoon salt, the bay leaf, and broth. Raise the heat and boil uncovered until the liquid has disappeared and holes appear in the surface of the rice, about 8 minutes. Stir in the pine nuts and currants with a fork and cover the saucepan with 2 layers of paper towels and a tight-fitting lid. Set aside for 15 minutes in a warm spot such as the back of the unheated oven.

Fill a large saucepan with water and bring to a boil. Trim off the stems from 32 medium or 40 smaller leaves and set aside.

Add the remaining leaves to the boiling water, 5 or 6 at a time, and blanch 3 seconds if canned, 5 seconds if fresh. Remove with a slotted spoon, spread between layers of paper towels, and blot dry. Line a heavy shallow nonreactive and flameproof baking dish or skillet, large enough to hold the *dolmáthes* in a single tightly packed layer, with these leaves, glossy sides facing down. Blanch the reserved leaves, drain, and blot dry.

Remove the bay leaf from the rice and, with a fork, stir in most of the dill, the parsley, the juice of half a lemon, and salt and pepper to taste.

Place a grape leaf on a clean work surface, glossy side down and stem end towards your wrist. Use 1 heaped teaspoon filling each for first course *dolmás,* 1 tablespoon filling for main course *dolmás.* Place the filling in the center of the leaf at its widest part, pull the stem end over, and fold in both sides. Firmly roll up the package towards the point of the leaf. Repeat with the remaining leaves and rice; as you finish each *dolmás,* place it in the dish pressing tightly against the next one.

Pour over 2 tablespoons of the remaining olive oil and the juice of another half lemon and add enough water to barely reach the top of the *dolmáthes.* Cover with a plate slightly smaller than the dish and place a weight (such as a large can of fruit) on top. Set the dish over medium-low heat and bring just to a boil, reduce the heat, and simmer small *dolmáthes* 25 minutes, larger ones 30 minutes. There should always be some liquid in the dish; if necessary add more water to barely reach the top of the *dolmáthes.*

Remove from the heat and, with the plate and weight still in place, set aside for 5 minutes if serving warm, or let cool.

Transfer the *dolmáthes* to a platter or individual plates and sprinkle with the remaining olive oil and lemon juice. Surround with the lemon wedges, or arrange them between the *dolmáthes,* and garnish with the remaining dill.

Note For a Cretan touch, substitute Green Grape Sauce (page 430) for half the water used to cook the *dolmáthes*. The sauce tenderizes the grape leaves to make lovely velvety *dolmáthes*.

Stuffed Grape Leaves with Avgolémono Sauce

Dolmáthes me Avgolémono

**Serves 8 as first course,
4 as a main course**

These *dolmáthes* are more substantial than the previous version, filled with lamb and rice and flavored with allspice and fresh fennel. They are especially good with a rich *avgolémono* sauce, but try them as well with the simpler *latholémono* sauce (page 262).

¼ cup extra-virgin olive oil

1 cup finely chopped onion

½ pound lean lamb, finely ground

1 teaspoon ground allspice

Sea salt and freshly ground black pepper to taste

⅔ cup long-grain rice

1⅓ cups light Meat Stock (page 467) or water

*32 medium grape leaves or 40 smaller leaves, fresh or canned,
plus extra leaves to make 1 layer in the baking dish*

*2 tablespoons finely chopped fresh fennel leaves or 2
tablespoons fresh mint leaves, torn into small pieces*

½ cup finely chopped flat-leaf parsley

Juice of 2 large lemons

2 egg yolks   *(continued)*

Heat 2 tablespoons of the olive oil in a heavy saucepan and sauté the onion over low heat until soft, about 8 minutes. Add the meat, raise the heat, and sauté until lightly browned, breaking up any lumps with a wooden spoon. Add the allspice, salt and pepper and rice, and cook 1 minute, stirring. Add the stock and boil uncovered until the liquid has disappeared and holes appear in the surface of the rice, about 8 minutes. Cover the saucepan with 2 layers of paper towels and a tight-fitting lid and set aside for 20 to 25 minutes in a warm spot such as the back of the unheated oven.

Prepare the grape leaves and line a dish as directed on page 262.

With a fork, stir the fennel, most of the parsley, half the lemon juice, and salt and pepper into the rice. Make the *dolmáthes* as directed on page 262. Pour the remaining 2 tablespoons olive oil and lemon juice over the *dolmáthes* and add enough water to barely cover them. Cover with a plate slightly smaller than the dish and place a weight on top. Set the dish over medium-low heat and bring to a boil, reduce the heat, and simmer small *dolmáthes* 25 minutes, larger ones 30 minutes. There should always be enough liquid to reach the top of the *dolmáthes;* add more water if necessary.

Pour off 1¼ cups of the cooking liquid and strain it. Replace the plate and weight and set the dish aside in a warm spot.

Beat the egg yolks with a hand whisk or electric mixer until pale and frothy. Gradually add the remaining lemon juice and whisk 1 minute longer. Slowly add the strained cooking liquid, whisking constantly. Transfer to the top of a double boiler set over hot water and stir over low heat, using a figure-8 motion, until the sauce is thick enough to lightly coat the back of the spoon, about 6 minutes.

Arrange the *dolmáthes* on a warm platter or individual plates and pour over the sauce. Sprinkle with the remaining parsley and serve immediately.

Stuffed Grape Leaves and Zucchini Blossoms

Dolmáthes Kolokithokorfáthes

Serves 8

A delight of late spring in Greece is a beautiful platter of stuffed grape leaves and stuffed zucchini blossoms, garnished with fresh fennel and wedges of lemon. Both are designed as tiny treats, small enough to be eaten in one mouthful, and stuffed with an aromatic flavored rice. Stuffed zucchini blossoms may sound a trifle exotic but do try them—they're delicious and well worth the effort. Serve these as part of a buffet or a picnic.

⅓ cup extra-virgin olive oil

1 cup finely chopped scallions, including the best green parts

¼ cup coarsely chopped fresh fennel leaves or 1 tablespoon ground fennel seed

1 cup long-grain rice

Sea salt to taste

2 cups fat-free Chicken Broth (page 461) or water

25 small grape leaves (each no more than 3 inches across at its widest point), fresh or canned, plus extra leaves to make 1 layer in the baking dish

15 zucchini blossoms or additional grape leaves

⅓ cup finely chopped flat-leaf parsley

Strained juice of 2 large lemons

Freshly ground black pepper to taste

FOR SERVING

Sprigs of fresh fennel, optional

Lemon wedges

(continued)

Heat 2 tablespoons of the olive oil in a heavy saucepan and sauté the scallions over low heat until soft, about 5 minutes. Stir in the fennel and cook 1 minute. Add the rice stirring with a wooden spoon to coat with the oil. Add salt to taste and the broth, raise the heat, and boil uncovered until the liquid has disappeared and holes appear in the surface of the rice, about 8 minutes. Cover the saucepan with 2 layers of paper towels and a tight-fitting lid and set aside for 20 minutes in a warm spot such as the back of the unheated oven.

Prepare the grape leaves and line a dish as directed on page 262 (trim the 25 small leaves before blanching).

To prepare the zucchini blossoms, gently pull out the stamens, trim the stems, and rinse them by dipping in a bowl of cold water. Shake off excess water and carefully wrap in a kitchen towel or paper towels to dry.

With a fork, stir the parsley, the juice of half a lemon, salt, and pepper into the rice to make a highly-seasoned mixture with a distinct flavor of fennel.

Make the *dolmáthes* as directed on page 262. To fill a zucchini blossom, hold it in the palm of one hand and, with your thumb, gently push 1 heaped teaspoon of stuffing inside, taking care not to break the flower. Fold 1 petal over the stuffing, then fold in the other petals to make a secure little package. Arrange in the dish with the stuffed vine leaves.

Sprinkle all the *dolmáthes* with 2 tablespoons of the remaining olive oil and the juice of half a lemon and add water to barely reach the top of the *dolmáthes*. Place a plate slightly smaller than the dish on top of the *dolmáthes* and set a weight (such as a large can of fruit) on the plate. Place the dish over medium-low heat and bring to a boil, reduce the heat to low, and simmer 25 minutes. There should always be liquid in the dish; add a little more water if necessary to barely reach the top of the *dolmáthes*. Remove from the heat and, with the plate and weight still in place, set aside to cool to room temperature.

To serve, arrange the *dolmáthes* on a platter and sprinkle with the remaining olive oil and lemon juice, and salt and pepper to taste. Garnish with the fennel sprigs and surround with the lemon wedges.

Note To store, let cool, transfer the *dolmáthes* to a nonreactive airtight container, and refrigerate for up to 2 days. Serve at room temperature.

Baked Eggplants with Tomatoes and Féta Cheese

Melitzánes me Féta

Serves 8

A slightly sweet, nutty flavor is the hallmark of this dish, and the secret lies in the quantity of olive oil used and in the preliminary cooking of the eggplants. An ideal buffet dish served hot or cold, especially with barbecued meats, this can easily be prepared for large numbers of people.

———

4 large eggplants (2 to 2½ pounds)

Sea salt

¾ to 1 cup extra-virgin olive oil (to taste)

12 ounces féta cheese, cut into 8 slices

½ tablespoon cracked black pepper, or to taste

*4 large ripe tomatoes, peeled, seeded, and
diced, juices reserved*

2 tablespoons tomato paste diluted with ¼ cup water

1 teaspoon honey

8 bay leaves

FOR SERVING

Juice of 1 large lemon

½ cup coarsely chopped flat-leaf parsley

Trim the ends from the eggplants and cut lengthwise in half. Sprinkle with 2 tablespoons salt and set aside for 30 minutes to sweat.

Heat the oven to 350°F. Set a large heavy skillet over medium heat and add ¼ cup of the olive oil. Thoroughly dry the eggplants with paper towels and fry half of them until the cut sides are dark golden brown and the skin is shriveled and darkened, about 12 minutes. Drain between layers of paper towels. Heat 2 tablespoons of the remaining olive oil in the skillet and fry the remaining eggplants. Drain.

(continued)

Arrange the eggplants, cut sides up, in a heavy baking dish just large enough to hold them in a single layer. Sprinkle with the pepper and place a slice of *féta* on top of each one.

Combine the tomatoes and their juices, tomato paste, honey, and remaining olive oil and spoon over the *féta* and eggplants. Place a bay leaf on top of each and add just enough water to the dish to cover the bottom. Bake uncovered for 30 to 40 minutes, or until the eggplants are very soft. There should be about 2 cups of sauce in the pan; add more water if necessary.

Serve directly from the baking dish, leaving the bay leaves in place as garnish. Sprinkle with the lemon juice, parsley, and salt and pepper to taste. Serve hot or warm.

Note To grill eggplants, trim the eggplants, cut in half, and sweat. Set a grill rack about 4 inches above hot coals and brush both eggplants and grill with olive oil. Grill on both sides until dark golden brown and soft. Meanwhile, heat the oven and make the tomato sauce. Drain the eggplants on paper towels, arrange in the baking dish as directed, and bake.

Baked Summer Vegetables

Briámi Mystrás

Serves 6

Magnificent baked vegetable casseroles have been part of Greek life for centuries. The ingredients may vary from season to season, but they always have a rich, satisfying character and fresh flavor. Here the vegetables are slowly baked in an onion and tomato sauce until they have absorbed most of the spicy sauce; a cheesy bread-crumb topping adds a golden crusty finish. Serve with country bread, a green salad and slices of mild *féta* cheese. It's also a perfect accompaniment to grills.

———

2 medium eggplants (about ¾ pound)

Sea salt

2 green bell peppers, roasted and peeled (page 460)

¾ cup extra-virgin olive oil, or to taste

1 cup thinly sliced onion

1 large clove garlic, finely chopped

6 large ripe tomatoes, peeled and diced, juices reserved

1 tablespoon honey

1 tablespoon ground cumin

3 tablespoons dried rígani (page 14)

⅓ cup coarsely chopped flat-leaf parsley

Freshly ground black pepper to taste

1 pound new potatoes

1 pound zucchini, cut into ¼-inch slices

⅓ cup hot water

½ cup lightly toasted fresh bread crumbs

½ cup grated kasséri or parmesan cheese

FOR SERVING

Juice of 1 large lemon

Trim the ends from the eggplants and cut into 1½-inch cubes. Sprinkle with 1 tablespoon salt and set aside in a colander to sweat for 30 minutes. Slice the tops off the peppers, discard the cores and seeds, rinse off any remaining seeds, and cut lengthwise into ¼-inch strips.

Heat ¼ cup of the olive oil in a large heavy skillet and sauté the onion over medium-low heat until soft, about 8 minutes. Add the garlic, tomatoes and their juices, honey, cumin, rígani, half the parsley, salt, and pepper. Raise the heat, bring to a boil, and simmer 10 minutes, or until reduced by about one third, stirring occasionally with a wooden spoon.

Heat the oven to 375°F. Place a second large heavy skillet over medium heat and add ¼ cup of the remaining olive oil. Thoroughly dry the eggplant with paper towels and fry until golden brown on all sides, about 10 minutes. Drain between layers of paper towels.

(continued)

Peel the potatoes and cut into ¼-inch slices. Arrange them in the bottom of a deep heavy baking dish. Combine the eggplant, pepper, and zucchini and spread over the potatoes. Pour over the sauce, remaining ¼ cup olive oil, and the hot water, firmly shake the dish to distribute the sauce, cover, and bake 15 minutes. Reduce the oven temperature to 350°F and bake 20 minutes longer. Stir the vegetables, taking care not to break the potatoes, and bake uncovered 25 minutes longer or until the potatoes are just tender.

Taste the sauce and add salt and pepper if desired. Combine the bread crumbs and cheese and sprinkle over the vegetables; with the back of a spoon gently press down on the vegetables so a little of the juices reaches the bread crumbs. Bake, uncovered, 15 minutes longer or until golden brown.

Sprinkle with the lemon juice, pepper, and the remaining parsley. Serve hot, warm, or at room temperature.

Note To make in individual casseroles, divide the ingredients among 6 small casseroles. Bake covered at 375°F for 15 minutes, uncovered at 350°F for about 25 minutes.

Honey-Glazed Onions

Kremíthia sto Foúrno

Serves 4

Baked in a honey and wine mixture aromatized with pungent cloves, these onions emerge from the oven beautifully glazed in a light sauce. Meltingly soft and sweetly spicy, they are delicious with grilled or roasted meats and game.

---

2 pounds boiling onions (about 1 inch in diameter)
peeled (page 472)

2 tablespoons unsalted butter

2 tablespoons Kalamáta olive oil

1 cup Mavrodaphne or Madeira wine and 1 tablespoon honey,
preferably Hymettus, or 1 cup fat-free Chicken Broth
(page 461) and 2 tablespoons honey,
preferably Hymettus

4 whole cloves

Sea salt and freshly ground black pepper to taste

1/2 cup coarsely chopped flat-leaf parsley

1 tablespoon finely chopped Preserved Lemon (page 19) or
1 tablespoon finely grated lemon zest

Heat the oven to 325°F. Arrange the onions in a heavy baking dish large enough to hold them in a single layer and dot with the butter and olive oil. Combine the wine and honey, ½ cup water, cloves, and salt and pepper in a small saucepan. Bring to a boil over medium-low heat and pour over the onions. Cover and bake 1 hour or until there is about ½ cup of light syrupy sauce and the onions are very soft.

Chop the parsley, Preserved Lemon, a pinch of salt, and a generous amount of pepper together to mix. With a wooden spoon, gently roll the onions around in the sauce to glaze, and transfer to a warm platter, discarding the cloves. Pour over any remaining sauce and sprinkle with the parsley mixture. Serve hot or warm.

Zucchini with
Olive Oil and Herbs

Kolokitháki me Elaiólatho

Serves 4

When preparing this as a side dish for grilled or roast meat or fish, I often bake a few extra zucchini—the next day they provide an instant *mezé* or salad or make an unusual omelet filling for a quick and tasty lunch.

1½ pounds baby zucchini (2 to 3 inches long)

¼ cup extra-virgin olive oil, or to taste

Juice of 2 lemons

Sea salt and freshly ground black pepper to taste

⅓ cup coarsely chopped flat-leaf parsley

1 tablespoon dried rígani (page 14), briefly pounded in a mortar

Heat the oven to 350°F.

Trim the zucchini and rub with a kitchen towel to remove any fuzz. Arrange in a heavy shallow baking dish large enough to hold them in a single layer. Pour over the olive oil and half the lemon juice and add ½ cup water. Sprinkle with salt and pepper and bake uncovered for 10 minutes. Roll the zucchini around in the cooking liquid to coat, reduce the oven temperature to 300°F, and bake 40 minutes longer, or until the zucchini are barely soft. Roll them around in the cooking liquid once or twice during baking, and add a few tablespoons of water if needed—there should always be at least ¼ cup of liquid in the dish.

Transfer the zucchini to a warm platter and sprinkle with a few tablespoons of the cooking liquid, the remaining lemon juice, the parsley, *rígani*, and olive oil, salt, and pepper to taste. Serve hot, warm, or cold.

Note To serve as a *mezé* or salad, refrigerate the zucchini in the cooking liquid, covered, in a nonreactive container for up to 24 hours. Remove from the liquid and cut into ½-inch slices. Sprinkle with lemon juice, olive oil, coarse-grain sea salt and cracked black pepper, a generous amount of finely chopped parsley, and *rígani*.

To use as a filling for an omelet, remove the zucchini from the cooking liquid, cut into thin slices, and drain on paper towels. Add to a barely set omelet, with a little finely chopped parsley, dried basil, freshly ground pepper, and a few tablespoons grated *féta* cheese.

Potatoes in a Clay Pot

Patátes sto Foúrno

Serves 4

The tradition of cooking in unglazed cooking pots dates from the Minoan period, the earliest Western civilization, but it thrives in modern Greece, and with good reason. Vegetables cooked this way need only to be scrubbed, no special care is needed in baking them, and they not only acquire a unique earthy flavor but also retain almost all their vitamins and minerals. Potatoes cooked in a clay pot develop a delightful slightly sweet flavor, making them especially good in salads or as a side dish for a delicately flavored main course such as Baked Sole in Grape Leaves (page 133). This cooking method is also excellent for beets—during baking their natural crimson color deepens to a rich dark purple and the texture turns velvety smooth.

1½ pounds small new potatoes of a similar size

FOR SERVING

Coarse-grain sea salt and cracked black pepper to taste

Fresh lemon juice

1 to 2 tablespoons extra-virgin olive oil or unsalted butter

Finely chopped flat-leaf parsley, optional

Prepare the pot following the manufacturer's instructions or immerse it for 5 minutes in warm water. Pour out the water, add the potatoes, and cover with the lid.

(continued)

Place in a cold oven and set the oven temperature to 325°F. Bake 1¼ to 1¾ hours or until the potatoes are tender.

Transfer to a warm bowl and sprinkle with the salt and pepper, lemon juice, olive oil, and parsley.

Note You can bake the potatoes at a higher heat (425°F) for a shorter time (50 minutes) or at a lower heat (250°F) for a longer time (2 hours) if necessary, but always start with a cold oven. For easier cleaning, immerse the pot in hot water as soon as you remove the potatoes from it.

Beets in a Clay Pot
Panzária sto Foúrno

Prepare the pot as directed above. Trim the stem and root ends from 6 small beets, about 2 inches in diameter. Scrub with a stiff brush under cold running water, taking care not to break the skins. Add to the pot, cover, and place in a cold oven. Set the oven temperature to 325°F and bake 1½ hours or until the beets are tender.

When cool enough to handle, peel the beets and cut into quarters or slices. Sprinkle with sea salt and cracked pepper, the juice of 1 small lemon, extra-virgin olive oil to taste, 1 tablespoon fresh oregano or dried *rígani*, and finely chopped flat-leaf parsley. These are delicious with *piláfi*, *féta* cheese, or grilled meat or swordfish.

Note If you are using the beets in a salad, season while they are still warm.

Garlic Potatoes
with Juniper Berries
Patátes Skórthou

Serves 3 to 4

This is a dish for those who like strong flavors—the taste of these tiny baked potatoes is anything but subtle. The finished dish has a bold expressive character and it's perfect with herbed roast chicken (page 157) or pork dishes. Real garlic lovers can press out the soft centers of the baked cloves and spread them on the potatoes or on toasted bread.

---

3 tablespoons extra-virgin olive oil

2 tablespoons dried juniper berries, lightly crushed

8 large cloves garlic

1 ½ pounds small new potatoes

FOR SERVING

Juice of 1 small lemon

Coarse-grain sea salt and cracked black pepper to taste

Finely chopped fresh oregano or dried **rígani** *(page 14)*

Triangles of toasted whole-wheat bread, optional

Heat the oven to 350°F.

Pour the olive oil into a heavy shallow baking dish large enough to hold the potatoes in a single layer. Sprinkle the juniper berries over the oil and place the dish in the oven for a few minutes to warm. Trim off the stem ends of the garlic cloves and rub off any feathery outer skin. Place the potatoes and garlic in the warm dish and roll them in the olive oil to lightly coat. Bake 10 minutes and roll the potatoes and garlic in the olive oil once more. Reduce the oven temperature to 300°F and bake uncovered for 50 minutes or until the potatoes are just tender.

Roll the potatoes in the olive oil to coat once more and transfer to a warm platter. Sprinkle with the lemon juice, salt and pepper, and oregano. Serve hot or warm, with toast, if desired.

Fresh Fava Bean Salad
with Black Olives

Fassólia Saláta me Eliés

Serves 3 to 4

Sweet young fava beans and fresh fennel usually appear in the markets at the same time and their very individual flavors complement each other well. This enticing salad is particularly good with sausages, egg dishes, or cold roast pork.

---

3 pounds fava beans in their pods

Juice of 1 large lemon, or to taste

1/3 cup extra-virgin olive oil, or to taste

Coarse-grain sea salt to taste

1 teaspoon cracked black pepper, or to taste

*12 Ámfissa or other mild black olives,
cut in half and pitted*

1 small red onion, quartered and thinly sliced

*1/3 cup lightly packed fresh fennel leaves or coarsely
chopped flat-leaf parsley*

Shell the beans and reserve 2 tender pods. Blanch the pods and beans in lightly salted boiling water for 5 minutes, drain, discard the pods, and rinse the beans. Remove the skins from the beans and place the beans in a non-reactive bowl. Add the lemon juice, olive oil, salt, and pepper, and gently stir to mix. Cover and set aside for 1 to 2 hours.

To serve, add most of the olives, onion, and fennel to the beans and season to taste with salt, pepper, lemon juice, and/or olive oil. Transfer to a platter, garnish with the remaining olives, onion, and fennel.

Note Although it is not necessary to remove the skins of very young favas, Greek cooks prefer to remove the opaque skins to reveal the pretty shade of green within. Without their skins, favas also are easier to digest and have a subtly different flavor.

Variation

- Substitute 1½ pounds green beans, such as Romanos, for the favas. Trim both ends of the beans and with a small knife remove the strings along both sides. Cut into 1½-inch pieces, blanch in boiling salted water for 5 minutes or until barely tender, and rinse. Proceed as directed above.

Green Lentil Salad

Fakés Saláta

**Serves 8 to 10 as a *mezé*,
4 as a salad**

The ancient Greeks believed that the benign influence of green lentils could greatly improve a grouchy temper—I cannot verify this claim, but I have seen smiles of pleasure creep over the faces of my guests when they try this salad! Cumin, parsley, mint, and garlic enhance the rustic tones of the humble lentil and a *latholémono* dressing deepens all the flavors.

2 cups dried green lentils, picked over and rinsed

*1 tablespoon cumin seeds, lightly pounded in
a small mortar*

1 small red onion, cut into thin rings

Juice of 1 lemon

Coarse-grain sea salt and cracked black pepper to taste

½ cup coarsely chopped flat-leaf parsley

2 tablespoons fresh mint leaves or 1 teaspoon dried mint

1 large clove garlic, minced

¼ cup finely chopped Preserved Lemon (page 19)

¼ cup extra-virgin olive oil

2 tablespoons Strained Yogurt (page 8)

FOR SERVING

Pinch of cayenne pepper

(continued)

Place the lentils in a large saucepan and add cold water to cover by 3 inches. Bring to a boil, cover, reduce the heat, and simmer until soft but not disintegrating, about 30 minutes. Drain, gently shake the colander once or twice, and set aside to dry. Warm the cumin seeds in a small dry skillet over low heat until aromatic, about 1 minute.

Combine the onion, half the lemon juice, ½ tablespoon of the cumin, and a large pinch of salt in a nonreactive bowl. Chop 1 tablespoon of the parsley and the mint leaves together just to mix; add to the onion. Set aside.

Chop the garlic, 3 tablespoons of the Preserved Lemon, remaining cumin, half the remaining parsley, and a pinch of salt together to mix. Combine with the lentils, remaining parsley and lemon juice, the olive oil, and salt and pepper to taste. Carefully stir to mix.

Transfer to a platter and sprinkle with the onion and its marinade. Spoon the yogurt over the center and sprinkle with the remaining Preserved Lemon and parsley and the cayenne pepper. Serve at room temperature.

Note The lentils can be cooked and combined with their flavorings a day ahead, but do not marinate the onion until a few minutes before serving.

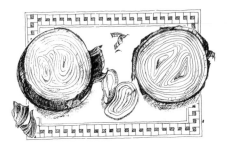

Black-Eyed Peas with Capers

Fassólia me Kápari

**Serves 8 as a mezé,
4 as a vegetable dish**

A *tavérna* favorite, this highly flavored dish is eaten as a quick snack, a *mezé*, or a side dish with grilled meats. The beans are mixed with a lively sweet-sour sauce, piquant with plump capers, and a bed of arugula supplies a refreshing complement. This dish can be prepared several hours ahead.

---

*2 cups dried black-eyed peas, soaked for 3 to 6
hours in cold water to cover*

1 tablespoon aromatic honey, such as Hymettus

3 tablespoons aged red-wine vinegar, or to taste

Coarse-grain sea salt and cracked black pepper to taste

⅓ cup Kalamáta olive oil, or to taste

3 tablespoons capers, rinsed, and coarsely chopped if large

⅓ cup coarsely chopped flat-leaf parsley

FOR SERVING

*1 cup arugula, torn into bite-sized pieces, or 1 cup
watercress sprigs*

1 small red onion, cut into thin rings

1½ cups Strained Yogurt (page 8)

Place the beans in a saucepan with cold water to cover. Bring to a boil, drain, and rinse out the saucepan. Return the beans to the pan, add cold water to cover by 3 inches, and bring to a boil. Cover, reduce the heat, and simmer 20 to 30 minutes or until tender; take care not to overcook. Drain and set aside in a colander for a few minutes to dry.

Combine the honey, vinegar, and salt and pepper in a large bowl and gradually whisk in the olive oil. Add the beans, capers, and parsley, and mix with a spoon. Season with vinegar, olive oil, salt and/or pepper.

Line the edges of a platter or shallow bowl with the arugula and place the beans in the center. Scatter over the onion and serve the yogurt separately.

Vegetables and Salads

Summer Bean Salad

Kalokhérini Saláta Fassolión

**Serves 12 as a *mezé*,
6 to 8 as a salad or vegetable dish**

In Greece dried beans and peas are not limited to winter dishes, but appear in various guises all year round—and there's a very good reason for this. At the height of the Greek summer the daytime temperatures are such that slaving over a hot stove is not an activity undertaken with enthusiasm. This is the time to take maximum advantage of the communal village oven. Food preparation can be done in the cool early morning and the main meal of the day taken to the *foúrnos* for baking; it's common practice to take to the oven not just a meat dish, but also a pot of beans to be baked alongside it. If the beans are not eaten that day they make a lovely cold salad for the next. In this recipe the country flavor of the beans is complemented by the sweet freshness of juicy ripe tomatoes, peppery watercress or purslane, and the perfume of bay leaves, thyme, and parsley. Serve this pretty dish as a *mezé*, with crusty bread as a light lunch, or as a side dish for grilled meat, chicken, or liver.

---

*2 cups dried cannellini or great northern beans, soaked for 6
to 12 hours in cold water to cover*

1 onion, peeled and stuck with 2 whole cloves

1 small carrot, cut into 3 pieces

1 celery stalk, cut into 3 pieces

2 bay leaves

2 large sprigs of parsley

Juice of 1 large lemon

½ cup extra-virgin olive oil

Coarse-grain sea salt and cracked black pepper to taste

4 large ripe tomatoes, peeled and diced

Large pinch of sugar

1 large clove garlic, finely chopped

*2 tablespoons fresh thyme, finely chopped, or 1 tablespoon
dried thyme, crumbled*

1½ cups watercress leaves or 2 cups small purslane sprigs

FOR SERVING

1 small red onion, cut into thin rings

½ to 1 cup Elítses or Niçoise olives, drained

Place the beans in a saucepan and add cold water to cover. Bring to a boil, drain, and rinse out the saucepan. Return the beans to the saucepan along with the onion, carrot, celery, bay leaves, parsley, and water to cover by 4 inches. Bring to a boil, cover, reduce the heat, and simmer 50 minutes or until the beans are tender but not disintegrating. Drain and set aside in a colander for a few minutes to dry.

Combine the beans, half the lemon juice, ¼ cup of the olive oil, a large pinch of salt, and 1 teaspoon pepper in a large bowl. Stir to mix, taking care not to break up the beans. Cover and set aside for up to 1 hour.

Place the tomatoes in a sieve over a bowl and sprinkle with the sugar and a pinch of salt. Set aside.

Whisk together the remaining lemon juice, garlic, thyme, a large pinch of salt, and pepper to taste in a small nonreactive bowl. Add the remaining ¼ cup olive oil in a thin steady stream, whisking constantly. Add to the beans along with the watercress and tomatoes, and season to taste.

Transfer to a platter and sprinkle with the onion and olives. Serve at room temperature.

Note To bake, soak the beans for 6 to 12 hours in cold water to cover, drain, and place in a large saucepan with cold water to cover. Bring to a boil, drain, and transfer to a large deep casserole. Add the onion, carrot, celery, bay leaves, parsley, and water to cover by 4 inches. Cover and bake 3 to 4 hours at 250°F or 2 hours at 350°F (the temperature can be varied to suit your oven schedule). Or, to reduce the baking time by 30 minutes, bring to a boil before placing the casserole in the oven.

Country Salad
Khoriátiki Saláta

Serves 6 to 8

No Greek table is complete without a salad; unfortunately, the "Greek salads" served to tourists often fall very short of the real thing. *Khoriátiki saláta* is the real thing, and it changes with the seasons. In summer the main ingredients are tomatoes, cucumbers, salad greens, and bell peppers; in winter thinly shredded cabbage is dominant. To these are added crumbly *féta* cheese, local black olives, capers, perfumed *rígani*, and a well-flavored olive oil. Present the salad on a good-sized platter and provide warm bread for your guests to dip into the flavorful juices.

---

1 large English hothouse cucumber or 2 small cucumbers

4 large ripe tomatoes, peeled if desired

½ teaspoon sugar

Coarse-grain sea salt to taste

1 small green bell pepper, roasted and peeled (page 460), seeds wiped off, and cut lengthwise into thin strips

2 cups salad greens, such as watercress or purslane sprigs or bite-sized pieces of escarole, arugula, or romaine

1 small red onion, cut into thin rings

12 to 16 Kalamáta olives, drained

8 toursí peppers, homemade (page 439) or bottled, drained, optional

½ pound féta cheese, drained and crumbled into large pieces

2 tablespoons small capers, drained

3 tablespoons dried rígani (page 14)

¼ cup finely chopped flat-leaf parsley

½ cup Kalamáta olive oil, or to taste

Strained juice of 1 small lemon, optional

Cracked black pepper to taste

Trim and peel the cucumber. Cut in half lengthwise, then into ½-inch slices to make half moons. (If cucumbers are not the hothouse variety, peel them, cut lengthwise in half, scoop out the seeds, and then slice.) Core the tomatoes and cut into wedges. Sprinkle with the sugar and salt and set aside for 15 minutes. Spread the pepper strips on paper towels to dry.

Arrange the greens around the edge of a serving platter. Make a circle of the tomatoes on the inner part of this border of greens, and arrange a circle of the cucumbers inside it. Sprinkle over the bell pepper, onion, olives, and *toursí* peppers. Pile the cheese in the center and sprinkle with the capers. Chop the *rígani* and parsley together to mix, and sprinkle over the salad, along with the olive oil, lemon juice, and pepper.

Note For a winter salad substitute 1 small head of white or green cabbage (about 1 pound) for the tomatoes and cucumbers. Core and rinse the cabbage, then slice very thinly or shred with a large-holed grater. Lightly mix together the cabbage and salad greens and arrange on a platter. Serve as described above.

Vegetables and Salads

283

Traditional Tomato Salad

Domáta Saláta Patroparádoti

Serves 4

Thick wedges of sweet juicy tomatoes, crumbly *féta* cheese, richly flavored olives, fruity olive oil, and aromatic hillside herbs make a distinctively Greek combination. This salad, the centerpiece of every *tavérna* table in summer, is the first dish I order each time I cross the border into Greece—just to prove to myself that I've really arrived!

---

4 large ripe tomatoes, peeled if desired

Coarse-grain sea salt and cracked black pepper to taste

¹/₂ teaspoon sugar

*6 scallions, trimmed, with the best green parts left intact,
and thinly sliced*

¹/₃ cup coarsely chopped flat-leaf parsley

12 Kalamáta olives, drained

¹/₂ cup crumbled féta *cheese*

*2 tablespoons dried rígani (page 14), briefly pounded in a
small mortar, or 3 tablespoons fresh oregano leaves*

¹/₃ cup Kalamáta olive oil, or to taste

1 tablespoon fresh lemon juice

Core the tomatoes, cut into wedges, and arrange on a platter. Sprinkle with salt and pepper and the sugar, loosely cover, and set aside for 1 hour.

To serve, sprinkle the scallions, parsley, olives, and *féta* over the tomatoes. Sprinkle the *rígani,* olive oil, and lemon juice over the salad, add olive oil and/or pepper to taste, and serve at once.

Tomato Salad with Arugula and Tiny Olives

Domatosaláta me Rókka ke Eliés

Serves 4

Arugula (*rokka*), said to be a native of the Greek islands, is mentioned frequently in myth and legend and still grows wild in the Greek countryside. A century ago, brought to the United States by Italian immigrants, it was a familiar sight on our tables, but unaccountably it fell from favor and only reappeared a few years ago with the emergence of "California cuisine." Be sure to choose arugula that's crisp and bright green. With its slightly bitter, mustardy flavor arugula has a wonderful affinity with tomatoes, amply demonstrated by this summer salad. It's especially good with cheese dishes.

---

4 large ripe tomatoes, peeled if desired

Coarse-grain sea salt and cracked black pepper to taste

1/2 teaspoon sugar

1 small bunch of arugula, trimmed and torn into large pieces

1 small red onion, cut into thin rings

24 Elítses or 12 Niçoise olives, drained

2 tablespoons fresh lemon juice

1/3 cup extra-virgin olive oil, or to taste

Core the tomatoes, cut into wedges, and sprinkle with salt and pepper and the sugar. Cover and set aside for 1 hour.

To serve, spread the arugula on a platter and arrange the tomatoes on top. Scatter over the onion and olives and sprinkle with the lemon juice, olive oil, and pepper. Serve immediately.

Orange Salad Cretan-Style
Saláta Kritikí

Serves 6

Folklore has it that the Lasithi plateau on the island of Crete is the birthplace of watercress, and the Cretans certainly are very fond of its peppery bite. Watercress appears in a variety of classic recipes, including this vibrantly colorful traditional favorite.

---

4 small beets, cooked in a clay pot (page 274), peeled, and cut into julienne (large matchsticks)

Juice of 1 small lemon

⅓ cup extra-virgin olive oil

Coarse-grain sea salt and cracked black pepper to taste

3 large navel oranges

2 cups watercress sprigs

8 ounces féta cheese, drained and cut into ½-inch dice

12 Elítses or Niçoise olives, drained

2 tablespoons dried rígani (page 14), briefly pounded in a small mortar

Combine the beets, most of the lemon juice, 2 tablespoons of the olive oil, and salt and pepper in a nonreactive bowl. Cover and set aside.

Peel the oranges and remove any white pith with a sharp knife. Cut the oranges crosswise into ¼-inch slices. Remove the pithy centers with the point of the knife. Spread the slices on a plate, tightly cover, and refrigerate until chilled.

To serve, line the edges of a chilled serving platter with the watercress and lay the orange slices in a single overlapping layer on the inside edge of this border. Make a circle of the beets inside the oranges and drizzle their marinade over. Place the *féta* in the center of the platter. Sprinkle the oranges with a little salt, and the beets and cheese with the *rígani* and olives. Sprinkle the remaining lemon juice and olive oil and pepper over the salad and serve at once.

Green Salads

Prásines Salátikes

Contrary to popular opinion, a green salad course did not originate with the French or the Italians but with the ancient Greeks. It was the custom to end a great feast with a simple salad, to refresh the palate after the excesses of a rich and heavy meal and, it was believed, to induce drowsiness (although we might suspect that the drowsiness had more to do with the copious quantities of wine consumed).

When Greeks order a green salad they expect to be served a traditional bowl of either romaine (*kos*) lettuce or one of a variety of wild greens such as purslane, watercress, chicory, or young dandelions. With the exception of those composed of the delicately sweet romaine lettuce Greek salads have in common an earthy, slightly bitter, flavor that's much appreciated by the peoples of the Eastern Mediterranean. This special flavor derives from the particular character of the soil of the region and cannot really be reproduced here. But in our markets we can occasionally find purslane, dandelion, and several varieties of chicory and, more frequently, arugula and watercress. Romaine lettuce is usually available year-round; in the spring, when it is at its best, use the whole head of lettuce for these salads; in other seasons select just the tender sweet heart. The natural astringency of these greens finds perfect partners in the mellow richness of olive oil and the simple flavors of fresh lemon juice or red-wine vinegar and sea salt.

Green Salad with Féta Cheese and Olives

Salatiká me Féta

Serves 6 to 8

A refreshing and popular salad, perfect for a simple lunch or a side dish. When a variety of greens is available I like to make it with hearts of romaine, chicory frisée, watercress, arugula, and tender young spinach leaves in about equal proportions. Be sure to use good-quality mild *féta* cheese or firm and crumbly goat's cheese.

---

2 small heads of romaine lettuce or 2 hearts of larger heads or
6 cups of a mixture of young spinach leaves, watercress sprigs,
curly endive, escarole, chicory frisée, arugula,
and young dandelion leaves

Strained juice of 1 lemon

Coarse-grain sea salt and cracked black pepper to taste

¹⁄₃ cup Kalamáta olive oil, or to taste

¹⁄₃ cup coarsely chopped flat-leaf parsley

18 Kalamáta olives

¹⁄₂ pound mild féta cheese, cut into ¹⁄₂-inch dice

6 scallions, trimmed, the best green parts left intact,
and thinly sliced, or 1 small red onion, quartered
and thinly sliced

3 tablespoons dried rígani (page 14)

Prepare the greens (page 289).

Combine the lemon juice and salt and pepper in a nonreactive bowl. Whisk in the olive oil in a thin steady stream. Combine the greens, parsley, olives, *féta*, and scallions in a serving bowl and pour the dressing over. Toss with a wooden spoon and fork, taking care to break up the cheese as little as possible. Sprinkle with the *rígani* and serve.

Easter Greens Salad with Latholémono Sauce

Salatiká Paskhaliná

Serves 4

Aclassic salad of mixed greens, scallions, and Preserved Lemon, scented with fresh dill and parsley and tossed in an olive oil and lemon juice dressing. This is one of the salads on the traditional Easter table.

---

2 small heads of romaine lettuce or 4 cups of curly endive, chicory frisée, young dandelion leaves, young spinach, arugula, and/or watercress or purslane sprigs

6 scallions, trimmed, the best green parts left intact

Strained juice of ½ small lemon, or more to taste

⅓ cup coarsely chopped fresh dill or 1 teaspoon dill seeds (soaked for a few minutes in the lemon juice)

Coarse-grain sea salt and freshly ground black pepper to taste

¼ cup extra-virgin olive oil, or to taste

⅓ cup coarsely chopped flat-leaf parsley

2 tablespoons finely chopped Preserved Lemon (page 19) or ½ tablespoon finely grated lemon zest, blanched in boiling water for 5 seconds and drained

Discard any stems and imperfect leaves from the greens, rinse well, and tear into large bite-sized pieces. Spin dry in a salad spinner or shake off any excess water and loosely wrap in a kitchen towel. Refrigerate for up to 12 hours.

To serve, cut the scallions lengthwise into quarters, then into 1-inch lengths. Combine the lemon juice (and dill seeds) and salt and pepper in a nonreactive bowl and gradually whisk in the olive oil. Combine the greens, scallions, fresh dill, parsley, and Preserved Lemon in a serving bowl, and pour the *latholémono* sauce over. Toss with a wooden spoon and fork and add lemon juice, salt, and/or pepper to taste. Serve immediately.

(continued)

Note Greek cooks take pride in slicing romaine lettuce as thinly as possible. This does indeed produce a sophisticated salad but also results in the loss of much vitamin C contained in the leaves. I prefer to tear the green leaves, minimizing the loss of this delicate vitamin.

Island Greens Salad

Salatiká Nisiótika

Serves 6 to 8

Chicory frisée is now sometimes available in our markets, and its flavor is very similar to that of the wild greens popular throughout Greece and the islands. Escarole lettuce is from the same botanical family and its tender, mildly astringent inner leaves are a delicious addition to a green salad. If you cannot find these bitter greens add a finely sliced Belgian endive or a few beautiful deep crimson radicchio leaves to give your salad an intriguing bite and lift it out of the ordinary. Choose Belgian endives with tightly closed heads, and buy the freshest chicory greens you can find—the flavor changes to an unpleasant bitterness once they're past their peak. For this popular island salad choose several contrasting types of salad greens. Fresh lemon juice is the perfect dressing—as a general rule, the more bitter the greens, the more lemon juice you'll need.

5 cups of watercress, chicory frisée, spinach leaves,
curly endive, romaine, young dandelion, radicchio,
purslane, and/or arugula

2 slices whole-wheat bread, crusts removed and
cut into ½-inch dice

Coarse-grain sea salt and freshly ground black pepper to taste

¼ cup extra-virgin olive oil, or to taste

1 large clove garlic, cut into 2 or 3 pieces

2 tablespoons finely chopped Preserved Lemon (page 19) plus
2 tablespoons of its oil (see Note)

Juice of ½ small lemon, or to taste

⅓ cup coarsely chopped flat-leaf parsley

24 Elítses or 18 Niçoise olives, drained

1 small red onion, quartered and thinly sliced

3 tablespoons fresh herbs such as marjoram, basil, or oregano
or 2 tablespoons dried rígani (page 14)

Prepare the greens (page 289).

Sprinkle the bread dice with salt and a generous amount of pepper. Warm 2 tablespoons of the olive oil in a large heavy skillet and sauté the garlic over low heat until it becomes aromatic, 2 to 3 minutes. Remove with a slotted spoon and discard. Raise the heat to medium and fry the bread dice until golden brown on all sides. Drain between layers of paper towels.

Combine the Preserved Lemon and its oil, lemon juice, and pepper to taste, in a nonreactive bowl, and gradually whisk in the remaining 2 tablespoons olive oil.

Combine the greens, parsley, olives, onion, herbs, and croutons in a serving bowl. Pour over the dressing and toss with a wooden spoon and fork. Add salt and pepper, olive oil, and/or lemon juice to taste and serve at once.

Note You can substitute the juice of 1 whole lemon plus 2 tablespoons extra-virgin olive oil for the Preserved Lemon, oil, and juice of half a lemon if necessary.

Purslane Salad

Salatiká Glistrítha

Serves 4

If you have a garden, purslane is very easy to grow, and it can be made into a wonderfully refreshing salad, either on its own or with other salad greens for variety in taste and texture. Or try adding other vegetables to the greens, such as beets, potatoes, fresh fava beans, tomatoes, or garbanzos and other dried beans.

---

4 cups purslane sprigs or 1 cup purslane sprigs and 3 cups arugula, escarole, chicory frisée, romaine, and/or young spinach leaves

2 scallions, trimmed, the best green parts left intact, and thinly sliced, optional

Coarse-grain sea salt and cracked black pepper to taste

Strained juice of 1 lemon, or to taste

⅓ cup extra-virgin olive oil, or to taste

Thoroughly rinse the purslane and remove the small fleshy leaves in clusters (the stems are easily broken with your thumbnail). Prepare the greens (page 289).

Combine the greens and scallions in a salad bowl and sprinkle with salt and pepper, lemon juice, and olive oil. Toss with a wooden spoon and fork and add salt, pepper, and/or lemon juice to taste. Serve immediately.

Purslane and Young Beets

Salatiká Glistrítha ke Panzária

Serves 4

Sweet young beets and crunchy peppery purslane make an appealing combination. With its pretty crimson-green contrast, this is an attractive side dish for grilled meat, chicken, or fish and egg dishes. Other Mediterranean greens such as arugula, watercress, young dandelion leaves, or chicory frisée can be substituted for the purslane.

————

3 medium young beets, baked in a clay pot (page 274)
or boiled and peeled

Large pinch of ground cloves

Coarse-grain sea salt and cracked black pepper to taste

Strained juice of 1 large lemon

⅓ cup extra-virgin olive oil, or to taste

3 cups purslane sprigs

2 scallions, white parts only, thinly sliced

Cut the beets into julienne (large matchsticks). Place in a nonreactive bowl, sprinkle with the cloves, salt and pepper, and half the lemon juice and olive oil. Gently toss together, taking care not to break the beets. Cover and set aside for 1 hour or refrigerate for up to 4 hours.

Thoroughly rinse the purslane and remove the small fleshy leaves in clusters.

Combine the beets, purslane, and remaining lemon juice and olive oil in a salad bowl. Add salt and pepper to taste, sprinkle with the scallions, and serve immediately.

Wild Leaf Greens
Ágria Khórta

To Greeks *khórta* means green vegetables or wild greens, sometimes even including grass; to compound the confusion wild greens are occasionally called wild herbs, and all of these may be called *salatiká*! For the sake of clarity, here the term refers only to wild leaf greens, such as mustard, dandelions, and chicory, and green leafy vegetables (such as beet and turnip greens and radish tops).

The tenderest leaves may be used in green salads but the most popular method of preparing *khórta* is to boil the greens and serve as a vegetable, warm or at room temperature, dressed with olive oil and vinegar. Crusty bread, yogurt, country cheeses, and olives are traditional accompaniments. *Khórta* is also a favorite filling for pies (page 120) and a delicious addition to casseroles.

After the first fall rains wild greens grow in abundance on the hillsides and in the fields and the sight of village women picking their favorites for the family meal is common; during the season Greek markets also stock many different varieties of *khórta*. Among them is tender *vlíta*, known in the United States as amaranth greens and sometimes available in specialty markets. Some Chinese markets offer purple or water spinach, which has a similar sweet/sour flavor and makes a delicious substitute for spinach in Cretan pies (page 118). Purslane, dandelion greens, radish tops, turnip and beet greens and broccoli rabe also are all occasionally available.

Wild greens continue to grow in Greece throughout the winter and short spring. Wild chicory (*rathíki*), in particular, is at its best in March and April, just before its clear blue flowers appear, and a bowl of this bitter green has pride of place as an accompaniment to the Paschal lamb on the traditional Easter table. Come the early summer, however, the dry season and a shortage of water means the absence of the traditional and healthy *khórta* dishes from Greek tables until the fall.

Wild Leaf Greens Salad

Khórta Salatiká

Serves 4

The combination of bitter greens, mustard, vinegar, olive oil, and sea salt creates a delicious explosion of flavors in this salad. Choose only fresh young tender leaves and tear them into pieces, rather than chopping, to preserve as much vitamin C as possible. Cast-iron pots produce an unpleasant flavor in *khórta* and also reduce the valuable vitamin content, so always cook them in a stainless steel or enamel-lined saucepan. Wild greens do not shrink in cooking as much as spinach, so you need allow only about 2 packed cups of torn leaves per person.

1¼ pounds wild greens such as turnip greens,
radish tops, amaranth greens, water spinach,
or wild mustard (charlock)

½ teaspoon mustard

2 to 3 tablespoons aged red-wine vinegar (to taste)
or juice of 1 small lemon

⅓ cup extra-virgin olive oil

Coarse-grain sea salt and cracked black pepper to taste

Rinse the greens in several changes of cold water. Remove any tough stems from the turnip greens and radish tops and tear the leaves into bite-sized pieces. Break off the tender sprigs of leaves from the amaranth greens, water spinach, or wild mustard and discard any tougher stalks.

Steam the greens, or place in a saucepan, add ¼ cup boiling water, and cook, stirring once or twice with a fork: Amaranth greens take only 1 to 2 minutes, turnip greens and radish tops take 3 to 4 minutes, and water spinach and mustard around 5 minutes—take care not to overcook. Drain well in a colander, pressing the greens against the sides with a wooden spoon.

To serve, combine the mustard and vinegar and whisk in the olive oil. Pour over the greens and sprinkle with a generous amount of salt and pepper. Serve warm or at room temperature.

Vegetables and Salads

Beet Greens Salad
Salatiká Panzária

Serves 3

Greek cooks would not dream of throwing away the crisp green leaves of young beets. Instead they cook them (reserving the vitamin-rich cooking liquid for soup) and turn them into this healthful salad.

Fresh green leaves from 6 young beets

¼ cup boiling water

Juice of 1 small lemon or 2 tablespoons aged red-wine vinegar

¼ cup extra-virgin olive oil, or to taste

1 teaspoon dried rígani (page 14), briefly pounded in a small mortar

½ teaspoon coarse-grain sea salt, or to taste

Cracked black pepper to taste

Remove the thicker stems from the beet greens but leave tender thin stems intact. Rinse well, and tear into bite-sized pieces.

Place in a stainless steel or enamel-lined saucepan, add the boiling water, cover, and boil until barely tender, about 2 minutes. Drain in a colander, pressing the greens against the sides with a wooden spoon to extract as much moisture as possible.

Transfer to a platter and gently separate the leaves with a fork. Sprinkle with the lemon juice, olive oil, *rígani,* salt, and pepper. Serve warm or at room temperature.

Dandelion Greens Salad

Rathíki Salatiká

Serves 4

Most Greek markets boast several varieties of dandelion greens and those snapped up the most quickly are always the wild ones. Our own garden dandelions are often tough and not usually suitable for cooking, but Italian, Chinese, and specialty produce markets sell cultivated dandelions in season and they make a delicious *khórta*.

---

1 pound young dandelion leaves

½ cup boiling water

1 small clove garlic, finely chopped

Juice of 1 small lemon, or to taste

¼ cup extra-virgin olive oil

*Coarse-grain sea salt and cracked black
pepper to taste*

Discard the coarse dandelion stems, thoroughly rinse the leaves, and tear the leaves into 2- to 3-inch pieces.

Place in a stainless steel or enamel-lined saucepan, add the boiling water. Cover, and boil 1 to 2 minutes. Drain well in a colander, pressing the greens against the sides with a wooden spoon.

Transfer to a platter and gently separate the leaves with a fork. Whisk together the garlic, lemon juice, and olive oil and pour over the greens. Sprinkle generously with salt and pepper and serve warm or at room temperature.

Note If you use wild dandelion leaves, blanch them in boiling water for 1 minute to remove bitterness and drain before boiling a second time.

Pilafs and Pastas

Piláfi ke Macarónia

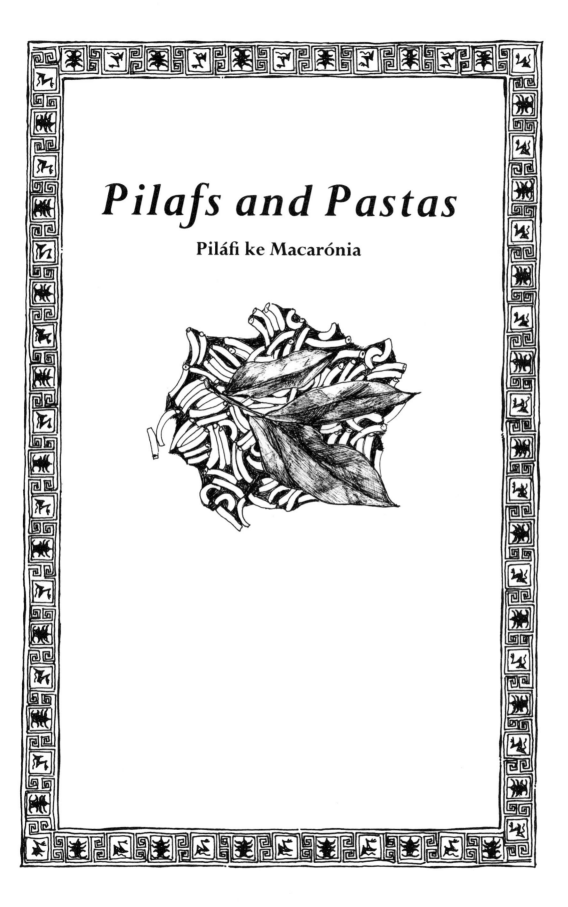

Savory rice dishes are known in Greece as *piláfi*. The rice is always cooked according to a basic method; to it are added meat, vegetables, or fish and one of a range of aromatic sauces to create any number of variations.

For any pilaf dish good-quality long-grain rice, such as Carolina or Patna, is essential. This is first cooked in olive oil or butter and then all the broth is added at once. The rice is removed from the heat and left in a warm spot while the grains absorb the liquid. For a successful pilaf, therefore, both rice and broth must be carefully measured; the amount of broth should be exactly double the quantity of rice.

In a properly made pilaf the rice grains are dry, firm, and separate and have a pleasantly mild and nutty flavor. The simple instructions for the *piláfi* included should produce perfect results every time. *Piláfi* is the ideal accompaniment to casseroles and stews and vegetable pilaf the perfect one-dish meal.

There are two types of Greek *macarónia*, or pasta. One, made with un-bleached all-purpose (soft-wheat) flour, is used to make thin flat strips like noodles or tagliatelle or shapes like ravioli, and cooked while fresh. The second type is made from durum (hard-wheat) flour and is dried and stored. Because of its high gluten content and an ability to retain its shape during cooking, this type is ideal for baked dishes such as *youvétsi* (spiced meat and *macarónia*) and *pastítsio* (page 317). Many of these *macarónia* are simple to make at home and their delicate flavor and ability to absorb aromatics makes them a perfect foil for sauces.

One unusual *macarónia* still made in villages, though difficult to dupli-cate here, deserves special mention. *Trahanás* is made from a stiff dough of hard-wheat flour, eggs, and yogurt or soured milk. The dough is rolled out, spread out to dry in the sun for a day or two, then forced through a special sieve to make an oatmeal-textured pasta. *Trahanás* is sometimes served as a pasta course but more often appears in a soup flavored with lemon juice, wine, egg yolks, or tomatoes.

Greek grocery stores sometimes sell fine-ground *farína* (semolina), a durum (hard-wheat) flour particularly suited to *macarónia*. *Macarónia* made with farína have a deliciously authentic country flavor and are ideal for use in oven-baked dishes such as Stuffed Macarónia in Country Broth (page 323). However, making *macarónia* with *farína* is not easy, and a machine is necessary to work the dough to the right texture. Greek grocery stores are also the place to find the long thin rolling pin needed to stretch the dough out and the special rolling pin covered with indented squares for cutting *macarónia* squares for Macedonian Pie (page 320).

As wheat was cultivated in Greece well before classical times, it's highly probable that *macarónia* has been produced there since antiquity—and there is indeed archaeological evidence to point in that direction. That being so, the simple and flavorsome recipes included here, popular all over Greece and the islands in regional variations, are based on a rich and ancient culinary tradition.

Rice Dishes
Piláfi

Perfect Pilaf
Piláfi

Serves 4

This simple bay-scented pilaf is excellent with casseroles and grilled dishes. A good fruity olive oil and a well-flavored broth produce the best results and a last-minute sprinkling of parsley and paprika adds a touch of color. (If necessary, it can be reheated over a heat diffuser mat or in a double boiler.)

———

(continued)

2 tablespoons extra-virgin olive oil

1½ cups long-grain rice, such as Carolina or Patna

3 bay leaves

1 teaspoon sea salt, or to taste

3 cups hot fat-free Chicken or Meat Broth

(pages 461 and 467) or water

FOR SERVING

Juice of ½ lemon

Finely chopped flat-leaf parsley

Pinch of paprika

Cracked black pepper to taste

Heat the olive oil in a heavy saucepan and stir the rice over low heat until the grains whiten, about 2 minutes. Add the bay leaves, salt, and broth, raise the heat to medium, and boil uncovered, without stirring, until the liquid has disappeared and holes appear in the surface of the rice, about 10 minutes. Remove from the heat, cover with a clean kitchen towel and a tight-fitting lid, and set aside for 30 to 40 minutes in a warm spot such as the back of the unheated oven. The grains will become firm, dry, and separated.

Transfer the rice to a warm platter or bowl and lightly separate the grains with a fork. Discard the bay leaves and sprinkle the pilaf with the lemon juice, parsley, paprika, and pepper. Serve hot or warm.

Pilaf with Currants and Pine Nuts

Piláfi me Stafíli Korinthiakó

Serves 4

The strong clove, ginger root, and orange zest flavorings reveal the Eastern influences behind this spicy pilaf. Currants and pine nuts are traditional additions sometimes cooked with the rice, sometimes added at the last minute. Adding them after the rice has absorbed all the liquid seems the best way to preserve their textures and distinctive flavors. Always served cold, this is especially good with game.

––––––––

¼ cup extra-virgin olive oil, or to taste

1½ cups long-grain rice, such as Carolina or Patna

4 whole cloves

1-inch piece of fresh ginger root, peeled

*1 bouquet garni (2 bay leaves, 3 sprigs of parsley,
and 1 sprig of thyme, tied together)*

2-inch strip of orange zest

3 cups hot fat-free Chicken Broth (page 461) or water

1 teaspoon sea salt, or to taste

*⅔ cup currants, soaked in 2 tablespoons Mavrodaphne
wine or warm water for 1 hour*

½ cup lightly toasted pine nuts or coarsely chopped walnuts

FOR SERVING

Juice of 1 small lemon

½ small red onion, thinly sliced

*2 tablespoons finely chopped flat-leaf parsley or
coarsely chopped fresh coriander*

*1 tablespoon finely chopped Preserved Lemon
(page 19), optional*

Cracked black pepper to taste

Heat 2 tablespoons of the olive oil in a heavy saucepan, add the rice, and stir over low heat until the grains whiten, about 2 minutes. Add the cloves, ginger root, bouquet garni, orange zest, broth, and salt. Raise the heat to medium and boil uncovered, without stirring, until the liquid has disappeared and holes appear in the surface of the rice, about 10 minutes. Stir in the currants and pine nuts with a fork and remove from the heat. Cover with a clean kitchen towel and a tight-fitting lid and set aside for 30 to 40 minutes in a warm spot such as the back of the unheated oven.

Discard the ginger root, bouquet garni, and orange zest, and turn the pilaf out onto a platter. Lightly separate the grains with a fork and set aside to cool.

To serve, sprinkle with the lemon juice, onion, parsley, Preserved Lemon, salt, pepper, and remaining 2 tablespoons olive oil.

Pilafs and Pastas

Eggplant Pilaf
with Glazed Tomatoes

Piláfi me Melitzánes ke Domátes

Serves 4

Serve this flavorful pilaf, garnished with thin strips of smoky broiled peppers and caramelized tomatoes, as a side dish for grilled meats or chicken, *souvlákia*, or sausages. For vegetable lovers it makes a satisfying lunch or supper.

———

2 medium eggplants

Coarse-grain sea salt

¼ cup extra-virgin olive oil

1½ tablespoons unsalted butter

⅓ cup fides (vermicelli) broken into small pieces

1 small onion, finely chopped

1¼ cups long-grain rice, such as Carolina or Patna

4 whole cloves

2 bay leaves

*2½ cups hot fat-free Chicken or Meat Broth
(pages 461 and 467) or water*

*⅓ cup lightly toasted almonds or walnuts,
coarsely chopped*

⅓ cup currants or small dark seedless raisins

12 large cherry tomatoes

½ teaspoon sugar, or to taste

Cracked black pepper to taste

2 medium green or yellow bell peppers

Juice of ½ lemon

¼ cup coarsely chopped flat-leaf parsley

Strained Yogurt (*page 8*)

Trim the ends from the eggplants and cut into ¾-inch dice. Sprinkle with ½ tablespoon salt and set aside for 30 minutes to sweat.

Dry the eggplant with paper towels. Heat 3 tablespoons of the olive oil in a large heavy skillet and lightly brown the eggplant on all sides over medium heat. Drain between layers of paper towels and set aside.

Melt the butter in a heavy saucepan and cook the vermicelli over low heat until the butter turns a deep golden brown, about 6 minutes; take care not to burn the butter. Add the onion and cook 5 minutes. Stir in the rice, cloves, and bay leaves and cook, stirring, until the grains whiten, about 2 minutes. Add the broth and ½ teaspoon salt, raise the heat to medium, and boil uncovered, without stirring, until the liquid has disappeared, and holes appear in the surface of the rice, about 10 minutes. Stir in the eggplant, almonds, and currants with a fork. Remove from the heat, cover with a clean kitchen towel and tight-fitting lid, and set aside for 30 to 40 minutes in a warm spot such as the back of the unheated oven.

Fifteen minutes before you are ready to serve, heat the broiler. With a sharp knife, slash open the top of each tomato and sprinkle the insides with a pinch of salt, the sugar, and a generous amount of pepper. Arrange the bell peppers on a broiler pan and broil 2 inches from the heat, turning, until the skin is shriveled and darkened. Remove from the pan and arrange the tomatoes on the pan. Brush with the remaining 1 tablespoon olive oil and broil until the tops are darkened and slightly caramelized. While the tomatoes are cooking, remove the core and seeds from the peppers. Rub off the skin and any remaining seeds with your fingers, dry with paper towels, and cut into thin strips. Turn the pilaf out onto a warm platter. Arrange the peppers on top, surround with the tomatoes, and sprinkle with the lemon juice and parsley. Serve hot or warm, with bowls of yogurt.

Pilaf with Green Lentils
Piláfi me Fakés

Serves 4

Those who are fond of the flavor of good olive oil will appreciate this dish. Coriander, allspice, and bay leaves perfume the lentils and rice, and when they are cooked, a sweet-and-sour honey, vinegar, and olive oil sauce is poured over them. The result is a highly seasoned pilaf with an unusual combination of flavors. Fresh Fava Bean and Sweet Carrot Pilaf (page 307) is the spring version of this winter dish.

---

*⅔ cup green lentils, picked over, rinsed, and soaked
for 2 hours in cold water to cover*

⅓ cup extra-virgin olive oil

1 medium onion, cut into quarters and thinly sliced

*1½ tablespoons dried coriander seeds, crushed, or
1 tablespoon ground coriander*

½ teaspoon ground allspice

3 bay leaves

*¾ pound carrots, halved or quartered lengthwise
and cut into 1-inch lengths*

¾ cup long-grain rice, such as Carolina or Patna

*2 cups hot fat-free Chicken or Meat Broth
(pages 461 and 467) or water*

1 teaspoon sea salt, or to taste

1 tablespoon aromatic honey, such as Hymettus

1 tablespoon aged red-wine vinegar

3 tablespoons finely chopped flat-leaf parsley

1 tablespoon dried rígani (page 14), crumbled

½ teaspoon cracked black pepper, or to taste

FOR SERVING

Strained Yogurt (page 8)

Drain the lentils and place in a saucepan with water to cover. Bring to a boil, drain, rinse, and set aside.

Heat 2 tablespoons of the olive oil in a heavy saucepan and sauté the onion over low heat until soft, about 6 minutes. Stir in the coriander, allspice, and bay leaves, add the carrots, and cook, stirring occasionally, 5 minutes longer. Stir in the rice and cook, stirring, until the grains whiten, about 2 minutes. Add the lentils, broth, and ¾ teaspoon of the salt. Raise the heat to medium and boil uncovered, without stirring, until the liquid has disappeared and holes appear in the surface of the rice, about 10 minutes. Remove from the heat, cover with a clean kitchen towel and tight-fitting lid, and set aside for 30 minutes in a warm spot such as the back of the unheated oven.

Combine the honey and vinegar in a small saucepan, stir in the remaining olive oil, and heat to warm. Stir in the parsley, *rígani*, pepper, and remaining ¼ teaspoon salt. Turn the pilaf out onto a warm platter and pour over the honey sauce. Serve hot with bowls of yogurt.

Fresh Fava Bean and Sweet Carrot Pilaf

Piláfi me Fáva ke Karótta

Serves 4

When the first fresh fava beans and tender young carrots appear in the market this popular spring dish is served in homes throughout Greece. The carrots cook to a sweet velvety texture with the rice, the crunchy beans are added at the last minute. Served warm or cold, with a bowl of yogurt and a green salad or wild greens dish, this is a satisfying meal on its own. It's also a perfect complement to grilled lamb.

———

(continued)

2 tablespoons extra-virgin olive oil

2 shallots, finely chopped

1 pound young carrots, halved or quartered lengthwise
and cut into 1-inch lengths

¾ cup long-grain rice, such as Carolina or Patna

1 teaspoon sea salt, or to taste

1 teaspoon honey

2 bay leaves

¾ cup hot fat-free Chicken Broth (page 461) or water

¾ cup hot water

1½ cups shelled fresh fava beans
(about 1½ pounds in the pod)

Juice of 1 lemon

Cracked black pepper to taste

FOR SERVING

Small sprigs of fresh dill or young mint, torn into
small pieces just before using

Heat 1½ tablespoons of the olive oil in a heavy saucepan and sauté the shallots over low heat until soft, about 5 minutes. Add the carrots and cook 2 to 3 minutes, stirring with a wooden spoon. Add the rice and cook, stirring, until the grains whiten, about 2 minutes. Add ¾ teaspoon of the salt, the honey, bay leaves, and broth. Raise the heat to medium and boil uncovered, without stirring, until the liquid has disappeared, and holes appear in the surface of the rice, about 10 minutes. Remove from the heat, cover with a clean kitchen towel and tight-fitting lid, and set aside for 30 to 40 minutes in a warm spot such as the back of the unheated oven.

Peel the skins from the fava beans. Heat the remaining ½ tablespoon olive oil in a small saucepan, add the beans, cover, and cook 4 minutes over low heat to soften. Add half the lemon juice, the remaining ¼ teaspoon salt, and pepper.

Stir the beans and cooking juices into the pilaf with a fork and turn out onto a warm platter. Sprinkle with the remaining lemon juice and the dill.

Saffron Rice with Mussels

Mýthia me Rísi

Serves 4

On the last day of one of the cooking courses I ran on the island of Crete a large basket was delivered to one of my students. Inside was a marine treasure trove—sea urchins, baby squid, mussels, shrimp, cuttlefish, razor clams, and sea anemones. Using this generous gift, we made a lovely saffron pilaf. Here is a simpler version of that delightful dish—try it also with baby squid, cuttlefish, shrimp, or a combination of seafood.

———

1 teaspoon saffron threads

32 to 40 mussels

3 tablespoons extra-virgin olive oil

3 shallots, finely chopped

1¼ cups long-grain rice, such as Carolina or Patna

2 bay leaves

2 cups hot water

½ cup lightly toasted pine nuts

⅓ cup currants or small dark seedless raisins

¼ cup finely chopped flat-leaf parsley

Sea salt and cracked black pepper to taste

Juice of ½ lemon

FOR SERVING

Lemon wedges

Heat the saffron in a small dry skillet until aromatic, about 1 minute. Set aside.

Discard any open mussels and those with broken shells. With a stiff brush, thoroughly scrub the mussels under cold running water and pull off their "beards." Place in a large saucepan, cover, and set over medium-high heat. Holding the lid firmly in place, shake the saucepan once or twice.

(continued)

After a minute or two all the mussels should have opened; discard any that do not open. Pour the mussel broth into a small bowl, crumble in the saffron, and set aside. Remove all but 8 mussels from their shells, reserving the juices, and set aside.

Heat 1½ tablespoons of the olive oil in a heavy saucepan and sauté half the shallots over medium-low heat until pale golden, about 5 minutes. Stir in the rice, and cook, stirring, until the grains whiten, about 2 minutes. Strain the saffron broth and add to the rice with the bay leaves and hot water. Raise the heat to medium and boil uncovered, without stirring, until all the liquid has disappeared and holes appear in the surface of the rice, about 10 minutes. Stir in the pine nuts and currants with a fork. Remove from the heat, cover with a clean kitchen towel and tight-fitting lid, and set aside for 30 minutes in a warm spot such as the back of the unheated oven.

Five minutes before you are ready to serve, heat the remaining 1½ tablespoons olive oil in a small skillet and sauté the remaining shallots over low heat until soft, about 3 minutes. Add the parsley, salt and pepper, and half the lemon juice and heat to warm. Add the shelled mussels, cover, and heat 1 minute over very low heat.

Stir the mussels and parsley mixture into the pilaf with a fork, turn out onto a warm platter, and sprinkle with the remaining lemon juice and reserved mussel juices. Surround with the lemon wedges and the mussels in their shells and serve at once.

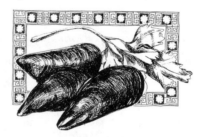

Spiced Shrimp Pilaf

Piláfi Aromatikó me Garíthes

Serves 4

Although this island pilaf is simple to make, it looks splendidly exotic and colorful, with its coriander- and turmeric-flavored rice, sweet tomato and shrimp sauce, and garnish of yogurt, parsley, and piquant capers. Although saffron is popular for coloring and flavoring *piláfi*, the Greeks use it only in dishes made with a very light broth, which preserves its delicate fragrance and color. As this pilaf is cooked in a heavier broth, the preferred aromatic is the less subtle (less expensive) turmeric.

———

1 1/2 pounds medium shrimp in the shell

1/4 cup extra-virgin olive oil

1 cup chopped onion

1/2 cup chopped celery

3 bay leaves

2 shallots, finely chopped

1 teaspoon ground coriander

1/2 teaspoon turmeric

1 1/4 cups long-grain rice, such as Carolina or Patna

1/2 teaspoon sea salt, or to taste

3 ripe medium tomatoes, peeled, seeded, and diced

Pinch of sugar

1/2 teaspoon cracked black pepper, or to taste

1 teaspoon dried rígani (page 14), crumbled

FOR SERVING

1/3 cup Strained Yogurt (page 8)

2 tablespoons finely chopped flat-leaf parsley

1 tablespoon capers, rinsed and coarsely chopped

(continued)

Rinse the shrimp, and shell all but 4 reserving the shells. Devein all the shrimp, cover, and refrigerate.

Heat 1½ tablespoons of the olive oil in a heavy saucepan, and sauté the onion and celery over low heat until golden, about 15 minutes. Add the shrimp shells (or 2 shelled shrimp), 1 of the bay leaves broken into 2 pieces, and 2 cups water. Bring to a boil over medium heat, cover, reduce the heat, and simmer 40 minutes. Strain the broth through a fine sieve into a bowl, pressing the solids against the sides of the sieve with the back of a wooden spoon. Add water if necessary to make 2½ cups and set aside.

Heat 1 tablespoon of the remaining olive oil in a heavy saucepan and sauté the shallots over low heat until pale golden, about 6 minutes. Stir in the coriander, turmeric, rice, and remaining 2 bay leaves. Cook, stirring, until the rice whitens, about 2 minutes. Add the shrimp broth and salt, raise the heat to medium, and boil uncovered, without stirring, until the liquid has disappeared, and holes appear in the surface of the rice, about 10 minutes. Remove from the heat, cover with a clean kitchen towel and tight-fitting lid, and set aside for 30 minutes in a warm spot such as the back of the unheated oven.

Heat the remaining 1½ tablespoons olive oil in a heavy skillet. Sauté the shrimp in their shells 2 minutes over medium-low heat and add the shelled shrimp. Cook, stirring occasionally, until pink and opaque all the way through, 3 to 5 minutes. Remove with a slotted spoon and keep warm. Add the tomatoes, sugar, and pepper to the skillet. Cook 1 minute, add the *rígani,* and return the shelled shrimp to the skillet. Lower the heat, simmer 1 minute longer, and season to taste. Warm the yogurt in a small saucepan over low heat.

Turn the pilaf out onto a warm platter, pour over the tomato and shrimp sauce, and spoon the yogurt on top. Sprinkle with the parsley and capers and garnish with the shrimp in the shell. Serve at once.

Pasta

Macarónia

Serves 4 (Makes about 1½ pounds dough)

Although you can use a pasta machine to do some of the work in making *macarónia*, I usually prefer to roll out the dough by hand.

Macarónia cut in ¼-inch-wide strips (what the Italians call tagliatelle) are easy to produce without a machine. For a soft and pliant dough all the ingredients should be at room temperature and the dough should be well kneaded.

2½ cups unbleached all-purpose flour

3 large eggs

Mound 2¼ cups of the flour on a large clean work surface and make a deep hollow in the center. Break the eggs into the hollow and lightly beat them with a fork. Little by little draw in the flour with your fingers and mix it with the eggs. Continue until you have incorporated all the flour; add some or all of the remaining flour if the dough feels sticky. Knead the dough for at least 5 minutes, until the dough leaves the work surface clean, adding a little more flour if necessary. Tightly wrap the dough in plastic wrap and set aside for 10 to 30 minutes; do not refrigerate.

Lightly dust a rolling pin and a clean work surface with flour. Divide the dough into 6 portions and roll out each as thin as possible without tearing. Use the rolling pin to push, rather than press, the dough into a large rectangular shape. Trim the sides of each sheet and loosely roll it up into a cylinder. With a sharp knife, cut each cylinder crosswise into strips of desired width. Separate the strips, and spread them on kitchen cloths or a pasta drying rack to dry slightly, about 15 minutes, before cooking. They are ready to cook when they are no longer sticky but are not so dry that they would crack if folded.

Macarónia with Olive, Anchovy, and Sweet Tomato Sauce

Macarónia me Eliés ke Sáltsa Domátas

Serves 4

Strong flavors and bold color contrasts make this simple dish exceptionally attractive and appetizing. The cooked *macarónia* is coated with an anchovy-garlic paste, and then a sweet tomato sauce is poured over it. Interestingly enough, although basil is seen growing in pots all over Greece, this is one of the few basil-flavored Greek dishes I know.

---

*3 whole salted anchovies (page 460), filleted, or 6
salted anchovy fillets*

¹/₂ cup extra-virgin olive oil, or more to taste

2 cloves garlic, thinly sliced

*12 Náfplion or other Greek green olives, blanched in boiling
water for 3 seconds, patted dry, pitted, and coarsely chopped*

6 large ripe tomatoes, peeled

1 teaspoon honey

Sea salt to taste

¹/₂ teaspoon cracked black pepper, or to taste

*2 tablespoons fresh basil or 1 tablespoon chopped
fresh thyme or oregano*

*1 recipe Macarónia (page 313), cut into ¹/₄-inch
strips and dried for 15 minutes*

Soak the anchovy fillets in cold water for 5 minutes. Rinse, pat dry, and cut into small pieces. Place in a small bowl with 2 tablespoons of the olive oil and set aside.

Fill a large pot with lightly salted water and bring to a boil. Meanwhile, heat 2 tablespoons of the remaining olive oil in a small heavy skillet and sauté the garlic over low heat until aromatic; do not let it color. Transfer the garlic and oil to a wooden mortar or bowl, add the anchovies and their oil, and pound together until mixed but not smooth. Return the mixture to the skillet, add the olives, and heat to warm.

Cut the tomatoes in half, squeeze out the seeds, and slice into thin wedges. Heat 1 tablespoon of the remaining olive oil in a second small skillet over medium heat and add the tomatoes, honey, salt, and pepper. Cook just until the tomatoes begin to lose their shape, about 1 minute. Tear the basil leaves into small pieces and stir into the tomatoes. Add the *macarónia* to the boiling water and cook only until they rise to the surface, about 3 minutes; drain immediately.

Combine the *macarónia* and olive sauce in a warm shallow bowl. Pour over the tomatoes, sprinkle with the remaining 3 tablespoons olive oil, and serve at once.

Pilafs and Pastas

Macarónia with Chicken and Wild Greens

Macarónia me Kotópoulo ke Khórta

Serves 4

This popular dish is simple and quick to prepare but it does require top-quality ingredients. Be sure to use a well-flavored olive oil, plump olives, and the freshest young beet or dandelion greens you can find.

———

1½ cups thin 1-inch-long strips of cooked chicken

2 tablespoons aged red-wine vinegar or 1 tablespoon balsamic vinegar

½ teaspoon freshly ground black pepper, or to taste

¼ cup extra-virgin olive oil, or to taste

1 clove garlic, cut into 2 or 3 pieces

2 cups tender young beet greens or dandelion greens, tough stems removed, and leaves torn into small pieces

¼ cup boiling water

⅓ cup lightly toasted pine nuts

24 Elítses or 12 Niçoise olives, drained, pitted, and coarsely chopped

1 recipe Macarónia (page 313), cut into ¼-inch strips and dried for 15 minutes

Sea salt to taste

FOR SERVING

Grated aged **myzíthra, halloúmi,** *or* **kasséri** *cheese*

Combine the chicken, vinegar, pepper, and 1 tablespoon of the olive oil in a bowl, toss to mix, and set aside.

Heat 2 tablespoons of the remaining olive oil in a large heavy skillet and sauté the garlic over low heat until pale golden; don't let it burn. Discard the garlic and set aside the skillet.

Fill a large pot with lightly salted water and bring to a boil. Meanwhile, place the greens in a heavy saucepan, add the ¼ cup boiling water, cover, and gently boil 1 minute. Drain well, spread between layers of paper towels, and blot dry.

Return the skillet to low heat and add the chicken, pine nuts, and olives. Cook 3 minutes, stirring occasionally with a fork. Add the greens and heat through. Add the *macarónia* to the boiling water and cook only until they rise to the surface, about 3 minutes; drain.

Combine the chicken mixture and *macarónia* in a warm earthenware bowl and toss to mix. Sprinkle with the remaining 1 tablespoon olive oil, salt, and pepper to taste. Serve at once, with bowls of the cheese.

Macarónia and Spicy Meat in a Pie

Pastítsio

Serves 8

This traditional dish, composed of layers of *macarónia*, a sweet and spicy meat sauce, and a creamy cheese sauce, makes no pretensions to elegance but its heady aroma, beautiful bubbling and golden-crusted appearance, and utterly delicious taste are pleasure enough. It needs only the simplest of accompaniments—a salad of wild greens (page 295) is ideal.

(continued)

1/3 cup extra-virgin olive oil

2 cups finely chopped onion

1 1/2 pounds lean beef or lamb or a mixture
of both, ground

1/2 cup red wine or 2 tablespoons aged red-wine vinegar

6 large ripe tomatoes, peeled, seeded,
and diced, juices reserved

1 1/2 to 2 tablespoons ground cinnamon

Large pinch of cayenne pepper

1 tablespoon dried marjoram, crumbled

1/2 cup finely chopped flat-leaf parsley

Sea salt and cracked black pepper to taste

WHITE SAUCE

5 tablespoons all-purpose flour

4 tablespoons unsalted butter

4 cups warm milk

1/2 teaspoon grated nutmeg

3 eggs, separated

2 egg yolks

1 1/2 pounds elbow macaroni or penne

1 cup small-curd cottage cheese, drained

1/2 cup grated féta cheese

2 tablespoons unsalted butter, melted

1 cup fresh fine bread crumbs, dried
5 minutes in a low oven

1/4 cup grated kasséri or parmesan cheese

8 Elítses or Niçoise olives, drained, pitted, and cut in half

Warm 3 tablespoons of the olive oil in a heavy skillet and sauté the onion
over medium-low heat until pale golden, about 5 minutes. Add the meat,
raise the heat, and cook, stirring and breaking up any lumps with a spoon,

until lightly browned, about 6 minutes. Add the red wine and boil until reduced by half. Add the tomatoes and their juices, 1 tablespoon of the cinnamon, and the cayenne pepper, and cook until the liquid is reduced by half. Add the marjoram, half the parsley, a pinch of salt, and a generous amount of pepper. Simmer 5 minutes longer and add cinnamon, salt and pepper to taste; the sauce should be highly flavored.

Fill a large pot with lightly salted water and bring to a boil. Meanwhile, melt the 4 tablespoons butter in a heavy saucepan and stir in the flour with a wooden spoon to make a roux. Cook, stirring, over low heat until the roux is smooth and light gold in color. Stir in the milk ½ cup at a time, adding more only when the sauce is smooth. Cook, stirring, until the sauce comes to a low boil. Remove from the heat, stir in the nutmeg and 5 egg yolks, and set aside.

Arrange a rack in the center of the oven and heat the oven to 350°F.

Cook the macaroni in the boiling water until barely soft, about 10 minutes. Drain and rinse briefly under cold running water. Shake the colander once or twice and set aside to dry.

Stir the cottage cheese, 6 tablespoons of the *féta* cheese, and a little pepper into the white sauce. Whisk the egg whites until they hold soft peaks and fold half of them into the white sauce. Combine the remaining egg whites and 1 tablespoon *féta* cheese, the parsley, 1 cup of the white sauce, a pinch of cinnamon, and the macaroni in a large bowl.

Brush a baking dish with half the melted butter and 1 tablespoon of the remaining olive oil, and sprinkle with half the bread crumbs. Spread one third of the macaroni mixture over the bottom of the dish and cover with half the meat filling. Spread a thin layer of macaroni over the meat, cover with the remaining filling and then the remaining macaroni. Cover with the white sauce, lightly smooth the top with a spatula, and sprinkle with the remaining bread crumbs and the *kasséri* cheese. Set 2 olive halves, cut sides down, in the center of each of what will be 8 serving portions and sprinkle with the remaining olive oil and melted butter.

Bake 40 minutes, or until a deep golden brown. Let rest for 10 minutes before cutting into serving portions.

Macedonian Pie

Lagánes

Serves 10

I once spent a week in a Macedonian village where the inhabitants seemed
to exist solely on this glorious dish. *Lagánes* (from which the Italian word
lasagna derives) is an extravagant pie of thin *macarónia* squares, layered
with three sauces, spicy sausages, and wild greens, and topped with *kasséri*
cheese and bread crumbs. Freshly baked, with each component in perfect
balance, this dish is a triumphant success.

----

*3¹/₂ cups unbleached all-purpose flour or semolina
(farína, page 462) or a mixture of both*

4 large eggs

MEAT SAUCE

2 tablespoons extra-virgin olive oil

1 cup finely chopped onion

1 pound lean beef, finely ground

¹/₄ cup finely chopped flat-leaf parsley

1 tablespoon dried rígani (page 14), crumbled

1 teaspoon ground allspice

¹/₂ cup dry white wine

2-inch strip of orange zest

3 bay leaves

Sea salt and cracked black pepper to taste

SAUSAGE FILLING

*Two 4- to 5-inch sausages (pages 233, 235 or 238), casings
discarded, cut into small dice or 1 cup finely diced lean
prosciutto*

1 tablespoon extra-virgin olive oil

*Fresh leaves from 6 young beets, cooked, drained, and chopped
(page 296) or ¹/₂ pound fresh spinach, chopped*

WHITE SAUCE

3 cups milk

3 tablespoons unsalted butter

3 tablespoons unbleached all-purpose flour

½ teaspoon grated nutmeg

3 egg yolks

1 cup grated graviéra or Gruyère cheese

2 tablespoons unsalted butter, melted

3 tablespoons extra-virgin olive oil

*1 cup fresh fine bread crumbs, briefly dried
in a low oven*

1 cup small-curd cottage cheese, drained

½ cup grated féta cheese

*3 cups Tomato Sauce (page 431), made with
cinnamon and parsley*

2 tablespoons grated kasséri or parmesan cheese

Make a dough with the 3½ cups flour and 4 eggs, as directed on page 319. Wrap the dough in plastic wrap and set aside.

To make the meat sauce, heat the olive oil in a heavy skillet and sauté the onion over medium-low heat until pale golden, about 8 minutes. Add the meat, raise the heat, stirring with a wooden spoon to break up any lumps, and cook, until lightly browned, about 5 minutes. Add the parsley, *rígani*, allspice, wine, orange zest, bay leaves, and salt and pepper, and simmer until most of the liquid has evaporated. Set aside.

To make the sausage filling, heat the olive oil in a second skillet and lightly brown the sausage dice. Drain on paper towels, combine with the beet greens and set aside.

Divide the dough into 6 portions. Dust a rolling pin and a clean work surface with flour. Roll out each portion as thin as possible into a 6-inch-wide strip. Trim the edges and cut in half lengthwise, then into 3-inch squares. Lightly dust with flour and spread on clean kitchen towels for a few minutes to dry. Fill a large saucepan with lightly salted water and bring to a boil.

(continued)

Meanwhile, to make the white sauce, heat the milk just to a simmer and remove from the heat. Melt the butter in a heavy saucepan and stir in the flour with a wooden spoon. Cook, stirring, over low heat until smooth and light gold in color. Briskly stir in the milk ½ cup at a time, adding more only when the sauce is smooth. Cook, stirring, until the sauce comes to a low boil. Remove from the heat, stir in the nutmeg, egg yolks, and *graviéra* cheese, and set aside.

Add the *macarónia* squares to the boiling water, 4 or 5 at a time, and cook until they rise to the surface, about 4 minutes. Drain on paper towels.

Arrange a rack in the center of the oven and heat the oven to 375°F. Brush a large heavy baking dish, at least 2½ inches deep, with half the melted butter and 2 tablespoons of the olive oil and sprinkle with half the bread crumbs. Cover the bottom of the dish with a single layer of *macarónia*. Remove the orange zest and bay leaves from the meat sauce and spoon half the meat sauce over the *macarónia*. Combine the cottage cheese, *féta* cheese, and ½ teaspoon pepper, and spoon half of this mixture over the meat. Spoon over ½ cup white sauce and cover with a third of the remaining *macarónia*. Spread the sausage filling over the *macarónia*, cover with half the tomato sauce, and then with half the remaining *macarónia*. Spoon over the remaining meat sauce and cottage cheese mixture, and then ½ cup of the white sauce. Cover with the remaining *macarónia*, tomato sauce, and, finally, the white sauce. Sprinkle with the remaining bread crumbs, the *kasséri*, and remaining 1 tablespoon olive oil and melted butter.

Bake 30 minutes, or until golden brown and aromatic. Let rest 10 minutes before cutting into serving portions.

Stuffed Macarónia in Country Broth

Macarónia Yemistá

Serves 4

These stuffed *macarónia* are traditionally served at celebrations, and I first sampled them at a country wedding on the island of Crete. Squares of *macarónia* are stuffed with a spicy meat or chicken mixture, baked until golden brown, and served in large shallow bowls with broth to moisten and plump the *macarónia* and a sprinkling of olive oil. Bowls of cheese, warm yogurt, or tomato sauce and a salad of wild greens (page 295) are traditional accompaniments.

⅓ cup extra-virgin olive oil, or more to taste

1 large onion, finely chopped

¾ pound lean beef or lamb, finely ground twice

*4½ cups Meat or Chicken Broth or Meat Stock
(pages 461 and 467)*

1 teaspoon ground cinnamon, or to taste

½ teaspoon sea salt, or to taste

1 teaspoon freshly ground black pepper, or to taste

1 tablespoon dried rígani (page 14), crumbled

¼ cup finely chopped flat-leaf parsley

*2½ cups unbleached all-purpose flour or semolina (farína,
page 462) or a mixture of both*

3 large eggs

FOR SERVING

*Grated aged myzíthra, or kasséri, or
parmesan cheese, or*

3 cups Strained Yogurt (page 8), or

*Tomato Sauce (pages 432 and 433), made with rígani or
parsley, warmed*

(continued)

Pilafs and Pastas

Heat 2 tablespoons of the olive oil in a heavy skillet and sauté the onion over medium-low heat until golden, about 12 minutes, stirring frequently. Add the meat and cook, stirring to break up any lumps, until lightly browned and any meat juices have evaporated. Spread on paper towels to drain, drain off the fat from the skillet, and wipe it out. Return the meat and onion mixture to the skillet, add ½ cup of the broth, the cinnamon, salt, pepper, *rígani*, and parsley. Simmer 5 minutes over low heat and set aside.

Make a dough with the 2½ cups flour and 3 eggs as directed on page 319. Divide into 6 portions and let rest for 10 minutes. Dust a rolling pin and clean work surface with flour and stretch and roll out each as thin as possible without tearing. Trim the edges and cut into 2-inch strips, then into 2-inch squares. You should have about 40 squares.

Heat the oven to 375°F. Place 1 teaspoon of filling in the center of each square and, with lightly dampened forefinger and thumb, gently pull 2 opposite corners of each square up and together. Repeat with the other 2 corners so they all meet in the center to make a neat packet.

Brush a heavy baking dish, at least 2 inches deep and large enough to hold all the *macarónia* in a single layer, with olive oil. Arrange the *macarónia* in it and brush them with olive oil. Bake 10 minutes, then reduce the oven temperature to 350°F and bake 10 to 15 minutes longer, or until light golden brown. Season the remaining broth to taste and pour into the dish. Bake 15 to 25 minutes longer, or until the *macarónia* are tender; taste one to test.

Divide the *macarónia* and broth among individual shallow bowls, sprinkle with the remaining olive oil, and serve with bowls of the cheese, yogurt, or Tomato Sauce.

Variations

- Cooked chicken cut into tiny dice can be substituted for the meat, or substitute the filling for Baked Cheese and Spinach Pies (page 116). Use ½ cup white wine and 4 cups Chicken Broth instead of Meat Broth or Meat Stock.

Stuffed Macarónia with Tomato Sauce

Macarónia Yemistá me Sáltsa Domátas

Serves 4

This is the Greek version of ravioli—*macarónia* stuffed with a nutmeg-spiced chicken and cheese mixture.

2½ cups unbleached all-purpose flour

4 large eggs

2 quarts Chicken Broth (page 461) or water

1 cup finely diced cooked chicken

2 tablespoons finely chopped flat-leaf parsley

2 egg yolks

2 tablespoons minced scallion

¼ teaspoon grated nutmeg

¼ cup grated féta or kasséri cheese

½ cup small-curd cottage cheese, drained

Sea salt and cracked black pepper to taste

FOR SERVING

1 cup Scorched Tomato Sauce (page 434)

½ cup Rich Chicken Broth (page 461)

Extra-virgin olive oil, to taste

Grated aged myzíthra or féta cheese

Make a dough with the 2½ cups flour and 3 of the eggs, as directed on page 319. Divide into 6 portions and let rest for 10 minutes. Lightly dust a rolling pin and clean work surface with flour and roll out the dough as thin as possible without tearing. Trim the edges, cut into strips 2½ inches wide, then into 2½-inch squares; you should have at least 24. Spread them out to dry for a few minutes. Bring the broth to a low boil. (*continued*)

Meanwhile, combine the chicken, parsley, egg yolks, scallion, nutmeg, *féta*, cottage cheese, and salt and pepper. Beat the remaining egg with a little water. Place 1 tablespoon of the filling in the center of each *macarónia* square, lightly brush the edges of each square with the beaten egg, and fold over to form a triangle. Trim into half-moons with a pastry wheel, firmly pressing the edges together to seal.

Add half the *macarónia* to the broth and cook until they rise to the surface, about 6 minutes. Drain, keep warm, and cook the remaining *macarónia*.

To serve, combine the Scorched Tomato Sauce and Rich Chicken Broth in a saucepan, season to taste, and heat to warm; do not boil. Transfer the *macarónia* to a warm earthenware bowl and pour over the tomato sauce and olive oil. Gently toss together and serve at once, with bowls of the cheese.

Variations

• Substitute a cheese (page 114), cheese and spinach (page 116), wild greens (page 118), or meat (page 120) filling for the chicken filling; you will need only half the quantity of filling those recipes make.

Kritharáki with Brown Butter and Cheese

Kritharáki me Voútiro ke Tyrí

Serves 4 to 6

Archaeological evidence suggests that *kritharáki* may have been an early "convenience food," sold in the marketplaces of ancient Greece. The tiniest grains of *kritharáki* are no larger than pearl rice, the largest are the size of cantaloupe seeds; you can find it in Greek or Middle Eastern stores—it is also called *manéstra* or *órza*. Goat's butter is the traditional flavoring but brown butter and lemon juice makes a fine substitute. Be generous with the cheese and fresh herbs.

---

2 cups medium-size **kritharáki**

7 cups Meat or Chicken Broth (page 461), Meat Stock (page 467), or water

6 tablespoons unsalted butter

Juice of 1 large lemon, or to taste

1 cup finely grated aged **myzíthra** *or* **kasséri** *cheese*

¼ to ½ cup fresh herbs, snipped or finely chopped

½ cup coarsely chopped flat-leaf parsley

6 scallions, best green parts only, finely sliced

Coarse-grain sea salt and cracked black pepper to taste

Bring the broth to a boil in a large saucepan. Add the *kritharáki* and simmer until barely tender, about 10 minutes. Drain, and briefly refresh under cold running water.

Meanwhile, heat the butter in a small heavy saucepan over very low heat until deep golden brown, about 10 minutes. (Keep the heat very low or the solids in the butter will burn.) Strain through 2 layers of cheesecloth into a bowl and add most of the lemon juice.

(continued)

Pilafs and Pastas

327

Rinse out the large saucepan and return the *kritharáki* to the pan. Add the butter mixture, the cheese, herbs, parsley, scallions, salt and pepper, and remaining lemon juice. Stir just to mix, heat to warm, and transfer to a warm serving bowl. Serve at once.

Note Your choice of herbs to flavor *kritharáki* depends on what is available and the dish it is to be served with. The quantity of herbs you use depends on their strength. Fresh oregano, chervil, thyme, borage, or coriander are all good choices. Herbs with a mild flavor, such as chervil, are simply snipped into small pieces, but stronger herbs, such as oregano, must be finely chopped.

Breads

Psomiá

Bread is a fundamental part of Greek life—it appears in some form at every meal and special festive breads are of great significance in religious festivals and family celebrations. Greek bakeries, piled high with breads of every conceivable size and shape, have a special magic. In rural communities bread is still baked in the *foúrnos* and the village baker supplies a range of breads, from the basic everyday loaf to wonderful crusty whole-wheat, barley, or stone-ground breads, as well as one or two savory or fruit breads.

Savory breads are seasonal and vary from region to region and baker to baker. The one essential common ingredient is a good fruity olive oil, which results in a wonderfully supple dough with an appealing aroma and the characteristic flavor and texture of all Greek breads. Flavored with cheese, olives, fennel, or herbs these savory breads invariably appear as round loaves but you may prefer to make the dough into rolls. And if you have savory bread left over, just sprinkle slices of the bread with olive oil and crisp them in a low oven; dipped into red wine and accompanied by fresh cheese and olives, they are a delectable, traditional, and quickly made snack.

Sweet breads, such as Currant Bread (page 352), are enjoyed all year round and *paximáthi,* a sweet anise-flavored hard bread, is a universal treat with coffee. The flavorings used in sweet breads hint at their ancient origins—mastic (page 467), *petimézi* (page 411), cinnamon, allspice, vanilla, and nutmeg are all traditional.

Both sweet and savory breads play a central role in Greek religious life, as part of Orthodox ritual and as celebration food. The women of each church congregation make a dense-textured bread for the celebration of the Eucharist, and a special bread flavored with mastic is made for Saints' days. These church breads are known as *ártos,* the ancient Greek word for bread. A flat sesame seed bread called *lagána* is baked to mark the first day of Lent; later, this important fast is broken by the sharing of the rich Easter bread (page 348). At Christmas and New Year's more festive sweet breads (pages 349 and 350) appear—ornately decorated or shaped and gleaming with sugary glaze. And throughout the year, for any celebration—an engagement, a wedding, the birth of a child—there is the all-purpose festive bread called *tsouréki* (page 346).

Many of these breads are not difficult to make at home, although they do take a little time. Most can be frozen very successfully, so you can make extra loaves or rolls to serve with Greek meals later, and they also keep extremely well.

Notes on Successful Bread Making

Making bread is wonderfully satisfying and not at all difficult if you follow some simple guidelines. These tips should help you succeed in making a variety of delicious breads, both savory and sweet.

Equipment you will need

Large mixing bowl

Dough scraper

Measuring cups and spoons; heavy baking sheets

Oven thermometer; clean kitchen towels; plastic wrap; an uncluttered, clean work area

Draft-free warm spot

Loaf pans are useful but not essential

Ingredients

Flour: These recipes use whole-wheat flour, pastry flour, graham flour, and unbleached all-purpose flour. Other flours, such as stoneground, can be substituted; you will usually need to use less of them and to knead the dough for a longer time. Cup measures, although simple to use, can be far from accurate; the important thing is to add enough flour to make the dough the required texture.

Salt: Salt serves two primary functions in bread making: It helps retain moisture in the dough and acts as a flavor enhancer. Use only sea salt—the taste of the chemical additives in other salts is intensified in bread. Salt must be dissolved before it is incorporated into the dough; fine-grain sea salt dissolves the most quickly.

Olive oil: The "secret" ingredient in Mediterranean breads, it makes a pliant, easy-to-handle dough. Pungent extra-virgin olive oil gives the most authentic taste, but use less-expensive refined olive oil, if you prefer.

Yeast: For convenience, these recipes use active dry yeast. However, do use fresh yeast if you can find it since it gives a better flavor; 1 small cake is equivalent to 1 tablespoon active dry yeast. Dissolve in liquid heated to 85°F to 90°F instead of 110°F.

Techniques

Temperature: Temperature is an important factor during all stages of bread making. Yeast is a living organism; it weakens and dies if overheated, refuses to work if too cold. It is activated only at specific temperatures, and once activated, will die if left too long (usually more than about 12 minutes) without a "host" (the flour). Mixing bowls should be lukewarm. Kneading warms the dough so that it will rise. The oven must be hot enough for a quick rise, but not too hot or the dough may collapse. After 10 minutes or so the temperature is usually reduced so that the loaf cooks through. Oven temperatures must be exact—use an oven thermometer.

Kneading dough: Use a lightly floured board or work surface for kneading dough, and press into the dough with your knuckles each time you fold it over. Kneading enables the dough to rise. A few minutes practice is all you need to become competent, and it is a very satisfying culinary skill but, if you prefer, you can use the dough hook attachment on an electric mixer.

Rising: To rise properly, bread dough needs warmth and contact with the yeast microorganisms that exist in the air. High humidity can cause bread to rise faster so be prepared to reduce the rising time if the atmosphere is humid. Cold will slow down the rising process: if you have to leave the dough for more than 2 or 3 hours, refrigerate it to prevent overrising and breaking. If it should overrise and collapse, knead again and bake immediately.

Flavor: In addition to the type of flour used and any added flavorings, the taste of bread is also affected by:

Yeast—too much adversely flavors the dough

Salt—without it the bread, whether savory or sweet, will be flat-tasting

Water—any unpleasant flavors in treated water are intensified in bread, use bottled water for best results

Rising—the longer the rise, the greater the flavor—cover the dough or bowl with plastic wrap to minimize contact with the air and slow down the rising

Making a good crust: A simple way to create a good bread crust is to spray the dough with a plant mister once or twice during baking. Slashing the top of the dough with a clean razor blade or very sharp knife gives the bread an attractive appearance; this can be done either before the second rise, in which case the crust will separate quite dramatically during baking, or just before baking. Wet doughs (such as that for spinach bread) cannot be slashed, nor can overrisen dough. Greek bakers usually slash only round loaves; a traditional design is 2 or 3 parallel lines cut diagonally across the center.

Country Bread

Khoriátiko Psomí

Makes 2 loaves

This is the flavorful bread that appears daily on village tables. It's easy to make, has an excellent crumb, and a good strong flavor enhanced with honey and olive oil.

---

2 tablespoons active dry yeast

1 cup tepid (110°F) water

2 tablespoons honey

2 teaspoons fine-grain sea salt

1 egg, lightly beaten

¾ cup milk, heated to tepid (110°F)

2 tablespoons olive oil

2 tablespoons unsalted butter, melted

5 to 5½ cups whole-wheat flour or 3 cups whole-wheat flour and 2 to 2½ cups graham flour (available in health food stores)

Sprinkle the yeast over ¼ cup of the tepid water and set aside in a warm spot for 10 minutes, or until foamy.

Combine the honey, salt, egg, milk, remaining ¾ cup water, 1 tablespoon of the olive oil, and half the butter in a bowl. Sift 3 cups of the flour into a large mixing bowl, make a well in the center, and stir in the yeast and honey mixtures. Knead 10 minutes, gradually adding enough of the remaining flour to make a firm, smooth, and elastic dough. Tightly cover the bowl and set aside in a warm draft-free spot for 1½ hours, or until doubled in bulk.

Lightly oil a heavy baking sheet. Knead the dough 1 minute. Form into 2 round loaves and place well apart on the baking sheet. Cover with a clean kitchen towel and set aside for 1 hour in a warm spot to rise.

Heat the oven to 375°F.

Brush the loaves with the remaining 1 tablespoon olive oil and butter and bake 40 minutes, or until lightly browned and, when tapped on the bottom, sound hollow. Cool on a rack.

Shepherd's Bread

Ártos Voskoú

Makes 2 round loaves or 10 rolls

This strongly flavored, densely textured bread is sometimes made into a large round loaf, often with a hole in the center, sometimes into long or round rolls. Greeks have been baking tasty country bread like this for centuries; originally made with oat bran and barley meal it's now more commonly made with oat and wheat brans and stone-ground flour. This bread is delicious served with grilled meats, salads, and sheep's or goat's cheeses or just dipped in olive oil or red wine. Try making it with fresh sheep's milk (available in health food stores) instead of water, as the ancient Greeks did!

2 tablespoons honey

3 teaspoons sea salt

⅓ cup olive oil

1 cup wheat bran

1 cup oat bran

2 cups lukewarm water or sheep's or goat's milk

3½ to 4 cups whole-wheat flour

Combine the honey, salt, 3 tablespoons of the olive oil, the wheat bran, oat bran, and water in a large jar. Tightly cover and set aside for 18 to 22 hours in a warm draft-free spot to ferment. After about 12 hours the mixture should begin to give off an aroma rather like that of fresh beer; let ferment longer. Don't worry if it takes a few hours longer to give off the characteristic aroma.

Sift 1½ cups of the flour, mix it into the fermenting bran mixture with a wooden spoon, replace the lid, and set aside for 4 hours longer in the same warm spot. The dough will have developed a sponge-like texture.

Sift 2 cups of the remaining flour into a large mixing bowl, make a well in the center, and pour in the bran mixture. Knead thoroughly for at least 5 minutes, adding additional flour if necessary to make a firm dough—it will never feel as smooth or as elastic as dough made with yeast.

(continued)

Lightly brush a heavy baking sheet with some of the olive oil. Form the dough into 2 round loaves or 10 round or long rolls and arrange on the sheet, spaced well apart. Cover with plastic wrap and set aside for 2 to 3 hours in a warm draft-free place to rise. The dough will increase in bulk by only about one third.

Heat the oven to 350°F.

Brush the loaves or rolls with the remaining olive oil and bake 15 minutes, then reduce the oven temperature to 325°F. Bake loaves 50 minutes longer, rolls 30 minutes longer, or until they sound hollow when lightly tapped on the bottom. Cool on a rack.

Pantry Bread

Paximáthi me Saláta

Serves 4 to 6

Bread quickly becomes stale in hot climates, and this bread is a country solution to the problem. Baked until it becomes hard and dry, it can be stored almost indefinitely. Then, when it is needed, it is soaked in wine, olive oil, or water and almost magically regains its dense and delicious texture. A village neighbor spreads chopped sweet tomatoes over the bread and sprinkles them with pungent herbs, making a simple and delicious summer lunch. Serve with Purslane Salad (page 292) and bowls of olives and cheese.

The Greeks also double-bake rolls and thick slices of bread, but the method works only with coarse or densely textured bread; softer, loose-textured loaves just become soggy if revived in the same way.

---

1 round loaf Shepherd's Bread (page 335),
cut in half horizontally

½ cup water

Juice of 1 lemon

6 large ripe tomatoes, peeled, seeded if desired, and diced

½ teaspoon sugar

1 teaspoon coarse-grain sea salt, or to taste

1 to 2 teaspoons cracked black pepper (to taste)

¾ to 1 cup extra-virgin olive oil (to taste)

1 small red onion, cut into thin rings

¼ cup finely chopped flat-leaf parsley

2 tablespoons dried rígani (page 14) or 1 tablespoon
dried thyme, crumbled

Heat the oven to 225°F.

Place the bread, cut sides up, on a heavy baking sheet, and bake 30 minutes or until hard, turning once. Cool on a rack.

Place the bread on a plate and sprinkle the water and lemon juice evenly over it. Set aside for 30 minutes, or until the liquids are absorbed. Sprinkle the tomatoes with the sugar, salt, and pepper, and set aside.

Pour ½ cup of the olive oil over the bread, set aside for a few minutes, then spoon over the tomatoes. Scatter the onion over the tomatoes and sprinkle with the parsley, *rígani,* and remaining olive oil. Serve at once.

Pita Bread

Píta

Makes 6 medium pita breads

The perfect bread to accompany *souvlákia* and other grilled meats, *píta* is soft-textured and mildly sweet. It's also straightforward to prepare and well worth making since the flavor of homemade *píta* is far superior to that of the bland commercial product. It keeps well for a few days and can be frozen. There are a surprising number of ways to make it, but the following is the one I find works best.

———

1 teaspoon light honey

¾ to 1 cup tepid (110°F) water

1 tablespoon active dry yeast

1 teaspoon fine-grain sea salt

3 tablespoons olive oil

1½ cups whole-wheat flour

1 cup unbleached all-purpose flour

Combine the honey and ¼ cup of the tepid water in a bowl and sprinkle the yeast over. Set aside for 10 minutes in a warm spot. Dissolve the salt in ½ cup of the remaining tepid water and add 1½ tablespoons of the olive oil.

Sift the whole-wheat flour and ½ cup of the all-purpose flour into a large bowl, make a well in the center, and pour in the yeast and salt mixtures. Mix with your hands, adding up to ¼ cup additional water or up to ½ cup additional all-purpose flour if necessary to make a moist but firm dough. Transfer to a lightly floured surface and knead 10 to 15 minutes, until smooth and elastic. Transfer to a lightly oiled bowl, and brush with olive oil. (The oil keeps the dough moist while rising.) Cover the bowl with a slightly damp kitchen towel and set aside in a warm draft-free spot for 2 hours, or until at least doubled in bulk.

Arrange 1 rack close to the bottom of the oven, 1 to the top, and heat the oven to 425°F.

Knead the dough 2 minutes and divide into 6 portions. Set aside for 10 minutes in a warm spot to rest, then flatten each portion with your palm. Lightly flour a work surface and roll the dough into ¼-inch-thick rounds or ovals. Brush a heavy baking sheet with the remaining olive oil and slide the pita rounds onto it, spacing them at least 4 inches apart. (Don't brush the pitas or they will not rise properly.)

Place the baking tray on the lower oven rack and bake 3 minutes. Quickly transfer to the top rack and bake 3 or 4 minutes longer, or until the pitas are puffy but not even lightly browned. They should still be soft. (If your oven is small and you need to use 2 baking sheets or more, place the second sheet in the oven when you move the first to the top rack.)

Stack between warm and very slightly damp clean kitchen towels and set aside in a draft-free spot until cool. Seal in plastic bags to store.

Olive Bread

Eliópsomo

Makes 1 large round loaf or 2 small ones

This aromatic bread changes its character with the seasons. In spring it's gently perfumed with fresh rosemary or fennel; in winter dried thyme or mint gives it a more pungent but less subtle flavor. Olive bread has a long-standing tradition in Greek life and is believed to have appeared on Minoan tables three thousand years before the birth of Christ. This is a modern version of an ancient recipe, made with added yeast, but it retains all the rustic simplicity and taste of the original. Cut it into thin slices and serve with *mezéthes*, sausages, or omelets.

---

1 teaspoon honey

1 cup tepid (110°F) water

1 1/2 tablespoons active dry yeast

1/2 cup extra-virgin olive oil

1 teaspoon fine-grain sea salt

3 1/2 to 4 cups whole-wheat flour

12 plump Greek or other imported oil-cured olives, pitted

1 cup finely chopped onion

*1 tablespoon fresh rosemary or fennel leaves, finely chopped,
or 1 tablespoon dried thyme or mint, crumbled*

Dissolve the honey in the water in a small bowl and sprinkle the yeast over. Set aside in a warm place until foamy, about 10 minutes. Whisk in 3 tablespoons of the olive oil and the salt.

Sift 2 cups of the flour into a large mixing bowl, make a well in the center, and add the yeast mixture. Knead 10 minutes, adding enough of the remaining flour to make a firm but elastic dough. Set aside in a warm draft-free place for 2 hours, or until at least doubled in bulk.

Heat 3 tablespoons of the remaining olive oil in a heavy skillet and sauté the onion over low heat until pale golden, about 10 minutes. Set aside.

Blanch the olives in boiling water for 1 second; drain and dry with paper towels. Cut 5 of the olives into small pieces and finely chop the rest. Add the olives and rosemary to the onions and stir to mix. Add to the dough and knead 1 minute.

Brush a heavy baking sheet with olive oil. Form the dough into 1 or 2 slightly flattened round loaves on the sheet, spaced well apart. Cover with a clean kitchen towel and set aside for 1 hour in a warm draft-free spot.

Heat the oven to 375°F.

Bake the bread 10 minutes, reduce the oven temperature to 350°F, brush with the remaining 2 tablespoons olive oil and bake 25 minutes to 35 minutes longer, or until the bread is deep golden brown and sounds hollow when tapped on the bottom.

Note Also try plump fleshy Ámfissa olives instead of the more pungent oil-cured ones.

Cheese Mint Bread

Tyrópsomo Thiósmou

Makes 3 small loaves

The characteristic, rather musty, flavor of *halloúmi* cheese is particularly suited to bread made with olive oil. If it is unavailable, *féta* cheese makes a perfectly good substitute, but it should be drained well before using. This densely textured bread, fragrant with mint, is traditionally made in small loaves, ideal for picnics or to serve with salads.

———

⅓ to ⅔ cup tepid (110°F) water

1 tablespoon active dry yeast

⅓ cup extra-virgin olive oil

1 teaspoon fine-grain sea salt

3 cups whole-wheat flour

2 tablespoons dried mint, finely crumbled

Scant ½ pound **halloúmi** *or* **féta** *cheese, cut or crumbled into small pieces*

1 tablespoon fresh lemon juice

Pour ⅓ cup of the water into a small bowl and sprinkle the yeast over. Set aside in a warm place until foamy, about 10 minutes. Whisk in ¼ cup of the olive oil and the salt.

Sift the flour into a large mixing bowl, make a well in the center, and pour in the yeast mixture. Knead 10 minutes, adding up to ⅓ cup additional water if necessary to make a firm elastic dough. Transfer to a lightly oiled bowl, and brush the dough with olive oil. Tightly cover the bowl with plastic wrap and set aside for 2½ hours in a warm draft-free spot. It will not quite double in bulk, but the long resting time produces a well-flavored bread.

Knead in the mint. Divide the dough into 3 portions. Form each into a ball, then flatten on a board to a thickness of ¾ inch. Place one third of the cheese in the center of each and bring up the edges of the dough to barely enclose the cheese, but do not seal. Transfer to a lightly oiled heavy baking sheet, cover with a clean kitchen towel, and set aside for 1 hour in a warm draft-free spot.

Heat the oven to 350°F.

Combine the remaining olive oil and the lemon juice and lightly brush the loaves with this mixture. Bake 10 minutes, reduce the oven temperature to 325°F, and bake 40 minutes longer or until golden brown.

Rígani Cheese Bread

Tyrópsomo Riganáto

Makes 1 large round loaf

I first tasted this delicious bread at a picnic high in the Pindus mountains—an appropriate setting for a bread heavily scented with mountain herbs. The great round loaf, with its glistening olive oil glaze and rich cheese flavor, was the delicious centerpiece of the outdoor feast; around it were spread olives, *Kephtethákia* (page 38), Smoked Fish Salad (page 36), and *mezéthes* of eggplant and other vegetables.

(continued)

1 tablespoon active dry yeast

1 cup tepid (110°F) water

3 tablespoons olive oil

½ teaspoon fine-grain sea salt

3 to 3½ cups whole-wheat flour

2 tablespoons dried rígani (page 14), crumbled

½ tablespoon dried mint, finely crumbled

¾ pound féta cheese, well drained and finely crumbled

1 egg yolk beaten with 2 tablespoons warm water

Sprinkle the yeast over the water and set aside in a warm place until foamy, about 10 minutes. Whisk in 2 tablespoons of the olive oil and the salt.

Sift 3 cups of the flour into a large mixing bowl, make a well in the center, and pour in the yeast mixture. Knead 10 minutes, adding the remaining ½ cup flour if necessary to make a firm elastic dough. Transfer to a lightly oiled bowl, tightly cover with plastic wrap, and set aside for 2 hours in a warm draft-free spot.

Knead in the *rígani*, mint, and *féta* until evenly distributed throughout the dough. Lightly oil a heavy baking sheet and place the dough in the center. Form into a round loaf and flatten to a thickness of 2 inches. Cover with a clean kitchen towel and set aside for 1 hour in a warm draft-free spot. The dough will rise only slightly.

Heat the oven to 350°F.

With a sharp thin blade, slash the top of the loaf diagonally in 2 or 3 parallel lines, brush with the remaining olive oil, and bake 25 minutes. Brush with the beaten egg yolk and bake 15 minutes longer, or until the bread is deep golden brown and sounds hollow when tapped on the bottom.

Fennel Bread

Marathópsomo

Makes 1 large or 2 smaller loaves

Fennel Bread changes its character during the year, according to the type of fennel used to flavor it. The finest-flavored loaves appear on Greek tables in early spring when succulent young fennel is at its best. Later in the season finely chopped larger fennel sprigs are used, and, for the rest of the year, the bread is made with pulverized fennel seeds. This exquisite bread is the perfect complement to a light meal of Beets Island-Style (page 244), olives, and *myzíthra* cheese (page 11). Its distinctive flavor is also superb with grilled fish, chicken, or pork.

---

1 tablespoon active dry yeast

1 cup tepid (110°F) water

⅓ cup extra-virgin olive oil

1 teaspoon fine-grain sea salt

3 to 3½ cups whole-wheat flour

2 cups fennel sprigs or ¼ cup fennel seeds

1½ cups finely chopped mild onion

Juice of 1 large lemon

¼ pound féta cheese, well-drained and finely crumbled

1 teaspoon coarse-grain sea salt

*6 Elítses or Niçoise olives, blanched in boiling water
for 5 seconds, drained, pitted, and halved*

Sprinkle the yeast over the water and set aside in a warm place until foamy, about 10 minutes. Whisk in 2 tablespoons of the olive oil and ½ teaspoon of the fine-grain salt.

Sift 3 cups of the flour into a large bowl, make a well in the center, and pour in the yeast mixture. Knead 10 minutes, adding the remaining ½ cup flour if necessary to make a firm elastic dough. Transfer to a lightly oiled bowl, brush the dough with olive oil, tightly cover with plastic wrap, and set aside for 2 hours in a warm draft-free spot. The dough will not quite double in bulk.

Blanch fresh fennel in boiling water for 5 seconds, pat dry with paper towels, and chop finely. (Or pound fennel seed and the remaining ½ teaspoon fine-grain salt in a mortar, or grind in a coffee grinder until almost pulverized, just before the seeds become a powder.) Combine the fresh fennel and remaining ½ teaspoon fine-grain salt (or the pounded fennel), onion, most of the lemon juice, and 2 tablespoons olive oil, and knead into the dough along with the cheese.

Lightly oil a baking sheet. Form the dough into 1 or 2 round loaves and flatten to 2 inches. With a clean thin blade, slash 2 parallel lines diagonally across the top of the loaf(ves), and set aside for 1 hour in a warm draft-free spot. The slashes will open as the dough rises.

Heat the oven to 350°F.

Sprinkle the coarse-grain salt inside the slashes and gently press the olives into the tops of the loaf(ves), cut sides down. Brush with the remaining olive oil and lemon juice and bake smaller loaves 35 minutes, 1 large loaf 50 minutes, or until browned and the bread sounds hollow when tapped on the bottom.

Spinach Bread

Spanakópsomo

Makes 1 large round loaf or 2 smaller ones

Traditionally this bread is made with wild greens. Spinach gives a smoother, lighter bread (and is easier to find), but you may like to try the ancient *khórta* version too. This flattish, chewy bread with its distinctive flavor is perfect with salads, egg dishes, and cheese and olives.

1 teaspoon honey

2 teaspoons fine-grain sea salt

¾ cup tepid (110°F) water

1 tablespoon active dry yeast

⅓ cup extra-virgin olive oil

3½ cups whole-wheat flour

2 pounds fresh spinach

2 cups finely chopped mild onion

1 large clove garlic, finely chopped

1½ tablespoons cumin seeds or 1 tablespoon
ground cumin

Juice of 1 large lemon

½ cup well-drained crumbled féta cheese, optional

Combine the water, honey, and 1 teaspoon of the salt in a medium bowl and sprinkle the yeast over. Set aside in a warm place until foamy, about 10 minutes. Whisk in 2 tablespoons of the olive oil, then sift in 1 cup flour and stir to mix. Set aside in a warm draft-free spot for 1 hour, or until sponge-like in texture.

Meanwhile, rinse the spinach in several changes of cold water, remove the tough stems and leaves, and cut the tender leaves into ¼-inch strips. Set aside. Heat 2½ tablespoons of the olive oil in a large heavy skillet and sauté the onion over low heat until pale golden, about 15 minutes. Heat the cumin in a small dry skillet until aromatic, and pulverize it in a mortar or grinder. Add the cumin, garlic, and remaining 1 teaspoon salt to the onion. Stir in the spinach and cook 5 minutes, stirring frequently, until soft. Sprinkle with the lemon juice and drain in a colander set over a bowl. Set aside, reserving the cooking liquid.

Sift 2 cups of the remaining flour into a large bowl, make a well in the center, and pour in the yeast sponge. Knead 10 minutes, adding enough of the reserved cooking liquid to make a firm but elastic dough. Transfer to a lightly oiled bowl, tightly cover with plastic wrap, and set aside for 2 hours in a warm draft-free place.

Add the *féta* to the dough and knead 1 minute. Add the spinach mixture, sprinkle with the remaining flour, and quickly mix together—the dough will be quite moist and loose; do not knead it again.   (continued)

Brush a baking sheet with olive oil and place the dough on it. Form into 1 large round loaf or 2 smaller ones spaced well apart. Cover with a clean kitchen towel and set aside for 1 hour in a warm draft-free spot.

Heat the oven to 375°F.

Bake the bread 20 minutes, reduce the oven temperature to 350°F, brush with the remaining olive oil, and bake 20 to 30 minutes longer, until golden brown.

Festive Bread

Tsouréki

Makes 2 braided loaves or 3 long loaves

During any major religious festival, this shiny glazed celebration bread is attractively displayed in every Greek cake shop and coffeehouse window, and laden baskets of the loaves hang from the ceiling of every bakery. However, many Greeks still prefer to make their own *tsouréki*, and every family has a favorite flavoring—orange, lemon, mastic, vanilla, allspice, or cloves and bay are the most popular. The traditional shape is a braided or round loaf, but forming the dough into long loaves makes it easier to store and cut. It makes delicious toast, and it keeps well for up to 1 week.

———

¾ cup packed light brown sugar

½ cup tepid (110°F) water

2 tablespoons active dry yeast

3 cups unbleached all-purpose flour

2½ to 3 cups unbleached pastry flour

½ cup plus 2 tablespoons milk, heated to tepid (110°F)

2 tablespoons olive oil

5 eggs

Juice of ½ orange

2 tablespoons finely grated orange zest, briefly dried in a low oven and pulverized in a mortar with ½ teaspoon sugar, or 1½ tablespoons orange extract

¹/₂ teaspoon vanilla extract

*1 teaspoon ground allspice or 1 teaspoon mastic
granules (page 467), pulverized in a mortar
with ¹/₂ teaspoon sugar*

1 teaspoon fine-grain sea salt

4 tablespoons unsalted butter, melted

1 egg yolk

1 tablespoon honey

¹/₄ cup sesame seeds or ¹/₄ cup blanched slivered almonds

Dissolve 1 teaspoon of the brown sugar in the water and sprinkle the yeast over. Set aside in a warm place until foamy, about 10 minutes.

Sift 2 cups of the all-purpose flour into a large bowl, make a well in the center, and pour in the yeast mixture. Knead and gradually add the ½ cup milk, remaining 1 cup all-purpose flour, and 1½ cups of the pastry flour, or enough to make a light, smooth, and elastic dough. Turn out onto a lightly floured surface and knead 10 minutes. Transfer to a lightly oiled bowl, and brush with olive oil. Cover with a warm damp kitchen towel and set aside in a warm draft-free place for 1 hour, or until at least doubled in bulk.

Beat the eggs in a large bowl until light and frothy and beat in the remaining brown sugar, the orange juice, orange zest, vanilla, allspice, and salt. Add to the dough with 3 tablespoons of the melted butter and knead in enough of the remaining 1½ cups pastry flour to make a soft dough. Transfer to a lightly floured surface and knead 3 minutes.

Divide the dough into 6 portions. With the palms of your hands, roll each into a 9-inch rope, slightly fatter in the middle and with pointed ends. Brush a large heavy baking sheet with the remaining melted butter. Lay 3 ropes on it side by side, loosely braid, and tuck the pointed ends underneath so the loaf ends are rounded. Repeat with the remaining 3 ropes, spacing the 2 braided loaves well apart. To make long loaves, either form the dough into loaves on the baking sheet or place in buttered loaf tins. Loosely cover with plastic wrap and set aside in a warm draft-free place for 2 hours, or until doubled in bulk.

Heat the oven to 400°F.

Whisk together the egg yolk, honey, and the 2 tablespoons milk and brush the loaves with this mixture. Sprinkle with sesame seeds and bake 10 minutes. Reduce the oven temperature to 350°F and bake 20 minutes longer, or until a beautiful honey brown. Transfer to racks to cool.

Easter Bread

Lambrópsomo

Makes 2 braided or large round loaves

The almond-topped bread that breaks the Lenten fast has pride of place on the Easter Sunday table. Rich in eggs and butter (foods forbidden during Lent), these shiny loaves display all the baker's artistry with their splendid decorations of spring flowers, leaves, or berries shaped in dough. Many of these Easter breads are so beautifully crafted that they are used as wall decorations throughout the year. Red eggs, signifying both rebirth and the blood of Christ, are an important part of the decoration—they delight the children but, unlike our traditional Easter eggs, are never eaten.

---

6 white eggs, at room temperature

2 teaspoons red food coloring

A few drops of blue food coloring

1 tablespoon olive oil

*1 recipe Festive Bread dough (page 346), made
without allspice or mastic*

½ cup blanched slivered almonds

Half fill a stainless steel saucepan with water, bring to a boil, and add the food colorings. Gently boil the eggs 20 minutes; add a little more coloring if necessary to produce deep crimson eggs.

Let the eggs cool in the water, remove them, and set aside to dry. Dip a paper towel in the olive oil, and rub each egg all over with it.

Form the dough into 2 braided (page 347) or round loaves on buttered baking sheets; if making round loaves reserve a little of the dough for decoration. Roll the reserved dough into thin ropes with the palms of your hands and break off small pieces to make into spring symbols, such as flowers, leaves, or berries. Decorate the tops of the round loaves with these shapes. Set the loaves aside for 2 hours in a warm draft-free spot to rise.

Heat the oven to 400°F.

Place the eggs either around the centers of the round loaves or between the decorations, or arrange the eggs between the braids. Brush with the egg and honey glaze, sprinkle with the almonds, and bake 10 minutes. Reduce the oven temperature to 350°F and bake 20 minutes longer, or until golden brown, transfer to racks to cool.

Discard the eggs once the bread is cut.

Christmas Bread

Christópsomo

Makes 2 shaped or round loaves

This enticingly festive bread is the focal point of a strong religious tradition. After midnight mass on Christmas Eve, each family gathers together to share the loaf, in great anticipation of who will find the lucky coin baked inside. The head of the household first breaks off a piece and sets it aside "for Christ"; then pieces are given to guests sharing the celebration. The next two pieces are for himself and the female head of the household, and finally the remainder is shared among the others at the table, men first, then women and, lastly, the children. Whoever finds the coin will be blessed with good luck; if it is found in the piece reserved for Christ, the money is given to the church or to charity. For a traditional Christmas table the bread is baked in the shape of any "blessing" the family would like to give thanks for, such as livestock or produce of the fields, and many city-dwelling cooks still shape their Christmas breads into these ancient symbols of good fortune.

---

1 recipe Saint Basil's Bread (page 350), substituting:

*3 whole cloves, 2 bay leaves, and one 2-inch
cinnamon stick for the aniseed;*

*2 tablespoons lemon zest or lemon extract for the orange zest,
optional; and ¾ cup blanched slivered almonds
for the sesame seeds*

2 egg whites

⅓ cup superfine sugar

Pinch of salt

12 small walnut halves

⅓ cup mixed candied fruit, cut into tiny dice   (*continued*)

Form the dough into 2 loaves on a buttered baking sheet and let rise a second time (page 351).

Heat the oven to 375°F.

Whisk the egg whites until thick but not stiff, then whisk in the sugar and salt. Brush the loaves generously with this glaze. Arrange the walnut halves on top, gently pushing them onto the dough, then sprinkle over the candied fruit. Lightly brush with the remaining glaze and bake 40 to 50 minutes, or until deep chestnut brown. Cool on a rack.

Saint Basil's Bread

Vasilópitta

**Makes 1 large round loaf,
2 long loaves, or 18 rolls**

Named for a founding father of the Orthodox church, this is the traditional New Year's bread and, like Christmas Bread, has a lucky coin baked inside. At the last chime of midnight on New Year's Eve the head of the family breaks the bread and divides it among those gathered for the celebration. Appropriately, for a bread made in honor of a Byzantine saint, the Eastern spice *mahlépi* is a favorite flavoring, but aniseed is also popular and whole aniseed gives the bread an interesting texture and a pungent festive aroma. This delectable loaf is a year-round favorite in nontraditional households. The traditional shape is a very large round loaf with a smaller loaf on top, but it's easier to store if you make it into two long loaves or rolls. It keeps well and can also be frozen.

———

2 tablespoons whole aniseed or 1 tablespoon mahlépi *seeds
(available in Greek and Middle Eastern stores), lightly crushed*

2 tablespoons active dry yeast

1 cup plus 2 tablespoons milk, heated to tepid (110°F)

*3 cups unbleached all-purpose flour and 3 to 4 cups
whole-wheat flour or 6 to 7 cups unbleached
all-purpose flour*

7 eggs

¾ cup honey

1 teaspoon fine-grain sea salt

¾ cup superfine sugar

12 tablespoons unsalted butter, melted

⅓ cup light olive oil

*2 tablespoons finely grated orange zest, briefly dried in a low
oven and pulverized in a mortar with 1 teaspoon sugar,
or 2 tablespoons orange extract*

¾ cup sesame seeds

Combine the aniseed and ½ cup water in a small pan, bring to a boil, and simmer 1 minute. Set aside to cool. Strain and set aside the liquid (or set aside both seeds and liquid).

Pour the 1 cup milk into a medium bowl, sprinkle the yeast over, and set aside for 10 minutes in a warm spot, or until foamy. Stir 1 cup of the all-purpose flour into the yeast with a wooden spoon, tightly cover, and set aside in a warm draft-free spot for 1 hour, or until it has become spongelike in texture.

With a wire whisk or electric mixer, beat 6 of the eggs, the honey, salt, and all but 2 teaspoons of the sugar in a large bowl until light and frothy. Sift the remaining 2 cups all-purpose flour and 2 cups of the whole-wheat flour into another large bowl, make a well in the center, and pour in the yeast sponge, aniseed liquid (and seeds if desired), about ⅔ cup of the butter, ¼ cup of the olive oil, the orange zest, and the egg mixture. Knead 5 minutes, transfer to a lightly floured surface, and knead 10 minutes longer, adding enough of the remaining flour to make a soft smooth dough. Transfer to a lightly oiled bowl and brush the dough with the remaining olive oil. Tightly cover and set aside in a warm draft-free spot for 2 hours, or until at least doubled in bulk.

Transfer to a lightly floured surface and knead 5 minutes. Divide into 2 portions, one twice as large as the other. Liberally butter a baking sheet with the remaining butter and place the larger portion on the sheet. Form it into a round loaf about 2 inches thick, and flatten the top slightly with your palm. Form the smaller portion into a round loaf about 1 inch thick, flattening it on the bottom, and center it on top of the larger one. (To make long loaves, either form into loaves on the baking sheet or place in buttered loaf pans. To make rolls, divide the dough into 18 portions and form into round or long rolls on a buttered baking sheet, spaced at least 3 inches

Breads

351

apart.) With a wooden skewer or equivalent, write the year on top for New Year's bread or make a simple design. Loosely cover with plastic wrap and set aside for 30 minutes in a warm draft-free spot.

Heat the oven to 375°F.

Beat the remaining egg with the reserved 2 teaspoons sugar and the 2 tablespoons milk and liberally brush the dough with this glaze. Sprinkle over the sesame seeds and bake 40 to 50 minutes, or until deep chestnut brown. Cool on a rack.

Currant Bread

Stafithópsomo

Makes 2 medium loaves or 12 rolls

With a more refreshing and lighter flavor than the familiar sweet raisin bread, this currant loaf is easy to make and has an attractive country character. It can be shaped into loaves or rolls and it makes perfect breakfast bread with yogurt, honey, and fresh fruit. Or try it toasted, with jam or preserves.

---

¹/₂ cup plus 1 tablespoon honey

2 tablespoons unsalted butter, melted

1¹/₂ teaspoons fine-grain sea salt

1¹/₄ cups milk, heated to tepid (110°F)

2 tablespoons active dry yeast

3¹/₂ cups whole-wheat flour

1¹/₂ cups unbleached all-purpose flour

¹/₂ teaspoon ground cloves

2 eggs, lightly beaten

1 tablespoon light olive oil

1¹/₂ cups currants

With a whisk, combine the ½ cup honey, 1 tablespoon of the butter, the salt, and 1 cup of the milk in a small bowl. Sprinkle the yeast over and set aside in a warm place until foamy, about 10 minutes.

Sift both flours and the cloves into a large mixing bowl; remove and set aside 1½ cups. Make a well in the center of the remaining flour, and stir in the yeast mixture and the eggs. Turn out onto a floured work surface and knead 4 to 5 minutes, or until the dough is light, smooth, and elastic. Transfer to a lightly oiled bowl, brush the dough with the remaining olive oil, tightly cover with plastic wrap, and set aside in a warm draft-free place for 30 minutes, or until increased in bulk by one third.

Sprinkle the currants and half the reserved flour mixture over the dough, and knead 5 minutes, adding some or all of the remaining flour, if necessary, to make a firm elastic dough. Cover the bowl and set aside in a warm draft-free place for 2 hours, or until doubled in bulk.

To make loaves Divide the dough into 2 portions. Lightly brush two 9- by 5-inch loaf tins with the remaining melted butter. Place 1 piece of dough in the center of each, or roll each piece into a 9- by 12-inch rectangle. Starting with a shorter side, roll up each rectangle to make a 9-inch loaf.

To make rolls Divide the dough into 12 portions and shape into rolls. Brush a heavy baking sheet with the remaining melted butter and set the rolls on it, spaced well apart.

Cover the loaves or rolls with a clean kitchen towel and set aside for 1 hour in a warm draft-free place, to rise.

Heat the oven to 375°F.

Whisk together the 1 tablespoon honey and the remaining ¼ cup milk and lightly brush the top of the dough to glaze. Bake loaves 1 hour, rolls 25 minutes, or until they sound hollow when tapped on the bottom. Transfer to a rack to cool.

Pies, Pastries, Cakes, and Cookies

Glykés, Píttes, Tártes, ke Biscotákia

Greeks have a great fondness for syrup-drenched pastries, pies, and cakes, but they rarely end a meal with them. Fresh fruit is the usual dessert and the Greek sweet tooth is satisfied between meals, most often at a pastry shop. Every village has at least one of these *zacharoplastía,* and in large cities the visitor is tempted at every turn by ornate examples of sculptured sweetness.

The skill of the *zacharoplástis* ("sugar sculptor") elevates cake and pastry making to fine art and the range of these sugary concoctions is breathtaking. Gloriously honeyed pastries such as *baklavá,* syrup-laden *kataïfi* (page 361), and creamy Phýllo Custard Pie (page 358) are displayed alongside regional specialties such as the wonderful lemon pie from the island of Kos.

To mark historic occasions the pastry maker bakes special celebration cakes; for festivals he bakes traditional sweet breads (pages 346–348), tiny sweet pies (page 364), and a variety of fragrant honey cakes (page 378), just as Greek bakers have done since ancient times.

Many of these traditional pastries and cakes are known as *glyká tou tapsioú,* meaning "sweets from the baking pan." After baking they are drenched in honey or syrup perfumed with orange flower water or rosewater or an aromatic spice. These, and the other pastries included here, are ambrosial. Serve them as snacks or dessert and, in the Greek fashion, provide Greek Coffee (page 453) and tall glasses of ice-cold water—perfect complements to the richness of these sweets.

Phýllo

Makes 1 pound dough

The golden pies in the windows of Greek pastry shops owe their crisp beauty to *phýllo* pastry. Paper-thin sheets of *phýllo* are difficult to make at home, but excellent *phýllo* is available ready-made, fresh or frozen. It is generally sold in 1-pound packages, each containing between 16 and 26 sheets of pastry, measuring 12 inches by 18 inches. Frozen *phýllo* must be allowed to thaw slowly in the refrigerator or it will become soggy. Unopened commercial *phýllo* can be refrigerated for up to 5 days but, once opened, it should be used within 24 hours.

Working with *phýllo* is straightforward if you bear in mind that, since it contains little oil, it must be kept moist or it will dry out and become impossible to manipulate. So cover it first with plastic wrap, then with a slightly damp kitchen towel (if the pastry touches the towel it will disintegrate). You can also protect the *phýllo* by working quickly but carefully.

If you would like to make your own *phýllo* you will need a large smooth tabletop or marble slab, a long thin rolling pin—and patience. *Phýllo* dough must be stretched as thin as possible. In some small Greek villages, making *phýllo* is a group effort, requiring four people: One stands at each corner of the rolled-out dough and each helps to pull and stretch out the pastry until it is paper-thin.

---

3 cups all-purpose flour

1 teaspoon fine-grain sea salt

¾ to 1 cup cold water

2 tablespoons olive oil

Sift 2½ cups of the flour and the salt into a large mixing bowl and gradually add enough of the water to make a firm but moist dough. Transfer to a floured work surface and knead 15 minutes, or until smooth and elastic. Sprinkle with half the olive oil and continue kneading, then sprinkle with the remaining olive oil and knead until it has all been incorporated. Tightly wrap in plastic wrap and refrigerate 1 hour to firm.

(continued)

Lightly flour a table top or marble slab. Break off an egg-sized piece of dough and roll it out, rolling first in one direction, then turning the dough and rolling again. Lightly flour the board as necessary. As the sheet becomes larger and thinner, use the rolling pin to help turn the dough, or a broom handle if the rolling pin is too short. When the pastry is paper thin, trim the edges, cut into rectangles about 12 by 18 inches, and stack between lightly floured kitchen towels. Set aside to dry for 10 minutes before using or storing. Repeat with the remaining dough.

To freeze, stack half the *phýllo* on waxed paper, cover with another sheet of waxed paper, and roll up loosely. Repeat with the remaining *phýllo*, wrap each roll in plastic wrap, and store in sealed freezer bags for up to 3 months.

Phýllo Custard Pie

Galaktoboúreko

Serves 12 to 15

This magnificent syrupy pie is best eaten very fresh. The light custard filling is scented with vanilla and lemon; the syrup, poured hot over the baked pie, is sharpened with lemon and orange—or, often, perfumed with cloves and rosewater (page 363). Be sure to use unsalted butter, which is essential to the subtle and fragrant flavor.

CUSTARD

5 cups milk

5 large eggs, separated

*1 cup vanilla sugar (page 16) or 1 cup superfine sugar
and 1 teaspoon vanilla extract*

1 cup fine-grain semolina (farína, page 462)

1 tablespoon unsalted butter

One 1-pound package phýllo *(page 357)*

*1 cup clarified butter (page 12) or 8 ounces
unsalted butter, melted*

SYRUP

1 cup honey

1 cup superfine sugar

Zest of 1 orange, removed in thin strips

Juice of 1 small lemon

3 tablespoons orange flower water, or to taste

FOR SERVING

Sifted confectioner's sugar

Ground cinnamon

Heat the milk to just below a boil. Remove from the heat and set aside. With an electric mixer or whisk, beat the egg yolks and sugar (and vanilla) in a large bowl until pale and creamy. Beat in the semolina and gradually beat in the hot milk. Rinse out the saucepan and return the custard mixture to low heat. Cook, stirring constantly in a figure-8 motion with a wooden spoon, until the custard is firm enough to come away from the sides of the pan, about 6 minutes. Transfer to a bowl. Secure the butter on the tip of a knife and rub it over the surface of the custard; the butter will immediately melt to make a thin oily layer, preventing a skin from forming. Lightly press waxed paper on top and set aside to cool.

Arrange a rack in the center of the oven and heat the oven to 375°F. Remove the packet of *phýllo* from the refrigerator and set aside unopened.

With a wire whisk, beat the custard until smooth. Whisk the egg whites in a copper or other mixing bowl until they hold stiff peaks. Stir one third of the whites into the custard to lighten it, then quickly fold in the remainder.

Divide the *phýllo* into 2 portions. Rewrap 1 and refrigerate. Lightly brush a 9- by 13-inch baking pan with melted butter. Line with 1 pastry sheet, carefully pushing it up the sides with your knuckle (fingernails tear *phýllo*). Lightly brush with butter and lay another sheet on top. Repeat with the remaining unrefrigerated *phýllo*, but do not brush the last sheet. Pour the custard into the pan, taking care not to disturb the *phýllo* lining the sides. Lightly smooth with a spatula and gently fold over any *phýllo* extending beyond the edges of the pan.

Remove the second portion of the *phýllo* from the refrigerator. Lay 1 sheet on top of the custard letting it hang over the sides of the pan and lightly brush with butter. Repeat with the remaining *phýllo*, but do not butter the last sheet. Ease the fingers of one hand down between the edge of the pie and the sides of the pan. Gently pull the bottom edges of the pie slightly towards the center and lightly tuck the top sheets in around the bottom of the pie. Liberally butter the top sheet. With a thin sharp knife, score the top 2 sheets into 3-inch squares or into diamonds with 2-inch-long sides.

Reduce the oven temperature to 350°F. Bake 40 minutes, or until the pastry is a deep golden brown and the custard is set: Gently shake the pie—it should sway only slightly; loosely cover with aluminum foil if it seems to be browning too quickly.

Meanwhile, combine the honey, sugar, orange zest, and 2 cups of water in a sugar pan or heavy saucepan. Bring slowly to a boil and simmer 10 minutes, or until the syrup lightly coats the back of a metal spoon. Set aside.

As soon as you remove the pie from the oven, immediately cut down through the score marks to the bottom of the pan. Add the lemon juice and orange flower water to the syrup, strain, reserving the zest, and pour over the hot pie. Cover the pan with a clean kitchen towel, making sure the towel does not touch the top of the pastry, and set aside; the trapped steam softens the top layers of *phýllo*. Refrigerate if serving time is more than 2 hours away.

To serve, cut through the score marks once more to loosen the pieces. Liberally sprinkle with the confectioner's sugar, lightly sprinkle with the cinnamon, and scatter the reserved orange zest over. Spoon over any syrup remaining in the pan, or serve the syrup separately if you prefer.

Kataïfi Nut Rolls with Caramel Syrup

Kataïfi Bourekákia

Makes approximately 24 pastries

Aromatic nut-filled pastries made from very thin strands of vermicelli-like dough, *kataïfi* are sumptuous honey-sweet treats. The dough, also called *kataïfi*, is available frozen in Greek and Middle Eastern stores, and the preparation, although it sounds complicated, is really not difficult. For best results make these a day ahead and pour on the hot syrup as soon as you remove the baking pan from the oven: The *kataïfi* will be sticky-sweet underneath but will remain crisp and golden on top. My favorite filling is made with pistachio nuts but almonds or walnuts are also good. For a dish of unashamed extravagance serve with Rich Cream (page 415).

---

2 cups finely chopped unsalted skinned (page 407) pistachio nuts, walnuts, or blanched almonds

1 egg white

1½ cups aromatic honey, such as Hymettus

1 teaspoon ground cinnamon, or more to taste

1¼ cups clarified butter (page 12) or 10 ounces unsalted butter, melted

One 1-pound package kataïfi

1 cup sugar

Strained juice of ½ lemon

Heat the oven to 350°F.

Whisk the egg white in a small bowl until it holds stiff peaks. Stir in the nuts, ¼ cup of the honey, the cinnamon, egg white, and 2 tablespoons of the butter and set aside.

Loosen the strands of *kataïfi*: Place the *kataïfi* in the center of a clean work surface, pull off a small amount, and gently squeeze it in one hand. With your other hand pull apart the stands, but avoid tearing them. Repeat with all the dough but work fast (don't spend more than 1 minute doing this—*kataïfi* dries out very quickly).

Lay a small handful in the palm of one hand and form into a rectangular shape. Place 1 tablespoon filling in the center, fold over the edges, and roll up towards your fingertips to make a parcel. As you finish each pastry, arrange it in a 10-inch round or 9- by 13-inch baking pan in tight concentric circles (round pan) or lines (rectangular pan). Spoon the remaining butter evenly over the pastries and bake 40 minutes, or until crisp and deep golden brown.

Meanwhile, melt the sugar in a sugar pan or small heavy saucepan and cook over a low heat until a deep gold (light caramel). While the sugar cooks, combine the remaining 1¼ cups honey with 1¼ cups water in a heavy saucepan, slowly bring to a boil, and simmer 6 minutes, or until it lightly coats the back of a metal spoon. Wrap your hand in a kitchen towel and carefully spoon the honey syrup into the caramel—don't pour: Caramel can spit and burn. Stir in the lemon juice.

As soon as you remove the pastries from the oven, pour the hot syrup over them. Cover the pan with a clean kitchen towel, making sure it does not touch the pastries, and set aside to cool. Serve the pastries directly from the baking pan or piled high on a platter.

Kataïfi and Custard Pie
in Rosewater Syrup
Kataïfi me Kréma

Serves 16 to 20

This easy-to-make pie is composed of layers of crisp golden *kataïfi* and smooth rich custard. The *kataïfi* are saturated with an exotic perfumed syrup of honey, cloves, lemon juice, and rosewater and the result is mouth-watering. Serve with Rich Cream (page 415) and Greek Coffee (page 453).

⅓ cup rice flour

1 cup superfine sugar

3 cups milk

5 egg yolks

1 teaspoon vanilla extract

One 1-pound package **kataïfi** *(page 361)*

1¼ cups clarified butter (page 12) or 10 ounces unsalted butter, melted and strained through cheesecloth

1½ cups aromatic honey (page 18)

6 whole cloves

Strained juice of 1 small lemon

3 tablespoons rosewater, or to taste

FOR SERVING

Kaymáki *rolls* **(page 415),** *optional*

Combine the rice flour with ¼ cup of the sugar and enough of the milk to make a smooth paste. Warm the remaining milk over low heat and whisk it into the paste. Rinse out the saucepan, return the milk mixture to the pan, and slowly bring to a boil, stirring constantly with a wooden spoon. Reduce the heat to very low and simmer, stirring, 3 minutes or until smooth and thick. Beat together the egg yolks and vanilla, and briskly whisk into the

Pies, Pastries, Cakes, and Cookies

milk mixture. Cook, stirring, 1 minute longer; don't let the custard boil. Set aside to cool.

Heat the oven to 350°F. Loosen the strands of *kataïfi* as directed on page 361 and place in a large bowl. Brush two 9- or 10-inch cake pans, one at least 3 inches deep, with melted butter and add the remaining butter to the *kataïfi*. With your fingers, quickly coat the stands with butter, divide between the pans, and spread evenly. Bake 30 to 40 minutes, or until crisp and a deep golden brown. Set aside to cool in the pans.

While the *kataïfi* is baking, combine the honey, cloves, remaining ½ cup sugar, and 1½ cups water in a heavy saucepan. Bring to a boil, then gently boil 10 minutes, or until the syrup coats the back of a metal spoon. Set aside to cool slightly.

Discard the cloves and stir the lemon juice and rosewater into the syrup. Pour two thirds of the warm syrup over the cooled *kataïfi* in the deeper tin. Set aside for 5 minutes, or until the syrup is absorbed by the pastry.

Cover with the custard and place the second *kataïfi* layer on top. Gently press down on it and spoon over the remaining syrup. Cover the pan with a clean kitchen towel and set aside for at least 1 hour. Cut into slices and serve.

Small Phýllo Pastries

Bourekákia

Makes approximately 24 pastries

Traditionally shaped into triangles, squares, rectangles, cigars, or coils, these crisp golden glazed pastries are stuffed with a range of delectable fillings. Pistachio nuts, almonds, or walnuts are favorites, combined with honey and cinnamon, custard, or fresh cheese. For a spectacular display on a buffet table make them in a variety of shapes and with a choice of fillings. For this recipe, you can make either one of the two fillings given below or one of the fillings detailed on pages 361, 368, and 370.

———

NUT FILLING

1 cup finely chopped walnuts

1 cup finely chopped blanched almonds

½ cup aromatic honey (page 18)

1 teaspoon finely grated lemon zest

1 teaspoon ground cinnamon

1 egg, lightly beaten

CUSTARD FILLING

2½ cups milk

4 large eggs, separated

*½ cup vanilla sugar (page 16) or ½ cup superfine
sugar and ½ teaspoon vanilla extract*

½ cup fine-grain semolina (farína, page 462)

1 tablespoon unsalted butter

*1¼ cups clarified butter (page 12) or 10 ounces
unsalted butter, melted*

One 1-pound package phýllo (page 357)

SYRUP

1 cup aromatic honey (page 18)

½ cup superfine sugar

Zest of 1 lemon, removed in thin strips

Juice of ½ lemon

2 tablespoons rosewater or orange flower water, optional

FOR SERVING

Sifted confectioner's sugar

*½ cup finely chopped unsalted pistachio nuts, walnuts,
or blanched almonds*

To make the nut filling, combine the ingredients in a large bowl.

To make the custard filling, heat the milk to just below a boil. Remove from the heat and set aside. With an electric mixer or whisk, beat the egg yolks and sugar (and vanilla) in a large bowl until pale and creamy. Beat in the semolina and gradually beat in the hot milk. Rinse out the saucepan and return the custard mixture to low heat. Cook, stirring constantly in a figure-8 motion with a wooden spoon, until firm enough to come away from the sides of the pan, about 5 minutes. Transfer to a bowl. Secure the butter on the tip of a knife and rub it over the surface of the custard. Lightly press waxed paper on top of the custard and set aside to cool.

Heat the oven to 350°F. Brush 2 baking sheets with some of the melted butter.

Divide the *phýllo* into 2 portions. Rewrap 1 and refrigerate. Fold half the remaining sheets in half, loosely cover with plastic wrap and then a slightly damp kitchen towel, and set aside. Lay the remaining sheets, stacked on top of each other, on the table, with a shorter side facing you.

To make triangles Cut the sheets lengthwise into 4 strips and stack the strips on top of each other. Lightly brush the top strip with melted butter and carefully remove from the pile, then lightly butter a second strip and place it on top of the first. Place 1 tablespoon nut filling or 2 tablespoons custard filling on the bottom end of the buttered strips. Take the bottom right corner of both strips between finger and thumb and fold over to the left side to make a triangle. Gently pull up the bottom left corner and fold up to make a second triangle. Continue folding until you reach the top. Place seam side down on the baking sheet. Repeat with the remaining *phýllo* and filling.

To make rolls Cut the *phýllo* sheets lengthwise into 3 strips and stack on top of each other. Lightly brush the top strip with melted butter and carefully remove from the pile, then lightly butter a second strip and place it on top of the first. Spread 1½ tablespoons nut filling or 3 tablespoons custard filling along the bottom of the strip, leaving a ¾-inch border along the lower edge and the sides. Fold the lower edges of the strips over the filling and roll over twice, then bring both sides over the filling, lightly brush with butter, and roll up the strip. Place seam side down on the baking sheet.

Cigars are small, thin rolls; rectangles and squares are made similarly but folded up, not rolled. If you prefer, all can be made with 1 *phýllo* strip instead of 2.

To make coils Cut the *phýllo* sheets lengthwise into 3 strips and stack on top of each other. Lightly brush the top strip with melted butter and carefully remove from the pile. Spread 1 tablespoon nut filling or 2 tablespoons custard filling along the bottom, leaving a ¾-inch border along the lower edge and the sides. Fold the lower edge over the filling and fold over both sides. Firmly roll up, and lightly brush with butter. Place a finger on one end of the cylinder and, with the other hand, wrap it around to make a tight coil. Tuck the outside end in and under, and set seam side down on the baking sheet.

Brush the pastries with the remaining melted butter and bake 20 to 25 minutes, or until crisp and golden.

While the pies are baking, combine the honey, sugar, lemon zest, and 1 cup water in a sugar pan or heavy saucepan. Bring to a boil and simmer 10 minutes, or until the syrup lightly coats the back of a metal spoon. Set aside to cool slightly, then add the lemon juice and rosewater.

Dip the hot pastries in the warm syrup a few at a time and pile on a platter. Sprinkle with the confectioner's sugar and nuts, and serve warm or cold. Serve any remaining syrup in a bowl.

Nut Pastries in Fragrant Honey Syrup

Floyéres

Makes approximately 24 pastries

With regional variations these crisp nut pastries are made throughout Greece and the islands. Sometimes they are baked, sometimes fried, and they may be shaped into half-moons, small circles, or squares. The filling given here is heady with cinnamon and cloves; these can also be made with the filling for Sweet Cheese Pastries (page 370) or any of those suggested for Small Phýllo Pastries (page 364), and honey can be substituted for the syrup.

———

(continued)

Pies, Pastries, Cakes, and Cookies

PASTRY

2 cups unbleached all-purpose flour

Pinch of salt

2 tablespoons confectioner's sugar

2 tablespoons unsalted butter, melted

2 tablespoons olive oil

2 egg yolks, lightly beaten

1 tablespoon finely grated orange zest, briefly dried in a low oven and pulverized in a mortar with 1 teaspoon sugar, or 1 teaspoon orange extract

Juice of 1 small orange

FILLING

2 egg whites

1¾ cups unsalted peeled (see page 407) pistachio nuts, walnuts, or blanched almonds, chopped

½ teaspoon ground cloves

1 teaspoon ground cinnamon

⅓ cup aromatic honey, such as Hymettus

10 tablespoons unsalted butter, melted

2 egg yolks, lightly beaten with 2 tablespoons water

SYRUP

1 cup aromatic honey, such as Hymettus

One 3-inch cinnamon stick, broken in half

4 whole cloves

Zest of 1 lemon, removed in thin strips

3 tablespoons orange flower water, or to taste

FOR SERVING

¼ cup unsalted peeled pistachio nuts, walnuts, or blanched almonds, chopped

Sifted confectioner's sugar

To make the pastry, sift the flour, salt, and sugar into a large bowl. Add the butter, olive oil, egg yolks, orange zest, and orange juice, and knead well for 5 minutes. Add cold water if necessary to make a smooth and elastic dough. Tightly cover with plastic wrap and refrigerate for 1 hour.

To make the filling, beat the egg whites until they just hold soft peaks. Combine the nuts, cloves, cinnamon, honey, and egg whites, and set aside.

Heat the oven to 350°F. Lightly brush 2 baking sheets with melted butter.

Divide the dough in half, rewrap 1 portion, and refrigerate it. Lightly flour a clean work surface. Roll out the dough as thin as possible and cut into 3-inch circles with a cookie cutter or inverted glass or into 2-inch squares with a knife. Place 1 tablespoon filling in the center of half the circles or all the squares. Dip your forefinger in water and lightly dampen the pastry edges. Place a second circle on top of the first, or pull the corners of each square almost into the center to make a smaller square with a little filling exposed, and lightly press the edges together. Seal each circle by pressing the edge with the tines of a fork or pastry wheel, or pinch the edge at ½-inch intervals to make a decorative border. Set the pastries 1 inch apart on the baking sheets, and repeat with the remaining dough and filling.

Brush with the remaining butter and bake 15 minutes, or until the pastry is set. Brush with the beaten egg yolks and bake 10 minutes longer, or until a deep golden brown. Transfer to a rack to cool.

Combine the honey, 1½ cups water, cinnamon stick, cloves, and lemon zest in a sugar pan or heavy saucepan. Bring to a boil and simmer 5 minutes. Add the orange flower water and keep the syrup hot over low heat. Dip the warm pastries in the syrup a few at a time and pile high on a warm platter. Sprinkle with the nuts and confectioner's sugar, and serve warm.

Sweet Cheese Pastries

Skaltsounákia

Makes approximately 24 pastries

A specialty of the island of Crete, these are made with a lemon-scented pastry and filled with a sweetened mixture of *myzíthra* and *féta* cheeses. Serve with bowls of warm Hymettus honey or syrup fragrant with orange flower water (page 18 or 20).

PASTRY

2 cups unbleached all-purpose flour

Pinch of salt

*1 tablespoon finely grated lemon zest, briefly dried
in a low oven and pulverized in a mortar
with 1 teaspoon sugar*

8 tablespoons unsalted butter, cold, cut into small pieces

2 egg whites

1 teaspoon vanilla extract

1 to 3 tablespoon cold milk or water

FILLING

*2 cups fresh myzíthra cheese (page 11) or 2 cups
drained small-curd cottage cheese, pressed
through a fine sieve*

¼ cup grated féta cheese

2 egg yolks, lightly beaten

½ cup aromatic honey, such as Hymettus

1 teaspoon vanilla extract

2 tablespoons brandy, optional

1 teaspoon ground cinnamon, or to taste

4 tablespoons unsalted butter, melted

2 egg yolks, lightly beaten

FOR SERVING

Ground cinnamon or orange flower water

Sifted confectioner's sugar

To make the pastry, sift the flour into a large bowl. Stir in the salt and lemon zest, add the butter, and lightly rub the mixture together with your fingers until it resembles coarse meal. Whisk the egg whites until they just hold soft peaks. Add the whites and vanilla to the flour and knead well, adding milk or water if necessary to make a smooth and elastic dough. Tightly cover with plastic wrap and refrigerate for 1 hour.

To make the filling, lightly mash the *myzíthra* in a bowl. Add all the remaining filling ingredients and mash lightly with a fork until well mixed but not smooth. Set aside.

Heat the oven to 350°F. Lightly brush 2 baking sheets with melted butter.

Divide the dough in half, rewrap 1 portion, and refrigerate it. Lightly flour a clean work surface. Roll out the dough as thin as possible and cut into 4-inch circles with a cookie cutter or inverted glass or into 4-inch squares with a knife. Place 1 heaped tablespoon filling in the center of each. Dip your forefinger in water and lightly dampen the pastry edges. Fold over circles to make half-moons and seal by gently pressing the edges together with a pastry wheel or the tines of a fork; or pull the corners of each square almost into the center to make a smaller square with a little filling exposed and lightly press the edges together. Set the pastries 1 inch apart on the baking sheets, and repeat with the remaining dough and filling.

Brush with the remaining butter and bake 15 minutes, or until the pastry is set. Brush with the beaten egg yolks and bake 10 minutes longer, or until golden brown. Cool on a rack.

Sprinkle with the cinnamon (or orange flower water) and sugar, and serve warm or at room temperature, with bowls of honey or a syrup of your choice.

Kos Lemon Pie

Lemonópitta tou Kó

Serves 10 to 12

A strong refreshing lemon flavor is the hallmark of this easy-to-make island specialty. For best results use whole blanched almonds and grind them yourself. And use a light touch when making the dough; the essence of this pie is its melt-in-the-mouth pastry and the perfect blend of the fresh natural ingredients. Serve this attractive midsummer dessert surrounded by lemon leaves if available.

————

PASTRY

1 cup unbleached all-purpose flour

¼ cup confectioner's sugar

½ tablespoon finely grated lemon zest

Pinch of salt

8 tablespoons unsalted butter, cold, cut into small pieces

2 egg yolks

1 teaspoon vanilla extract

FILLING

8 tablespoons unsalted butter, at room temperature

⅓ cup honey

5 egg yolks

1½ cups finely ground blanched almonds

Strained juice of 2 lemons

*¼ cup smooth Rich Cream (without crust, page 415)
or heavy cream*

½ cup superfine sugar

Zest of 2 lemons, removed in thin strips

Juice of 1 lemon

Sifted confectioner's sugar

To make the pastry, sift the flour and confectioner's sugar into a large cold bowl, stir in the lemon zest and salt, and add the butter. Quickly and lightly rub the mixture together with your fingers until it resembles coarse meal. Beat the egg yolks and vanilla together and stir into the flour mixture. Pull the dough together into a ball with your fingers, adding cold water only if necessary to make a soft dough. Tightly cover with plastic wrap and refrigerate for 30 minutes.

Set a rack in the center of the oven and heat the oven to 375°F.

Lightly flour a work surface and roll out the pastry to fit a 9- or 10-inch tart pan with a removable bottom. To transfer the pastry, wrap it around the rolling pin, lift above the pan, and unroll over the rim. With your thumb or knuckle, gently press the pastry into the pan, then roll the rolling pin over the rim to trim the edges. Line with aluminum foil and bake 6 to 8 minutes or until just set. Set aside, and lower the oven temperature to 325°F.

To make the filling, beat the butter and honey with an electric mixer or by hand until pale and creamy. Beat in the egg yolks one at a time. Then stir in the almonds, the juice of 2 lemons, and the cream. Pour into the pastry shell and lightly smooth the top with a spatula. Bake 30 to 40 minutes, or until golden brown and set.

Meanwhile, combine the sugar, lemon zest, and ½ cup water in a sugar pan or small heavy saucepan. Slowly bring to a boil, then simmer 6 minutes or until the syrup lightly coats the back of a metal spoon. Set aside to cool slightly.

Add the lemon juice to the barely warm syrup and strain, reserving the zest. Pour the syrup over the warm pie, remove from the pan, and liberally sprinkle with confectioner's sugar and the reserved zest. Serve immediately.

Note To make the pastry in the food processor, chill the processor bowl and metal blade in the refrigerator for 1 hour. Working very quickly, process the flour, sugar, lemon zest, and butter until the mixture resembles coarse meal. Add the egg yolks and vanilla and pulse just to mix. (It is unlikely that you will need to add water.) Wrap and refrigerate.

Pies, Pastries, Cakes, and Cookies

Yogurt Cake

Yiaourtópitta Glýkisma

Serves 14 to 18

When the occasion calls for a really sticky cake, with lashings of syrupy sweetness, this is the treat to make. It's one of the best examples of the Greek tradition of *glýka tou tapsioú,* meaning "sweets from the baking pan." In a traditional version there would be even more of the sticky lemon syrup. Increase the amount of syrup if you like, but it's quite sweet as is. This cake can be made in advance and in fact tastes even better if the flavors are allowed to mellow for a day. Serve, cut into slices, with Greek Coffee (page 453).

---

*2 cups aromatic honey, such as Hymettus or
orange blossom*

Zest of 1 lemon, removed in thin strips

¾ cup superfine sugar

6 tablespoons unsalted butter, melted

4 eggs, separated

2 to 2¼ cups unbleached all-purpose flour

2 teaspoons baking powder

2 cups Strained Yogurt (page 8), beaten until smooth

Juice of ½ lemon

Combine the honey, lemon zest, 6 tablespoons of the sugar, and 2 cups water in a sugar pan or heavy saucepan. Bring to a boil and simmer 10 minutes, or until the syrup lightly coats the back of a metal spoon. Set aside to cool.

Meanwhile, remove the zest from the cooled syrup and stir in the lemon juice.

Set a rack in the center of the oven and heat the oven to 375°F. Brush a round 9-inch cake pan at least 2½ inches deep with 1 tablespoon of the melted butter and place on a baking sheet.

With an electric mixer, beat the egg yolks and remaining 6 tablespoons sugar together until pale and thick. Sift in 1¼ cups of the flour and the baking powder and stir to mix. Stir in the remaining butter and the yogurt. Sift in enough of the remaining flour to make a dough stiff enough to come away from the sides of the bowl. (The consistency of the yogurt affects the quantity of flour needed.)

Whisk the egg whites until they hold stiff peaks and stir one third of the whites into the flour mixture. Fold in the remaining whites and pour into the cake pan. Bake 35 minutes, or until golden brown and a cake tester is clean when removed.

As soon as you remove the cake from the oven, spoon the syrup over the top, letting it run down the sides. Cover the pan with a clean kitchen towel and set aside until cool.

Note For a traditional version of this cake, increase the quantity of syrup by half: Use 3 cups honey, zest of 1½ lemons, ½ cup sugar plus 1 tablespoon, 2 cups water, and juice of 1 small lemon.

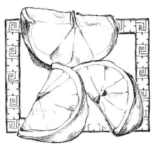

Almond Cake in Honey Syrup

Revaní

Serves 15 to 20

This cake has a pleasant almond and yogurt flavor and the syrupy coating can be orange- or lemon-scented, according to your taste. It will keep for up to one week in an airtight container, but it is likely to magically disappear long before that. Serve it cut into squares or diamond shapes, with *kaymáki* rolls (page 415) and Greek Coffee (page 453).

———

(continued)

1½ cups aromatic honey (page 18)

1½ cups superfine sugar

Zest of 1 large navel orange or 2 lemons, removed
in thin strips

1½ tablespoons unsalted butter, melted

6 eggs, separated

1½ cups fine-grain semolina (farína, page 462)

½ cup blanched almonds, coarsely ground

1 cup Strained Yogurt (page 8), beaten until smooth

½ cup chopped blanched almonds

Strained juice of 1 large navel orange or 2 lemons

2 tablespoons orange flower water, or to taste

Combine the honey, ½ cup of the sugar, the zest, and 1½ cups water in a sugar pan or heavy saucepan. Bring to a boil, and simmer 10 minutes or until the syrup lightly coats the back of a metal spoon. Let cool.

Heat the oven to 350°F. Brush a 9-inch square cake pan, at least 2½ inches deep, with the melted butter.

With an electric mixer or by hand, beat the remaining 1 cup sugar and the egg yolks together until pale and thick, about 5 minutes. Stir in the semolina, ground almonds, and yogurt. Whisk the egg whites until they form stiff peaks and stir one third into the semolina mixture. Fold in the remaining whites, pour into the cake pan, and sprinkle with the chopped almonds. Bake 40 to 45 minutes, or until golden brown.

Meanwhile, stir the orange juice and orange flower water into the cooled syrup.

As soon as you remove the cake from the oven, spoon the syrup and zest over the top, letting it run down the sides. Cover the pan with a clean kitchen towel and set aside for at least 2 hours before serving.

Honey Puffs
Loukoumáthes

Makes about 36 pastries

Tucked away in the back streets of many Greek towns are tiny cafés that serve only these light fluffy puffs of yeast batter bathed in a velvety honey and cinnamon syrup. The pastries are made to order and served with a glass of ice water to cleanse the palate after the sweetness.

Make the batter at least two hours ahead. It should be of a pouring consistency but only just. As a *loukoumáthes* cook once explained to me, the batter is right "when the dough needs a little help to leave the hand or the spoon." Then fry the pastries when your guests are ready to eat—and not a minute before.

---

2 teaspoons active dry yeast

3 tablespoons plus 1 teaspoon superfine sugar

¾ to 1¼ cups tepid (110° F) water

2 cups unbleached all-purpose flour

Pinch of salt

2 tablespoons olive oil

Peanut or corn oil, for deep-fat frying

2 cups aromatic honey, such as Hymettus

2 tablespoons fresh lemon juice

2 tablespoons rosewater, or to taste, optional

FOR SERVING

1½ tablespoons ground cinnamon

Dissolve the yeast and 1 teaspoon of the sugar in ¼ cup of the tepid water and set aside until foamy, about 10 minutes.

Sift the flour and salt into a large bowl and add the yeast mixture, olive oil, and ½ cup of the tepid water. Beat with a wooden spoon or an electric mixer to make a soft dough, adding more warm water if necessary to make it just firm enough to need scooping off a spoon. Tightly cover and set aside in a warm draft-free spot for 2 to 3 hours to rise. The dough is ready when the surface bubbles and blisters; if the batter seems thin, beat in a little more sifted flour. Knead 2 minutes and set aside.

Heat the oil to 375°F (or until a little batter dropped in sizzles immediately) in a large saucepan or deep-fat fryer. Dip a spoon in the hot oil, then scoop up about a tablespoon of dough, and use a second spoon to push it off into the oil. Don't hold the spoons too high above the oil or you will be splashed. Fry 5 or 6 *loukoumáthes* at a time until deep golden brown on all sides, about 3 minutes. Remove with a slotted spoon and drain on paper towels.

Combine the honey and 1 cup water in a heavy saucepan, bring to a boil, and simmer 3 minutes. Stir in the lemon juice and rosewater. Remove from the heat. Dip the *loukoumáthes* in the syrup a few at a time and heap on a warm platter or individual plates (5 to 6 per person). Mix the cinnamon with the remaining sugar and sprinkle over the pastries. Drizzle over a few threads of syrup and serve immediately.

Honey Cakes
Melomacárona (Finíkia)

Makes 24 small cakes

These light and crumbly cakes, Phoenician in origin, are offered to all visitors at Christmas and New Year's gatherings. The dough is shaped into small flat ovals and marked with a crisscross design; after baking each cake is dipped into a sweet syrup and sprinkled with nuts, cinnamon, and sugar for an attractive finishing touch. *Melomacárona* can be kept for up to one week in an airtight container.

———

8 tablespoons unsalted butter, melted

½ to ¾ cup olive oil

1 cup fine-grain semolina (farína, page 462)

5 tablespoons superfine sugar

2 tablespoons brandy, optional

*1 tablespoon finely grated orange zest, briefly dried in a low
oven and pulverized in a mortar with 1 teaspoon sugar,
or ½ tablespoon orange extract*

2 cups aromatic honey, such as Hymettus

1 to 1¼ cups unbleached all-purpose flour

1 teaspoon baking powder

¼ teaspoon grated nutmeg

½ teaspoon ground cloves

Strained juice of ½ lemon

*Strained juice of 1 small orange or 2 tablespoons
orange flower water*

FOR SERVING

1 cup finely chopped walnuts or blanched almonds

1 teaspoon ground cinnamon

Combine ½ cup of the olive oil and the remaining butter in a large bowl. Gradually stir in the semolina, 2 tablespoons of the sugar, the brandy, orange zest, and ½ cup of the honey. Sift together the flour, baking powder, nutmeg, and cloves, and stir into the semolina mixture. Turn out onto a lightly floured surface and knead 10 minutes, or until soft and pliant. If it seems stiff, add a little more oil; if thin, more flour.

Heat the oven to 350°F. Brush 2 baking sheets with some of the melted butter.

Form the dough into egg-sized ovals and set them 2 inches apart on the baking sheets. With the back of a fork, lightly press down twice on top of each oval to make a crisscross design, slightly flattening them at the same time. Bake 20 minutes, or until lightly browned. Transfer to a rack to cool.

While the cakes are cooling, bring the remaining 1½ cups honey and 1½ cups water to a boil in a saucepan and simmer 4 minutes. Remove from the heat and add the lemon and orange juices. With a spoon, place the barely warm cakes in the hot syrup a few at a time. Leave them in the syrup 1 minute, and transfer to paper muffin cups or a serving platter.

Combine the nuts, cinnamon, and remaining 3 tablespoons sugar, and sprinkle over the cakes.

Pies, Pastries, Cakes, and Cookies

Shortcakes

Kourabiéthes

Makes about 36 shortcakes

No festive table in Greece would be complete without a large platter piled high with these snowy white, sugar-dusted shortcakes. Scented with cloves and rosewater, these buttery treats are perfect with fruit desserts and spoon sweets. Their flavor improves with age—store them at room temperature in an airtight container with confectioner's sugar sprinkled over each layer, and dust with fresh sugar before serving. A variation of these can be made with blanched almonds (see below).

---

1 pound unsalted butter, at room temperature

1/2 cup superfine sugar

1 teaspoon vanilla extract

2 egg yolks

2 tablespoons brandy, optional

3 to 3 1/2 cups all-purpose flour

1 teaspoon baking powder

2 tablespoons unsalted butter, melted

12 to 36 whole cloves, as desired

FOR SERVING

3 tablespoons rosewater

1 1/2 cups confectioner's sugar

With an electric mixer or by hand, beat the room-temperature butter in a large bowl until light and fluffy. Beat in the sugar, vanilla, egg yolks, and brandy. Sift in 2 cups of the flour and the baking powder and beat to mix. Gradually stir in enough of the remaining flour to make a soft dough. (Traditional cooks use their fingers to do this; it is easier to judge the right moment to stop.) Tightly cover and refrigerate for 1 hour.

Heat the oven to 325°F. Lightly brush 2 baking sheets with the melted butter and dust them with flour.

Break off pieces of dough the size of very small eggs and shape into balls, ovals, pears, S-shapes, or crescents. Set 2 inches apart on the baking sheets.

Press 1 clove into each of 12 of the shortcakes or into every one if you prefer. Bake 15 minutes, or until firm and very pale gold. Transfer to racks to cool.

Sprinkle the shortcakes with the rosewater. Spread ¾ cup of the confectioner's sugar on a plate and arrange the shortcakes side by side on the sugar. Liberally dust with the remaining sugar.

Variations

- Substitute 1 cup finely ground lightly toasted blanched almonds for 1 cup of the flour.
- In a small mortar, pulverize 1 teaspoon mastic (page 467) with 1 tablespoon sugar, and add with the eggs. Omit the brandy and the cloves.

Hazelnut Cookies

Foundoúkia Biscotákia

Makes 30 to 36 cookies

The perfect accompaniment to fruit desserts and cream desserts, these sweet and spicy mouthfuls are easy to make—and they are irresistible!

———

2 tablespoons unsalted butter, melted

2 tablespoons all-purpose flour

8 ounces unsalted butter, at room temperature

¼ cup superfine sugar

*½ cup aromatic honey, such as Hymettus or
orange blossom*

3 eggs

3 cups hazelnuts or walnuts, finely ground

½ teaspoon ground cloves

1 teaspoon ground cinnamon

FOR SERVING

1 cup confectioner's sugar

Heat the oven to 325°F. Lightly brush 2 baking sheets with the melted butter and dust with flour.

Beat the room-temperature butter and the sugar in the bowl of an electric mixer or a large mixing bowl until pale and creamy, about 5 minutes. Beat in the honey, then beat in the eggs 1 at a time. Stir in 2 cups of the hazelnuts, the cloves, and cinnamon. Add some or all of the remaining hazelnuts to make a mixture just stiff enough to hold its shape.

Place heaped tablespoons of the mixture 2 inches apart on the baking sheets, and use your fingers to pull each gently up into a cone shape. Bake 20 to 25 minutes or until firm but not hard. Transfer to racks to cool.

Liberally dust with the confectioner's sugar and pile high on a platter.

Fruit Desserts, Puddings and Creams, and Candy

Froúta, Kréma, ke Glýkisma

For most Greeks, after a meal, juicy refreshing fruit is the dessert of choice. Fruits of all kinds appear on Greek tables in various seasons—although it's said that modern Greeks have nowhere near the choice of fruits that were available to their classical ancestors: For example, it is believed that there were over 100 varieties of pear in ancient Greece.

The fruits most commonly associated with Greece are the grape and the fig. Legend has it that Hercules ate vast quantities of figs and that, on one campaign, Alexander the Great's army survived for a time on only figs, so it's not surprising that even modern Greeks believe figs to be a source of strength and stamina! The wild figs of the Greek countryside are usually small and often seedless but filled with the most heavenly sweet nectar. In the early 1900s Greek immigrants took cuttings of Smyrna figs, a particularly luscious variety, to California, where they now produce magnificently plump and juicy Calimyrna figs, a lovely green-amber fruit perfect for drying. More widely available in the United States is the deep rich purple Mission fig. Either of the figs is perfect for the desserts, jams, and spoon sweets included here. Grapes, in contrast, are a relative newcomer to Greek dessert tables. Until recent years, they were grown only for wine making or drying.

Also based on fruits (although young vegetables and nuts can be used) are spoon sweets, *glyká tou koutalioú,* a very Greek specialty. Preserving ripe fruits and nuts in honey was a technique much favored by both the Minoans and the ancient Greeks. These honey-coated delicacies are a fundamental part of the Greek expression of friendship and welcome, and every guest entering a Greek house is offered a lace-covered tray holding small silver bowls of spoon sweets along with a glass of ice water, a small cup of thick strong coffee, and a small glass of liqueur. The rims of the bowls are indented to hold long-handled spoons with which the visitor scoops up the mellifluous treat. In this ritual the sweet offering is a traditional symbol of hospitality: It is extremely impolite to refuse it.

Spoon sweets are probably best described as a cross between a jam and a

preserve. Almost any fruit can be used to make them, but those made with tiny whole fruits are the most treasured of all. Spoon sweets made from sour cherries and fragrant citrus blossoms are especially delectable. All of these sweets are excellent with ice cream, pancakes, and, surprising as it may sound, with pungent goat's or sheep's cheeses.

Puddings, creams, and candies are rarely eaten straight after a meal in Greece but instead at various times throughout the day or night—whenever the need for something sweet overwhelms! In summer the whole family may go out to the pastry shop or café late in the evening to enjoy ice creams, candies, velvety smooth rice puddings, creams made from pistachios or almonds, and elaborate honeyed pastries. Many of these sweet treats have been enjoyed by generations of Greeks since antiquity—the chewy honey-sesame candies called *pastéli*, for example, were presented to victorious athletes at the classical Olympic games. And many other creams, puddings, candies, and spoon sweets are based on ancient flavors and fragrances. With their unusual tastes, textures, and aromas they are unmistakably Greek.

Platter of Fresh Fruits
Fréska Froúta

Serves 4

Magnificent platters of prepared fresh fruit must have been one of the earliest Greek desserts. Use only fruit in perfect condition and keep the arrangement simple but colorful. Since most fruits discolor very quickly, prepare them just a few minutes before serving. Allow half a dozen pieces of fruit per person.

Choose from any of the following:

½ small sweet melon such as honeydew or Persian

¼ small watermelon

1 crisp sweet apple, cored and cut into 8 wedges

1 ripe pear, cored and cut into quarters

½ pound large sweet grapes, cut into 4 clusters

1 large cactus pear, peeled (page 401), and cut into quarters

8 strawberries, with their stems if possible

16 cherries, with their stems if possible

4 ripe figs, halved

2 peaches or nectarines, peeled, pitted, and cut into quarters

FOR SERVING

Green leaves such as those of the fig, strawberry, lemon or apple, rinsed and patted dry

12 ounces **myzíthra** *cheese, cut into 8 slices*

Hymettus or other aromatic honey

Remove the seeds from the honeydew melon, cut it into 4 slices, and cut off the rind. Cut the watermelon flesh into 4 or 8 chunks.

Line a serving platter with the leaves and arrange the fruit attractively on the leaves. Serve with a plate of the sliced cheese and small bowls of the honey.

Note Mulberries, apricots, plums, and quince are other traditional Greek fruits. For breakfast, serve with Strained Yogurt (page 8), honey, and Currant Bread (page 352).

Fruit in Sweet Wine and Honey

Froúta Glýkisma

Serves 6

At summer tables today it is still traditional to dip fresh fruit into a glass of sweet wine before eating it, but the fruit also can be poached in wine. For this versatile, not-too-sweet dish you can use a wide variety of fruits, including peaches, nectarines, plums, apricots, cherries, figs, pears, apples, and quinces or melons. The fruit should be ripe but it does not have to be perfect to produce a special dessert. Here the flavoring for the poaching syrup is vanilla, coriander, and lemon but you can also try cinnamon, cloves, or orange (see below). For a particularly delicate flavor add the pits of fruits such as apricots to the poaching liquid. Serve poached fruit on its own or with cookies, Rich Cream (page 415), and chilled Samos wine.

————

2 cups sweet Samos wine or 1 cup Mavrodaphne wine

¹/₂ cup aromatic honey, such as Hymettus

One 2-inch piece of vanilla bean or 1 teaspoon vanilla extract

24 whole coriander seeds

Zest of ¹/₂ small lemon, removed in thin strips

6 portions of any of the fruits mentioned above

Combine the wine, water, honey, vanilla, coriander seeds, and lemon zest, and enough water to cover the fruit in a large saucepan, slowly bring to a boil, and simmer 5 minutes.

Meanwhile, remove the stems from the fruit (or trim those of figs), and remove any pits carefully so the fruit does not lose its shape. Use a pitter for cherries and a small paring knife for plums and apricots. Cut melon into bite-sized pieces. Peel apples, pears, and quinces and cut into slices. If you

Fruit Desserts, Puddings and Creams, and Candy

are poaching apricots, crack a few pits with a nutcracker, remove the kernels, and add to the poaching liquid.

Add the fruit to the poaching liquid in small batches, slightly raise the heat, and return to a gentle simmer. Poach until barely tender: figs, grapes, or melons 1 to 2 minutes, apricots or gooseberries about 4 minutes, plums or cherries about 6 minutes, and apple, pear, or quince slices about 8 minutes. Transfer to paper towels to drain and place in a serving bowl.

Raise the heat and boil the poaching liquid until it is slightly syrupy and lightly coats the back of a metal spoon. Let cool slightly, strain, and pour over the fruit. Set aside for up to 2 hours, or cover and refrigerate for up to 24 hours. Serve at room temperature.

Note Strawberries, other soft berries, and citrus fruit segments need no poaching; just macerate them in a little honey or sugar before pouring the warm syrup over them.

Peaches in Sweet Wine and Honey
Glýkisma me Rothákina

Choose 6 small or 3 large ripe peaches with no bruise marks or soft spots, and handle them carefully; do not peel until after poaching so the fruit retains flavor and color. Substitute 3 whole cloves and one 3-inch cinnamon stick for the vanilla and coriander. Cut larger peaches in half and discard the pits; to pit a small peach, hold it firmly, insert the point of a paring knife into its stem end, carefully loosen the pit, and then push it out from the other end. Poach small peaches or peach halves 5 minutes, larger whole peaches 8 minutes.

Note Nectarines can be substituted for the peaches.

Fragrant Apricot Ice Cream

Veríkoka Pagotá Aromatiká

Serves 6

Apricots, said to originate in China, are thought to have been brought to Greece by the Phoenicians. In those days they were probably made into creams or candies, but modern Greeks are more likely to use this ancient flavor in ice creams. Make this rich ice cream in early summer when apricots are ripe and sweet. Serve it prettily decorated with toasted almonds and small colorful flowers, and accompanied by glasses of sweet Samos liqueur.

---

2 pounds fresh apricots

1 teaspoon vanilla extract

½ cup aromatic honey (such as Hymettus), or to taste

3 eggs, separated

*⅓ cup Rich Cream (without crust, page 415)
or ⅔ cup heavy cream*

2 tablespoons Samos liqueur or apricot ratafia, optional

FOR SERVING

Toasted slivered almonds

*A few citrus blossoms or borage flowers or other fragrant,
decorative (nonpoisonous) flowers*

Fill a large saucepan with water and bring to a boil. Drop the apricots into the boiling water, remove the saucepan from the heat, count to 3, then carefully remove the apricots with a slotted spoon. Peel with a small paring knife, cut each in half, and discard the pits. If they are not quite ripe, bring about ½ cup water to a boil in a heavy saucepan, add the apricots, and simmer 5 minutes. Drain and reserve the cooking liquid. Process the apricots until smooth in a food processor fitted with the plastic blade. Add the vanilla and most of the honey. Add the remaining honey to taste, and add some of the reserved cooking liquid if necessary to produce a mixture the consistency of heavy cream.

(continued)

Place 1 cup of this purée in a nonreactive bowl, tightly cover, and refrigerate. Whisk the egg yolks until thick and pale and gradually add the remaining purée, whisking constantly. Transfer to a small heavy saucepan or the top of a double boiler set over hot water. Heat over low heat, stirring constantly, until thick enough to lightly coat the back of the spoon, about 5 minutes. Immediately transfer to a bowl. Let cool.

Stir the Rich Cream until smooth (or whisk heavy cream until slightly thickened), and lightly whisk it into the cooled custard. Transfer to an ice cream machine and freeze according to the manufacturer's instructions. When the mixture is almost frozen, whisk the egg whites until they hold soft peaks, fold into the custard, and freeze until firm.

Add the liqueur to the reserved purée. Stir in honey to taste if desired and add some of the reserved juice or water if necessary to give a pourable consistency.

To serve, spoon the sauce onto chilled plates, place small scoops of ice cream in the center of the sauce, and sprinkle with the toasted almonds and blossoms. Serve immediately.

Note You can also freeze this ice cream in the freezer. Pour the cooled custard into metal pans and freeze, stirring occasionally, until almost firm. Whisk the egg whites until they hold firm peaks and fold them into the custard until thoroughly combined. Freeze until firm.

Honey Ice Cream with Fresh Fig Compote

Pagotó me Síka ke Khímo Rothión

Serves 6

In early fall tall glasses of honeyed ice cream topped with a syrupy compote of figs and pomegranate juice are served in pastry shops throughout Greece. It's an elegant and refreshing dessert, rich with the deep, luscious flavors of the two best fruits of the season. Serve it with Almond Shortcakes (page 380) or Hazelnut Cookies (page 382).

2 large ripe pomegranates

1 tablespoon fresh lemon juice

¹/₂ cup honey, preferably Hymettus

*1 pound fresh figs, peeled and cut into
4 or 6 wedges each*

1 cup milk

*One 2-inch piece of vanilla bean, split, or
1 teaspoon vanilla extract*

4 egg yolks

1 tablespoon superfine sugar

*²/₃ cup Rich Cream (without crust, page 415)
or 1 cup heavy cream*

Scoop out the flesh and seeds from the pomegranates and place in a food processor bowl fitted with the plastic blade. Blend at low speed just until the flesh is separated from the seeds, about 15 seconds. (A gentle touch is essential or the juice will be tannin-flavored, a result of working the membranes too vigorously.) Strain the juice through 2 layers of cheesecloth into a nonreactive bowl. Stir in the lemon juice and 2 tablespoons of the honey, then add the figs. Tightly cover and refrigerate for 2 to 3 hours, shaking the bowl occasionally, to redistribute the figs in the sauce.

Place the milk and vanilla bean in a heavy saucepan and heat over low heat until very hot, but not boiling. Remove from the heat. With a hand whisk or electric mixer, whisk the egg yolks and sugar until pale and frothy, about 2 minutes. Gradually add the hot milk, whisking constantly. Return the custard to the rinsed-out saucepan and gently heat, whisking constantly, until it lightly coats the back of a spoon. Transfer to a bowl and set aside to cool.

Remove the vanilla bean from the custard and discard. Add the remaining honey to taste. Whisk the *kaymáki* until smooth (whisk the heavy cream until thick), and stir into the custard. Transfer to an ice cream machine and freeze according to the manufacturer's instructions, or pour into metal pans and freeze until firm, stirring occasionally.

To serve, place 2 or 3 small scoops of ice cream in tall parfait glasses and spoon over the fig and pomegranate compote.

Fresh Fig Custard

Fréska Síka Afróthi

Serves 6

This fluffy custard is perfect for figs that are too battered to serve on their own. You can use any variety of fig, although deep purple Mission figs will give the custard the most spectacular color. Adding the optional egg white will produce a custard somewhat like a soufflé although it will not rise very high. You can make this in a large soufflé dish or individual dishes, and it can be served hot or at room temperature.

¾ cup superfine sugar

*1 pound ripe figs, preferably Mission, peeled, and cut
into 4 or 6 wedges each*

8 tablespoons unsalted butter

3 tablespoons all-purpose flour

¾ cup milk

One 2-inch piece of vanilla bean or 1 teaspoon vanilla extract

4 large eggs, separated

1 egg white, optional

FOR SERVING

Sifted confectioner's sugar

Heat the oven to 425°F. Combine ½ cup of the sugar and ¼ cup water in a sugar pan or heavy saucepan and bring to a boil over low heat. Raise the heat and boil rapidly for 3 to 4 minutes, or until the syrup lightly coats the back of a metal spoon. Add the figs, gently shake the saucepan to coat the figs, and reduce the heat to very low. Simmer 6 to 8 minutes, or until the figs darken a little. Set aside.

Melt 4 tablespoons of the butter in a heavy saucepan over low heat. Stir in the flour with a wooden spoon and cook, stirring, 2 minutes longer, or until this roux turns a medium gold. Meanwhile combine the milk, 1 tablespoon of the remaining sugar, and the vanilla in another saucepan and heat to just under a boil. Whisk the milk into the roux and cook, whisking constantly, until the custard reaches a low boil. Reduce the heat, simmer a few minutes longer, and remove from the heat.

Brush a 6-cup soufflé dish with the remaining 4 tablespoons butter and sprinkle with the remaining 3 tablespoons sugar. Invert over the sink and tap sharply to remove excess sugar.

Remove the vanilla bean from the custard and stir in the egg yolks one at a time. Stir in the figs and their syrup just to combine. With a hand whisk or an electric mixer, whisk the egg whites until they hold stiff peaks. Stir one third of the whites into the fig custard, then lightly fold in the remaining whites and transfer to the soufflé dish. Reduce the oven temperature to 375°F and bake 30 minutes. Gently shake the dish—it should wobble only slightly. Bake another 5 to 10 minutes if necessary.

Dust the custard with the confectioner's sugar and serve immediately. Or let cool, dust with the sugar, and serve warm or at room temperature.

To make individual custards Butter small (1-cup) soufflé or other oven-proof dishes, sprinkle with sugar, and divide the custard equally among them. Bake 20 to 25 minutes at 350°F.

Variation

• Double the quantity of vanilla and add ½ cup sieved fresh *myzíthra* cheese (page 11) or ¼ cup Rich Cream (page 415) to the custard after the egg yolks. Bake at 350°F and increase the baking time by 5 to 10 minutes; if the custard browns too quickly, loosely cover with aluminum foil. This custard is especially good warm.

Fruit Desserts, Puddings and Creams, and Candy

Baked Figs

Síka sto Foúrno

Serves 4

Firm but not underripe figs are the kind to choose for this dish. They are baked whole in a honeyed orange juice syrup until they are soft, sweet, and shiny. Arranged on a white serving platter, sprinkled with syrup and fragrant orange flower water, they make an elegant and delicious dessert. Also try baking figs in Mavrodaphne or Samos wine instead of orange juice. Fresh *myzíthra* (page 11) is the traditional accompaniment.

------

12 to 16 small fresh figs or 8 large figs

*¼ to ⅓ cup honey, preferably Hymettus,
or superfine sugar (to taste)*

½ teaspoon vanilla extract

*Strained juice of 1 large orange or ½ cup
Mavrodaphne or sweet Samos wine*

FOR SERVING

2 tablespoons orange flower water, optional

Heat the oven to 325°F. Rinse the figs and trim the stems. Arrange in a single layer, stem ends up, in a heavy baking dish.

Combine the honey, vanilla, and orange juice in a small saucepan and gently heat until the honey has dissolved. Pour over the figs and add enough water to cover the bottom of the dish. Bake, uncovered, 15 minutes and baste the figs with the juices in the dish. Bake small figs 40 minutes longer, large figs 1 hour longer, basting occasionally; add a few tablespoons water if necessary so there is always some liquid in the dish.

Transfer the figs to a platter, spoon over the syrup, sprinkle with the orange flower water, and serve.

Anoula's Dried Figs

Síka Xserá

Serves 6

This recipe comes from my neighbor on Crete, Anoula. Each year she dries hundreds of figs, first laying them out in the sun for 3 days on a bamboo frame covered with dried grass, then completely drying them in a low oven. The most attractive figs from this abundance are packed into wooden boxes to be given as gifts; others are threaded on long grass strings and hung from storage room rafters, to serve later as a *mezé;* and still others are kept for spicy sweet desserts like this one.

---

18 plump dried imported or Calimyrna figs

6 bay leaves

One 2-inch cinnamon stick

One 1-inch piece of lemon zest

3 cups Mavrodaphne wine or strong freshly brewed
tea, strained

½ to 1 cup sugar

18 lightly toasted blanched almonds

FOR SERVING

2 tablespoons fresh lemon juice or orange flower water

Rinse the figs, trim the stems, and combine the figs, bay leaves, cinnamon stick, lemon zest, and wine in a nonreactive bowl. Cover and set aside overnight.

Transfer to a heavy saucepan and slowly bring to a boil. Simmer 10 minutes, then transfer the figs with a slotted spoon to paper towels to drain. Measure the cooking liquid, return it to the saucepan, and add half as much sugar as measured liquid. Raise the heat and boil 10 minutes, or until the syrup lightly coats the back of a metal spoon. Strain and set aside.

With a small knife, make an incision in each fig just below the stem. Insert an almond into each fig, leaving the tip exposed. Place the figs in a

bowl and pour over the syrup. Let cool, tightly cover, and set aside for 2 to 6 hours.

To serve, arrange the figs on a platter with the almonds upwards, pour over any remaining syrup, and sprinkle with the lemon juice.

Dried Apricots with Sweet Samos Wine
Veríkoka Xserá me Krasí Samiótiko

Substitute sun-dried apricots for the figs and sweet Samos wine for the Mavrodaphne. Omit the bay leaves and cinnamon. Simmer only 2 minutes.

Minoan Dates and Prunes
Mourmáthes Xserá ke Damáskina

Serves 6

Dried prunes were exported to Egypt by the Minoans; dates imported from Egypt by the same route. This ancient dish remains a favorite of Cretan islanders. An attractive dessert, it is easy to prepare. When choosing the fruit, select large California prunes and dates if possible (avoid sticky shiny dates, which are too sweet for this recipe).

---

12 large prunes, soaked in 2 cups Mavrodaphne wine or strong freshly brewed tea for 4 to 12 hours

¹/₃ to ¹/₂ cup sugar

12 large dates

1 cup Rich Cream (without crust, page 415) or mascarpone cheese

12 toasted blanched almonds, coarsely chopped

Transfer the prunes and their liquid to a heavy saucepan and slowly bring to a boil. Simmer 2 minutes, then, using a slotted spooon, transfer the prunes to paper towels to drain. Measure the cooking liquid, return it to the saucepan, and add half as much sugar as the measured liquid. Raise the heat and boil 10 minutes, until the syrup lightly coats the back of a metal spoon. Set aside.

Make a lengthwise incision in each fruit and carefully remove the pits. For a neat appearance, tuck in the sides of the prune incisions with the point of a small knife. Arrange the prunes and dates on a platter.

Beat the Rich Cream until firm enough to hold its shape and divide in half. Using one half, place a spoonful of cream in each date. Whisk 3 tablespoons of the syrup into the remaining cream and whisk until stiff. Fill each prune with a spoonful of this mixture.

Sprinkle the almonds over the prunes, and sprinkle with some or all of the remaining syrup if desired. (Dates need no added sweetness.) Serve immediately.

Morello Cherry Spoon Sweet
Víssino

Makes 6 to 7 cups

Morello cherries are much loved by Greeks and have been popular since classical times. The delicious summer fruit is eaten both fresh from the tree, juicy and sharp, or as a preserve, mellowed by sugar and brandy. Dried cherries are eaten with strong country cheese as a simple *mezé*, cherry juice is fermented into liqueur, and plump and luscious cherries are made into this delicious spoon sweet. Morello cherries are occasionally available in our markets; sweet cherries are not a perfect substitute, but they too can be made into a satisfactory spoon sweet (recipe follows). The perfect accompaniment for both versions is *myzíthra* cheese (page 11).

---

2 pounds Morello (sour) cherries

2¼ pounds sugar

1 teaspoon vanilla extract

2 tablespoons fresh lemon juice

Thoroughly wash and sterilize four 1-pint jars and set aside in a warm spot.

Working over a bowl to catch any juices, remove the pits from the cherries with a cherry-pitter or small paring knife. Reserve the juice. Crack 12

Fruit Desserts, Puddings and Creams, and Candy

of the pits and remove the kernels. Wrap these in a small square of cheese-cloth, tying up the edges to make a bag. Set aside.

Combine the sugar, any reserved juices, and ¼ cup water in a large heavy saucepan and melt the sugar over very low heat. Raise the heat to medium-low and boil 1 minute, stirring vigorously. Add the cherries and bag of kernels and boil 12 minutes. Remove any froth with a slotted spoon, taking care not to stir it into the syrup. With the slotted spoon, transfer the cherries to paper towels to drain, leaving as much syrup as possible in the pan. Discard the bag of kernels. Add the vanilla to the syrup, raise the heat, and boil rapidly until the syrup reaches 235°F to 240°F on a candy thermometer (or a little syrup dropped into a glass of cold water immediately forms a soft ball). Add the lemon juice, and set aside to cool slightly.

Divide the cherries among the sterilized jars and add enough syrup to cover. (Use any remaining syrup for drinks or to pour over ice cream.) Let cool, tightly cover, and store at room temperature for up to 6 months.

Sweet Cherry Spoon Sweet
Kerási

Use 2½ pounds small ripe but firm sweet cherries, 2 pounds sugar, 2 teaspoons vanilla extract, and the juice of 1 small lemon. Boil the cherries in the syrup for 10 to 15 minutes or until they are plump and a little translucent. Drain and proceed as directed above.

Fresh Fig and
Honeydew Spoon Sweet

Síka ke Pepóni Glykó

Makes 6 to 8 cups

Perfectly ripe melons and figs need no adornment and are deliciously refreshing to eat just as they are. But bruised or less-than-perfect fruits can be made into this ancient spoon sweet, an ideal way to enjoy all their juicy flavor.

———

One 2-pound honeydew or other sweet melon

1 pound fresh figs, trimmed, peeled, and cut into 6 or 8 wedges (about 3 cups)

Strained juice of 2 large lemons

3 to 4 cups sugar

Thoroughly wash and sterilize eight ½-pint jars. Cut the melon in half, remove the seeds, and dice the flesh (you should have about 3 cups). Place the figs, melon, and lemon juice in a large heavy saucepan and simmer 20 to 30 minutes, or until the fruit is soft. Transfer to a nonreactive sieve set over a bowl and press the fruit through with a wooden spoon.

Measure the purée, return it to the rinsed-out pan, and add exactly the same quantity of sugar. Slowly bring to a boil to dissolve the sugar, then raise the heat. Boil rapidly, stirring occasionally to prevent sticking or burning, until the syrup reaches 235°F to 240°F on a candy thermometer (or a little syrup dropped into a glass of cold water immediately forms a soft ball), about 20 minutes. The mixture will be thick and a deep reddish-brown. Let cool slightly.

Fill the jars, let cool completely, and cover tightly. Store at room temperature for up to 4 months.

Lemon Blossom Spoon Sweet

Glykó Lemónanthos

Makes approximately 3 cups

The perfumed blossoms of rose, orange, grapefruit, jasmine, and honeysuckle can all be made into delectable spoon sweets, but the most exquisitely fragrant of them all is made from lemon blossom. For this recipe you need the flower petals only, so enlist a friend's help to gather them. One of you holds a bag under a blossom-laden branch while the other gently shakes the flowers so that the petals fall into the bag. (Be sure to leave some blossom on the tree so that, in a few months' time, you can gather a harvest of perfumed juicy lemons!)

———

1 tightly packed cup lemon petals

2 cups sugar

Juice of 1 lemon

Thoroughly wash and sterilize four ½-pint jars.

Combine the petals with the sugar and set aside, uncovered, for 4 to 6 hours. With your fingers, toss the petals occasionally, gently rubbing them together so they bruise lightly. Your kitchen will smell wonderful!

Slowly bring ½ cup water and half the lemon juice to a boil in a large heavy nonreactive saucepan. Add the petals and sugar, reduce the heat to very low, and cook until the sugar has dissolved. Raise the heat, gently boil 20 minutes, and set aside to cool.

Strain through a sieve, preferably plastic, set over a bowl and discard the solids. Return the syrup to the rinsed-out pan, add the remaining lemon juice, and boil until the syrup reaches 235°F on a candy thermometer (or a little syrup dropped onto a cold plate retains its shape). Let cool slightly.

Fill the jelly jars, let cool completely, and cover tightly. Store at room temperature for up to 3 months.

Cactus Pear Spoon Sweet
Glykó Frangósika

Makes approximately 4 cups

The large cactus pear bush (also known as prickly pear) is a common sight all around the eastern Mediterranean. Its sweet ruby-red fruits, available here in produce markets in the fall, taste wonderful chilled, with a little lemon juice sprinkled over them. Or choose tender cactus pears to make this colorful spoon sweet, especially good with *myzíthra* (page 11) or pungent *kephalotýri* cheese (page 10).

---

8 medium to large cactus pears (about 3 pounds)

1½ to 2 cups sugar

Strained juice of 1 small lemon

Thoroughly wash and sterilize five ½-pint jars and set aside in a warm spot.

Without touching it—or your hand will be covered with tiny hair-like spines—secure 1 cactus pear with a fork and slice off each end with a sharp knife. Make 4 or 5 lengthwise incisions through the skin, slip the knife blade under each strip of skin, and lift it off. Without letting the exposed fruit touch the work surface (to avoid the spines), transfer it to a clean cutting board and cut into small pieces. Repeat with the remaining fruit.

Place the fruit, including the seeds, in a large heavy saucepan and simmer until tender, about 10 minutes. Transfer to a sieve, preferably plastic, set over a bowl, and press the fruit through it. Discard the seeds. Measure the purée, return it to the rinsed-out pan, and add the lemon juice and ¾ cup sugar for every 1 cup purée. Slowly bring to a boil over medium-low heat. Raise the heat and rapidly boil, stirring occasionally to prevent sticking or burning, until the purée reaches 235°F to 240°F on a sugar thermometer (or a little purée dropped onto a cold plate retains its shape). Let cool slightly.

Fill the jelly jars, let cool completely, and cover tightly. Store at room temperature for up to 3 months.

Fruit Desserts, Puddings and Creams, and Candy

Vanilla Rice Pudding

Risógalo me Vaníllia

Serves 6

The enticing moist and creamy rice puddings of Greece, never thick or overly sweet, bear no resemblance to any versions remembered from childhood. Greeks enjoy them as a snack as well as a satisfying end to a meal and this vanilla-flavored pudding is one of the most popular. Other traditional flavorings are mastic (page 467), lemon (page 18), and orange (page 20).

⅔ cup round or short-grain rice

3 cups milk

⅓ cup plus 1 tablespoon superfine sugar or vanilla sugar (page 16), or more to taste

½-inch strip of orange zest

Pinch of salt

1 tablespoon unsalted butter

1 egg

½ teaspoon vanilla extract, or to taste

1 tablespoon fresh lemon juice, or more to taste

⅓ cup Rich Cream (without crust, page 415) or ½ cup heavy cream

FOR SERVING

Ground cinnamon

Sifted confectioner's sugar

Place the rice in boiling water and leave for 5 seconds; drain, and rinse. Bring the milk almost to a boil in a heavy saucepan, and stir in the rice, the ⅓ cup sugar, the orange zest, salt, and butter. Reduce the heat to very low and simmer uncovered, stirring occasionally to prevent sticking, for 1 hour, or until thick and creamy. Remove from the heat and set aside.

Whisk together the egg, vanilla, lemon juice, and remaining 1 tablespoon sugar until pale and thick, about 2 minutes. Remove the orange zest from

the rice mixture and stir half the rice into the egg mixture. Return this to the saucepan and stir to combine. Gently cook over low heat, stirring well, for 2 minutes. Stir in the Rich Cream and add more sugar or lemon juice if desired. (If using heavy cream, beat until slightly thickened, then stir into the rice mixture.) Divide among individual dishes and chill.

To serve, liberally dust with the cinnamon and confectioner's sugar.

Aromatic Rice Pudding

Risógalo Aromatikó

Serves 6

M astic, the resin of the mastic tree, was greatly valued by the ancient gourmets as a flavoring for puddings, spoon sweets, and bread (page 346).

There is no substitute for the strong, rather mysterious taste and perfume of mastic—look for small packets of the granules in Greek and Middle Eastern stores. It is particularly good combined with other flavors of antiquity such as those of Baked Figs in the oven (page 394), Glazed Sweet Chestnuts (page 410), or the spoon sweets (pages 397 to 401). Serve small quantities of this delectable pudding, since the flavors are strong and too much can be overpowering.

½ cup round or short-grain rice

4 cups milk

Pinch of salt

1 tablespoon unsalted butter

*¼ cup vanilla sugar (page 16) or ¼ cup superfine sugar
and ½ teaspoon vanilla extract, or
more sugar to taste*

1 tablespoon mastic granules

1 tablespoon fresh lemon juice

FOR SERVING

Sifted confectioner's sugar

Finely chopped toasted almonds   (continued)

Fruit Desserts, Puddings and Creams, and Candy

Place the rice in boiling water and leave for 5 seconds; drain, and rinse. Bring the milk almost to a boil in a heavy saucepan, and add the rice, salt, butter, all but 1 tablespoon of the sugar, and the vanilla. Reduce the heat to very low and simmer uncovered, stirring occasionally to prevent sticking, for 1 hour, or until soft and creamy. Remove from the heat before all the liquid evaporates; the mixture thickens on cooling. Set aside.

Pound the mastic in a mortar with the remaining sugar to a fine powder (or grind in a clean coffee grinder). Stir this powder, the lemon juice, and more sugar if desired into the warm rice. Divide among individual dishes, let cool, cover, and chill.

To serve, dust with the confectioner's sugar and sprinkle with the almonds.

Lemon Rice Pudding

Risógalo me Lemóni

Serves 6

These refreshing, meltingly creamy puddings can be served on their own, or with Lemon Blossom Spoon Sweet (page 400). With their golden brown topping of caramelized sugar, they look extremely pretty.

––––––––––

²/₃ cup round or small-grain rice

Finely grated zest of 1 lemon

3 cups milk

¹/₂ cup superfine sugar, or to taste

Pinch of salt

1 tablespoon unsalted butter

3 eggs, separated

¹/₂ teaspoon vanilla extract

Strained juice of 1 lemon, or to taste

¹/₃ cup heavy cream

FOR SERVING

Sifted confectioner's sugar

Place the rice with the lemon zest in boiling water and leave for 5 seconds; drain, and rinse. Bring the milk nearly to a boil in a heavy saucepan and stir in the rice and lemon zest, ¼ cup of the sugar, the salt, and butter. Reduce the heat to very low and simmer uncovered, stirring occasionally to prevent sticking, for 1 hour, or until thick and creamy. Set aside.

Set a rack in the center of the oven and heat the oven to 350°F. Whisk together the egg yolks, vanilla, 2 tablespoons of the remaining sugar, and most of the lemon juice until pale and creamy; lightly beat the cream until slightly thickened. Add the cream and the egg yolk mixture to the rice, and add sugar and the remaining lemon juice to taste. Whisk the egg whites in a large copper or mixing bowl until they hold stiff peaks. Stir one third of the whites into the rice, and lightly fold in the remaining whites. Divide among 6 dishes and smooth the tops.

Place in a shallow baking pan and add water to come 1 inch up the sides of the dishes. Bake 25 minutes, or until barely set.

Meanwhile, heat the broiler. Place the puddings on the broiler rack and sprinkle with the remaining 2 tablespoons sugar. Broil 3 to 4 inches from the heat source until caramelized and golden brown, about 2 minutes.

Serve warm, at room temperature, or chilled, lightly dusted with the confectioner's sugar.

Orange Rice Pudding
Risógalo me Portokáli

Substitute the juice of 2 oranges and the finely grated zest of 1 orange for the lemon juice and lemon zest.

Remove the zest of the second orange with a stripper or zester. Combine an additional ½ cup sugar and ½ cup water and boil to a light syrup, about 8 minutes. Add the orange zest and simmer 5 minutes longer. Remove the zest with a slotted spoon, drain on paper towels, and coarsely chop. Reserve the syrup.

To serve, sprinkle the puddings with chopped orange zest, some of the syrup, and orange flower water if desired. Dust with confectioner's sugar and a pinch of cinnamon.

Fruit Desserts, Puddings and Creams, and Candy

Almond Creams
Kréma Amígdalou

Serves 6

The perfect dinner party dessert after a rich main course, these light creams have a delicate sweet almond flavor enhanced with a subtle hint of mace. Decorated with a scattering of honeyed almonds and fresh or candied flowers, they have an elegant appearance and an unusual exotic taste. The almond cream must be prepared at least 6 hours before serving to allow the flavors to develop.

———

3 tablespoons cornstarch

2 tablespoons ground rice (available in health food stores)

2 cups milk

¼ cup aromatic honey, such as Hymettus

1 egg yolk

1¼ cups freshly ground blanched almonds

¼ teaspoon ground mace

FOR SERVING

Sifted confectioner's sugar

¼ cup honeyed blanched almonds (see Note), lightly crushed, or ¼ cup toasted blanched almonds, finely chopped

Fresh or candied violets or rose petals, optional

Combine the cornstarch and ground rice with ¼ cup of the milk and stir until smooth. Warm the remaining 1¾ cups milk in a large saucepan and whisk it into the cornstarch mixture. Return it to the rinsed-out saucepan and slowly bring to a boil, stirring. Simmer 1 minute, stirring, then transfer to a nonreactive bowl. Stir in the honey, egg yolk, almonds, and mace. Let cool, cover, and refrigerate for at least 6 hours, or overnight.

Set a sieve, preferably plastic, over a bowl and press the almond cream through with a wooden spoon. Divide among individual bowls, lightly dust with the confectioner's sugar, and sprinkle with the almonds. Serve cold, decorated with the flowers.

Note To make honeyed almonds, heat the oven to 300°F. Toast 24 whole blanched almonds, turning once so they brown evenly, until pale golden brown, about 10 minutes. Combine with enough honey to coat (about 3 to 4 tablespoons) and spread on a lightly buttered baking sheet. Bake 8 minutes, or until the honey coating hardens. Cool on the baking sheet, and store in an airtight jar between layers of waxed paper.

Pistachio Creams

Kréma Fistikioú

Serves 6

The aromatic flavor of pistachio nuts in this beautiful pale green cream is enhanced with fragrant honey and vanilla. For an elegant and sophisticated dessert, serve with a bowl of perfectly ripe pears.

———

1 cup unsalted pistachio nuts

2 tablespoons cornstarch

2 tablespoons semolina (farína, page 462)

2 cups milk

¼ to ½ cup aromatic honey, such as Hymettus (to taste)

One 2-inch piece of vanilla bean or 1 teaspoon vanilla extract

2 egg yolks

FOR SERVING

Sifted confectioner's sugar

Wrap the pistachio nuts in a kitchen towel, rub briskly, and remove the loosened skins with your forefinger and thumb. Coarsely chop about 6 nuts and set aside for garnish. Finely chop the remaining nuts and set aside.

(continued)

Fruit Desserts, Puddings and Creams, and Candy

Combine the cornstarch and semolina with ¼ cup of the milk and stir until smooth. Warm the remaining 1¾ cups milk in a large saucepan and whisk it into the cornstarch mixture. Return it to the rinsed-out saucepan and slowly bring to a boil, stirring well. Add the honey and vanilla and simmer 2 minutes, stirring. Transfer to a nonreactive bowl, and stir in the egg yolks and finely chopped nuts. Let cool, cover, and refrigerate for at least 6 hours or overnight.

Set a sieve, preferably plastic, over a bowl and press the pistachio cream through with a wooden spoon. Discard the vanilla bean. Divide among individual bowls, lightly dust with the confectioner's sugar, and sprinkle with the reserved nuts. Serve cold.

Sweet Chestnuts and Lemon Cheese

Kástana Glýkisma me Kaymáki

Serves 8

The chestnut season is always anticipated with relish in Greece and, for a few weeks in the fall, small braziers appear at every street corner and the debris of roasted chestnuts covers the sidewalks. Syrupy chestnut desserts are popular, especially this treat, based on thick and mellow *kaymáki* cream, perfumed with lemon, vanilla, and cloves. You can use heavy cream instead of *kaymáki* with no great loss of character to the dish, but make the lemon cheese at least four hours in advance for the richest flavor and texture.

―――――

LEMON CHEESE

2 cups Rich Cream (without crust, page 415)
or heavy cream

Finely grated zest of 1 lemon

Strained juice of 1 lemon

½ cup superfine sugar

3 egg whites

1½ pounds chestnuts, shelled and skinned (page 410)

*¼ cup vanilla sugar (page 16) or ¼ cup superfine
sugar and ½ teaspoon vanilla extract*

1 cup milk

3 whole cloves

FOR SERVING

*½ cup unsalted pistachio nuts, shelled, skinned
(page 407), and coarsely chopped*

To make the lemon cheese, line a sieve, preferably plastic, with a single layer of damp cheesecloth large enough to hang over the sides and set over a bowl.

Whisk together the Rich Cream, lemon zest, lemon juice, and sugar in a bowl until the mixture is just stiff enough to hold its shape. Take care—it will curdle if overworked. Whisk the egg whites until they hold stiff peaks and fold quickly and lightly into the cream. Transfer to the sieve, pull the corners of the cheesecloth up and together, and tie with string to make a bag. Hang the bag over the bowl or the sink, away from heat or direct sunlight, and let drain 4 hours, occasionally giving the bag a firm squeeze to remove as much moisture as possible. Set aside, or refrigerate in the cheesecloth bag for up to 4 hours.

Prepare the chestnuts no more than 2 hours before serving. Combine the chestnuts, sugar, vanilla, milk, and cloves in a heavy saucepan and simmer until all the milk is absorbed, about 15 minutes. Discard the cloves. Fit a food mill with the medium disk and pass the chestnuts through into a bowl.

Lightly spoon one third of the chestnut mixture into a glass serving bowl. Don't flatten the top—that would spoil its airy texture. Gently smooth half the cheese over the top, then carefully add half of the remaining chestnut mixture. Add another layer of cheese, reserving a little for garnish, and finish with a layer of the remaining chestnut mixture. Garnish with the reserved cheese and the pistachio nuts. Serve immediately, or refrigerate for up to 6 hours.

Glazed Sweet Chestnuts
Zakharotá Kástana Glýkisma

Serves 4

During the long slow baking of this sweet and spicy dish the fruity aromatic Mavrodaphne wine permeates the chestnuts and glazes them with a deep red syrup. Easy to make, this dessert is ideal for dinner parties since it can be made a day ahead. It is equally delicious warm or cold and is traditionally accompanied by fresh *myzíthra* cheese (page 11), Rich Cream (page 415), or Lemon Cheese (page 408).

---

16 fresh plump chestnuts (see Note)

¼ cup honey or superfine sugar

¼ teaspoon ground allspice

1½ cups Mavrodaphne wine

Heat the oven to 300°F. Fill a medium saucepan with water and bring to a boil. Using a small knife with a strong blade (or a special chestnut knife), make an incision around the middle of each chestnut shell, beginning and ending on the flat side; take care not to cut into the chestnut. Add to the boiling water, and boil 10 minutes; then turn off the heat. Remove 2 or 3 chestnuts at a time and, as soon as they are cool enough to handle, carefully peel off the shells and inner skins, leaving the chestnuts whole. Work quickly—warm chestnuts are much easier to peel. Arrange in a single layer in a heavy baking dish just large enough to hold them.

Combine the honey, allspice, and wine, and pour over the chestnuts. Bake uncovered 1½ hours, gently turning the chestnuts in the syrup about every 20 minutes. Handle the chestnuts with care; they break easily. At the end of the baking time there should be about ⅓ cup syrup: add a little more wine or water if necessary, or bake 15 to 30 minutes longer to reduce the syrup.

Cool in the dish, then gently roll the chestnuts in the syrup. Transfer to a shallow serving dish or individual dishes and pour over any remaining syrup. Serve at room temperature or cold.

Note To use canned chestnuts, rinse, drain, and dry with paper towels. Bring the wine, honey, and allspice to a boil in a large saucepan, add the chestnuts, and gently simmer 5 minues. With a slotted spoon, transfer the chestnuts to paper towels to drain. Rapidly boil the cooking liquid until it is syrupy and coats the back of a metal spoon, about 8 minutes. Transfer the chestnuts to a serving dish and pour the syrup over. Let cool and serve.

Moustalevriá Candies

Moustalevriá Glýkisma

Makes approximately 18 pieces

This jellylike candy, made from grape must and flour, was probably one of the very first candies (page 385). It was a popular sweet in ancient Greece and down through the centuries Greeks have had a special fondness for its unusual flavor. In the villages *moustalevriá* is still made in the traditional way: The grapes are trodden by women (men tread the grapes for wine) and the must is first clarified with wood ash from the *foúrnos*, then boiled until it forms a light syrup called *petimézi*. This is then thickened with flour, semolina, or cornstarch to make the candy. The exact moment for removing the candy from the heat is judged in dramatic fashion by slipping a piece of flaming charcoal into the mixture—if the flame stays alive it is ready! For this recipe, you need to prepare the grape juice a day or two before making *petimézi*, a true must is grape juice that is just beginning to ferment. However, *petimézi* can be prepared ahead and stored for up to three months. Use it to flavor fruit salads, cookies, breads, cakes, and Moustalevriá Pudding (page 413) as well as these candies.

———

(continued)

5 pounds large sweet grapes

2 tablespoons wood ash (available from stores specializing in equipment for homemade wine)

⅓ cup honey

6 to 8 tablespoons sifted all-purpose flour

A few drops of olive oil

Ground cinnamon

About ¼ cup lightly toasted sesame seeds

Fill a large saucepan with water and bring to a boil. Stem the grapes and add them all at once to the boiling water. Count to 5 and drain.

Peel the grapes with your fingernail or a small paring knife and, with a wooden spoon, press them through a sieve, preferably plastic, set over a bowl. Strain the juice through cheesecloth into a saucepan and discard the pulp. There should be about 7 cups juice.

Cut out a 6-inch square of a double layer of cheesecloth, place the wood ash in it, and tie up the edges to make a bag. Add to the juice, bring to a boil, and simmer 10 minutes. Discard the bag of ash and pour the juice into a nonreactive bowl. Cover and set aside for 1 to 2 days.

Line a sieve with 2 layers of cheesecloth and set it over a saucepan. Strain the must into the saucepan, add the honey, and boil until it reaches 225°F to 230°F on a candy thermometer, the light thread stage. To test, dip the tip of a pair of scissors into the syrup. Remove them and open them—if the syrup (*petimézi*) forms a thread between the blades, it is ready. Set aside to cool. Measure the *petimézi*, and place 2 tablespoons flour for each cup in a bowl. Add enough *petimézi* to make a thin paste, and bring the remaining *petimézi* to a boil in a large saucepan. Whisk the boiling *petimézi* into the paste, and return it to the rinsed-out saucepan. Simmer over low heat, stirring frequently with a wooden spoon, until it reaches the soft ball stage on a candy thermometer (234° to 238°F), or test by dropping a small amount of the *moustalevriá* onto a cold plate: It should keep its shape.

Lightly wipe a baking sheet with the olive oil and carefully pour on the *moustalevriá* to make a ½-inch layer. Set aside to cool.

Sprinkle the cinnamon on a plate and sesame seeds on another. Cut the *moustalevriá* into 1-inch squares and gently roll them first in the cinnamon, then in the sesame seeds. Store in an airtight container between layers of waxed paper for up to 1 month.

Moustalevriá Pudding

Moustalevriá

Serves 4

A variation of the mixture used for making *moustalevriá* candies makes an unusual pudding. Here raisin juice is used for a quicker and easier version of *moustalevriá*. Do not be tempted to use grape juice—it is not a successful substitute and produces an unpleasant flavor in this pudding.

———

2 cups small dark seedless raisins soaked in ½ cup
Mavrodaphne wine
and ½ cup hot water for 2 hours or 1½ cups petimézi
(page 411)

⅓ cup semolina (farína, page 462)

1 tablespoon honey

FOR SERVING

⅓ cup finely chopped walnuts or blanched almonds
or ¼ cup lightly toasted sesame seeds

Ground cinnamon

Fit a food mill with the fine blade and pass the raisins and their liquid through into a bowl. (Or process in a blender or food processor.) Set a sieve over a bowl and press the mixture through with a wooden spoon. Add water if necessary to make 1½ cups liquid.

Combine the semolina, honey, and ¼ cup of the raisin juice to make a paste, then stir in the remaining juice. Transfer to a heavy saucepan and slowly bring to a boil. Simmer over very low heat until the mixture comes away from the sides of the saucepan, about 4 minutes, stirring constantly with a wooden spoon; take care not to let it burn.

Divide among small bowls and let cool. Cover tightly and refrigerate until chilled, or up to 2 days.

To serve, sprinkle with the nuts and cinnamon.

Fruit Desserts, Puddings and Creams, and Candy

Honey Sesame Candies

Pastéli

Makes 16 pieces

In summer the cry of the *pastéli* vendor is a familiar sound in every Greek village and town and he has no lack of customers for this traditional sweet, rich, and nourishing candy. It's also very good crushed and sprinkled over ice cream.

1¼ *cups sesame seeds*

1½ *cups aromatic honey, such as Hymettus or orange blossom*

2½ *tablespoons fresh lemon juice*

1½ *tablespoons unsalted butter, melted*

1 *tablespoon orange flower water, optional*

Heat the oven to 350°F. Line an 8- by 4-inch loaf pan with waxed paper.

Spread the sesame seeds on a baking sheet and bake 5 minutes to toast lightly. Set aside.

Combine the honey and ¼ cup water in a small saucepan and slowly bring to a boil. Add the lemon juice and sesame seeds and gently boil until the mixture reaches the soft ball stage (234° to 238°F) on a candy thermometer, or a small amount forms a slightly misshapen ball when dropped into a glass of cold water.

Brush the prepared pan with the melted butter and pour in the honey and sesame mixture. Sprinkle with the orange flower water and set aside to cool.

Turn out, peel off the paper, and, with a sharp knife, cut into pieces about ¾ inch by 2 inches. Store up to 1 month between layers of waxed paper in an airtight container.

Rich Cream

Kaymáki

Makes 1 to 1¼ cups (plus the crust)

Thick rich eastern Mediterranean *kaymáki* (literally, "frothy cream") is unique, but two more readily available products have a similar flavor and texture. Imported English clotted (Devon) cream and Italian mascarpone cheese both make good substitutes, or you can make your own. Make this when you plan to be in the kitchen for a couple of hours—for an even smooth texture and a thick crust you need to stir the hot cream at regular intervals. Be sure to use meticulously clean utensils and keep the cooking heat very low (or use a heat diffuser mat). *Kaymáki* should be made at least 18 hours before you need it; it can be stored for up to a week.

---

1 quart heavy cream

Slowly bring the cream almost to a boil in a heavy saucepan, stirring occasionally with a wooden spoon. Reduce the heat to as low as possible, or place the saucepan on a heat diffuser mat. Lift a ladleful of cream about 12 inches above the saucepan, and pour it back in a thin steady stream; repeat 2 or 3 times. Repeat this procedure every 10 minutes or so over the next 1½ hours, and stir the cream occasionally to make sure it does not stick.

Leave the cream undisturbed over the lowest heat for 30 minutes longer; it will have reduced by at least two thirds. Remove the saucepan from the heat and let cool.

Loosely cover with a clean kitchen towel and set aside for 2 hours.

Remove the kitchen towel, tightly cover, and refrigerate for at least 12 hours, or overnight.

Cut the crust on top of the cream into 1-inch-wide strips. Gently fold one end of a strip over the handle of a wooden spoon and roll it up (cut in half if the roll becomes too thick or unwieldy), and slide off onto a plate. Repeat with the remaining strips. The remaining *kaymáki* will have the texture of thick airless cream. It can be refrigerated in a tightly covered container for up to 1 week; refrigerate the rolls for up to 3 days.

(*continued*)

Fruit Desserts, Puddings and Creams, and Candy

Note Serve *kaymáki* rolls on their own or with desserts such as Kataïfi Nut Rolls (page 361) or Almond Cake (page 375). *Kaymáki* cream can be added to ice cream (page 389) or rice pudding (page 402) for an especially good flavor. Or whisk it together with a little sweet wine or lemon juice for a perfect accompaniment to fresh or poached fruit or sweet pastries.

Sauces

Sáltses

The philosopher Plato believed that, although anyone can grill food, only a skilled chef could flavor a sauce. It may be impudent to disagree with the great man but if that were true most of us would immediately abandon any attempt at sauce making.

Greek sauces are generally not awesomely complex—the ubiquitous *latholémono* (lemon juice and olive oil) and *lathóxsitho* (vinegar and olive oil) do not even require recipes since they are simple mixtures of oil and an acid, blended and seasoned to taste. The sauces in this chapter are those the visitor to Greece is likely to encounter most often. They range from two contrasting mayonnaises and the famous *avgolémono* and *skorthaliá* to creamy sauces based on walnuts, almonds, or pine nuts, a piquant anchovy sauce, and several very different tomato sauces. Throughout the book, of course, there are many more unusual sauce recipes detailed in individual recipes.

Many of these sauces have ancient origins and would traditionally be made with a wooden mortar and pestle. For modern cooks food processors and blenders now make speedy work of many of them and produce excellent results with fine flavors and textures.

A good sauce harmonizes all the flavors of a dish and brings out the essential character of the individual ingredients. These versatile sauces will add verve and vivacity to your Greek meals.

Avgolémono Sauce

Avgolémono

Serves 4

Avgolémono seems to add the perfect finishing touch to practically any dish, except those containing tomatoes or garlic. Its delicate flavor is ideally suited to fish dishes, turns a simple chicken dish into one of elegant subtlety, marries well with lamb or pork, enhances pungent grape leaves, and lifts plain vegetables into the luxury class.

Avgolémono is simply a mixture of eggs, lemon juice, and broth. For a rich deep-yellow sauce, suited to vegetables and roast meats, yolks alone are used. For casseroles and soups Greeks prefer a lighter sauce, made with whole eggs.

The key to a successful *avgolémono* is to use gentle heat, as high temperatures will cause the sauce to curdle, and to make it just before serving; this is not a sauce you can keep warm or reheat. The amount of lemon juice is adjusted to taste or to complement different dishes. *Dolmáthes,* for example, need little lemon juice because of the astringency of the grape leaves, while a mellow-flavored chicken dish benefits from a larger amount.

———

3 large egg yolks

⅓ cup strained fresh lemon juice, or to taste

1 cup strained hot broth (*from the dish to be sauced*)

Whisk the yolks, using a hand whisk or electric mixer, for 2 minutes, or until pale and frothy. Slowly add the lemon juice and whisk 1 minute longer. Add one third of the broth in a thin steady stream, whisking steadily, then quickly whisk in the remainder. Transfer to a small heavy saucepan or the top of a double boiler set over very hot water. Gently heat, stirring constantly in a figure-8 motion, until just thick enough to lightly coat the back of a wooden spoon, about 4 minutes. Do not stop stirring the sauce or let it boil or it will curdle. When it is ready, immediately remove from the heat (and saucepan) and serve.

(continued)

Whole Egg Avgolémono
for Soups and Casseroles

Serves 4 to 6

Avgolémono made with both egg whites and yolks is a beautiful pale lemony color. However, egg whites cook faster than yolks so there is a risk of the sauce looking stringy. To avoid this Greek cooks whisk the egg whites until stiff before adding the yolks and lemon juice.

———

2 large eggs, separated

½ cup strained fresh lemon juice, or to taste

½ cup hot soup or cooking liquid
(from the dish to be sauced)

Whisk the egg whites with a hand whisk or electric beater until they hold stiff peaks. Add the yolks, whisk 1 minute longer, then add the lemon juice. Continue whisking until very pale and frothy. Pouring from a height of about 12 inches, slowly add ½ cup of soup or cooking liquid to the egg and lemon juice mixture, whisking constantly. (By the time the liquid reaches the egg mixture it will no longer be hot enough to curdle the sauce.) Off the heat, add the *avgolémono* to the soup or casserole and stir or shake gently to blend the flavors. Set aside in a warm place for a few minutes; do not return to the heat. Serve immediately.

Garlic Almond Sauce

Skorthaliá

Serves 6 to 8

This thick and creamy blend of garlic, almonds, and olive oil has been a favorite since the days of the ancient Greeks. However, since almonds are now expensive, modern versions often substitute bread crumbs or potatoes for some or all of the ground almonds. For a truly excellent sauce use fresh sweet garlic and take a few minutes to blanch and grind fresh whole almonds. Serve *skorthaliá* with vegetable dishes such as fried zucchini and eggplants or baked beets or with grilled or baked fish or chicken.

¾ cup ground almonds or ½ cup ground almonds and ¼ cup fresh bread crumbs (made from white or whole-wheat bread, crusts removed)

4 to 6 large cloves garlic, crushed (about ¼ cup)

Sea salt to taste

½ teaspoon freshly ground white pepper, or to taste

¼ cup aged red-wine vinegar or the juice of 1 large lemon

¾ to 1 cup extra-virgin olive oil or ½ cup extra-virgin olive oil and ⅓ to ½ cup broth (from the dish to be sauced)

FOR SERVING

12 Elítses or Niçoise olives

Place the almonds (and bread crumbs), garlic, salt, and pepper in a food processor or blender container. With the machine running, slowly add 2 tablespoons of the vinegar and ¾ cup olive oil. Add some or all of the remaining vinegar and olive oil if necessary: The sauce should be creamy, with a slightly piquant flavor, and thick enough to hold its shape. Slightly more liquid is needed if you use bread crumbs. Serve immediately, or refrigerate for up to 24 hours in a tightly covered jar.

(continued)

To make the traditional way Pound the almonds, garlic, salt, and pepper in a large wooden mortar until well mixed and fairly smooth. Add the bread crumbs, if using, and pound to mix. Gradually add the vinegar and olive oil, pounding constantly, until you have a thick sauce. It will not be as smooth as a food processor version but will have a superior flavor produced by the continual working together of the ingredients.

Note You can remove the powerful garlic aroma from a wooden bowl by wiping with lemon juice or bicarbonate of soda.

Potato Skorthaliá

Skorthaliá me Patátes

Serves 6 to 8

This sauce should be made only in a mortar or bowl, as food processors ruin the texture of cooked potatoes. Use firm good-quality boiling potatoes and, for a sauce with a glorious deep yellow color and rich flavor, add an egg yolk.

---

*1 pound boiling potatoes or ½ pound boiling potatoes
and ½ cup fresh bread crumbs (made from white
bread, crusts removed)*

4 to 6 large cloves fresh garlic, crushed (about ¼ cup)

1 egg yolk, optional

Sea salt to taste

½ teaspoon freshly ground white pepper, or to taste

¼ cup aged red-wine vinegar, or more to taste

¾ to 1 cup extra-virgin olive oil

Fill a large saucepan with lightly salted water and bring to a boil. Cut the potatoes into halves or quarters, add to the boiling water, and cook 15 minutes, or until just tender. Drain, and peel when cool enough to handle.

Push the potatoes through a potato ricer or food mill into a large mortar or bowl; add the bread crumbs, if using, the garlic, egg yolk, salt, and pepper. With a pestle or wooden spoon, pound until fairly smooth and well mixed. Gradually add the vinegar and then the olive oil, pounding constantly, until the sauce is thick. Add more vinegar, if liked. Serve immediately, or refrigerate in an airtight container for up to 3 hours.

Piquant Almond Sauce

Amigdalósaltsa Pikantikí

Serves 2 to 3

Fresh young almonds are a favorite *mezé* wherever *rakí* is enjoyed—as I discovered when I lived in a Cretain village house surrounded by magnificent almond trees. Sitting under their beautiful flowering branches in my first spring there I contemplated the lovely dishes I would make when the almonds were ready in the fall—not realizing that my trees and their almonds were considered public property by the villagers! Along with everyone else I enjoyed "my" almonds in the village café where tables were piled high with them! The Greek love of almonds dates back to ancient times, as does this pungent sauce. Served with baked, poached, or steamed fish or chicken it elevates simply prepared food to the realms of elegance.

---

¹/₃ cup freshly ground almonds

2 tablespoons aged red-wine vinegar, or more to taste

1 ¹/₂ tablespoons dried rígani (page 14)

2 tablespoons finely chopped flat-leaf parsley

¹/₄ teaspoon ground mustard

1 teaspoon aromatic honey, such as Hymettus

Sea salt and freshly ground black pepper to taste

¹/₄ cup extra-virgin olive oil

*¹/₄ to ¹/₂ cup light Meat, Chicken, or Fish Broth
(pages 467, 461, and 463)*

(continued)

Place the almonds, vinegar, *rígani*, parsley, mustard, honey, and salt and pepper in a food processor or blender container. With the machine running, add the olive oil and then ¼ cup broth in a thin steady stream to make a thick sauce. For a thinner sauce, add up to ¼ cup additional broth. Add vinegar to taste, but its flavor should not be overpowering. Serve at room temperature or heat over low heat until warm.

Almond, Yogurt, and Coriander Sauce
Amigdalósaltsa me Yiaoúrti

Serves 3 to 4

This popular sauce, which can also be served as a *saláta*, is delicious with broiled meats, *souvlákia*, eggplants, *piláfi*, fried fish, or vegetables.

———

⅓ cup freshly ground almonds

½ teaspoon ground coriander

1 clove garlic, finely chopped

1 teaspoon aromatic honey, such as Hymettus

Juice of 1 small lemon

Sea salt and freshly ground black pepper to taste

½ to 1 cup Strained Yogurt (page 8)

¼ cup coarsely chopped flat-leaf parsley

¼ cup coarsely chopped fresh coriander

Place the almonds, ground coriander, garlic, honey, half the lemon juice, and salt and pepper in a food processor or blender container. With the machine running, add yogurt a tablespoon at a time until the sauce has the desired consistency. Add the parsley and fresh coriander and pulse or blend just to mix. Add salt, pepper, and/or lemon juice to taste and serve immediately.

Walnut Sauce

Karythósaltsa

Serves 6

Fresh walnuts are one of the incomparable delights of late summer and early fall on the Greek islands and this is the sauce islanders make with them. With its velvet texture and fine flavor it is the traditional accompaniment to fried mussels, grilled or fried fish, grilled or fried eggplants, and zucchini or chicken. New-crop walnuts with golden or pale brown inner skins are best for this sauce but if these are hard to find, use the freshest walnuts available. This sauce freezes exceptionally well—freeze it in small amounts and you'll have a delicious instant sauce for a variety of grilled and fried dishes. It can also be used to thicken and enhance the pan juices of baked chicken or fish dishes.

1½ cups walnut pieces

⅓ cup fresh bread crumbs (made from whole-wheat bread, crusts removed), soaked for 5 minutes in ¼ cup broth (from the dish to be sauced) or milk (see Note)

2 tablespoons extra-virgin olive oil (see Note)

1 large clove garlic, finely chopped

Sea salt and freshly ground white pepper to taste

2 to 4 tablespoons fresh lemon juice or white-wine vinegar (to taste)

OPTIONAL FLAVORINGS

½ teaspoon grated nutmeg or 1 teaspoon ground allspice (for chicken)

1 teaspoon finely grated fresh horseradish and ½ cup coarsely chopped flat-leaf parsley (for mussels, fish, or vegetables)

1 tablespoon finely chopped fresh thyme (for vegetables)

Walnuts with light-brown inner skins must be peeled: Blanch them in boiling water for 5 seconds and drain. Wrap in a kitchen towel, rub briskly to remove the skins, and set aside to dry. *(continued)*

Pulverize the walnuts and bread crumbs in a food processor bowl, then add the olive oil in a thin steady stream, processing until smooth. Add the garlic, salt, and pepper, half the lemon juice, and the chosen flavoring(s) and process until mixed. Add salt and pepper and/or the remaining lemon juice to taste. Add more broth if necessary to produce a thick but pourable sauce, or add more bread crumbs to thicken the sauce. Serve warm or cold.

To make the traditional way Pound the walnuts in a large wooden mortar with a pestle until the oil is released, 10 to 15 minutes. Add the bread crumbs and pound to mix. Slowly add the olive oil, pounding constantly. Add the garlic, salt, and pepper, lemon juice, and chosen flavoring and pound until creamy, fairly smooth, and pourable (it will not be as smooth as a machine-made sauce).

Note The amount of oil in walnuts varies, so the texture of the sauce may be different each time you make it. Be prepared to add varying amounts of broth, and/or olive oil.

Pine Nut Sauce

Koukounária Sáltsa

Serves 4

Along much of Greece's dramatic rocky coastline the magnificent umbrella-shaped Mediterranean pine dominates the landscape. Every three years the glossy brown cones mature and ripen, and inside each is the edible kernel known to us as the pine nut. This extended ripening period and the fact that these pine trees thrive only along coastlines mean that pine nuts have always been relatively scarce and, therefore, expensive. But the delicate creamy blend of nuts, lemon juice, olive oil, and fresh chives in this traditional sauce more than justifies the extravagance. Serve with grilled or baked chicken or fish.

1 1/4 cups pine nuts

1 small clove garlic, finely chopped, optional

Sea salt to taste

1/4 teaspoon freshly ground white pepper, or to taste

*2 tablespoons fresh lemon juice or 1 tablespoon aged
red-wine vinegar, or more to taste*

3 tablespoons extra-virgin olive oil, or more to taste

*1/4 to 1/3 cup broth (from the dish to be sauced)
or additional extra-virgin olive oil*

1/4 cup chopped fresh chives

Place the pine nuts, bread crumbs, if using, garlic, salt, and pepper in a food processor or blender container. With the machine running, gradually add the lemon juice, olive oil, and 1/4 cup broth and process until the sauce resembles thick cream. Add broth or olive oil if a thinner consistency is desired, and add salt or a few drops of lemon juice to taste; take care not to overpower the delicate flavor of the pine nuts. Add the chives and pulse just to mix. Serve immediately

To make the traditional way Place the pine nuts, garlic, salt, and pepper in a wooden mortar and pound with a pestle until smooth and well mixed, about 10 minutes. Add the bread crumbs, if using, and pound to mix. Gradually add the olive oil and broth, pounding constantly. The sauce will not be as smooth as a food processor version, but the flavor will be more distinctive. Stir in the chives just before serving.

Note Pine nut sauce can be refrigerated in an airtight container for up to 24 hours or frozen for up to 1 month, but do not add the chives until just before serving.

Mayonnaise

Mayonaíza

Serves 3 to 4

The flavor of mayonnaise is determined by the olive oil used. A light olive oil will produce the lightest mayonnaise, Kalámata or extra-virgin olive oils the fruity, traditional Greek version. Greek cooks sometimes add a few spoonfuls of yogurt to mayonnaise to lighten both color and flavor. Serve this mayonnaise with cold poached or baked fish, shellfish, chicken, and salads.

---

2 large egg yolks, at room temperature

Large pinch of ground mustard

½ cup extra-virgin olive oil

1 to 2 tablespoons fresh lemon juice to taste

Sea salt and freshly ground white pepper to taste

1 to 2 tablespoons Strained Yogurt (page 8), optional

Place the egg yolks and mustard in a large nonreactive bowl and whisk together 1 minute with a small whisk or 2 forks (held slightly apart, in the same hand). Add ¼ cup of the olive oil drop by drop, whisking constantly and pausing once or twice to add a few drops of lemon juice. Slowly add the remaining olive oil in a thin stream, whisking constantly. Add salt and pepper, whisk in the yogurt to taste, and serve.

Note To store, add 1 tablespoon boiling water to the finished mayonnaise. Cover tightly and refrigerate no longer than 4 hours.

To rescue curdled mayonnaise, place 1 room-temperature egg yolk in a clean bowl and slowly add the curdled mayonnaise, whisking constantly.

Garlic and Watercress Mayonnaise

Skórtho ke Kárthamon Mayonaíza

Serves 4

This piquant mayonnaise adds a delightful dash of the unexpected to *kephtéthes* or everyday grilled chicken, and it can be quickly made in the food processor.

---

1 bunch of fresh watercress, green leaves only (about 1 cup)

1 teaspoon finely grated fresh horseradish

¼ teaspoon ground mustard

1 tablespoon capers, rinsed and patted dry

2 to 4 large cloves garlic, finely chopped, to taste

Sea salt to taste

2 egg yolks, at room temperature

½ cup extra-virgin olive oil

Strained juice of ½ lemon, or more to taste

Blanch the watercress in boiling water for 5 seconds, drain, spread between layers of paper towels, and blot dry.

Place the horseradish, mustard, capers, garlic, salt, egg yolks, and watercress in a food processor or blender container and, with the machine running, add ¼ cup of the olive oil drop by drop. Gradually add the remaining ¼ cup olive oil and the lemon juice. Add more lemon juice and/or salt to taste and serve immediately.

To make the traditional way Boil 2 eggs for 4 minutes, peel, and remove the yolks with a small spoon. They should be soft but not runny. Chop together the blanched watercress, horseradish, mustard, and capers. Pound the garlic and a large pinch of salt to a purée in a large mortar or bowl. Add the egg yolks and watercress mixture and pound until well mixed. Add half the olive oil drop by drop, still pounding, then add the remaining olive oil and the lemon juice in a steady stream. The sauce should be thick and well mixed, but it will not be as smooth as a food processor version.

Green Grape Sauce

Agourítha

Makes approximately ⅔ cup

This unusual sauce is made from the juice of underripe grapes (known here as *verjuice*). Made in traditional homes on Crete, it is used to flavor pork and game dishes and Stuffed Eggplants (page 103). The small hard pickling grapes found in Chinese markets in early summer are exactly right for this sauce; if it proves impossible to find suitable grapes, *agourítha* can also be made with gooseberries, rhubarb, crab apples, or lemons or limes (see below). With its clear sharp tang, this is a particularly effective flavoring for baked fish and chicken dishes and a perfect marinade for lamb. It can be frozen; since only a little sauce is required to flavor a dish, freeze it in an ice cube tray and store the cubes in a bag, ready to use.

---

1 pound small hard white grapes (on the stem)

Blanch the grapes in boiling water, for 5 seconds, and remove with a slotted spoon. Drain between layers of paper towels and blot completely dry, then carefully separate the grapes from the stem.

Set a plastic sieve over a nonreactive bowl and push the grapes through with a wooden spoon. Don't be tempted to use a food processor because the metal blade reacts harshly with the sour juice, giving an unpleasant metallic flavor to the sauce. Even the plastic blade of a food processor will "overwork" the grape skins and spoil the delicate flavor. When you have extracted as much of the juice and pulp from the grapes as possible, rinse the sieve, line it with a layer of cheesecloth, and place over another clean nonreactive bowl. Press the purée through a second time; the result will be a lovely smooth sauce.

Refrigerate for up to 1 week in a covered jar or freeze for up to 2 months.

Substitutes

• Substitute ½ pound firm sour gooseberries for grapes; avoid large pink ones—they are usually sweet and watery. Snip off both ends with small scissors, and simmer 10 minutes in ¼ cup water. Large gooseberries may need a little longer to soften.

- Substitute ½ pound rhubarb, trimmed and the "strings" removed. Cut into ½-inch slices and simmer 10 minutes in ¼ cup water. Use pink rhubarb only when the green color of classic *agourítha* is not an integral part of the dish.
- Substitute 1 pound crab apples, peeled, cored, and cut into quarters. Simmer in a few tablespoons water until soft, about 30 minutes.
- If you can find neither underripe grapes nor a substitute, use the juice of 2 limes and 1 lemon (about ⅔ cup). However, this mixture does not have quite the same depth of flavor, nor does it have the property that turns the sauce slightly sweet when cooked, as do grapes, gooseberries, rhubarb, and crab apples, but it works well in such dishes as Stuffed Eggplants with Green Grape Sauce (page 103).

Tomato Sauce

Sáltsa Domátas

Makes approximately 1 quart

The secret of the deliciously sweet tomato sauces of Greece is vine-ripened tomatoes (although when they are unavailable Greek cooks cheat a little by adding a spoonful of honey). You can vary this basic sauce depending on the herbs and spices used. Make large quantities whenever there is a good supply of top-quality tomatoes, and store for use later.

———

(continued)

¼ cup Kalamáta olive oil

1 cup chopped onion

5 pounds ripe tomatoes, peeled and diced, juices reserved

¼ cup dry red wine or hot water

1 tablespoon tomato paste

1 tablespoon honey

Sea salt and freshly ground black pepper to taste

ANY ONE OF THE FOLLOWING GROUPS OF FLAVORINGS

1 teaspoon ground cinnamon or one 3-inch cinnamon stick and ¼ cup chopped flat-leaf parsley or fresh mint or 2 tablespoons dried rígani (page 14); or

12 sprigs of parsley and 4 bay leaves; or

4 tablespoons chopped fresh basil, parsley, or marjoram and 4 whole cloves and 1 large clove garlic, finely chopped; or

1 teaspoon ground cumin and 12 sprigs of parsley

Warm the olive oil in a large nonreactive skillet and sauté the onion over low heat until soft, about 10 minutes. Combine the red wine, tomato paste, and honey, and add to the skillet. Stir in the tomatoes, salt and pepper, and the flavorings. Raise the heat and boil uncovered, stirring occasionally, 30 to 40 minutes, or until thick enough to stay separated for a few seconds when a wooden spoon is drawn across the bottom of the skillet.

Set a sieve over a bowl. Remove the bay leaves or cinnamon stick, if using, and press the sauce through the sieve with the back of a wooden spoon. Add more salt and pepper to taste (if it is to be stored, season before using). Serve warm or cold.

Note To store, fill small sterilized jars with the sauce. Invert a metal spoon 1 inch above a jar and pour a thin stream of olive oil onto the spoon. It will reach the surface of the sauce at an angle, ensuring that it is not disturbed. Use only enough olive oil to make a thin layer for an airtight seal. Repeat with the remaining jars and cover tightly and refrigerate for up to 3 months. Use the sealing olive oil for cooking or stir into the sauce when serving.

Light Tomato Sauce
Sáltsa Domátas Elafriá

Makes 1 to 1½ cups

Make this elegant sauce when tomatoes are at their summer sweetest. Aromatized with cinnamon and pungent herbs it has a subtle fresh taste and a smooth thin consistency. It must be made as close as possible to serving time since the flavor begins to acidify in just a few hours. This sauce is excellent with *macarónia* or *piláfi*, grilled fish or eggplants, and simple summer vegetable dishes.

———

5 tablespoons extra-virgin olive oil, or to taste

¼ cup finely chopped onion

1 clove garlic, finely chopped, optional

4 large ripe tomatoes, peeled and diced

½ teaspoon honey

One 3-inch cinnamon stick, broken in half

Sea salt and freshly ground black pepper to taste

OPTIONAL FLAVORINGS

2 tablespoons fresh mint, parsley, marjoram, basil, or oregano; or

1 tablespoon dried rígani (page 14); or

1 teaspoon dried thyme; or

1 tablespoon Mavrodaphne or Madeira wine, or to taste

Warm 3 tablespoons of the olive oil in a heavy skillet and sauté the onion over low heat until barely soft, about 6 minutes. Chop the fresh herbs, if using, and add the garlic, tomatoes, honey, cinnamon stick, salt and pepper, and half the flavoring herb to the onions. Raise the heat and boil 3 minutes. Discard the cinnamon stick. Pour off any liquid in the skillet and set aside.

Set a sieve, preferably plastic, over a bowl and press the sauce through with a wooden spoon. Stir in the wine, if using, and the remaining 2 tablespoons olive oil. The sauce should be the consistency of thin cream; if too thick, add some or all of the reserved cooking liquid. Season with salt and pepper and stir in the remaining flavoring herb. Serve warm or cold.

Scorched Tomato Sauce

Sáltsa Domátas Kapsalisméni

Serves 3 to 4

When whole tomatoes are broiled until their skins blacken and blister, their flavor becomes wonderfully sweet and mellow—the perfect base for a full-flavored sauce. In *tavérnas,* where the grill is in constant use, this sauce is made in vast quantities. It's simple to make and a wonderful complement to broiled or barbecued fish, chicken, or lamb, and vegetable *piláfi.*

---

4 large ripe tomatoes

1 to 2 teaspoons aromatic honey, such as Hymettus

1 large clove garlic, minced

1 tablespoon dried marjoram or 1½ tablespoons dried rígani (page 14), crumbled

1 teaspoon ground paprika

Coarse-grain sea salt and cracked black pepper to taste

½ cup coarsely chopped flat-leaf parsley

¼ cup extra-virgin olive oil

Heat the broiler.

Set the tomatoes on a broiling pan and broil close to the heat until blackened and blistered on top, about 5 minutes. Remove from the heat and, when cool enough to handle, peel, discard the seeds, and place the pulp in a sieve set over a bowl. Set aside to drain for a few minutes, and reserve the juice.

Transfer the pulp to a food processor or blender container and add the honey, garlic, marjoram, paprika, salt and pepper, and half the parsley. Pulse to mix, and add the olive oil in a thin steady stream, pulsing until well mixed and fairly smooth. Stir in the remaining parsley and enough of the reserved juice to make the desired consistency, and season to taste with salt and pepper. Serve at room temperature or heat gently to warm.

To make the traditional way Prepare the tomatoes as directed above. Chop half the parsley, the garlic, marjoram, paprika, and salt and pepper together to mix. Place in a large wooden mortar, pound 1 minute, then add the tomato pulp and honey and pound to blend. Continue pounding as you add the olive oil. Stir in enough of the reserved juice to make the desired consistency, and stir in the remaining parsley. Season to taste.

Peloponnese Honey Sauce

Sáltsa Peloponíssou

Serves 3

This piquant sauce is perfect for broiled or grilled white-fleshed fish, especially bass or halibut, or for grilled pork, *souvlákia*, or sausages. It's simple to make but the flavors are complex and tantalizing. Make the sauce with a wooden mortar and pestle or in a china or glass bowl using a wooden spoon—metal bowls or utensils will interact with the flavor of the egg yolk and subtly alter the taste of the finished sauce. Serve warm or cold.

———

2 soft-boiled eggs (boiled 4 minutes)

2 tablespoons aromatic honey, such as Hymettus

Sea salt to taste

1 teaspoon cracked black pepper

¼ cup aged red-wine vinegar or 2 tablespoons balsamic vinegar diluted with 2 tablespoons warm water

1 tablespoon small capers, rinsed

2 tablespoons finely chopped flat-leaf parsley

Slice the top third off each egg and spoon out the creamy yolk into a wooden mortar or nonreactive bowl. Add the honey, salt and pepper, and pound until smooth. Add the vinegar a few drops at a time, pounding constantly.

Transfer to a sieve, preferably plastic, set over a bowl and press the mixture through with the pounder. Stir in the capers and parsley and salt and pepper to taste. Serve immediately, or gently heat until warm. Do not let the sauce become too hot or the egg yolks will curdle.

Sauces

Anchovy Sauce

Sáltsa Antsouyías

Serves 3 to 4

In a few Greek markets, such as Athinas in central Athens, it's still possible to buy whole anchovies preserved in brine, sometimes sold straight from the huge wooden barrels in which they were packed. Canned anchovies do not have the same special flavor but unless you can track down brine-preserved anchovies in a Greek or Middle Eastern store, they are the kind to use for this creamy sauce. Make the sauce as close to serving time as possible. It's especially good with broiled tuna or swordfish.

---

1 large shallot, chopped, or 2 scallions,
white parts only, chopped

1 large clove garlic, cut into 2 or 3 pieces

6 to 8 salted anchovy fillets, rinsed (to taste)

Finely grated zest of ½ lemon

1 tablespoon capers, rinsed

Juice of 1 small lemon, or to taste

⅓ cup extra-virgin olive oil, or to taste

2 tablespoons finely chopped flat-leaf parsley

½ teaspoon cracked black pepper, or to taste

Place the shallot, garlic, anchovies, lemon zest, capers, and lemon juice in a food processor or blender container. With the machine running, add the olive oil in a thin steady stream. Add the parsley and pepper and pulse just to mix. The sauce will have the consistency of fairly thick cream. For a thinner sauce add more lemon juice, which will give a more piquant flavor, or olive oil, which will mellow the flavor. Serve at room temperature.

To make the traditional way Finely chop the shallot, garlic, anchovies, and capers together. Place in a wooden mortar and pound with the pestle until well mixed and fairly smooth, about 10 minutes. Slowly add the lemon juice and about ½ cup olive oil, pounding constantly, until thick. Stir in the parsley and pepper.

Appendixes

Pickles

Toursiá

Although *toursiá* means "pickles," the term is generally now applied only to vegetables such as artichokes, cauliflower, cucumber, and peppers that have been traditionally prepared and flavored and stored in wine vinegar, sometimes spiced. Other vegetables and fruits of all kinds are also pickled in great quantities: lemons are salted and stored in olive oil (page 19), capers are packed in brine (page 16), and tomatoes sun-dried and stored in olive oil. *Toursiá* are served as *mezethákia* with *oúzo* or *rakí* (page 454), or with other *mezéthes,* such as preserved meats, cheeses, radishes, wild artichokes, and raw young fava beans. They are rarely served with a main course.

Vegetables used for pickling must be fresh, unblemished, and very clean. Use an enamel-lined, stainless steel, or other nonreactive saucepan and sterilized wide-necked jars with tight-fitting lids.

Pickled Peppers

Piperiés Mikrés Toursí

Yields approximately 3 quarts

For pickling the Greeks use long, slender, waxy yellow or pale green peppers. They can be very mild, almost sweet, or quite tangy. If your peppers are tangy, omit the honey and cinnamon in the spiced vinegar, and add dried red chili peppers to the jar. These are delicious with tomato or beet salads, or with *féta* cheese.

---

36 thin Anaheim peppers, 2 to 3 inches long,
stems trimmed to ¼ inch

3 tablespoons coarse-grain sea salt

6 dried red chili peppers, optional

5 cups Spiced Vinegar (page 441)

Olive oil, for sealing the jars

Place the peppers in a glass or china bowl, sprinkle with the salt, and add water to barely cover. Cover and set aside for 6 hours, occasionally stirring the peppers.

Rinse the peppers and spread on paper towels to dry. Loosely pack into 1-quart jars, add a red chili pepper to each jar, cover with the Spiced Vinegar, and seal with a thin layer of olive oil. Tightly cover and store at room temperature for at least 3 weeks, or up to 3 months, before using. Refrigerate after opening.

Pickled Tiny Stuffed Eggplants

Melitzanákia Yemistá Toursí

Makes approximately 5 pints

For this pretty, delicate pickle choose slender baby eggplants about 2 inches long. To keep the filling in place, you use the stronger "strings" removed from the celery stalks (for Filling 1) or the parsley or wild celery stems (for Filling 2). Store for up to eight weeks at room temperature, and refrigerate and use within one week once the jar is opened.

———

2 pounds small eggplants

FILLING 1

2 large cloves garlic, finely chopped

2 large ribs celery, tough strings removed and reserved, cut into 3- to 4-inch pieces

2 tablespoons finely chopped celery leaves (see wild celery, page 473)

1 red bell pepper, roasted, seeded, and peeled (page 460), rinsed, and cut into thin strips

3 tablespoons finely chopped flat-leaf parsley

1 tablespoon olive oil

FILLING 2

3 large cloves garlic, finely chopped

2 young carrots, peeled if desired, and grated

2 tablespoons finely chopped flat-leaf parsley

1 tablespoon finely chopped fresh mint

1 tablespoon olive oil

Pine nuts, small blanched almonds, or walnut pieces (1 for each eggplant)

Slender flat-leaf parsley or wild celery stems (see page 473) each with a few leaves attached (1 stem for each eggplant)

5 red chili peppers, optional

3 cups white-wine vinegar combined with 2 cups water and 2 tablespoons coarse-grain sea salt or 5 cups spiced vinegar (see Note)

Olive oil, for sealing the jars

Slice off the ends of the eggplants and carefully make a short lengthwise incision in each eggplant. Blanch in boiling salted water for 2 minutes, remove with a slotted spoon, and dry between layers of paper towels.

Blanch the celery pieces for 5 minutes, remove with the slotted spoon, and drain on paper towels; finely chop. Blanch the celery strings or the parsley stems for 6 seconds, and drain. Cut 6 of the pepper strips into ½-inch pieces and set aside; finely chop the rest.

Combine the garlic, celery, celery leaves, chopped bell pepper, parsley, and olive oil (for Filling 1), or combine the garlic, carrots, parsley, mint, and olive oil (for Filling 2). Loosely stuff the eggplants with the filling. Arrange the bell pepper strips along the eggplant incisions or place a pine nut in each eggplant. Firmly wrap a celery string around each eggplant (Filling 1) or wrap with a parsley stem, starting with the leafy end over the filling but leaving the pine nut slightly exposed (Filling 2). Place the eggplants upright in 1-pint jars, packing quite tightly. Push 1 red chili pepper down between the eggplants in each jar, cover with the vinegar, and seal with a thin layer of olive oil. Tightly cover the jars and set aside for 2 weeks before using.

Note To make Spiced Vinegar, combine 3 cups white-wine vinegar, 2 cups water, 2 tablespoons coarse-grain sea salt, 1 dozen whole allspice berries, 6 whole cloves, 1 teaspoon whole black peppercorns, one 2-inch cinnamon stick, and 1 tablespoon honey in a large saucepan and bring to a boil. Simmer 5 minutes, strain, and let cool.

Pickled Cucumbers

Angourákia Toursí

Yields approximately 3 quarts

Leave tiny (1 to 2 inches long) cucumbers whole, and cut larger ones lengthwise into quarters or into thick slices. Store at room temperature for at least two weeks or up to four months before using, and refrigerate after opening. Use these as a garnish for Pork in Aspic (page 44) or Fried Cheese (page 47), or serve with other small appetizers.

———

2 pounds pickling cucumbers, stems trimmed

2 large cloves garlic, cut into large slivers, optional

12 black peppercorns

6 sprigs of fresh dill or 1 tablespoon dill seeds

12 small fresh grape leaves, tough stems trimmed, blanched in boiling water for 5 seconds, optional

2 cups white-wine vinegar

3 tablespoons coarse-grain sea salt

½ teaspoon honey

Olive oil, for sealing the jars

Blanch the cucumbers in boiling water for 1 minute and dry between layers of paper towels. Fill three 1-quart jars with the cucumbers and divide the garlic, peppercorns, dill, and grape leaves among them. Combine the vinegar, salt, honey, and 1 cup water and pour over the cucumbers. Cover with a thin layer of olive oil and tightly cover the jars.

Jams and Preserves
Glyká

From the wide choice of fruits available to them, Greeks make a variety of delicious jams and preserves. Three of my particular favorites are those made from figs, quinces, and loquats. They are not difficult to make, calling for time, patience, and careful observation rather than professional skill, but the following tips may be helpful.

Jam sets thanks to the work of the enzyme pectin (present in large quantities in fruits such as apples and quince, in smaller amounts in other fruits—it's especially low in strawberries). But to work effectively pectin needs the help of both acid, in the fruit or in added lemon juice, and sugar, so it's important to judge the proportion of sugar to fruit carefully and to add the sugar at the right moment, usually when the fruit is already cooked or softened. At that point some of the fruit's own sugar will have started to work with the pectin. Once the sugar has been added, careful observation is crucial. If you do not boil the mixture sufficiently you will end up with a crystallized jam, while overboiling will give you a runny syrup instead.

Another common problem is the formation of mold on top of the stored jam. To guard against this it's a good idea to add some form of alcohol to the jam mixture—whisky, cognac, Armagnac, or, in true Greek fashion, *rakí*, all serve the purpose. The same result is achieved by pouring melted paraffin over the surface of the jam, but the alcoholic option is easy and adds flavor as well.

Fresh Fig Jam

Síka Glyká

For this richly flavored jam you can use any variety of fig but the fruit must be ripe. If you have unsprayed figs the skin can be left on the fruit (almost all store-bought figs are sprayed)—they give the jam a beautiful deep color, especially if you use deep-purple Mission figs. Otherwise the figs must be peeled. The tart apples in this recipe serve a dual purpose: Rich in pectin, they help the jam to set, and they are also an economical way of increasing the amount of jam you can produce from a reasonable quantity of the more expensive figs.

---

2 pounds fresh ripe figs, rinsed or peeled, and stems trimmed

1 pound tart apples, such as Granny Smiths

1 teaspoon whole fennel seeds

Finely grated zest of 1 lemon

Strained juice of 3 large lemons

2 pounds sugar

Thoroughly wash and sterilize five 1-pint jars.

Cut each fig in 6 or 8 pieces. Peel, core, and thinly slice the apples. Place the fennel seeds on a small square of cheesecloth and tie up the edges to make a bag.

Place the figs, apples, bag of fennel seeds, lemon zest, and lemon juice, in a large heavy saucepan, cover, and bring slowly to a boil. Simmer 30 minutes or until the figs are tender, stirring occasionally to ensure that the fruit does not stick. Discard the bag of fennel seeds, add the sugar, stir well with a wooden spoon, and raise the heat. Boil 5 minutes, or until the setting point (220°F to 222°F) is reached: To test, either use a candy thermometer or drop a small quantity of jam onto a chilled plate—if it appears to be covered by a light skin, it is ready. If not, boil a few minutes longer and test once more; remove the saucepan from the heat each time you test and, to prevent the figs from burning, stir vigorously with a wooden spoon.

Pour into the jars and cover the surface of the jam with circles of waxed paper or with melted paraffin. Tightly cover the jars and store at room temperature.

Quince Jam

Glyká Kidóni

Makes 7 to 8 cups

Throughout Greek myth and legend the quince is associated with love, marriage, and fertility, and it was actually a golden quince that Paris awarded to the goddess of love, Aphrodite, when he made the ill-fated judgement that sparked off the Trojan war. For Greeks the quince is still the love-fruit and its blossoms or fruit are an integral part of the Greek marriage ceremony.

In season Cretan markets display green-gold ripening quinces in abundance; in the United States, unfortunately, they are not so easy to find. If you spot quinces in your local market, do not hesitate to buy them. They are versatile fruits to cook with: The ancient Greeks made them into a candy, but they can also be poached (page 387) or baked like apples and, when cooked, take on a beautiful deep red color. They are lovely baked with a little sweet white wine, sugar, and a few cloves or a vanilla bean (rinse and core the quinces, and bake in a low oven until tender). Half a quince, finely chopped, is also a wonderfully aromatic addition to apple and pear pies and tarts. Or use their delicately perfumed flavor in this delicious jam. Be sure to choose firm underripe quinces; ripe yellow ones are pulpy, and not suitable for jam.

---

2 pounds underripe quinces

2 small lemons

2 pounds sugar

2 teaspoons vanilla extract

Thoroughly wash and sterilize four 1-pint jars.

Fill a large bowl with ice water. Quarter 1 lemon, squeeze the juice into the bowl, and add the quarters. Squeeze the juice from the remaining lemon and set aside. Wipe the quinces to remove the fuzzy down on their skins. Peel, quarter, and core, and tie the peelings and cores up in a piece of cheesecloth to make a bag. Thinly slice or julienne the quinces, dropping them into the ice water. When all are prepared, drain the quinces, pat dry with paper towels, and place in a large heavy saucepan. Add 3 cups water and the cheesecloth bag. Slowly bring to a boil, and simmer 15 minutes. Remove the cheesecloth bag, squeeze it over the pan to extract as much juice as possible, and discard.

Add the sugar, reserved lemon juice, and the vanilla to the quinces and simmer until the sugar is dissolved. Raise the heat and rapidly boil until the setting point is reached (as directed on page 444).

Fill the jars, cover the surface of the jam with circles of waxed paper or with melted paraffin, and tightly cover the jars. Store at room temperature for up to 6 months.

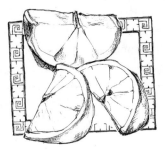

Loquat Preserve

Glyká Mespilónta

Makes 1 to 1½ cups

The refreshing, delicately flavored loquat is native to China but throughout southern Greece and Crete loquat trees, laden with clusters of small orange-gold fruits, are a common sight. The loquat conveniently ripens in late spring, at the end of the orange season and before summer fruits appear in the markets. This lovely jam is absolutely delicious with cookies, pancakes, or almond cakes and it is especially good with Rich Cream (page 415).

1½ pounds large unblemished loquats

Strained juice of 1 lemon

One 2-inch strip of lemon zest

1 to 1½ cups sugar

Thoroughly wash and sterilize three ½-pint jars. Rinse the loquats and trim out their flower ends with a small paring knife. Cut into pieces and discard the pits. Work quickly—the fruit discolors easily.

Place the loquats in a heavy saucepan with the lemon juice, zest, and ¼ cup water, cover, and bring slowly to a boil. Reduce the heat and simmer 30 to 40 minutes, or until the loquats turn deep auburn. (This slow cooking is essential to release the loquats' sugar and to make a well-flavored preserve.)

Fit a food mill with the fine blade and set it over a nonreactive bowl. Discard the lemon zest and pass the loquats through the food mill. Measure the pulp, return it to the rinsed-out saucepan, and add exactly the same amount of sugar. Slowly bring to a boil and simmer 5 to 20 minutes, or until the setting point (220°F to 222°F) is reached (test as directed on page 444).

Fill the jars, cover the surface of the jam with circles of waxed paper or with melted paraffin, and tightly cover the jars. Store at room temperature for up to 4 months.

Beverages

Potá

Greeks are connoisseurs of water and many will tell you without hesitation that cold water, pure and crystalline, is the only truly refreshing drink. As one English writer describes it, "The glass of water appears everywhere; it is an adjunct to every kind of sweetmeat and even to alcohol. It has a kind of biblical significance. When a Greek drinks water he *tastes* it and, pressing it against the palate, savors it." This fondness for water does not stop them, however, from delighting in a range of deliciously flavored nonalcoholic drinks. Some of the best are made with the syrup of spoon sweets or with the spoon sweet itself. Other popular traditional drinks are made with almonds, citrus fruits, and pomegranates.

Morello Cherry Syrup

Vissinátha

Apopular and thirst-quenching drink is made from the syrup remaining from Morello Cherry Spoon Sweet (page 397). Fill a tall glass with ice, add syrup to taste, and fill with cold water.

The syrup of any spoon sweet can be used in the same way—lemon blossom syrup (page 400) is especially good.

Submarines

Ypovríkhia

This is the colloquial name for a traditional way to serve spoon sweets. A long-handled spoon is used to scoop up the sweet and then is immersed in a tall glass of ice-cold water. The fondant-like spoon sweet remains attached to the spoon, hence the drink's name. Favorite versions are those made from vanilla, Morello cherries (page 397), or mastic (page 467). Sipping *ypovríkhia* under a shady tree is an exceedingly pleasant way to while away the afternoon.

Almond Drink

Soumátha

Makes about 4 cups syrup

This refreshing drink, especially delicious on a hot summer's day, is the traditional beverage to serve at weddings. The classic way to make the syrup is to pound the almonds and sugar in a mortar, but a food processor will produce a similar flavor using far less time and energy. Process only a small quantity at a time or the almonds will not be properly pulverized. The syrup keeps indefinitely in airtight bottles.

———

1 ¼ cups blanched almonds

3 cups sugar

4 cups water

*A few drops of bitter almond essence or
almond extract, optional*

With a nut grinder or a food processor, finely chop the almonds—but do not pulverize. Transfer ¼ cup of the chopped almonds to a mortar, or remove 1 cup from the processor bowl and set aside. Add 1 tablespoon each of sugar and water to the ¼ cup almonds and pulverize to a paste. Remove and set aside, and repeat with the remaining almonds, adding sugar and water to each ¼ cup.

Combine the remaining sugar and water in a heavy saucepan, bring to a boil, and gently boil 10 minutes. Stir in the almond paste with a wooden spoon and boil 10 minutes longer, stirring frequently to prevent sticking; do not leave unattended—the syrup easily boils over. Set aside to cool. Strain into a bowl through 2 layers of cheesecloth, and squeeze the cheesecloth to extract all liquid. Add almond essence if desired—the almond flavor should be unmistakable, but not overpowering. Store at room temperature in airtight bottles.

To serve, pour syrup to taste over crushed ice in a tall glass and add cold water.

Lemonade

Lemonátha

Makes about 3 cups syrup

This is a simple and unusual way to make any citrus drink. The light syrup keeps in the refrigerator for up to two weeks.

SYRUP

3 cups sugar

3 cups water

Zest of 1 lemon

1 whole clove

One 2-inch cinnamon stick

FOR SERVING

Freshly-squeezed lemon juice, to taste

Slices of lemon dipped in sugar

Combine the sugar, water, lemon zest, clove, and cinnamon stick in a heavy saucepan and bring to a boil. Gently boil 10 minutes and set aside to cool.

Strain into clean bottles or jars and refrigerate.

To serve, pour lemon juice and syrup to taste over ice in a tall glass, and add cold water. Balance a slice of lemon dipped in sugar on the rim of the glass.

Pomegranate Drink

Graníta

Serves 4

The flavor of this sweet and pretty drink is best when the pomegranates are juiced within an hour or two of serving.

———

4 large ripe pomegranates

Juice of ½ small lemon

⅓ cup sugar, or to taste

FOR SERVING

A few drops orange flower water or rosewater, optional

Use a lemon squeezer or juice extractor, or a blender fitted with the plastic blade, or food processor to juice the pomegranates (page 391).

Strain the juice through 2 layers of cheesecloth into a nonreactive pitcher. Stir in the lemon juice and sugar with a wooden spoon and stir until the sugar has completely dissolved. Chill.

Serve over crushed ice, and sprinkle with orange flower water or rosewater if desired.

Coffee / Kafés

Old ways die hard in Greece and, although tradition is now changing slowly, the best coffee is still to be found in the *kafeníon* (café)—an exclusively male domain. Women generally drink coffee at home or in the *zacharoplasteíon* (pastry shop). Coffee is rarely served in *tavérnas* or restaurants.

Greeks make coffee the way it is made throughout the Middle East—in a long-handled small brass pot (*bríki*) with a broad lip, tapering towards the top. It is almost always served already sweetened, in tiny straight-sided cups. When you order coffee you are asked how you would like it made, as sugar is added to the coffee grounds at the same time as the water. Some Greeks assert that there are at least 50 ways to make and flavor coffee but, in general, you are likely to be offered only *skéto* ("unsweetened"), *métrio* ("with some sugar"), and *glykó* ("sweet").

Greek coffee is made with thoroughly pulverized, well-roasted coffee beans. Brazilian is the coffee bean of choice although it is the length of time the beans are roasted that really defines Greek coffee's special character. Since the coffee grounds are poured into the cup it's essential that they are powder fine.

To make Greek coffee at home you will need a *bríki*. They are available in a range of sizes, from 1-cup to generous 8-cup versions. Both *bríkia* and traditional cups can be bought from Greek and Middle Eastern stores; if you prefer to use larger espresso cups, increase the quantity of coffee and sugar by one half. Serve the coffee steaming hot.

Greek Coffee

Kafés

Serves 4

Greek coffee is always served with tall glasses of ice water.

---

4 coffee cups water

4 teaspoons powder-fine ground coffee, or heaped to taste

4 teaspoons sugar, or heaped to taste

Bring the water to a boil in a 4- to 6-cup *bríki*. Remove from the heat and sprinkle the coffee and sugar over the water. Bring to a boil again, and remove from the heat. Stir until the froth has disappeared, and return to a high heat. Remove from the heat, stir until the froth disappears, and bring to a boil one more time. (This process is necessary to infuse the coffee and make a thick froth; the alternative is a thin liquid.)

Divide the froth among the cups (it's said to bring good luck!) and carefully pour in the coffee to the brim. The froth will rise to the surface. Serve at once.

Herb Teas / Tsaï Vótana

In Greek villages tea means *faskómilo,* an infusion of the three-lobed sage (*salvia triloba*), a more aromatic member of the same botanical family as garden sage (*salvia officinalis*). Village folklore attributes great powers to sage tea, as a blood purifier or euphoric or to help relieve chest colds and upset stomachs. The sage is infused in boiling water for 3 to 5 minutes, according to taste, and the sweetener is honey.

Many other ancient herb teas are still enjoyed by Greeks today. Like sage tea these are not only refreshing and reviving drinks, but also have medicinal properties. Chamomile (*kamomíli*) is the favorite, especially as a relaxing night-time tea or to ease head colds. Mint (*thiósmos*) is taken for a fever, thyme (*thimári*) when bronchitis threatens, and Cretan dittany (*dictámos*) when health or spirits are low. Most of these teas can be bought in Greek grocery stores. Or, if you feel adventurous, take your symptoms to a herbalist in a Greek market, and try the recommended concoction!

Alcoholic Drinks / Potá Einopnevmatótha

In Greece grapes are used to make a variety of alcoholic drinks in addition to wine. Once the grapes have been harvested, the vine remnants are distilled to produce two distinctive popular and highly potent liquors.

Aniseed-flavored *oúzo* is the traditional accompaniment to *mezéthes* throughout most of Greece. In the old-style cafés it is served straight, in a small glass, with a tall glass of cold water. Serving *oúzo* over ice is a modern innovation. The *oúzo* sold in Greece is usually much stronger than exported varieties.

Rakí has a markedly different flavor, often somewhat similar to that of tequila. It is not bottled commercially so can only be drunk in areas where it is produced (or in households with relatives in those areas). Until recently, it was made at home, or communally in the village, but today its manufacture requires a license. On the islands of Crete and Santorini and in other ancient wine-producing areas *rakí* is the favorite liquor to drink with *mezéthes*. Good *rakí* is delicious; bad *rakí* best avoided.

Other alcoholic drinks produced in Greece include brandy; *mastíha,* a mastic-flavored liquor; a refreshing lager-style beer; and a number of flavored liqueurs.

The Wines of Greece

Dionysus, the Greek god of wine, was the son of Zeus and the Theban princess Semele. The story runs that he passed on to the Greeks the secrets of wine making he had learned from the satyr Silenus. That much is myth: What is fact is that as their empire expanded the Greeks introduced both the vine and wine making to the rest of Western Europe.

Wine, along with bread and olives, has been part of Greek culture since the very earliest times and the poets of antiquity, Greek and Roman, praised the delights and variety of Greek wines. There is still an enormously rich variety of wine in Greece, and modern Greece has inherited grape varieties yielding wines that are often quite different in color, aroma, and flavor from Western wines.

Much of the best Greek wine is produced by small firms and cooperatives and, unfortunately, rarely leaves the confines of the community in which it is made. But more Greek wines are now being imported into the United States, as a growing interest in Mediterranean foods has led to an interest in the flavors associated with them.

The Greek relationship with wine, as you might expect between old friends, is easy and natural. Greeks enjoy wine without fuss or unnecessary ceremony, without heated discussions of vintages or close scrutiny of labels. In general, Greek society still follows the precepts of the physician Hippocrates, who advised that wine was beneficial if taken at the right time and in the right quantity.

For Greeks the right time to drink wine is with food, whether a full meal, *mezéthes,* or a snack. Greek wine is the natural accompaniment to Greek food: A *tavérna* meal and a glass of local wine, taken outside in the warm pine-scented air, perhaps with a view of the sea or the vine-covered hillsides, may not be the "hautest" of cuisines but it is a moment of inspired magic.

More importantly, the experience of Greek wine and food together brings us exciting new harmonies of flavor. Particularly stimulating to non-Greeks are the unexpected aromas of wines produced from grapes indigenous to Greece but unknown outside the country.

The wine most associated with Greece is, of course, *retsína*. The Greek taste for *retsína* dates back three thousand years; it is the pine-laced wine of the ancients. This very individual wine is not to everyone's taste but a chilled glass of *retsína* or *kokkinéli* (the rosé version), with its surprising stringency, is just right with *mezéthes*.

Retsína is a legacy of the ancient Greeks' experiments with preserving and flavoring. Its origins probably lie in the fact that local pinewood was used at some stage of wine production and/or that pine resin was used to seal the huge amphorae (wine storage jars). Wine makers soon realized that resinated wines remained stable longer than unresinated wines, an important consideration in a hot country—and with a product that could only be made once a year.

In some quarters *retsína* is not taken very seriously, a pity since the finest *retsína* from Attica and Evia, made from the *savátiano* grape, has a delicate aroma and a distinctive, pleasant, and very refreshing flavor. *Retsína* is the true traditional accompaniment to the Easter feast of Paschal Lamb and *kokorétsi* (page 190), and it marries well with dishes accompanied by a garlic sauce.

However, if you are entertaining friends at a Greek meal you may prefer a choice of wines. A growing number of unresinated wines are also becoming available in the United States and a significant proportion of these are far above average in quality and character. Below you will find a consumer guide to dry unresinated Greek wines and suggestions on wines to serve with specific dishes.

Once you start to sample Greek wines, you will begin to appreciate that they have a very special color, aroma, and flavor and that they enhance the dishes in this book as no other wines can. If you would like to know more about Greek wines, I recommend you wholeheartedly to *The Wines of Greece*, by Miles Lambert-Gócs (Faber & Faber, 1990)—a treasure trove of information on the subject.

EIS IYEIAN!
Your Health!

Consumer's Guide to Greek Wines

Major Private Wine Companies

Producer	Type	Label
Boutari	Red	Naousa
		Grande Reserve
		Boutari
(Paros)		Paros
(Cyclades)	White	Santorini
		Chateau Matsa
Tsantalis (Macedonia)	Red	Naousa
		Cava Tsantalis
	White	Ayioritiko
Porto Carras (Macedonia)	Red	Chateau Carras
		Domaine Carras Grand Vin Rouge
	White	Carras Reserve
		Domaine Carras Blanc de Blancs
Calligas (Cephalonia)	Red	Calliga Ruby
		Monte Nero
		Cava Calliga
	White	Robola of Cephalonia

Cooperatives

Wines from Greek wine cooperatives appear sporadically in the United States but they are well worth looking out for:

Nemea (Peloponnese)	*Red*	Cava Nemea
		Nemea
Patraïki (Peloponnese)	*Red*	Santa Laura
	White	Santa Laura
		Patras
GAOS (Cephalonia and Naousa)	*White*	Robola of Cephalonia
	Red	Naousa
		Cava Vaeni
Peza (Crete)	*Red*	Logado
	White	Logado
	Rosé	Logado
CAIR (Rhodes)	*Red*	Chevalier de Rhodes
	White	Ilios
EOSS (Samos)*	*White*	Samena

* Samos is mainly famous for sweet muscat wines—one is available in the United States under the EOSS label.

This is a list of the Greek wines most frequently available in the United States at the present time.

Glossary

Anchovies No Greek market would be complete without its large wooden barrels of anchovies, which owe their unique flavor to the traditional preservation methods used. The small whole anchovies (just the heads are removed) are immersed in heavy brine, lightly dried in the sun until the brine crystallizes into salt, and then packed into barrels. A good anchovy packer uses the same brine several times and it's in this recycling that the secret of Greek anchovies lies. Anchovies packed in reused brine have the strong traditional flavor familiar to the ancient Greeks, and these are the ones most sought after by today's connoisseurs. They can occasionally be found in Greek stores here; only the two fillets are used—lift each one from the backbone with the tip of a small knife. Imported canned anchovy fillets packed in olive oil are the best substitute.

Avgolémono Probably the best-known Greek flavor, this blend of lemon juice and eggs can become a delicious sauce for fish, chicken, or vegetables or a fine delicate soup based on a good Chicken Broth (page 461).

Beans Buy only unblemished, crisp, brightly colored fresh beans. Small young tender beans (e.g., Kentucky Wonders and Romanos) need only the ends trimmed off; larger beans have tough strings down the sides that should be removed. To do this quickly, hold a small paring knife firmly in one hand and trim the stem end of the bean from its outside curve nearly through to the inner side; the string will come away with the stem.

Bell Peppers The distinctive flavor bell peppers impart to Greek dishes is thanks to a method of roasting (scorching) them over an open flame or hot embers. In Greece large fleshy bell peppers are always stuffed; Greek cooks choose slender, mildly flavored varieties similar to Anaheim peppers for roasting. These are difficult to find here but you can obtain a similar flavor by "scorching" bell peppers. Using tongs, hold the pepper over an open flame or hot embers (or use a broiler), turning it until it is blistered and blackened on all sides. Cool in a paper bag or in a bowl covered with plastic wrap to make removing the skin easier. Remove the core and seeds and rub off the skin and any remaining seeds with your fingers. Do not rinse—water affects flavor and storage life. To store, cut roasted peppers into strips, place in clean jars, cover with olive oil, and seal with a lid. Store for up to 2 months. Once the peppers are used, the storage oil can be used for flavorful grilling or cooking or on salads.

Cephalopods (squid, cuttlefish, and octopus) The name *cephalopod* derives from the Greek for "head and legs"—these sea creatures consist of just a head, tentacles, and a body bag or sac. Apart from the larger cuttlefish, which has a single bone in its sac, cephalopods have no bones. What they do have, however, is an ink sac that nature has provided for their protection. Under threat of attack from a predator the cephalopod squirts out ink and, under cover of the ensuing darkness, it slips away to safety. This ink not only protects the cephalopod but is useful to the cook too. It has a slight salty flavor, lends a unique color and sheen to sauces, and acts as a thickener. Some fish purveyors will clean cephalopods for you (even tiny ones retain grains of sand in their body bags) but avoid any that are already cleaned since these may not be fresh. See also Octopus and Squid.

Chicken Broth Although Greek chickens are often scrawny, they are invariably free-range and have a superb flavor.

To make approximately 8 cups of excellent broth: Cut up a chicken into 6 or 8 pieces, discard excess fat, trim the giblets, discarding the liver, and rinse the chicken and giblets. Place the chicken pieces and giblets in a large saucepan or stockpot along with 1 carrot (unpeeled), cut into large pieces; 1 rib celery, cut into large pieces; 1 medium onion, peeled and quartered; 3 bay leaves; 3 sprigs of parsley; 12 peppercorns; pinch of cayenne pepper; 2 whole cloves; ½ teaspoon saffron threads, gently heated in a small skillet until fragrant; and 10 cups water (or enough to cover). Bring slowly to a boil, skim off any froth, cover, reduce the heat, and simmer 1¼ hours. Strain broth and make fat-free (see Meat Broth) and, if desired, reduce for easier storage by rapid boiling. To make **Rich Chicken Broth** boil the fat-free broth until reduced by one third. Use the chicken meat in pies, salads, or sandwiches. See also Meat Broth, Lamb Broth, Fish Broth, Vegetable Broth, and Meat Stock.

Cleaning and Scaling Fish Cleaning a fish means to gut it, leaving head and skin intact. To gut a fresh fish, which should be done as soon as possible, slit open the belly with a sharp knife and pull out everything in the cavity;

run your finger and thumb along the inside of the fish to check. Trim the fins with scissors and pull out the gills; if necessary, loosen them with a small paring knife. With a scaling knife or the back of a table knife, remove the scales by scraping from the tail to the head, and thoroughly rinse the fish. If you plan to grill a large fish do not scale it—the scales will protect it from the fierce grilling heat; just gut and thoroughly rinse the fish. See also Fish, Filleting Fish, and Scoring Fish.

Croutons Crunchy, olive oil–rich croutons give Greek soups and salads a very special character.

To make croutons: Remove the crusts from densely textured white or whole-wheat bread, and cut the bread into ¼-inch cubes. Add a ⅛-inch layer of extra-virgin olive oil to a heavy skillet and heat over moderate heat. Fry the bread cubes until golden brown on all sides. Drain on paper towels.

The secret of successful croutons is to use fruity olive oil and not to allow it to reach smoking temperature. In Greece it is common to see packets of croutons of very hard dark bread, made by the baker when he bakes Pantry Bread (page 336).

Dolmás (Dolmáthes) These are small parcels of grape-leaf wrapped rice and herbs; sometimes meat and/or vegetables are added (pages 261 and 263). Tiny *dolmáthes*, suitable for a *mezé*, are called *dolmathákia*. In winter *dolmáthes* are made with cabbage leaves (page 112); in spring with zucchini flowers (page 265).

Elítses Tiny purple-brown olives grown extensively on Crete. Use whenever a mildly flavored olive is called for; if unavailable, substitute French Niçoise olives.

Farína (Semolina) Available in Greek stores and health food stores. Fine-ground *farína* has the texture of coarse flour and is used to make *macarónia* (pages 313, 320, and 323). Medium- or coarse-grain *farína* is used in puddings (pages 407 and 413) and coarse-grain *farína* is used in custards (pages 378, 358, 364, and 375).

Fatback (pork) Available cut in very thin slices from good butchers. It is used to cover meats and game to protect them from fierce grill or oven heat and keep them moist during cooking.

Fava This "Old World" bean is one of the most frequently used in Greek cooking. Very young favas are shelled and eaten raw as a *mezé*, or cooked in the pod. Fresh favas are made into a *saláta* (page 150), oven-baked with lamb (page 200) or chicken, eaten cold as a salad (pages 72 and 276) or warm as a vegetable dish (page 259). They are dried for the winter and made into one of the most popular Greek *mezéthes* (page 52).

Féta A flaky white sheep's milk cheese that varies in flavor and texture from area to area, season to season. The best *féta* is a deliciously fresh-tasting, slightly salty cheese, perfect on the *mezé* table or as a quick snack with crusty bread and olives. In cooking, *féta* flavors shrimp (page 148) and eggplant (page 267). For further information, see page 9.

Filleting Fish Agres of Rhodes, in the second century A.D., is said to have been the first person to think of filleting fish. Fish filleted just before cooking has the best flavor, so always fillet fish yourself. It is easy to remove fish fillets with a filleting knife, which has a long, thin, supple blade. First, to remove the skin, ease the point of the knife under the skin at the tail and firmly pull the skin toward the head. Then, run the point of the knife around the side of the fish and lift off the fillet.

Fish When buying fish your best guide is your nose—fresh fish smells good. It's also a good idea to inspect the head—this is the first part of a fish to go bad. (In Greece all fish except fresh anchovies and sardines are sold with their heads intact; headless fish are assumed to have been frozen). Check the eyes too—they should be dark, clear, and except for deepwater fish such as the grouper, protruding. Gills should be red and the flesh spring back when prodded. If you are in any doubt, pick the fish up by its tail; if the body bends, do not buy it! See also Cleaning and Scaling Fish, Scoring Fish, Filleting Fish, and Fish Broth.

Fish Broth Bony fish make the best-flavored broth, and including fish heads in the broth will produce a smooth velvety texture. In Greece favorite fish to use as a base for broth are the John Dory (page 465) and the scorpion fish (*scorpéna*).

To make approximately 4 cups broth: Place 1½ pounds cleaned, gutted, and scaled fish (see Cleaning and Scaling Fish, page 461) or fish pieces in a large saucepan and add 1 sliced onion; 1 carrot (unpeeled), cut into large pieces; 2 bay leaves; 4 sprigs of parsley or ¼ cup parsley stems; 1 rib celery, cut into large pieces, or a small handful of wild celery leaves (page 473); a large pinch of saffron threads, heated in a frying pan over low heat until fragrant, optional; 1 tablespoon olive oil; 6 peppercorns; and water to cover. Bring slowly to a boil, reduce the heat, and simmer 1 hour. Strain through a large sieve lined with 2 layers of cheesecloth, let cool, and refrigerate for up to 2 days. Any flakes of fish can be seasoned and coated in a *rígani*/parsley-flavored *latholémono* sauce and served with olives and cheese, as a *mezé*. Or lightly mix them with some Mayonnaise (page 428) or add to a *piláfi* (page 301).

Foúrnos The traditional clay oven that was once part of every Greek house (see page 25). Today when Greeks speak of the *foúrnos* they usually mean the local bakery. The baker will cook his customers' food in his oven once the day's bread is baked, saving time and money (the upkeep of a *foúrnos* is very expensive now). Casseroles, breads, pies, and vegetables baked in a *foúrnos* have a unique taste.

Game When dealing with game it is helpful to understand the principle of hanging, the process by which game is tenderized. Wild birds and animals, because of the action of internal bacteria, do not putrify but rather dry after death. Domestic animals and birds, by contrast, are invaded by external bacteria that quickly cause decomposition, the effects of which are harmful to us. Therefore, it is essential that you know the origin of any bird or animal you wish to hang. Game that has been quickly and cleanly killed, that has only a few shot holes, can be hung; if the flesh is torn or the game has come into contact with our environment it should be prepared for the table right away. To hang game choose a cool place inaccessible to flies (a cellar is ideal). The length of hanging time will depend on the weather, age of the game, and, above all, personal taste. The right moment is usually when a tail feather can be plucked. To enjoy game safely avoid any you have not seen in its fur or feathers and cook only that which you have seen hung. For those who dislike the idea of dealing with hanging game, marinating is the answer. Game immersed in acids, such as wine or vinegar, undergo a process similar to hanging, and the meat is tenderized and flavor improved. See also Hare, Kid, Partridge, Pigeon/Squab.

Grape Leaves The grape leaves used to make *dolmáthes* (page 462) must be tender enough to be edible, so they are picked from the top third of the vine and only a few are taken from each plant, in the spring and early summer. The leaves used to protect baked or grilled foods are discarded before the dish is served, so they are picked from any part of the vine, throughout the summer. For a delicious country flavor cover trays of stuffed vegetables or whole fava beans with grape leaves before baking (page 259) or wrap *kephtéthes* (page 211, made with rice instead of bread) in grape leaves and bake moistened with water, olive oil, and lemon juice. Both fresh leaves and those preserved in brine are used to make *dolmáthes;* only fresh leaves are used in grilled dishes.

Hare A hare is larger than a rabbit, usually weighing around 7 to 8 pounds (5 pounds after skinning). To cut a hare into serving pieces, cut off the front and back legs. Cut the body in half down the backbone. Cut each half into 4 or 5 pieces, similar in size to the legs. Hare meat can be tough, so it should be marinated for 1 to 2 days before cooking (page 174).

John Dory (*Christópsaro*) John Dory, with its firm white flesh and sweetly delicious flavor, is popular in Europe for use in filleted fish dishes (page 133). However, since most of the fish is head and belly, it is the perfect choice for soups and dishes requiring a rich broth such as *Psária Plakí* (page 129). Its Greek name, meaning "Christ's fish," derives from the two black spots behind the enormous head, said by some Greek fishermen to be the fingerprints of St. Christopher, who plucked it from the water while he was carrying Christ on his back.

Kalamátas Large, glossy, pungent purple-black olives perfect in salads and as a snack. To use these olives in cooking, first blanch them for 5 seconds in boiling water. See also pages 3 and 5.

Kephtéthes Aromatic round, oblong, or square croquettes of meat, chicken, fish, or vegetables, unchanged in form and flavor since antiquity. *Kephtéthes* vary in size from very small (*kephtethákia*), for a *mezé*, to large enough for a main course. They can be grilled, fried, or poached and are served with a variety of sauces (pages 38, 40, and 211).

Khórta Wild greens that grow in Greek meadows and on hillsides during the fall, winter, and spring. These greens are rich in vitamins and minerals and have in common a slightly bitter flavor that makes them delicious with *latholémono* (page 466) or *lathóxsithi* (an olive oil and vinegar sauce). Served cold, as a cooked greens salad, *khórta* becomes *khórta salatiká* (page 295).

Kid In Greece kid often replaces the Paschal Lamb (page 188) for the Easter Sunday feast. Spit-roasted kid makes an unusual centerpiece for an outdoor party. Whole kid can be bought during spring from Italian butchers in our larger cities; leg of kid is often available through early summer. It can be prepared with the marinade on page 193. Usually older and larger than lamb when slaughtered, kid needs a longer roasting time, so the fire heat must be steadier and constant. Build the fire with coals spread out over a large area and leveled. When the fire is ready, arrange the spit about 2 feet above the glowing coals but slightly to one side. Roast a 22- to 25-pound kid 3 to 3½ hours, slowly bringing the turning spit closer to the embers, until the kid is only 5 to 6 inches away from the heat. Baste frequently, catching the juices in a pan. Near the end of the cooking time be especially careful that the less fleshy sections of meat do not burn—push most of the embers under the rump, leaving only a shallow layer under the shoulders and rib cage.

Kléphtiko This term refers to dishes baked in paper, an ancient and practical cooking method (page 206) that seals in all the delicious juices of the meat or fish. Modern cooks have discovered that vegetables taste delectable when cooked this way too.

Lamb Broth Light and distinctively flavored lamb broth is a delicious ingredient of *souvlákia* (page 472) and casseroles.

To make approximately 6 cups broth: Place 2 pounds cracked lamb bones and any scraps of lamb meat in a large heavy saucepan with 12 black peppercorns; 1 carrot (unpeeled), cut into large pieces; ½ cup sliced onion; 1 celery rib, cut into large pieces; and water to cover. Bring to a boil, cover, reduce the heat, and simmer 3 hours. Strain and make fat-free (see Meat Broth). Use within 2 days or freeze.

Latholémono A light blend of fruity extra-virgin olive oil and perfumed lemon juice, this is a fresh-tasting and traditional sauce for salads and sautéed or grilled meat and fish. Made with red-wine vinegar instead of lemon juice *latholémono* becomes *lathóxsithi*, a sauce made in the kitchens of antiquity.

Lobster For home cooks, the easiest method of killing a live lobster is to plunge it headfirst into a large pot of rapidly boiling water. Add 1 tablespoon salt and ¼ cup vinegar for each quart of water. Once the water returns to the boil after the lobsters have been added, reduce the heat slightly and cook 6 (1- to 1½-pound lobsters) to 10 (larger ones) minutes longer. Drain, and blot dry with a cloth.

Macarónia Greek pasta; homemade pastas are also known as *zimariká* (literally, "dough"). A wide variety of *macarónia* is available here in Greek and Middle Eastern stores; one popular type of small pasta is called *kritharáki* (page 327).

Mastic (*Mastikha*) The resin collected from the bark of a small bush, mastic is a flavoring unique to the Eastern Mediterranean. It is sold as small hard granules—pulverize them in a clean coffee grinder or mortar, with double the quantity of sugar, before using. Mastic flavors cookies (page 381), breads (pages 347 and 348), and rice pudding (page 402).

Meat Broth Greeks have great faith in the sustaining powers of good meat broth; it is excellent on its own as a broth or as a basis for heartier soups, sauces, and casseroles. Most butchers will give you bones (veal bones produce a lovely gelatinous broth).

To make approximately 10 cups broth: Add 3 tablespoons olive oil to a heavy baking dish or roasting pan. Arrange 4 pounds beef, veal, or lamb bones (including shin, knuckle, and marrow bones, sawn through by the butcher and thoroughly rinsed) in it in a single layer, and add 1 large onion, sliced in half, cut sides down. Bake 1 hour at 375°F or until well browned. Transfer to a large stockpot or saucepan, add 10 cups water, bring to a boil, and remove any froth from the surface with a slotted spoon. Add 1 tablespoon black peppercorns; 2 bay leaves; 1 whole clove; 12 sprigs of parsley; ½ teaspoon dried thyme; 2 large carrots (unpeeled), cut into large pieces; 1 small turnip, peeled and cut in half; and 2 diced tomatoes. Bring to a boil, reduce the heat, and simmer 3 to 4 hours. (Do not allow to boil.)

Strain through a large sieve lined with 2 layers of cheesecloth and set aside to cool. Remove the fat from the surface of cooled broth with a spoon to produce almost fat-free broth. To make the broth completely fat-free, strain again through 2 layers of cheesecloth, or clarify as directed for Meat Stock (see below). Refrigerate for up to 2 days or freeze. Or reduce, if desired, to half the original volume by rapid boiling in an uncovered saucepan (to use in these recipes, use equal parts reduced broth and water). Cool before refrigerating or freezing. For **Light Meat Broth** use 2 parts broth and 1 part water. See also Chicken Broth, Fish Broth, Lamb Broth, Vegetable Broth, and Meat Stock.

Meat Stock Greek cooks make a wholesome and delicious meat stock by enriching Meat Broth (see above).

To make approximately 8 cups stock: Add 3 tablespoons olive oil to a heavy baking dish or roasting pan. Arrange a single layer of about 2 pounds beef shin bones (sawn through by the butcher and thoroughly rinsed) in it, and bake 1 hour at 375°F or until well browned. Transfer to a large stockpot or saucepan, add 10 cups Meat Broth, and bring to a boil. Cover, reduce the heat, and simmer 4 to 5 hours. Strain through a large sieve lined with 2 layers of cheesecloth, let cool, and remove the fat from the surface of the broth to make it almost fat-free. Refrigerate for up to 2 days or freeze. For Light Meat Stock, use 2 parts stock and 1 part water.

To make completely fat-free Meat Stock, reduce the stock by rapid boiling to 5 cups, and let cool. Add 2 egg whites and bring slowly to a boil, stirring with a wooden spoon. Simmer uncovered, without stirring, for 15 minutes. Slowly strain the stock through a sieve lined with 2 layers of cheesecloth into a bowl, 1 ladleful at a time, disturbing the sediment on the bottom of the pot as little as possible. Remove any remaining fat by blotting the surface with paper towels. See also Chicken Broth, Lamb Broth, Fish Broth, and Vegetable Broth.

Mezé (Mezéthes) A small, usually savory, dish served with *oúzo* or *rakí* (page 454) or wine. From 4 to 25 *mezéthes* are served at one time to compose a *mezé* table. Small *mezéthes,* such as olives, cucumber or tomato chunks, cheese, and almonds, are known as *mezethákia.* See Appetizers and First Courses (page 29).

Myzíthra A soft white cheese with a delicious and unusual flavor, fresh *myzíthra* is perfect as a dessert with honey and fresh fruit or spoon sweets (pages 397–401); as a *mezé* with olives, preserved meats, or figs; or as a snack anytime. (To make fresh *myzíthra,* see page 11.) Pale yellow aged *myzíthra,* available in Greek stores, is grated over *macarónia* (page 313) or enjoyed in the same way as fresh *myzíthra.*

Octopus Remnants of Minoan and Classical Greek pottery adorned with strange and beautiful octopus-inspired motifs have been found on island and mainland archaeological sites, and they testify to a Greek fascination with the octopus stretching back to antiquity.

The traditional way to kill an octopus is for the fisherman to bite through the nerve center which passes behind the octopus' eyes. Traditionally too he tenderizes the octopus by beating it against a rock—40 times, say some fishermen, as many times as you can stand it, say others! Octopus is usually sold cleaned (but see Grilled Octopus, page 152), and tenderized (tenderizing must be done when the octopus is killed, so don't waste your time trying to pound a tough one to tenderness). Octopus must also be skinned but this is an easy job if you let the cooking do some of the work for you. Either simmer the octopus in wine, or braise it in its own juices in a covered baking dish in a low oven until all moisture has evaporated, at which point the octopus will be almost cooked and the skin will peel off easily. Never rub octopus with salt or add salt to the pot before it is almost cooked, or it will toughen beyond redemption.

Onion Juice This is used in Greece as a marinade to tenderize and flavor fish and meat before grilling (page 198). For the best flavor do not use metal utensils to prepare it.

To make onion juice: Chop 1 large onion, place it in a bowl, and stir in ¼ cup boiling water. Set aside to cool. Line a sieve with 2 layers of cheesecloth and set it over a bowl. Pour in the onion and any liquid, pull up the edges of the cheesecloth to make a bag, and squeeze as much juice as possible into the bowl. Use immediately.

Orange Flower Water Used to flavor syrups for *phýllo* pastries (page 358) and cakes (page 375). Available from Greek and Middle Eastern stores and gourmet shops.

Orange or Lemon Zest When a recipe calls for just a delicate hint of citrus zest, remove the zest from the fruit with a stripper or zester and either blanch it or dry it. To blanch zest, drop it into boiling water for a minute, then drain, cool, and blot dry with paper towels before using. To dry zest, spread the strips of zest on a baking sheet and dry them for 30 minutes in a very low oven. Store dried zest for up to 3 months in an airtight container and use it in casseroles and pastries.

Partridge In Greece these game birds are in season from late October through November. When choosing partridges, you need to know their age since this dictates the length of time you should cook them. (You can recognize an old partridge by the large knots on its lower legs, not present in younger birds.) One large partridge will serve two. They are delicious spit roasted; wrap first in grape leaves to flavor and to protect from the fierce roasting heat. Always request the giblets from your supplier; they improve the flavor of the accompanying sauce.

Pastoúrmas Highly spiced and salted veal or pork. Thin slices of *pastoúrma* are served with pickles as a *mezé*. *Pastoúrmas* also describes a type of flavor (page 235).

Glossary

469

Phýllo These very thin pastry sheets (the word means "leaves") are the basic ingredient for sublimely syrupy sweet pastries and aromatic savory pies. For information on making homemade *phýllo* dough and on using homemade or commercial *phýllo*, see page 357 and specific recipes.

Pigeon/Squab Pigeons, or squab, are best braised, as in recipes such as Hunter's Pot (page 178); simply roasted, they tend to become dry. Always request the giblets from the supplier; they add to the flavor of the accompanying sauce.

Pilaf A savory rice dish flavored with herbs, to which can be added vegetables, fish or shellfish, chicken, or meat (pages 299 to 312).

Pita Soft, flat bread, shaped into rounds or ovals (page 337) that can be split through the center to make "pockets" to hold *souvlákia* and/or salads. Perfect with grilled meats or dishes served with a sauce, or with *mezéthes*, especially *salátes* (see below).

Pork Caul Fat This is the outer lining of a pig's stomach. In Greece it is sold in small blocks by street vendors as well as in butcher shops; here it is available from many butchers, in the same block form. Pork caul fat (*pánes*) is stiff and easily torn; to separate the pieces, soak block in lightly vinegared tepid water. Use to make sausages or packets of ground or chopped meat for grilling, spit roasting, or baking. During cooking the fat melts away, leaving moist and tender aromatic meats.

Rígani *Rígani*, or wild oregano, covers the Greek hillsides, perfuming the air on warm days. It has a stronger perfume and flavor than Italian oregano. *Rígani* is sold dried in large bunches in Greek stores here; use the leaves on salads, on grilled foods, and in casseroles, and throw the twigs on a barbecue fire for a true Greek flavor. Italian oregano can be substituted, but the flavor will not be as authentic.

Rosewater A favorite flavoring for *phýllo* nut pastries (page 357) and *kataïfi* (Custard Pie, page 363).

Saláta (Salátes) Literally, this means "salad," but Greek salads do not always conform to our expectations of a salad. Many are purées (see the chapter on Appetizers and First Courses), others are composed vegetable salads. A green salad is called *salatiká,* and one consisting of wild greens, *khórta salatiká* (see the chapter on Vegetables and Salads).

Sardines in Olive Oil Greek sardines—lightly salted, immersed in fruity olive oil, and packed in barrels—have an unusual and appetizing flavor. Garnished with capers, cracked black pepper, and a little chopped mild onion they make a delicious *mezé.* Greek stores occasionally stock barrels of sardines from Greece; other imported canned sardines packed in olive oil are the best substitute.

Sausage Casings To make a long sausage for smoking you need a long intestine—the ancient Greeks used pig's intestine but villagers today use a sheep's intestine. It is scrubbed inside and out with vinegar or wine, rinsed well, and then stuffed (pages 235 and 238). Italian butchers occasionally stock cleaned and salted sheep's intestines; to prepare them, soak overnight and rinse thoroughly. Frozen sausage casings for 4- to 5-inch sausages are sold in most butcher shops—just rinse them before using.

Scoring Fish When grilling large fish you need to make sure they cook in the center but do not burn on the outside. To ensure that they cook through, make two or three deep parallel diagonal incisions on each side of the fish with a sharp knife.

Sea Urchins Only the roe (eggs) of sea urchins are eaten (page 150), and it is easiest to buy them ready to use. However, collecting sea urchins can be an enjoyable way to pass a few hours. You can find sea urchins in small clusters on rocks just below the water's surface (experienced divers will find a better harvest on rocks 12 to 15 feet below the surface). Look for female urchins, which are a deep reddish or chestnut brown. The greenish-black males can be left alone. The urchin's hard round shell is covered entirely in spikes except on the flattened underside where the mouth is. For the best harvest, gather sea urchins at the full moon. Greek sea urchins are usually quite small (1 to 3 inches across) but those found in American waters are larger. Sea urchins must be very, very fresh so either collect them yourself or use a reputable supplier; they are usually inexpensive.

Skorthaliá The best version of this pungent, powerful garlic sauce is made with almonds (page 421). Serve with Fried Fish (page 37), *khórta* (page 295), or as a dip, with pita bread (page 337).

Small Onions Choose onions ¾ to 1 inch in diameter. Blanching makes it much easier to peel them. Slice the root end off each onion and remove the feathery outside layer of skin. Blanch the onions in boiling water for 5 minutes, drain, and peel.

Snails Snails are very popular in Greece, especially on the islands, where they are made into a *mezé* (recipe, page 46), *piláfi,* and a winter casserole. Gathered after a rain (the only time villagers consider them safe to eat), they are kept in large baskets containing bran, to dry the snails, and thyme, to sweeten their flavor. To deter the snails from escaping salt is spread round the basket rim. The snails are left in a cool place for 3 or 4 days and thoroughly rinsed in lightly vinegared cold water before cooking.

When buying fresh snails make sure that the shell and the membrane covering the opening are both intact; at home discard any that break during preparation. Simmer snails 1 hour (or until cooked), adding a few tablespoons vinegar once the water boils (skim off the scum that forms on the surface). Remove membranes with a small paring knife, discard the tiny black "tail" of each snail—and they are then ready to use. Of course, although some flavor is lost it is much easier to buy canned snails—all you have to do is drain them!

Souvláki (Souvlákia) Flavorful chunks of meat, fish, or vegetables are threaded on a skewer (*soúvla*) and roasted over an open fire or grill. Lamb is the most popular meat but pork and chicken are also used and ground meat is wrapped in pork caul fat (see above) to make *sheftaliá* (page 233). These are more familiar to many of us as *kebabs,* the Turkish name for the ancient cooking technique used. See also page 196.

Squid In Greece, succulently tender, flavorful squid is a favorite summer dish. Larger squid are stuffed, tiny ones are fried whole. Squid is caught off both coasts of the United States and is often available in fishmarkets. Fresh squid is firm and shiny with a lightly mottled, pink skin.

To prepare squid: Gently pull the head from the body or bag and cut off the two attached fins. Discard the contents of the bag (use your finger, or slit the bag from end to end to check) except for the elongated ink sac—set this aside in a small bowl. Cut off and discard the strip containing the eyes and press out the tough beak. Thoroughly rinse the squid, rubbing both tentacles and body bag with your fingers to remove any sand or purplish skin. Leave the body bags of small squid (and those to be stuffed) intact; cut others into 1-inch strips for sautéing; leave in ice water until ready to use.

Tavérna Despite its name, the Greek *tavérna* is not primarily a drinking place but rather an eating place. Simpler, less expensive, and less pretentious than restaurants, many *tavérnas* are located in spectacularly beautiful places—on terraced hillsides, in village squares, alongside beaches. Many (even in the heart of Athens) have vine-covered or shady courtyards or terraces and in most the owner stamps his personality on the decor in a very idiosyncratic way!

The way to find the most interesting food in a *tavérna* is to follow the Greek example and take a look around at what's bubbling in the kitchen—written menus do not always alert the visitor to the day's specialty. Family-run *tavérnas* usually have a welcoming casual atmosphere with the emphasis on relaxation—so don't expect a meal in a hurry. *Tavérnas* often specialize—harborside establishments serve mostly fish, mountain *tavérnas* mainly meat, while others may make a specialty of a certain cooking method or type of dish.

Most *tavérnas* serve local wine measured by the jug and perhaps a few bottles of national brands too. You will not be offered fancy desserts—fresh fruit or perhaps yogurt and honey are traditional endings for a *tavérna* meal—nor is coffee usually available. These will be found at the nearby pastry shop, or *zacharoplasteíon*.

Toursí (Toursiá) Vegetables pickled by a traditional method and with a distinctive flavor (page 439).

Vegetable Broth This simple, fresh-tasting broth can be used as a substitute for meat or chicken broths. Celery is the dominant flavor but add or substitute turnips, parsnips, or leeks if you prefer.

To make approximately 4 cups broth: Combine 1 cup each finely diced celery and carrot, 1 cup chopped onion, 2 bay leaves, 2 sprigs of fresh dill (or fresh or dried thyme or marjoram), 2 sprigs of parsley, a pinch of salt, and 2 cups water in a heavy saucepan. Bring to a boil, cover, reduce the heat, and simmer 40 minutes. Discard the bay leaves and herb sprigs, transfer vegetables and cooking liquid to a blender or food processor, and purée until smooth. Or pass the vegetables through a food mill fitted with the fine disk into a bowl containing the cooking liquid. Set a fine-meshed sieve over a bowl and press the purée through with a wooden spoon. Discard any solids left in the sieve. Thin with water if desired, and season to taste with salt and pepper. Refrigerate for up to 2 days. See also Meat Broth, Chicken Broth, Fish Broth, and Meat Stock.

Wild Celery A very popular flavoring in meat and fish casseroles, soups, and salads, and the most commonly available celery in Greece. Its natural habitat is marshland near the sea but in Greece it is semicultivated. The leaves, similar in appearance to flat-leaf parsley, are a beautiful shade of dark green; they have a mild, almost sweet, flavor, without any trace of the slightly bitter aftertaste of the pale leaves of large cultivated celery. During spring and summer Italian markets stock wild celery; if unavailable, use the darkest leaves of rib celery, but first blanch them briefly in boiling water.

Menus
for Different
Occasions

ewcomers to Greek cooking may at first be unsure how to compose a balanced menu with dishes from various sections of this book. To help with this problem (although I am sure it will not remain a problem for long) I have suggested below a range of complete menus suitable for family meals, quick suppers, and for entertaining (both for small dinner parties and larger gatherings). Represented here are authentic, traditional dishes in which a variety of distinctively Greek flavors contrast and complement: Any of these menus will give you and your guests an ideal introduction to the enticing tastes and aromas of Greek food.

AN EASTER FEAST

Mezethákia, *page 32, served with Drinks*
Spit-Roasted Lamb Variety Meats, page 190
Three Marinated Salads, page 72
Easter Bread, page 348
The Paschal Lamb, page 188
Easter Greens Salad with Latholémono Sauce, page 289
Asparagus and New Potatoes Avgolémono, page 249
Kos Lemon Pie, page 372

A MEZÉ PARTY

Mezethákia, *page 32*

Fish Roe Saláta, *page 55*

Eggplant Saláta, *page 57*

Stuffed Grape Leaves with Latholémono Sauce, *page 261*

Kephtethákia, *page 38*

Lamb's Liver with Lemon Juice and Rígani, *page 43*

Honey-Glazed Onions, *page 271*

Fragrant Eggplants with Olives, *page 63*

Purslane and Young Beets, *page 293*

Tiny Cracked Potatoes, *page 76*

Smoked Fish Salad, *page 36*

Red Mullet in Savory Sauce, *page 138*

Souvlákia, *pages 196 and 198*

Píta Bread, *page 337*

A BARBECUE

Baked Green Beans in Grape Leaves, *page 259*

Marinated Olives, *page 33*

Black-Eyed Peas with Capers, *page 279*

Snails in Vinegar, *page 46*

Baked Cheese and Spinach, Sesame Spinach, and Marjoram Meat Pies,
pages 116 to 121

The Villagers' Grilled Lamb, *page 195*

Eggplant Pilaf with Glazed Tomatoes, *page 304*

Green Salad with Féta Cheese and Olives, *page 288*

Phýllo Custard Pie, *page 358*

Menus for Different Occasions

A SUMMER BUFFET

Mezethákia, *page 32*
Black Olives and Lentil Saláta, *page 49*
Beet Salad with Allspice, *page 246*
Cucumber Salad with Honey and Vinegar Sauce, *page 255*
Country Bread, *page 334, and/or Pita Bread, page 337*
Moussakás, *page 208*
Potatoes in a Clay Pot, *page 273*
Island Greens Salad, *page 290*
Nut Pastries in Fragrant Honey Syrup, *page 367*
Honey Cakes, *page 378*

A PICNIC

Marinated Olives, *page 33*
Peppered Dried Figs, *page 35*
Garbanzo Beans and Garlic Saláta, *page 54*
Island Eggplants, *page 66*
Cheese Mint Bread, *page 340, and/or Pita Bread, page 337*
Bay-Scented Chicken with Figs, *page 167*
Pilaf with Currants and Pine Nuts, *page 302*
Easter Greens Salad with Latholémono Sauce, *page 289*
Almond Cake in Honey Syrup, *page 375*
Platter of Fresh Fruits, *page 386*

A DINNER PARTY

Mezethákia, *page 32, served with Drinks*
Pork in Aspic, page 44
Marinated Olives, page 33
Purslane and Young Beets, page 293
Aromatic Beef in Red Wine, page 218
Potatoes in a Clay Pot, page 273
Island Greens Salad, page 290
Minoan Dates and Prunes, page 396

DINNER PARTY 2

Mezethákia, *page 32, served with Drinks*
Tiny Stuffed Vegetables, page 68
Cretan Chicken Pie, page 124
Green Salad with Féta Cheese and Olives, page 288
Honey Ice Cream with Fresh Fig Compote, page 390
Shortcakes, page 380

A CASUAL DINNER PARTY

Mezethákia, *page 32, served with Drinks*
Fish Roe Saláta, page 55
Pita Bread, page 337
Macarónia and Spicy Meat in a Pie, page 317
Country Salad, page 282
Platter of Fresh Fruits, page 386
Honey Sesame Candies, page 414

CASUAL DINNER PARTY 2

Mezethákia, *page 32, served with Drinks*
Baked Eggplants to Make the Sultan Swoon, page 98
Yogurt Lamb Souvlákia with Saffron Rice, page 198
Purslane and Young Beets, page 293
Kataïfi Nut Rolls with Caramel Syrup, page 361

A VEGETARIAN DINNER PARTY

Mezethákia, *page 32, served with Drinks*
Fried Cheese, page 47
Beets Island-Style, page 244
Mushrooms à la Grecque, page 288
Spinach Bread, page 344, and/or Pita Bread, page 337
Stuffed Eggplants with Green Grape Sauce, page 103
Green Salad with Féta Cheese and Olives, page 288
Baked Figs, page 394
Hazelnut Cookies, page 382

A QUICK DINNER FOR FRIENDS

Mezethákia, *page 32, served with Drinks*
Smoked Fish Salad, page 36
Macarónia with Chicken and Wild Greens, page 316
Easter Greens Salad with Latholémono Sauce, page 289
Fruit in Sweet Wine and Honey, page 387

Bibliography

While writing this book I consulted many written sources. Some were manuscripts and stored in archives, others were books long out of print and quite difficult to find. These are some of the more easily accessible works.

Brillat-Savarin, Jean Anthelme. *The Physiology of Taste.* Translated and annotated by M.F.K. Fisher. San Francisco: North Point Press, 1986.

Chantiles, Vilma Liacouras. *The Food of Greece.* New York: Avenel Books, 1979.

Clusells, Sylvain. *Cooking on the Turning Spit and Grill.* London: Arthur Baker Ltd., 1961.

D'Andrea, Jeanne. *Ancient Herbs in the J. Paul Getty Museum Gardens.* Malibu, CA: J. Paul Getty Museum, 1982.

David, Elizabeth. *Mediterranean Food.* Revised ed. London: Penguin Books, 1955.

Davidson, Alan. *Mediterranean Seafood.* London: Penguin Books, 1972.

Durrell, Lawrence. *Prospero's Cell.* London: Faber & Faber, 1963.

Fermor, Patrick Leigh. *Roumeli.* London: John Murray, 1966; Penguin Books, 1983.

Gissing, George. *By the Ionian Sea.* 1901. Reprint. London: Richards Press, 1956.

Graves, Robert. *Greek Myths.* 2 volumes. London: Penguin Books, 1956.

Gray, Patience. *Honey from a Weed.* London: Prospect Books, 1986.

Grigson, Jane. *Jane Grigson's Vegetable Book.* London: Michael Joseph, 1978.

Harrison, S. G.; Masefield, G. B.; and Wallis, Michael. *The Oxford Book of Food Plants.* Illustrations by B. E. Nicholson. London: Oxford University Press, 1969.

Homer. *The Odyssey.* (Many editions available.) London: Penguin Books, 1985.

———. *The Iliad.* (Many editions available.) London: Penguin Books, 1950.

McConnell, Carol and Malcolm. *The Mediterranean Diet.* New York: W. W. Norton & Co., Inc., 1987.

Marks, Theonie. *Greek Islands Cooking.* Boston: Little, Brown & Co., 1972.

Miller, Henry. *The Colossus of Maroussi.* 1941. Reprint. London: Penguin Books, 1963.

Niebuhr, Alta Dodds. *Herbs of Greece.* Sponsored by the New England Unit of the Herb Society of America, 1970.

Paradissis, Chrissa. *The Best Book of Greek Cookery.* Athens: P. Efstathiadis & Sons, 1976.

Salaman, Rena. *Greek Food.* London: Fontana Books, 1983.

Sculley, Victor. *The Earth, the Temple, and the Gods.* New Haven: Yale University Press, 1979.

Soyer, Alexis. *The Pantropheon.* New York: Paddington Press, 1977.

Stavroulakis, Nicholas. *Cookbook of the Jews of Greece.* New York: Cadmus Press, 1986.

Stobart, Tom. *Herbs, Spices, and Flavorings.* London: Penguin Books, 1977.

Stubbs, Joyce M. *The Home Book of Greek Cookery.* London: Faber & Faber, 1963.

Tselementes, Nicholas. *Greek Cookery.* New York: D. C. Divry Inc., 1950.

Wolfert, Paula. *Mediterranean Cooking.* New York: Quandrangle/The New York Times Book Co., Inc., 1977.

Index

mushrooms (*cont.*)
   à la grecque, 258–259
mussels, 145
   saffron rice with, 309–
      310
mustard sauce:
   pork cutlets with, 232–
      233
   spicy sausages with,
      235–237
mýthia me risi, 309–310
myzíthra cheese, 11, 468
   fresh, 11–12
   fried cheese pies, 114–
      115
   kritharáki with brown
      butter and, 327–328
   omelet, 92–93
   sweet cheese pastries,
      370–371

Náfplion olives, 3
nectarines in sweet wine
   and honey, 388
nisiótikes/melitzánes,
   66–67
nut(s), 17
   glazed sweet chestnuts,
      410–411
   hazelnut cookies, 382
   kataïfi rolls with cara-
      mel syrup, 361–362
   pastries in fragrant
      honey syrup, 367–
      369
   pine, pilaf with currants
      and, 302–303
   pine, sauce, 426–427
   small *phýllo* pastries,
      364–367
   sweet chestnuts and
      lemon cheese, 408–
      409
   see also almond(s); pis-
      tachio nut(s); wal-
      nut(s)
nutmeg, 15

octopus, 151, 461, 468–469
   grilled, 152–153
   skinning of, 469
okra, chicken and, 160–161
olive(s), 2–4, 462, 465
   black, and lentil *saláta,*
      49–50
   black, fresh fava bean
      salad with, 276
   black, green bean salad
      with, 277
   bread, 339–340

olive(s) (*cont.*)
   fragrant eggplants with,
      63
   green salad with *féta*
      cheese and, 288
   macarónia with an-
      chovy, sweet tomato
      sauce and, 314–315
   marinated, 33
   small appetizers, 32–33
   tiny, tomato salad with
      arugula and, 285
   traditional tomato salad,
      284
olive oil, 4–5
omelet:
   cheese, 92–93
   country vegetable, 97–
      98
   sausage and potato,
      93–94
   to season pan for, 92
   the villager's eggs, 91
omeléta, see omelet
onion(s), 472
   baked summer vegeta-
      bles, 268–270
   and carrots à la
      grecque, 256–257
   honey-glazed, 271
   juice, 469
   small, rabbit with, 172–
      173
   soup, the monks', 87–88
   stuffed, *avgolémono,* 109
   stuffed, with green
      grape sauce, 105
   tiny, marinated chicken
      with vinegar and,
      166–167
   vegetable broth, 473
orange(s), 19–20
   candied citrus peel,
      20–21
   rice pudding, 405
   salad Cretan-style, 286
   zest, 469
orange flower water, 469
oregano, 14
   see also rígani
orektiká, see appetizers
   and first courses
ortíkia tis skhára, 180–181
óstraka ke ostrakíthi, 145–
      150

*pagotó me síka ke khímo
   rothión,* 390–391
palamítha psití me khórta,
   143–144

pans, pots, and kitchen
   tools, 21–25
panzária, see beet(s)
papáki thessalías, 182–
   183
papoutsákia, 210
parsley, 14
partridge, 469
   hunter's pot, 178–179
pastas, 313–328
   kritharáki with brown
      butter and cheese,
      327–328
   Macedonian pie, 320–
      322
   see also macarónia
pastéli, 20, 414
pastítsio, 317–319
pastoúrmas, 469
pastries, 356, 364–371
   fried cheese pies, 114–
      115
   honey puffs, 377–378
   kataïfi nut rolls with
      caramel syrup, 361–
      362
   marjoram meat pies,
      119–121
   nut, in fragrant honey
      syrup, 367–369
   sesame spinach pies,
      118–119
   sweet cheese, 370–371
   see also phýllo
patátes, see potato(es)
paximáthi me saláta, 336–
   337
peaches in sweet wine and
   honey, 388
peas, carrots, and arti-
   chokes *avgolémono,*
   251–252
peas, split, *see* split
   pea(s), yellow
pepper, 16
pepper(s), bell, 460–461
   baked stuffed tomatoes
      and, 110–111
   baked summer vegeta-
      bles, 268–270
   country salad, 282–283
   to scorch, 460–461
   stuffed, *avgolémono,*
      107–108
   stuffed, with green
      grape sauce, 106
   stuffed, with tomato cu-
      min sauce, 102–103
peppered dried figs, 35
peppers, pickled, 439